Dickens's *Great Expectations*

Dickens's Great Expectations

Misnar's Pavilion versus *Cinderella*

Jerome Meckier

THE UNIVERSITY PRESS OF KENTUCKY

Publication of this volume was made possible in part
by a grant from the National Endowment for the Humanities.

Copyright © 2002 by The University Press of Kentucky

Scholarly publisher for the Commonwealth,
serving Bellarmine University, Berea College, Centre
College of Kentucky, Eastern Kentucky University,
The Filson Historical Society, Georgetown College,
Kentucky Historical Society, Kentucky State University,
Morehead State University, Murray State University,
Northern Kentucky University, Transylvania University,
University of Kentucky, University of Louisville,
and Western Kentucky University.
All rights reserved.

Editorial and Sales Offices: The University Press of Kentucky
663 South Limestone Street, Lexington, Kentucky 40508-4008

06 05 04 03 02   5 4 3 2 1

Library of Congress Cataloging-in-Publication Data
Meckier, Jerome.
  Dickens's Great expectations : Misnar's pavilion versus Cinderella /
Jerome Meckier.
       p. cm.
  Includes bibliographical references and index.
  ISBN 0-8131-2228-7 (cloth : alk. paper)
  1. Dickens, Charles, 1812-1870. Great Expectations. 2. Morell,
Charles, Sir, 1736-1765. Tales of the genii. 3. English fiction—19th
century—History and criticism. 4. Dickens, Charles, 1812-1870—
Knowledge—Folklore. 5. Dickens, Charles, 1812-1870—
Contemporaries. 6. Tales—Arab countries—History and
criticism. 7. Cinderella (Tale)—History and criticism. 8. English
fiction—Arab influences. 9. Cinderella (Legendary character).
10. Tragicomedy. 11. Parody. I. Title.
  PR4560 .M43 2002
  823'.8—dc21
  2001007149

This book is printed on acid-free recycled paper meeting
the requirements of the American National Standard
for Permanence in Paper for Printed Library Materials.

Manufactured in the United States of America.

*For my mother, Pauline,
my daughter, Alison,
and my grandson, Jacob*

Contents

Abbreviations   viii
Preface   xviii
1. Misnar versus Cinderella   1
2. Lever   41
3. Thackeray   76
4. *David Copperfield*   97
5. Collins   123
6. Mary Shelley   155
7. Charlotte Brontë   180
8. Emily Brontë   206
Synopsis A: The Tale of Misnar's Pavilion   228
Synopsis B: *A Day's Ride*   232
Notes   236
Index   268

Abbreviations for Works Cited

A William F. Axton. *Circle of Fire.* Lexington: Univ. of Kentucky Press, 1966.
AB Samuel Smiles. *Self-Help: with Illustrations of Conduct and Perseverance.* London: John Murray, 1958. Centenary Edition with an Introduction by Asa Briggs.
AD Alan Dundes, ed. *Cinderella: A Folklore Casebook.* New York: Garland, 1982.
ADR Charles Lever. *A Day's Ride: A Life's Romance.* Boston: Roberts Brothers, 1898; vol. 28 in the Copyright Edition.
AE Annabel Endicott. "Pip, Philip and Astrophil: Dickens's Debt to Sidney?" *The Dickensian,* 63 (autumn 1967), 158–62.
AED A.E. Dyson. *The Inimitable Dickens.* London: Macmillan, 1970.
AG Ann Grigsby. "Charles Reade's *Hard Cash:* Lunacy Reforms Through Sensationalism." *Dickens Studies Annual,* 25 (1996), 141–58.
"AH" George Levine. "The Ambiguous Heritage of *Frankenstein*." Levine and U.C. Knoepflmacher, eds. *The Endurance of Frankenstein.* Berkeley: Univ. of California Press, 1974, 3–30.
AH Aldous Huxley. *Antic Hay.* London: Chatto & Windus, 1923.
AK Arnold Kettle. *An Introduction to the English Novel: Defoe to the Present.* New York: Harper, 1968; revised edition.
AM Anne K. Mellor. *Mary Shelley: Her Life, Her Fiction, Her Monsters.* New York: Routledge, 1988.
AN Ada Nisbet. "Charles Dickens." *Victorian Fiction: A Guide to Research.* Lionel Stevenson, ed. Cambridge: Harvard Univ. Press, 1964.
AN Husain Haddawy, trans. *The Arabian Nights.* New York: Norton, 1990.
AS Anny Sadrin. *Great Expectations.* London: Unwin Hyman, 1988.

AW	Charles Dickens. *Great Expectations*. New York: Signet, 1963. With an "Afterword" by Angus Wilson.
AW	Gordon Ray. *Thackeray: The Age of Wisdom, 1847–1863*. New York: McGraw-Hill, 1958.
AY	Arlene Young. "The Monster Within: The Alien Self in *Jane Eyre* and *Frankenstein*." Studies in the Novel, 23 (fall 1991), 325–38.
B	*Blackwood's Magazine*, 81 (1857), 497.
BB	Bruno Bettelheim. *The Uses of Enchantment: The Meaning and Importance of Fairy Tales*. New York: Alfred A. Knopf, 1977.
B-C	Robin Gilmour. "Dickens and the Self-Help Idea." J. Butt and I.F. Clarke, eds. *The Victorians and Social Protest: A Symposium*. Newton Abbot: David & Charles, 1973, 71–101.
BD	Bernard Duyfhuizen. "Periphrastic Naming in Mary Shelley's *Frankenstein*." Studies in the Novel, 27 (winter 1995), 477–92.
BFL	Barbara Fass Leavy. "Wilkie Collins's Cinderella: The History of Psychology and *The Woman in White*." Dickens Studies Annual, 10 (1982), 91–141.
BG	Jack Zipes, trans. *The Complete Fairy Tales of the Brothers Grimm*. New York: Bantam, 1992.
BH	Bert G. Hornback. *Great Expectations: A Novel of Friendship*. Boston: Twayne, 1987.
BH	Charles Dickens. *Bleak House*. George Ford and Sylvère Monod, eds. New York: Norton, 1977.
BS	William Makepeace Thackeray. *The Book of Snobs*. John Sutherland, ed. New York: St. Martin's, 1978.
C	Micael M. Clarke. *Thackeray and Women*. DeKalb: Northern Illinois Univ. Press, 1995.
"CA"	K.J. Fielding. "The Critical Autonomy of Great Expectations." *Review of English Literature*, 2 (1961), 75–88.
CB	Chris Baldick. *In Frankenstein's Shadow: Myth, Monstrosity, and Nineteenth-Century Writing*. New York: Oxford Univ. Press, 1987.
C*GE*	David Paroissien, ed. *The Companion to Great Expectations*. Great Britain: Helm Information Ltd., 2000.
CH	Curt Hartog. "The Rape of Miss Havisham." *Studies in the Novel*, 14 (fall 1982), 248–65.
CHM	Carol Hanberry MacKay. "Serialization and the Redoubled Self: Fantasy in *David Copperfield* and *Pendennis*." Dickens Studies Annual, 14 (1985), 241–65.
CL	Lionel Stevenson. *Doctor Quicksilver: The Life of Charles Lever*. New York: Russell and Russell, 1969. Originally published 1939.

CM	Charles Mauskopf. "Thackeray's Attitude Toward Dickens's Writings." *Nineteenth-Century Fiction,* 21 (1966), 21–33.
CP	Catherine Peters. *The King of Inventors: A Life of Wilkie Collins.* Princeton, N.J.: Princeton Univ. Press, 1991.
DA	Doris Alexander. *Creating Characters with Charles Dickens.* University Park, Pa.: Penn State Univ. Press, 1991.
DC	David Cecil. *Victorian Novelists.* Chicago: Univ. of Chicago Press, 1935.
DC	Charles Dickens. *David Copperfield.* Jerome H. Buckley, ed. New York: Norton, 1990.
DD	William Makepeace Thackeray. *Denis Duval.* Charleston, S.C.: Martin and Hoyt, n.d.
DeM	Cynthia DeMarcus. "Wolves Within and Without: Dickens's Transformation of 'Little Red Riding Hood' in *Our Mutual Friend.*" *Dickens Quarterly,* 12 (March 1995), 11–17.
DG	David J. Geherin. "An Interview with Christopher Isherwood." *Journal of Narrative Technique,* 2 (Sept. 1972), 143–58.
DJ	W. Jerrold. *Douglas Jerrold.* London: Hodder and Stoughton, 1918.
DL	David Lodge. "Fire and Eyre: Charlotte Brontë's War of Earthly Elements." *Language of Fiction.* London: Routledge & Kegan Paul, 1966, 114–43.
DM	David E. Musselwhite. *Partings Welded Together: Politics and Desire in the Nineteenth-Century English Novel.* London: Methuen, 1987.
DT	Charles Dickens. *Great Expectations.* Charlotte Mitchell, ed. Introduction by David Trotter. London: Penguin, 1996.
DW	Dennis Walder. *Dickens and Religion.* London: Allen & Unwin, 1981.
EBC	Peter Bayne. *Essays in Biography and Criticism.* Boston: Gould, 1857.
ED	Edward Downey. *Charles Lever: His Life in His Letters.* Edinburgh: William Blackwood & Sons, 1906.
EK	Ella Kusnetz. "'This Leaf of My Life': Writing and Play in *Great Expectations.*" *Dickens Quarterly,* 10 (Sept. 1993), 146–60.
EM	Ellen Moers. *The Dandy: Brummel to Beerbohm.* New York: Viking, 1960.
EN	Nathaniel Hawthorne. *The English Notebooks.* Randall Stewart, ed. New York: MLA, 1941.
EP	E. Pearlman. "Inversion in *Great Expectations.*" *Dickens Studies Annual,* 7 (1978), 190–202, 259–60.
ES	Edward Said. *Culture and Imperialism.* New York: Vintage, 1994.
EW	Edmund Wilson. "Dickens: The Two Scrooges." *The Wound and the Bow.* New York: Oxford Univ. Press, 1965.
F	John Forster. *Life of Charles Dickens.* Andrew Lang, ed. New York: Charles Scribner's Sons, 1899.

F	Mary Shelley. *Frankenstein*. Johanna M. Smith, ed. Boston: St. Martin's Press, 1992.
FK	Frederick R. Karl. *A Reader's Guide to the Nineteenth-Century British Novel*. New York: Noonday, 1965.
FP	Charles Dickens. *Great Expectations*. "Introduction by Frederick Page." Edito-Service, S.A.: Geneva, Switzerland. Centennial Edition, n.d.
FR	Frederick William Roe, ed. *Victorian Prose*. New York: Ronald Press Co., 1947.
FT	Jack Zipes. *Fairy Tale as Myth, Myth as Fairy Tale*. Lexington: Univ. Press of Kentucky, 1994.
"FTO"	Harry Stone. "Fairy Tales and Ogres: Dickens' Imagination and *David Copperfield*." *Criticism*, 6 (1964), 324–30.
G	Robin Gilmour. *The Victorian Period*. London: Longman, 1993.
GA	Gillian Avery, ed. *Charles Dickens: Holiday Romance and Other Writings for Children*. London: J.M. Dent, 1995.
GBN	Gwendolyn B. Needham. "The Undisciplined Heart of David Copperfield." Pp. 794–805 in Buckley's Norton edition (see *DC*).
"GBS"	George Bernard Shaw. "George Bernard Shaw on *David Copperfield*." *The Dickensian*, 45 (1949), 118.
GC	G. Armour Craig. "The Unpoetic Compromise: On the Relation between Private Vision and the Social Order in Nineteenth-Century British Fiction." Charlotte Brontë. *Jane Eyre*. Richard J. Dunn, ed. New York: Norton, 1971, 476–78.
GE	Charles Dickens. *Great Expectations*. Margaret Cardwell, ed. Oxford: Clarendon, 1993.
GF	George Ford, ed. *Victorian Fiction: A Second Guide to Research*. New York: MLA, 1978.
G&G	Sandra M. Gilbert and Susan Gubar. *The Madwoman in the Attic*. New Haven, Conn.: Yale Univ. Press, 1979.
GKC	G.K. Chesterton. *Criticisms and Appreciations of the Works of Charles Dickens*. London: J.M. Dent, 1992. First published 1911.
GL	George Levine. *The Realistic Imagination: English Fiction from Frankenstein to Lady Chatterley*. Chicago: Univ. of Chicago Press, 1981.
GM	Goldie Morgentaler. "Meditating on the Low: A Darwinian Reading of *Great Expectations*." *Studies in English Literature*, 38 (autumn 1998), 707–21.
GS	Grahame Smith. *Charles Dickens: A Literary Life*. New York: St. Martin's Press, 1996.
H	Humphry House. *The Dickens World*. London: Oxford Univ. Press, 1961. First published 1941.

HD	Sir Henry Dickens. *The Recollections of Sir Henry Dickens.* London: Heinemann, 1934.
HH	Humphry House. "George Bernard Shaw on *Great Expectations.*" *The Dickensian,* 44 (1948), 63–70; 183–86.
HM	Huang Mei. *Transforming the Cinderella Dream: From Frances Burney to Charlotte Brontë.* New Brunswick, N.J.: Rutgers Univ. Press, 1990.
HR	Jerome Meckier. *Hidden Rivalries in Victorian Fiction: Dickens, Realism, and Revaluation.* Lexington: Univ. Press of Kentucky, 1987.
HS	Harry Stone. *Dickens and the Invisible World.* Bloomington: Indiana Univ. Press, 1979.
H&S	Wilkie Collins. *Hide and Seek.* Catherine Peters, ed. New York: Oxford Univ. Press, 1993.
HT	Charles Dickens. *Hard Times.* George Ford and Sylvère Monod, eds. New York: Norton, 1996.
HvS	Helen von Schmidt. "The Dark Abyss, the Broad Expanse: Visions of Self in *Jane Eyre* and *Great Expectations.*" *Dickens Quarterly,* 2 (Sept. 1985), 84–92.
I	Martin Amis. *The Information.* New York: Harmony Books, 1995.
IC	Iain Crawford. "Pip and the Monster: The Joys of Bondage." *Studies in English Literature,* 28 (1988), 625–48.
J	Edgar Johnson. *Charles Dickens: His Tragedy and Triumph.* New York: Simon and Schuster, 1952.
JAS	J.A. Sutherland. *Victorian Novelists and Publishers.* Chicago: Univ. Press of Chicago, 1976.
JB	Jerome Beaty. *Misreading "Jane Eyre": A Postformalist Paradigm.* Columbus: Ohio State Univ. Press, 1996.
JC	Charles Dickens. *Great Expectations.* Janice Carlisle, ed. New York: St. Martin's Press, 1995.
JCu	John Cunningham. "Christian Allusion, Comedic Structure and the Metaphor of Baptism in *Great Expectations.*" *South Atlantic Review,* 59 (1994), 35–51.
JDV	J.Don Vann. *Victorian Novels in Serial.* New York: MLA, 1985.
JE	Charlotte Brontë. *Jane Eyre.* Beth Newman, ed. Boston: St. Martin's Press, 1996.
JF	Judith Fisher. "Ethical Narrative in Dickens and Thackeray." *Studies in the Novel,* 29 (spring 1997), 108–17.
JHB	Jerome Hamilton Buckley. *Season of Youth: The Bildungsroman from Dickens to Golding.* Cambridge, Mass.: Harvard Univ. Press, 1974.
JHM	J. Hillis Miller. *Charles Dickens: The World of His Novels.* Bloomington: Indiana Univ. Press, 1963. First published in 1958.

JJ	John O. Jordan. "Partings Welded Together: Self-Fashioning in *Great Expectations* and *Jane Eyre.*" *Dickens Quarterly,* 13 (March 1996), 19–33.
JM	Jerome Meckier. "Dickens and *King Lear:* A Myth for Victorian England." *South Atlantic Quarterly,* 71 (winter 1972), 75–90.
JPM	John P. McGowan. "*David Copperfield:* The Trial of Realism." *Nineteenth- Century Fiction,* 34 (June 1979), 1–19.
JPR	Jack P. Rawlins. *Thackeray's Novels: A Fiction That is True.* Berkeley: Univ. of California Press, 1974.
JR	John Reed. *Dickens and Thackeray: Punishment and Forgiveness.* Athens: Ohio Univ. Press, 1995.
JS	Jay Stubblefield. "'What Shall I Say I Am—To-Day': Subjectivity and Accountability in *Frankenstein* and *Great Expectations.*" *Dickens Quarterly,* 14 (Dec. 1997), 232–42.
JTS	John T. Shawcross. *John Milton: The Self and the World.* Lexington: Univ. Press of Kentucky, 1993.
JuM	Julian Moynahan. "The Hero's Guilt: The Case of *Great Expectations.*" *Essays in Criticism,* 10 (1960), 60–79.
JZ	Jack Zipes. *The Brothers Grimm.* New York: Routledge, 1988.
K	Fred Kaplan. *Dickens: A Biography.* New York: Morrow, 1988.
KB	Karen Ann Butery. "Jane Eyre's Flights from Decision." *Third Force Psychology and the Study of Literature.* Bernard J. Paris, ed. Rutherford, N.J.: Fairleigh Dickinson Univ. Press, 1986, 114–35.
KC	Karen Chase. *Eros and Psyche: The Representation of Personality in Charlotte Brontë, Charles Dickens, and George Eliot.* New York: Methuen, 1984.
KF	Kathleen Ferris. *James Joyce and the Burden of Disease.* Lexington: Univ. Press of Kentucky, 1995.
KJF	K.J. Fielding. *Charles Dickens: A Critical Introduction.* Boston: Houghton Mifflin, 1965.
L	Walter Dexter, ed. *Letters of Charles Dickens.* Bloomsbury: Nonesuch Press, 1938.
LCB	Elizabeth Gaskell. *The Life of Charlotte Brontë.* Alan Shelton, ed. London: Penguin, 1975. First published 1857.
L&D	U.C. Knoepflmacher. *Laughter and Despair: Readings in Ten Novels of the Victorian Era.* Berkeley: Univ. of California Press, 1971.
L-E	Mary Lowe-Evans. "Reading with a 'Nicer Eye': Responding to *Frankenstein*" in Johanna M. Smith's edition; see *F,* 215–19.
LF	Lawrence Frank. *Charles Dickens and the Romantic Self.* Lincoln: Univ. of Nebraska Press, 1984.

LG   W. Laurence Gadd. *The Great Expectations Country.* London: Cecil Palmer, 1929.
LJS   L.J. Swingle. "Frankenstein's Monster and its Romantic Relatives: Problems of Knowledge in English Romanticism." *Texas Studies in Literature and Language,* 15 (spring 1973), 51–65.
LPP   Gordon N. Ray, ed. *The Letters and Private Papers of William Makepeace Thackeray, Vol. II: 1841–1851.* Cambridge, Mass.: Harvard Univ. Press, 1945.
LS   Lionel Stevenson. *The English Novel: A Panorama.* Boston: Houghton Mifflin, 1960.
MA   M.H. Abrams. *A Glossary of Literary Terms.* New York: Rinehart & Co., 1959.
MC   Michael Cotsell, ed. *Critical Essays on Great Expectations.* Boston: G.K. Hall, 1990.
McM   Juliet McMaster. "Novels by Eminent Hands: Sincerest Flattery from the Author of *Vanity Fair.*" *Dickens Studies Annual,* 18 (1989), 309–36.
MCr   Mark Cronin. "The Rake, the Writer, and *The Stranger:* Textual Relations between *Pendennis* and *David Copperfield.*" *Dickens Studies Annual,* 24 (1996), 215–40.
ME   Monroe Engel. *The Maturity of Dickens.* Cambridge, Mass.: Harvard Univ. Press, 1967.
MEd   Mary Edminson. "The Date of the Action in *Great Expectations.*" *Nineteenth-Century Fiction,* 13 (June 1958), 22–35.
MFD   Margaret Flanders Darby. "Listening to Estella." *Dickens Quarterly,* 16 (Dec. 1999), 215–29.
MG   Morris Golden. *Dickens Imagining Himself.* New York: Univ. Press of America, 1992.
MK   Michael C. Kotzin. *Dickens and the Fairy Tale.* Bowling Green, Oh.: Bowling Green Univ. Press, 1972.
ML   Michael Lund. *Reading Thackeray.* Detroit: Wayne State Univ. Press, 1988.
MS   Mark Spilka. *Dickens and Kafka.* London: Dennis Dobson, 1963.
MT   Martin Trapp. *Mary Shelley's Monster: The Story of Frankenstein.* Boston: Houghton Mifflin, 1977.
N   Ada Nisbet. "The Autobiographical Matrix of *Great Expectations.*" *Victorian Newsletter* (spring 1959), 10–13.
N*GE*   Charles Dickens. *Great Expectations.* Edgar Rosenberg, ed. New York: Norton, 1999.
NN   Wilkie Collins. *No Name.* Virginia Blaine, ed. New York: Oxford Univ. Press, 1986.
NR   Nick Rance. "Wilkie Collins in the 1860s: The Sensation Novel and

	Self-Help." Clive Bloom et al., eds. *Nineteenth-Century Suspense: From Poe to Conan Doyle*. London: Macmillan, 1998, 48–63.
O	Dinah Craik. *Olive: A Young Girl's Triumph Over Prejudice*. New York: Oxford Univ. Press, 1996.
OS	Charles Darwin. *The Origin of the Species*. Philip Appleman, ed. *Darwin*. New York: Norton, 1979.
OT	Charles Dickens. *Oliver Twist*. New York: Holt, Rinehart & Winston, 1962.
"P"	George Bernard Shaw. Preface to the Limited Editions Club *Great Expectations*. Edinburgh: R. & R. Clark, 1937, v-xxii.
PA	James Joyce. *Portrait of the Artist as a Young Man*. New York: Viking, 1958.
PB	Peter Brooks. "Repetition, Repression, and Return: The Plotting of *Great Expectations*." *Reading for the Plot: Design and Intention in Narrative*. New York: Vintage, 1984, 113-42.
PC	Philip Collins. *Dickens and Crime*. London: Macmillan, 1965.
Pen	William Makepeace Thackeray. *Pendennis*. London: J.M. Dent, 1962.
PL	*The Letters of Charles Dickens: The Pilgrim Edition*. Kathleen Tillotson, Graham Storey et al., eds. Oxford: Clarendon, 1965–.
PM	Philip Marcus. "Theme and Suspense in the Plot of *Great Expectations*." *Dickens Studies*, 2 (May 1966), 57–73.
PR	Phyllis Rose. *Parallel Lives: Five Victorian Marriages*. New York: Knopf, 1983.
PRS	Patricia R. Sweeney. "Mr. House, Mr. Thackeray and Mr. Pirrip: The Question of Snobbery in *Great Expectations*." *The Dickensian*, 64 (winter 1968), 55–63.
PT	Peter Thoms. *The Windings of the Labyrinth*. Athens: Ohio Univ. Press, 1992.
QDL	F.R. and Q.D. Leavis. *Dickens the Novelist*. New York: Pantheon, 1970.
RA	Richard D. Altick. *Victorian People and Ideas*. New York: Norton, 1973.
RC	Randall Craig. *The Tragicomic Novel*. Newark: Univ. of Delaware Press, 1989.
RCh	Richard Chase. "The Brontës, or, Myth Domesticated." William Van O'Connor, ed. *Forms of Modern Fiction*. Bloomington: Indiana Univ. Press, 1959, 102–19.
RD	Ross H. Dabney. *Love and Property in the Novels of Dickens*. London: Chatto & Windus, 1967.
RG	Robert Garis. *The Dickens Theatre*. Oxford: Clarendon, 1965.
RH	Robert Hughes. *The Fatal Shore: The Epic of Australia's Founding*. New York: Knopf, 1977.

RJD	Richard J. Dunn. "Dickens and the Tragi-Comic Grotesque." *Studies in the Novel*, 1 (summer 1969), 147–55.
RK	Robert Keefe. *Charlotte Brontë's World of Death*. Austin: Univ. of Texas Press, 1979.
RL	Robert Langbaum. "The Tempest and Tragicomic Vision." *The Modern Spirit*. New York: Oxford Univ. Press, 1970.
RLP	Robert L. Patten. *Dickens and His Publishers*. Oxford: Clarendon, 1978.
RMP	Robert M. Polhemus. *Erotic Faith: Being in Love from Jane Austen to D.H. Lawrence*. Chicago: Univ. of Chicago Press, 1990.
RMcM	Charles Dickens. *Great Expectations*. R.D. McMaster, ed. New York: Odyssey, 1966.
RP	Robert B. Partlow. "The Moving I: A Study of the Point of View in *Great Expectations*." *College English*, 23 (Nov. 1961), 122–26.
RR	George Ford. "Self-Help and the Helpless in *Bleak House*." Robert C. Rathburn and Martin Steinmann Jr., eds. *From Jane Austen to Joseph Conrad*. Minneapolis: Univ. of Minnesota Press, 1958, 92–105.
S	Algernon Swinburne. "Charles Dickens." *The Quarterly Review*, 196 (July 1902), 20–39.
SCL	George Eliot. *Scenes of Clerical Life*. David Lodge, ed. Harmondsworth, Middlesex, England: Penguin, 1973.
SF	Stanley Friedman. "Ridley's *Tales of the Genii* and Dickens's *Great Expectations*." *Nineteenth-Century Literature*, 44 (Sept. 1989), 215–18.
SG	Sandra M. Gilbert. "Plain Jane's Progress" in Newman's edition; see *JE*, 475–501.
SH	Samuel Smiles. *Self-Help with Illustrations of Conduct and Perseverance*. London: John Murray, 1908.
SI	Stephen Ingle. *George Orwell: A Political Life*. Manchester, England: Manchester Univ. Press, 1993.
SM	Sylvia Manning. *Dickens as Satirist*. New Haven, Conn.: Yale Univ. Press, 1971.
SM	George Eliot. *Silas Marner*. New York: Signet, 1960.
SR	"Great Expectations." *Saturday Review*, 12 (20 July 1861), 69–70.
SS	Samuel Smiles. *The Autobiography of Samuel Smiles*. Thomas Mackay, ed. New York: Dutton, 1905.
TB	H.G. Wells. *Tono-Bungay*. New York: Signet, 1961.
TC	Thomas Carlyle. *Past and Present*. New York: Charles Scribner's Sons, 1899. Vol. 10 in the Centenary Edition of *The Works of Thomas Carlyle*.
TC	Anthony Trollope. *The Three Clerks*. London: Penguin, 1993.
TG	Sir Charles Morell (Rev. James Ridley). *The Tales of the Genii*. London: Henry G. Bohn, 1861.

TJ	T.A. Jackson. *Charles Dickens: The Progress of a Radical.* New York: International Publishers, 1987. First published 1937.
TW	J.A. Sutherland. *Thackeray at Work.* London: Athlone, 1974.
UA	Gordon N. Ray, ed. *Thackeray: The Uses of Adversity, 1811–1846.* London: Oxford Univ. Press, 1955.
UCK	U.C. Knoepflmacher, ed. *A Christmas Carol by Charles Dickens and Other Victorian Fairy Tales.* New York: Bantam, 1983.
UT	Charles Dickens. *The Uncommercial Traveller and Reprinted Pieces.* London: Oxford Univ. Press, 1968.
V	Thomas Vargish. "Revenge and *Wuthering Heights.*" *Studies in the Novel*, 3 (spring 1971), 7–17.
VD	Hilary Shor. "'If He Should Turn to and Beat Her': Violence, Desire, and the Woman's Story in *Great Expectations.*" See JC, 541–57.
VF	William Makepeace Thackeray. *Vanity Fair.* New York: Modern Library, 1950.
VFT	Jack Zipes, ed. *Victorian Fairy Tales.* New York: Methuen, 1987.
VPR	J. Don Vann. "Dickens, Charles Lever and Mrs. Gaskell." *Victorian Periodicals Review*, 22 (summer 1989), 64–71.
W	George J. Worth, ed. *Great Expectations: An Annotated Bibliography.* New York: Garland, 1986.
WC	Nicholas Rance. *Wilkie Collins and Other Sensation Novelists: Walking the Moral Hospital.* Rutherford, N.J.: Fairleigh Dickinson Univ. Press, 1991.
WCP	Walter C. Phillips. *Dickens, Reade, and Collins: Sensation Novelists.* New York: Columbia Univ. Press, 1919.
WFA	William F. Axton, "Great Expectations, Yet Again." *Dickens Studies Annual*, 2 (1972), 278–93, 373–74.
WG	William R. Goetz. "Genealogy and Incest in *Wuthering Heights.*" *Studies in the Novel*, 14 (winter 1982), 359–76.
WH	Walter E. Houghton. *The Victorian Frame of Mind, 1830–1870.* New Haven, Conn.: Yale Univ. Press, 1957.
WH	Emily Brontë. *Wuthering Heights.* Linda H. Peterson, ed. Boston: St. Martin's Press, 1992.
WJF	W.J. Fitzpatrick. *Life of Charles Lever.* London: Chapman and Hall, 1879.
WM	Warren Montag. "'The Workshop of Filthy Creation': A Marxist Reading of *Frankenstein.*" See F, 300–11.
WP	George Orwell. *The Road to Wigan Pier.* New York: Berkley Medallion, 1961. First published 1937.
WW	Wilkie Collins. *The Woman in White.* Julian Symons, ed. Harmondsworth, Middlesex, England: Penguin, 1974.

Preface and Acknowledgments

Dickens's Great Expectations: *Misnar's Pavilion versus* Cinderella completes an informal trilogy. The first part of the trilogy, *Hidden Rivalries in Victorian Fiction: Dickens, Realism, and Revaluation* (1987), examined parodic revaluation in the nineteenth-century British novel generally; during the realism wars of the 1850s, social analysts certified the accuracy of their assessments by attempting to rescind a rival's credentials, usually Dickens's. Novelists as different from each other as Anthony Trollope, Elizabeth Gaskell, and George Eliot recast Dickens's critiques less scathingly so that his satire would appear excessive. (Even Wilkie Collins, a protegé, thought he could outdo "The Inimitable.") Forced to retaliate, Dickens wrote double-barreled narratives; besides contributing to the story in hand, these narratives darken characters, themes, and situations he found unrealistic in the work of less stringent competitors.

Innocent Abroad: Charles Dickens's American Engagements (1990), the second work of the trilogy, concentrated on one aspect of Dickens's career—his traumatic disappointment with America, especially during his first visit in 1842. In *American Notes,* Dickens rebuked Alexis de Tocqueville, Frances Trollope, and Harriet Martineau, whose travelogues either flattered the new country or failed to expose its pretensions harshly enough. Beginning with *Martin Chuzzlewit,* principally in the American chapters, Dickens revised downward his hopes for society and his opinion of human nature. This increasingly Juvenalian perspective dismayed the more sanguine novelists among his rivals, provoking them, in effect, to rewrite his later novels in theirs.

Dickens's Great Expectations focuses on what is arguably Dickens's finest novel. It counts the ways the recollection of Misnar's ingenious pavilion in Sir Charles Morell's *The Tales of the Genii*—"the Eastern story" that Pip summarizes in chapter 38's final paragraph (*GE*, 309–10)—repeatedly fired Dickens's imagination as he composed *Great Expectations*. To satirize Victorian expectancy and subvert the era's Cinderella complex, Dickens rewrote the cinder girl's story with a warning from Misnar's.

Pip recalls how the would-be usurpers are pulverized by the collapsible ceiling of a gorgeous pavilion built expressly to entrap them. Although he has tried to reenact *Cinderella,* he discovers a more appropriate analogue for his career in the Misnar tale. In an epiphanic moment, he likens the collapse of his expectations to the collapse of Misnar's pavilion. As Pip's Cinderella story turns into a reprise of "the Eastern story," Dickens's aptitude for revaluative parody culminates in the reconsideration of a famous fairy tale. But Dickens went even further. To repudiate the adoption of *Cinderella* as a cultural myth celebrating the rise of Victorian England, *Great Expectations* parodies half a dozen rival novels, accusing their authors of concocting fairy tales—unrealistic stories imbued with Cinderella motifs—instead of writing tragicomedy, Dickens's final word on what life is.

Unable to say "Pirrip," Pip's "infant tongue" can manage "nothing longer or more explicit than Pip" (*GE,* 3); as a result, he "came to be called Pip" with a vengeance. Magwitch designates his beneficiary by the only name extracted during their encounter on the marshes: "Pip, sir" (*GE,* 4). It is the basis for Miss Havisham's "cruel" farewell when Pip departs for London: "Good-bye Pip!— you will always keep the name of Pip, you know" (*GE,* 156). Having learned of Magwitch's stipulation from lawyer Jaggers, she pretends to have imposed this condition, thereby encouraging Pip to misconstrue her as his benefactor. Wemmick's note of warning—"DON'T GO HOME"—is addressed to "Philip Pip, Esquire" (*GE,* 364). Should Estella marry him, she would become, legally, Estella Pip. Nevertheless, it seems advisable to refer to the grown-up narrator of *Great Expectations* as Mr. Pirrip, reserving "Pip" for his experiencing younger self.[1] This convenient distinction preserves the tension between immediacy and recollection: Dickens pretended that his thirteenth novel was a memoir appearing in *All the Year Round* from the pen of a middle-aged autobiographer bent on fashioning his melodramatic life story into a timely admonishment.[2]

Dickens's Great Expectations relies on Margaret Cardwell's Clarendon edition of the novel for its text references but not for its chapter numbering. It makes more sense to follow the 1860–1861 serial version in which chapters run from 1 to 19 (First Stage), 20 to 39 (Second), and 40 to 59 (Third). Cardwell opted for the three-volume 1861 edition; confusingly, in both the Second Stage and the Third (namely, volumes 2 and 3), chapters begin again from 1 to 20, the common practice for a Chapman and Hall three-decker. I also ignore Cardwell's inexplicable preference for the novel's final line as it appeared in *All the Year Round* and the 1861 three-volume edition: "I saw the shadow of no parting from her" (*GE,* 480). In the 1862 one-volume edition and thereafter, Dickens finally got it right: "I saw no shadow of another parting from her" (*GE,*

480, n. 2). Unless otherwise specified, citations of the last line refer to the updated 1862 version.

Chapter 2, on Dickens's dealings with Lever, appeared previously as "'Dashing in Now': *Great Expectations* and Charles Lever's *A Day's Ride*," *Dickens Studies Annual*, 26 (New York: AMS Press, 1998), 227–64. I published the last section of chapter 4 as "*Great Expectations* and *Self-Help:* Dickens Frowns on Smiles" in *The Journal of English and Germanic Philology*, 100 (Oct., 2001), 537–54. A study of Dickens's negative reaction to Mary Shelley's use of *Paradise Lost* in *Frankenstein*, the final segment of chapter 6, was accepted by *The Dickensian* but has yet to appear. Thanks to the editors of the aforementioned journals for permission to incorporate these articles.

Several of my essays on *Great Expectations* are not included in this book but provide an ambiance. I wish there had been room for "Dickens, *Great Expectations*, and the Dartmouth College Notes," *Papers on Language and Literature*, 28 (spring 1992), 111–32; "Dating the Action in *Great Expectations:* A New Chronology," *Dickens Studies Annual*, 21 (New York: AMS Press, 1992), 157–94; "Charles Dickens's *Great Expectations:* A Defense of the Second Ending," *Studies in the Novel*, 25 (spring 1993), 28–59; and "*Great Expectations:* Symmetry in (Com)motion," *Dickens Quarterly*, 15 (March 1998), 28–49.

Harry Stone answered queries about nineteenth-century editions of *Cinderella* and *The Tales of the Genii*. George Worth provided information about the *Great Expectations* manuscript and Dickens's composition habits. Deborah Thomas explained William Makepeace Thackeray's fondness for "The Tale of the [Barber's] Fifth Brother" in *The Arabian Nights*. I have benefited repeatedly from David Paroissien's *Companion to Great Expectations* and from Edgar Rosenberg's Norton Critical Edition. To Jerome H. Buckley I credit my interest in the bildungsroman. I am grateful to him and his wife, Elizabeth, for their hospitality during my visits to Cambridge. I discussed Elizabethan tragicomedy with my late friend and colleague, Joseph A. Bryant Jr. In organizing my material, I have followed several suggestions from my longtime friend and former colleague John Clubbe.

Staffs at Harvard's Widener Library and the New York Public Library have been unfailingly cooperative. I have always been able to rely on Inter-Library Loan at the University of Kentucky. I wish to thank the university's Research Fund for a travel allowance that enabled me to visit the *Great Expectations* country; Paul Geoghehan, cab driver and native of Rochester/Chatham, drove me all over that area. Mrs. A.P.N. Everitt, headmistress of Gad's Hill School, gave me a tour of Dickens's residence.

Chapter 1
Misnar versus Cinderella

Several of Dickens's primary reasons for authoring *Great Expectations* have gone unobserved; these motivations determined the mood and manner in which he wrote his thirteenth novel and offer reliable clues as to what it is about and how it should be read.[1] Although these reasons constantly overlap, they may be listed in ascending order:

    1. To repay Charles Lever for hampering *All the Year Round* with an unpopular serial that Dickens came to consider unrealistic. A prime example of a Victorian novel written to push aside an allegedly inferior composition, Dickens's study of a snob's inner workings, a case history intended to be as psychological as it is sensational, should be read as a parodic revaluation of *A Day's Ride*.

    2. To place Dickens beyond the reach of other rivals as well, not all of them contemporaries. Independent, coherent statement though it is, *Great Expectations* contains a series of repudiations: every time it revised a rival text—parodying episodes from *Jane Eyre,* for example, or parts of *Frankenstein*—Dickens informed readers how *not* to read his own.

    3. To bridge the widening gap between Haves and Have-Nots. Dickens considered this gap one of the principal drawbacks to utopian fantasies about unstoppable progress, such as England's view of itself as heading toward, if not already at, civilization's apex. Psychologically, sociologically, economically, the Pip–Magwitch connection is arguably the most important relationship Dickens ever concocted. In a mordant parody of Cinderella and her fairy godparent, a vengeful outcast turns a blacksmith's apprentice into a London gentleman, yet the bond between them develops into a tragicomic masterpiece brimming over with irony and pathos.

4. To perfect a tragicomic perspective. Dickens paid homage to Shakespeare and Sophocles while reviving his talent for comedy; he developed a protomodern concept of the human condition as tragicomedy verging on tragic farce. Soon to be as temporally distant from us as Shakespeare is from the early Romantics, Dickens the tragicomedian remains close to both classic antecedents and the modern mode. The Victorian period's best weekly serial should be read as the crucial text for understanding the tragicomic novelist the later Dickens thought he had become.

5. To revalue *Cinderella* parodically. Dickens subverts the cinder girl's saga in order to belittle the age's inordinate expectancy, its confidence in better things steadily to come. Darkening what Harry Stone has called "fairy-tale method" (HS, xii), the capacity to comprehend the world with help from fairy lore, Dickens's anti–fairy tale not only turned *Cinderella* upside down but actually replaced it with a more pertinent paradigm for the nature of things. In Dickens's retelling of the century's favorite fairy tale, Cinderella's rise, which Pip thinks to emulate, turns into a fall, a replay of the collapse of Misnar's pavilion in *The Tales of the Genii*.

All of the novels from which Dickens wished to distinguish *Great Expectations* are imbued with Cinderella motifs. The list includes his own *David Copperfield,* Lever's *A Day's Ride,* Thackeray's *Pendennis,* Wilkie Collins's *The Woman in White,* Mary Shelley's *Frankenstein,* Charlotte Brontë's *Jane Eyre,* and Emily Brontë's *Wuthering Heights.* Parodying *Cinderella* enabled Dickens to assail several rival novelists for composing unrealistic fairy tales that they fobbed off on an all-too-credulous public as truthful social criticism. *Great Expectations* should be read as an irreverent revaluation of the many Cinderella stories in nineteenth-century fiction.

In a tragicomic world, Dickens warned, a Cinderella complex is unhealthy. No one should expect a life of unqualified ascent; by extension, no society should envision itself as a Cinderella among nations, as if providence were its fairy godparent. In effect, the parodic revaluator functions as myth breaker. Using Pip's autobiography to deflate *Cinderella,* Dickens exploded unwarranted cultural assumptions; he challenged Victorian England's exalted conception of itself as a chosen people. When Magwitch returns in chapter 39, Pip's life story ceases to chronicle a Cinderella-like rise; instead, it becomes clear that it has been building toward a tragicomic downfall not unlike the collapse of Misnar's pavilion upon pretenders to the sultan's throne.

As David Copperfield's days at Doctor Strong's academy draw to an end, he refers to his life as "a great fairy story" that he is "about to read" (*DC,* 235). But when Pip attempts to see himself as Cinderella, a realistic view of his situation calls for a less gratifying analogue. *Great Expectations* may be read as an "inverted fairy tale" (HS, 299)—*Cinderella* upside down, inside out, and in reverse. But simply skewering the cinder girl's story was not enough; full-fledged parodic revaluation demanded that it be pushed aside in favor of a cautionary tale better suited to life's tragicomic uncertainties. Two fairy tales unfold at once in *Great Expectations:* the one Pip thinks to duplicate, and a counterstory undermining it. Besides redoing Cinderella's fall and rise as Pip's rise and fall, *Great Expectations* retells the collapse of Misnar's pavilion. Pip suddenly discovers that he has been reliving the Misnar story despite trying to imitate Cinderella's.[2]

Cinderella goes from being her father's darling, to misery as her step-mother's lowliest servant, to glorious triumph as a prince's consort.[3] In contrast, Pip exchanges the drudgery of a blacksmith's apprentice for the life of a London gentleman, only to watch his new lifestyle collapse like the pavilion that crushes the usurpers of Misnar's throne in *The Tales of the Genii*. The sultan's splendid but deadly palace symbolizes the dangers inherent in setting up illusory goals and seeking unmerited rewards. Perhaps more provokingly than Dickens intended, it also stands for the insubstantiality of earthly attainments generally.

The task of replacing *Cinderella* with a caveat from Misnar falls to Mr. Pirrip, Pip's older self. In the last paragraph of chapter 38, Mr. Pirrip has Pip liken his social promotion and his plans to marry Estella to the construction and collapse of Misnar's pavilion. This 168-word allusion did not occur to Pip at the time his prospects actually collapsed. The autobiographer introduces it to herald Magwitch's return in chapter 39, due to which his younger self's snobbish expectations fall apart. Magwitch's return destroys them as effectively as the collapse of Misnar's pavilion pulverized the usurpers.[4]

In the last paragraph of chapter 38, Pip is made to realize that in removing himself from Joe's forge to a gentleman's chambers in London, he has reenacted the Misnar tale, not *Cinderella*. The passage prepares readers for the novel's epiphanic moment: Magwitch's unwelcome return, the catastrophe around which the plot of Mr. Pirrip's life story rotates. First Pip reprimands Estella for her willingness to "deceive and entrap" (*GE,* 309); then, through a process of association, he shifts to the bigger trap that was about to be sprung on him.

In the penultimate paragraph, Pip resolves to "pass on" from romantic frustrations "to the event that has impended over [him] longer yet": reunion with Magwitch, the outcome of actions that took place before Pip even "knew the world held Estella." Then, redolent with foreboding, comes the most important passage in *Great Expectations*—the concluding paragraph of the penultimate chapter in the next-to-last weekly installment for the "Second Stage." "In the Eastern story," says Pip, the heavy slab that was to fall on the bed of state in the flush of conquest was slowly wrought out of the quarry, the tunnel for the rope to hold it in its place was slowly carried through leagues of rock, the slab was slowly raised and fitted in the roof, the rope was rove to it and slowly taken through the miles of hollow to the great iron ring. All being made ready with much labour, and the hour come, the sultan was aroused in the dead of night, and the sharpened axe that was to sever the rope from the great iron ring was put into his hand, and he struck with it, and the rope parted and rushed away, and the ceiling fell. So, in my case; all the work, near and afar, that tended to the end, had been accomplished; and in an instant the blow was struck, and the roof of my stronghold dropped upon me" (*GE*, 309–10).[5]

Pip's marathon allusion to *The Tales of the Genii* was no mystery to Dickens's original audience, familiar with fairy tales from childhood. Today, readers need to be told that "The Enchanters; or, Misnar the Sultan of the East," Number VI of the *Tales,* has three parts. In "The History of Mahoud," Misnar ascends the throne amid prophecies that "the powers of enchantment shall prevail!" (*TG*, 139). At one point, Misnar, Horam (his faithful vizier), and the Princess of Cashmere are transformed into reptiles by Ulin, an enchantress. Although sultan and vizier regain their former powers and Ulin is destroyed, enchanters continue to aid Ahubal, Misnar's younger brother, in revolts against Misnar.

In the centerpiece, "Continuation of the Tale of the Enchanters," Horam builds Misnar an opulent pavilion designed to eclipse the "sumptuous pavilion" that Ahubal's troops have erected for their leader; Horam's structure will "far outshine in splendour every glory upon earth" (*TG*, 205). When Misnar's forces are compelled to retreat, his "magnificent pavilion" falls into enemy hands; Ahubal's chief advisors, the enchanters Ahaback and Desra, hold a victory banquet in the pavilion. Horam leads Misnar to a spacious cavern where, late at night, the sultan strikes with an axe, severing a strong rope from its ring of iron. It flies swiftly among the rocks and out through a hole in the cavern wall.

Unimpressed, Misnar sentences Horam to be hanged for dereliction of duty. Instead of building the pavilion and then remaining in the rear, his forces should have been fighting alongside Misnar's. The next morning, however, news arrives of the deaths of Ahaback and Desra, who were crushed by the pavilion's collapse. Revitalized, Misnar's armies fall upon Ahubal's, soundly defeating them. When a giant, Kifri, later kills Ahubal to avenge the enchanters, Misnar is finally secure. In the third part, "The History of the Princess of Cashmere," the princess is rescued and becomes sultana of India.

Horam explains to Misnar that the single "massy stone" for the pavilion's roof was hung on "four pillars of gold." The rope holding the stone aloft "passed through one of the golden pillars into the earth beneath, and by a secret channel . . . was carried . . . to a ring of iron in a cave hollowed out of the rock" (*TG*,

213). In severing the rope, Misnar frees the stone, in effect releasing the death trap's ceiling to execute the usurpers, who are "puffed up with their success." The manner of their deaths is summarized as follows: "Over the magnificent pavilion of the sultan, which Horam built for his master, the artful vizier had concealed a ponderous stone, which covered the whole pavilion. This, by some secret means, he contrived in the night to release from its confinement, while Ahaback and Desra were sleeping on the sofas beneath it . . . their bodies were crushed to atoms" (*TG*, 212).

Mr. Pirrip's younger self realizes that the future he built for himself out of false hopes has proven as deceptive and deadly as the pavilion that Horam constructed for Misnar. Using the tale of "The Enchanters," Dickens tells Pip's story—and retells Cinderella's—not in terms of miraculous elevation, not as the recovery of one's rightful status, but as a sudden crash, a violent comedown for overreachers. Cinderella's prerogatives are redone as Pip's presumptions: Dickens transforms snobbery—his protagonist's expressly Victorian "hankerings after money and gentility" (*GE*, 236)—from social climbing to the equivalent of usurpation.

Misnar's pavilion, Pip's life story, and Victorian England's moral condition become interchangeable: the first is an implicit analogue for the second, which is also a microcosm for the third. The pavilion stands—or rather falls—as an architectural reminder to a nation overly proud of its multiplying advantages that the roof can easily cave in if, like Pip, it mistakes ascendance for improvement, material prosperity for progress. In the novel's parodic counterstory, Dickens personifies false expectations as enchanters and treats their snares as forms of "enchantment," the word Pip uses to describe Estella's hold over him (*GE*, 239). Pip is spellbound three times over: trapped within Magwitch's schemes and enthralled by both Miss Havisham and Estella, he represents an enmeshed society obsessed with gentility, upward movement, and status over substance. Pip's snobbish pretensions symbolize the Victorian overconfidence in a seemingly endless growth of national prestige and material advancement. However, as did Misnar's fabulous but lethal pavilion, Pip's magnificent future as a London gentleman, informally engaged (so he thinks) to an heiress, suddenly caves in. To collapse one fairy tale, Mr. Pirrip has Pip invoke another. Novels modeled on *Cinderella* (stories with Cinderella motifs), Dickens objected, support a national ethos of accumulation and perpetual ascent; thanks to the Misnar analogue, *Great Expectations* rewards such hubris by building toward a spectacular breakdown.

In conventional fairy tales, *disenchantment* signals a return to mental and physical normalcy, but in *Great Expectations* it connotes *disillusionment.* When Magwitch returns, Pip emerges from three spells—he comprehends his actual relationship to Magwitch, Miss Havisham, and Estella. He also reverts from prince to pauper. An anti–Cinderella story after all, Pip's autobiography not only satirizes presumptuous expectancy; it also hints that expectation itself resembles a state of enchantment, pure folly in an indeterminate world.

Irony does not lie solely in Pip's recognition of himself as a failed Cinderella. Unfortunately, he is not Misnar either: unlike the sultan, he has been deposed. He resembles Horam only parodically in having built himself a collapsible palace out of daydreams. Admittedly, Pip's life at the forge exceeds the cinder girl's for dirt and grime, and "Mrs. Joe" Gargery, Pip's sister, is a close match for Cinderella's abusive stepmother.[6] But as Magwitch's tool for usurping gentility, Pip most clearly recalls the Eastern tale's overreachers, its doomed enchanters. Like Ahaback and Desra, Pip is struck down at the height of fortune; his hopes, like their limbs, are "crushed to atoms" (*TG*, 212), making his disaster just as ignominious.

From the tale of Misnar's pavilion, Dickens borrowed a fatal edifice to stand for the self-destructive allure of what Pip calls "ill-regulated aspirations" (*GE*, 236). Because these ambitions are as unstable as Misnar's pavilion, Magwitch's return exerts the same impact on them as the collapse of the sultan's palace had on the pretenders to his throne. In a stroke of genius, Dickens depicted Pip as both the enchanted and the enchanter: on one hand, Magwitch's victim; on the other, an impostor like Ahaback and Desra. Despite falling under several spells that he seems powerless to avoid, as do Misnar and Horam, Pip is the willing representative of an enchanted age, having imbibed the false values of his society.

Cinderella has been read as "an allegory for the Soul's discovery of its Image" (AD, 195). The glamorous Cinderella is a projection of the cinder girl's ideal or better self (AD, 199); her transformation enables her to reveal to the world that sense of inner worth all mortals would like to externalize permanently. In Cinderella, the prince's "sought-for" ideal also materializes. But when Pip beholds his true image, instead of a resplendent inner self, he discovers consanguinity with the deluded upstarts in the Misnar story.[7]

For Pip there is no slipper on the stair, no clue to Cinderella's whereabouts for him to find or leave. Instead, "at eleven o'clock," when he is startled to hear "a footstep on the stair" (*GE*, 311), the tread belongs to Magwitch, returning to reveal himself as Pip's undesirable fairy godfather. Only for Magwitch, with motives a mixture of gratitude and revenge, is Pip the long-sought ideal. Shock leaves Pip "too stunned" to go to bed "for an hour or more" (*GE*, 320). So his "stronghold" collapses once and for all at midnight, about the time that Cinderella's transformation wears off each evening. It is also in "the dead of the night" (*GE*, 310) that Misnar severs the rope to release the ceiling stone. Dickens parodies Cinderella's nightly relapse into "cinderhood" with Pip's permanent reversion from false hopes to crushed dreams, for which the collapse of Misnar's pavilion supplies the perfect parallel.

Robert Garis singled out *Great Expectations* as the only Dickens novel with a plot free from "contraptions"; that is, "consciously contrived theatrical scenes and rhetorical arguments" (RG, 206). Nevertheless, because of Pip's Misnar allusion, the novel contains a contraption par excellence, arguably Dickens's finest. Just as Horam designed Misnar's pavilion to cave in on pretenders trying to steal the sultan's throne, Dickens fashioned *Great Expectations* with punitive artistry to humble his allegedly inferior competitors.

Misnar's pavilion illustrates the process whereby Dickens's parodic revaluations collapse the fictions of his rivals: it exemplifies the paradox of construction through destruction at the heart of "the Eastern story" (*GE*, 309) and of parodic revaluation generally. Misnar regains his throne at the expense of the undeserving enchanters who thought to replace him; similarly, the parodic revaluator builds a case for one story by tearing down another, sabotaging *Cinderella* with the Misnar tale, for example, or *A Day's Ride* with *Great Expectations*.

The sultan's palace is a defensible entrapment unlike the "snares" Estella sets for Drummle, or Miss Havisham for Pip (*GE*, 358). *Great Expectations* functions as a sort of Misnar's pavilion in which rival novelists as diverse as Lever, Collins, Thackeray, and the Brontës are treated like usurpers; that is, not realists but enchanters whose spells must be dissolved. On one hand, *Great Expectations* is meant to "outshine" rival novels the way Misnar's pavilion outclassed the pavilion built for Ahubal, Misnar's rival for the throne (*TG*, 204–5); on the other hand, Dickens permits his rivals' themes, characters, and situations to enter his novel just as Ahaback and Desra infiltrated Misnar's pavilion, but only so that his parodic revisions can demolish them just as the sultan's palace caved in on the enchanters. Unlike Pip, Dickens could envision himself as both Misnar and Horam. The reigning sultan among novel writers, he had become a prospective target for every rising novelist seeking the top spot. Consequently, he had to be his own grand vizier, his own strongest protector against claimants to supremacy.

An example of precision engineering, Dickens's architectural symbol monumentalized his formula for holding together a good serial. If the serialist must "lay some one strong ground of suspended interest" (*PL*, 9:323–24), the identity of Pip's patron, the suspenseful delay preceding Magwitch's reappearance, is just such "strong ground"; the "heavy slab" overhanging the "bed of state" concretizes it (*GE*, 309). If a serial must be "strung . . . on the needful strong thread of interest" (*PL*, 9:321–22), the counterpart for this in Misnar's story is the rope stretching from the roof to the cavern's "great iron ring" (*GE*, 310). Symbolic of the novel's plot and the individual's lifeline, this rope is severed by a serialist imitating, as did Misnar, the workings of a retributive providence.

The sultan uses a sharp axe to cut the rope. Pip simply states that "the blow was struck" (*GE*, 310), which creates the impression of vast, impersonal forces at work—providence functioning within the historical process as a corrective agent with paradoxical characteristics: patience, but with a capacity for swift redress. Life stays on course and justice is done not through a three-day rise like Cinderella's, but as a result of deceptively sudden readjustments, apparently slow in arriving but headlong and unstoppable in retrospect. Patient delay before quick comeuppance is the serialist's stock in trade. Dickens's sensational realism, Misnar's pavilion, and so-called real life allegedly operate by similar rules.

The word "slowly" appears four times in the first sentence of chapter 38's last paragraph. Once stone and rope are carefully manufactured and meticulously installed—deliberate steps in Pip's synopsis—the pace quickens: the rope in the Misnar story "rushed away" to release the stone, and Pip's "stronghold" falls in "an instant" (*GE*, 310). His allusion to Misnar's pavilion not only makes visible the first principles of the serialist's art; it also reveals affinities between such artistry and providence's long-term plans.

In making Pip's allusion to *The Tales of the Genii* so dominant, Dickens risked implying that Misnar's pavilion is a satiric symbol for life itself, a commentary on the vanity of human wishes. It could be construed as a symbol for the temporal world's meretricious allure, its shortlived delights. Collapsibility stays central to both the Misnar tale and Pip's life story, despite the sultan's recovery of his throne and the latter's moral rehabilitation. Still, Dickens works hard to limit the catastrophism in his key symbol. Although "society itself is the trap" for Pip (MS, 110), the novel stops short of equating the human situation with such a trap. Unlike Thackeray's image of Vanity Fair, which it resembles yet rejects, the sultan's pavilion need not connote the eventual collapse of *all* earthly goals and aspirations—not if a supervisory providence, possibly theistic, schools Pip, turning him from false gentility into a real gentleman.

In the belated epiphany with which chapter 38 ends, Pip's reassessment of his career to date is a painful readjustment that entails a glimpse of the nature of things: sooner or later, every mortal's "stronghold" (*GE*, 310) collapses. Because the Cinderella story puts rise in place of fall and fulfillment in frustration's stead, it reverses grim facts. It must be inverted, a tactic employed from the very beginning when Magwitch turns Pip "upside down" in the churchyard (*GE*, 4). But the truth about life—what it is like to be alive—does not lie solely in Misnar's caved-in ceiling any more than it lies in Cinderella's fabulous rise. It resides as well in the tragicomic discrepancy between them. This is the gap that Mr. Pirrip's autobiography explores. When Pip's life story begins to recall the Misnar tale instead of *Cinderella,* the emphasis falls on disparity, not futility.

Dickens's world is as laden with disappointment and sorrow as Thackeray's, yet unlike his rival's description of the latter, Dickensian satire, no matter how indignant, is rarely "more melancholy than mirthful" (*VF,* xxix).[8] In *Great Expectations,* as compared with *A Tale of Two Cities* or *Little Dorrit,* Dickens reminded himself that he possessed a stronger sense than Thackeray's of the comic consequences of life's inadequacies. Granted, the world of *Bleak House* remains closer to *Vanity Fair* than to Middlemarch or Barchester, and Misnar's pavilion verges on becoming a satiric metaphor for life. From 1860 on, however, Dickens strove to be a "mirthful" rather than a melancholic tragedian.

Like Misnar's pavilion, *Great Expectations* was conceived to save a kingdom: *All the Year Round,* the journal whose circulation was being spoiled by Lever's *A Day's Ride*. It was also written to admonish a nation. Novels as different from each other as *A Day's Ride* and *The Woman in White*—both published in Dickens's own journal—relied on Cinderella motifs to woo readers. The ubiquity of such motifs, Dickens objected, encouraged an exaggerated sense of self-worth; by extension, they also permitted a nation to overestimate its accomplishments and inflate its potential.

For nearly two decades before *Great Expectations* opens, England struggled through the Napoleonic Wars; unpaid bills, political crises, and widespread labor unrest were the economic consequences (JC, 5–6).[9] Neither George III nor the Prince of Wales—the latter first as Regent, then as George IV—commanded the public's affections. By 1860, however, England had apparently come through: twenty-three years into her reign, Queen Victoria was widely esteemed and prosperity had returned. The tiny island had recently hosted the 1851 Great Exhibition, a gigantic world's fair; London, its capital, was the civilized world's financial hub. Thanks to "boom times," "sunlit years" whose brightness had never been seen before, England had become the "richest nation on earth"— the world's "foremost banker, shipper, supplier of manufactured goods" (RA, 12–13). A rebounding economy, coupled with social improvements, created a climate of "rising *expectations*" (JC, 5; italics added). "Growth of the *expectation* of change," Robin Gilmour has observed, was the "most significant intellectual development" between 1800 and 1850 (G, 19; italics added). By mid-century and increasingly thereafter, the Victorians may be characterized as an *expectant* people; despite numerous long-standing social evils and a plethora of new problems still unsolved today, they lived during the era of greatest material expectancy the world had ever seen.

Not surprisingly, Victorian England considered itself a Cinderella story of national proportions.[10] The country's recovery and the cinder girl's seemed to verify each other. The latter's rise could be elevated to a popular myth worth reading again and again in novels of the day, because it fit the seemingly miraculous changes that nineteenth-century England had undergone between the early 1800s and 1860: from beleaguered island to world power on the brink of global domination. When Victorian novelists imbued their fictions with Cinderella motifs, they ingratiated themselves with a middle-class reading public eager to be congratulated on its moral and material situation. If a drawing master could marry an heiress in *The Woman in White*, if the son of an apothecary could win the hand of a wealthy industrialist's daughter in *A Day's Ride*, if a governess could change from plain Jane Eyre to "Jane heiress," happily married to Mr. Rochester, then Victorian society reaffirmed itself. In mythologizing *Cinderella*, it could justify its own existence and trust its prospects for additional advancement. Through a wonderful symbiosis, Victorian novelists wrote success stories that catered to an appetite for the snobbish exaltation of self and country that such stories continued to stimulate.

Throughout the 1850s, Dickens sounded like a prophet of doom; he contradicted the prevailing ethos in a series of satirical novels that threatened his popularity even as they ensured his immortality. In *Bleak House*, he compared London's legal system to its stopped-up drains. In *Hard Times*, he enumerated the ravages of industrialism on both body and mind. In *Little Dorrit*, he anatomized a useless high society, damned crooked entrepreneurs, and exposed the willful incompetence of the nation's bureaucracy. Then he resurrected the specter of revolution in *A Tale of Two Cities*. England was a cloacal mess, an industrial dystopia; when not clogged, its administrative arteries ran in circles. To this list, despite a rich comic vein, *Great Expectations* added that the nation was a phony Cinderella.

Great Expectations should be read not just as Dickens's perspective on the 1860s but also as the climax to his fictions of the 1850s, arguably his greatest decade. He set the novel in the post-Napoleonic time period out of which the Victorians felt that England had climbed so gloriously. He collapsed the midcentury onto the Regency years. This strategy dispelled the pervasive aura of a miraculous rise; it infested the earlier time with cravings for wealth and status that Dickens alleged were ruining the later period. Progress achieved since the 1820s was a mirage—it had given rise to an increase of snobbery and money worship—or else these deficiencies were already threatening even then.

Dickens's "myth of England," according to Gillian Avery, "is derived . . . from T.B. Macaulay" (GA, xxiv), whose so-called Whig view of history is not incompatible with Cinderella's story. Macaulay's England takes a phenomenal leap forward during the century and a half prior to 1840, rising from humble circumstances before the Glorious Revolution to the top of the heap during Victoria's reign. Macaulay's worldview presupposed that "inevitable progress" had asserted itself as a virtual natural law in the late seventeenth century. Volume 1 of his *History of England* (1848) uses "England in 1685" as a point of departure for a comparison of "Past and Present." Unlike Carlyle's disquisition on the same subject in 1843, it shows the nation steadily improving, becoming "in the course of ages . . . not only a wiser, but also a kinder people" (FR, 153). "Our ancestors," Macaulay insisted, "were less humane than their posterity"— less charitable, less prosperous, less enlightened, less progressive.

By 1860, Carlyle had been Dickens's historian of choice for at least a decade: Cassandra instead of Pangloss. Dickens shared Macaulay's disdain for his country's benighted past but also echoed Carlyle's reservations about the present situation.[11] Macaulay considered it "unreasonable and ungrateful ... to be constantly discontented with a condition which is constantly improving" (FR, 154). His thoughts were tantamount to reading English history as a perpetual imitation of Cinderella's rise. Carlyle compared "the condition of England" (that is, industrialized countries) to that of King Midas: the land was cursed with "an enchanted wealth" (TC, 5) that left many of its citizens poor and starving. Macaulay toasted England as "the richest and most civilized spot in the world!" (FR, 85) In *Bleak House,* where "perpetual stoppage" is the rule (*BH,* 146), one finds "as much mud in the streets, as if the waters had but newly retired from the face of the earth" (*BH,* 3). Neither the London of *Bleak House* nor Coketown in *Hard Times,* Dickens responded, offers proof of continual progress; neither should be confused with a principality in utopia.

Prior to *Great Expectations,* Dickens's myth for his age came not from Macaulay as Avery claimed, but from Shakespeare's *King Lear,* which he revised as follows: "the hardhearted, deluded father-figure, who refuses or perverts the love he receives from an affectionate daughter, became mid-century England, industrialized, materialized, even Benthamized." Dickens blamed England for "casting out, in the persons of Nell, Florence, and Louisa, all the emotions, feelings, and attributes of the heart that [he] felt were essential to any genuine millennium" (JM, 76). In Nell and her grandfather (*The Old Curiosity Shop*); Mr. Dombey and his daughter, Florence (*Dombey and Son*); and Mr. Gradgrind with both his daughter, Louisa, and his ward, Sissy Jupe (*Hard Times*), Dickens reworked Lear's mistreatment of Cordelia. Underestimates or outright dismissal of the daughter figure symbolized England's increasingly selfish repudiation of its gentler, more humane tendencies in favor of a crass materialism—this view of the 1840s and 1850s squarely contradicting Macaulay's scenario.

As Cinderella motifs proliferated in Victorian novels, Dickens may have been perturbed by resemblances between *Cinderella* and his reworkings of *King Lear.* All four of Dickens's maligned heroines—Nell, Florence, Louisa, and Sissy, not to mention Cordelia—can be misconstrued as Cinderella types, variations on a theme rather than its refutation. Several Cinderella-like Cordelias await recognition that either never comes or arrives too late. Dickens's rephrasings of Shakespeare did not put enough distance between himself and *Cinderella.* Although Mr. Dombey tumbles, for example, Florence is restored to her proper station thanks to Walter Gay, a reasonable facsimile for the famous fairy tale's ardent prince.

Dickens's Lear-like father figures personify the state as an irresponsible or unnatural parent; the long suffering daughter figure remains passive. More culpable, Pip is a self-victimizer who pursues the Cinderella role that his upbringing has conditioned him to covet. Using the Misnar story to undercut *Cinderella* was not inconsistent with Dickens's earlier redoings of Lear and Cordelia. Both ridicule Macaulay's conception of a continually improving state of affairs. Nor is discrediting the cinder girl with the Misnar tale less subtle than adapting the Lear-Cordelia relationship from Shakespeare's play. However, Dickens's subversion of the century's best-known fairy tale seems intended to be more parodic, funnier yet just as serious. The breach between Lear and Cordelia is tragic but repairable; not so the gap between *Cinderella* and the Misnar tale, which is tragicomic and permanent.

Dickens's paramount reason for writing *Great Expectations* was to reconsider the prevailing climate of unrealistic expectancy, to discredit novelists whose use of Cinderella motifs fostered such a climate. He was convinced that reading novels in which the fate of hero or heroine vindicates Cinderella's was akin to living in a fairy tale, much as Pip attempts to do. It was like falling under an enchantment. To calumniate his rivals' fondness for Cinderella stories, Dickens employed *four* Cinderellas in *Great Expectations*—three disastrous failures and one ironic success. He debunked the Cinderella complex prevalent in nineteenth-century fiction by filling his thirteenth novel with parodic Cinderellas; besides Pip, the contingent includes Estella, Miss Havisham, and Biddy.

Cold-hearted, herself a victim, Estella symbolizes the futility of living life in terms of rewards deferred. The more Pip yearns for Estella, pining to be raised to her level, the less he accomplishes. His Cinderella complex is both an unsettling influence and a paralyzing agent. Moreover, the deferred reward turns out to be illusory: inasmuch as Estella is not really Miss Havisham's daughter, she was never a princess after all.[12] When Pip discovers her to be Magwitch's child, shrewd detective work though it is, the solution to Estella's parentage (ch. 50) parodies the prince's successful search for the young woman who captivated him at the ball. In Estella's rendition, the cinder girl is indifferent to others, totally unattainable, a fake or travesty who goes from riches to rags when her husband, Bentley Drummle, squanders her inheritance.[13] Ironically, Estella spurns Pip to marry a cruel parody of Prince Charming.

If Estella is a ruinous Cinderella, a heartbreaker, Miss Havisham is a ruined, heartbroken one. "She was dressed," Pip reports, "in rich materials—satins and lace, and silks—all of white. Her shoes were white. And she had a long white veil dependent from her hair, and she had bridal flowers in her hair, but her hair was white" (*GE,* 58). The last detail changes whiteness from virginal promise to superannuation, Cinderella as an old maid. Although "bright jewels sparkled on her neck and on her hands," everything about Miss Havisham, Pip realizes, "had lost its lustre, and was faded and yellow." The dress "had been put upon the rounded figure of a young woman," but "the figure on which it now hung loose, had shrunk to skin and bone" (*GE*, 59). Miss Havisham makes a grimmer mockery of expectancy than Estella does.[14] She is attired in a bride's decaying finery as if for a ball she will never attend. Nor will her missing shoe furnish the clue through which a prince can find her. This witchlike woman seems bewitched herself—under an unbreakable spell that arrests the hands of time. On three successive evenings, Cinderella's good luck runs out at midnight; Miss Havisham's luck ran out permanently "at twenty minutes to nine" on her wedding day (*GE*, 59). Her version of Cinderella is a victim whose rise or recovery never happens: Compeyson proves a false prince who defrauds Miss Havisham, then deserts her permanently.

Between them, these two false Cinderellas (Miss Havisham and Estella) prevent Pip, a would-be Cinderella, from recognizing the novel's only true cinder girl. After Biddy has been at the forge a year, Pip "imperceptively" notices "a change." Her "shoes came up at the heel, her hair grew bright and neat, her hands were always clean . . . she had curiously thoughtful and attentive eyes; eyes that were very pretty and very good" (*GE*, 124).[15] Gone is the unformed Biddy who arrived "with a small speckled box containing the whole of her worldly effects" (*GE*, 122). In her place, having matured through personal effort and by degrees rather than miraculously, stands a priceless young woman, "not beautiful" but "pleasant and wholesome and sweet-tempered" (*GE*, 124), whose wealth is her abundant good nature. Unfortunately for her and Pip, "remembrance of the Havisham days" (*GE*, 131), like a lingering enchantment, obscures his vision and scatters his wits. He daydreams that Miss Havisham will make his "fortune" (*GE*, 132) and marry him to Estella once he completes his apprenticeship. Pip's failure to return Biddy's love—indeed, he becomes a torment to her—seems almost criminal. Although Biddy would make a plausible Cinderella, thus imparting credence to the fairy story, Pip overlooks her, then puts her aside for a simulacrum. As a result, Pip is a parody of Cinderella many times over: he fails to be transformed into one, tries to wed a false one, and neglects to marry the real one.[16]

Dickens was no stranger to *The Tales of the Genii*. At the age of ten, he "was inspired to compose a tragedy entitled *Misnar, the Sultan of India* (founded on one of the *Tales of the Genii*)" (J, 1:23), his "first effort at authorship" (HS, 59). Dickens's father owned a copy of the *Tales;* so too does David Copperfield's father. It is among the "small collection of books" that, says David, "kept alive my fancy" (*DC*, 53). When Copperfield is exiled to his room by the Murdstones, stories like the *Tales* provide companionship; they also nourish a starved imagination. Temporarily forgetting his predicament by "reading as if for life," David entertains a "hope of something better beyond that place and time" (*DC*, 54).

The youthful author of "Misnar, the Sultan of India" probably never suspected that his source was not oriental, but Dickens surely knew this by the time he wrote *Great Expectations*. Like the other stories in *The Tales of the Genii; or, The Delightful Lessons of Horam, The Son of Asmar*, "The Enchanters; or, Misnar the Sultan of the East" pretends to be a translation from the Persian by Sir Charles Morell. Actually, the stories were written by the Reverend James Ridley, who was born in Stepney and died in 1765, the year after their publication. In substituting the Misnar story for *Cinderella*, Dickens replaced a fairy tale of French and German origins with a more pertinent one that was homespun.[17]

Pip refers to "the Eastern story" (*GE*, 309), so Mr. Pirrip appears to accept the *Tales* at face value. But he may simply be acknowledging their setting or implying that his youthful self considered the story authentically Persian. Mr. Pirrip entrusts the Misnar allusion to Pip, as if it were occurring to the latter on the spot, not as the autobiographer's retrospective embellishment. Pip remembers the Misnar material perfectly, recounting details with wonderful economy. He also displays a sensationalist realist's sense of pace: the five conjunctives in the second sentence of the last paragraph of chapter 38 impart to the synopsis a mounting suspense germane to his life story.

Just as Dickens's fascination with the Misnar story dates from childhood, his preoccupation with *Cinderella* was career-long. No fewer than six of Dickens's first seven novels are indebted to *Cinderella*. In most instances, the early Dickens subscribed to this fairy tale's promise of better days to come for those down on their luck. The cellar-dwelling Marchioness in *The Old Curiosity Shop* makes a passable Cinderella, with Dick Swiveler as her Cockney prince. In *Dombey and Son*, as has been noted, Walter Gay plays the prince for Florence. In *David Copperfield*, Emily is Cinderella gone awry, but David wins through to prosperity and Agnes.[18] Charity and Mercy Pecksniff in *Martin Chuzzlewit* are Cinderella's selfish stepsisters reincarnated.[19]

In *Nicholas Nickleby*, the eponymous hero may be called a Cinderella: Nicholas recovers the money and position his family lost through his late father's speculations. *Oliver Twist*, the earliest of Dickens's novels indebted to *Cinderella*, corroborates it the most. An orphan brought up "by hand" as is Pip (*GE*, 8), Oliver gains a father, mother, and sister in "one moment" of the penultimate chapter when Dickens sorts out the boy's salvationary ties to Mr. Brownlow, Mrs. Maylie, and Rose Fleming (*OT*, 397).[20] In contrast, Pip must give up Miss Havisham and Estella once Magwitch reappears. Having forfeited Biddy to Joe, Pip severs his connections with England as well.

For warmth Cinderella has to sleep, dusty and dirty, in the cinders on the hearth, but her innate worth eventually shines through. Like his grasp of the

King's English, Oliver's character remains unsullied even in a den of thieves. Earmarked for prosperity as surely as the cinder girl, he is never physically or morally blackened. Hardly Cinderella, Pip is no reaffirmation of Oliver. Having stolen to feed an escaped convict, he feels "contaminated" with "prison dust" even after his rise (*GE,* 263). During his apprenticeship at the forge, Pip dreads being seen as a cinderfella; that is, at his "grimiest and commonest . . . with a black face and hands" (*GE,* 107–8). Ironically, Magwitch's gifts—education, gentlemanly status, a regular stipend—tarnish Pip's already vulnerable better self, lessening his capacity for loyalty and friendship.

Biographically, Dickens testifies on both sides of the Cinderella issue—both for and against her plausibility. His rise from label paster in Warren's Blacking Warehouse to squire of Gad's Hill reads like a Cinderella story. In 1824 and 1825, the twelve-year-old future novelist was a reluctant child laborer in the shoe polish business, where, like Cinderella, he experienced what Bruno Bettelheim has called "the misery of being degraded" (BB, 249). A "poor little drudge" (F, 1:25), a genuine cinder boy, Dickens was ashamed of the "defiling polish that grimed his hands and fingernails" (K, 42). Thirty-two years later, on 14 March 1856, he purchased Gad's Hill Place, Rochester. At Gad's, Dickens was an internationally famous author who had returned to the scene of his youth to reclaim his patrimony. When Charles was ten, he and his father had often walked past this house, which John Dickens "promised that [young Charles] might himself live in . . . if he would only work hard enough" (F, 1:6).[21]

Within this outline, however, Dickens's life is a series of disappointments beginning with the absence of requital from his first love, Maria Beadnell, and the sudden death of his beloved sister-in-law, Mary Hogarth. In America, the democratic republic he had imagined never materialized. Besides being increasingly dissatisfied with his marriage to Catherine Hogarth, he chafed at the snail's pace of reform. The harm Lever was doing to *All the Year Round* illustrated the precariousness of success. In short, the forty-eight-year-old novelist was becoming steadily more aware of the impermanence of health, friendships, and love.[22]

By 1860, Dickens's career both was and was not a Cinderella story. A tragicomic patina had settled over his life, a sense of multiple disappointments despite many triumphs. His climb from Warren's to Gad's paralleled the country's rise from imperiled island to industrial powerhouse. But just as Dickens's career was pitted with setbacks and shortfalls, the nation's preeminence, he alleged, was deceptively Cinderella-like. To demonstrate this, Dickens curbed his lifelong interest in *Cinderella* with a subversive revaluation of it using the Misnar story, the subject of his earliest composition. Revised as a tragicomedy in place of *David Copperfield* and presented obliquely as Mr. Pirrip's autobiography, Dickens's life story dramatized the maturation of its author's philosophical outlook and the consummation of his aesthetic.

To read *Great Expectations* effectively, one must chart the darkening of Dickens's so-called fairy tale vision. The frequency with which fairy stories "entered his imagination and shaped his art" (HS, xi) never varied, but Dickens's attitude toward one such influx did. Nothing better illustrates the idea of Dickens as "of all the great Victorian writers . . . probably the one most antagonistic to the Victorian Age itself" (EW, 25) than his shift from supporter of fairy lore generally to saboteur of *Cinderella*.

In "Frauds on the Fairies," the lead article in the 1 October 1853 issue of *Household Words*, Dickens protected fairy tales in principle by parodying *Cinderella*. He scolded George Cruikshank, his former illustrator, for authoring pious retellings of famous fairy tales into which Cruikshank "interpolated social doctrines" (HS, 2). Such heavy-handed moralizing, Dickens protested, reduced fairy tales to propaganda. Having read *Hop-o'-my Thumb*, the first volume in Cruikshank's *Fairy Library*, Dickens wrote to W.H. Wills from Paris, asking his subeditor for "the most simple and popular version of *Cinderella* you can get me" (HS, 2).[23] To ridicule Cruikshank's didactic zeal, Dickens retold *Cinderella* as a temperance tract. After marrying her prince, Cinderella implements repressive eating and drinking policies to stamp out alcoholism; anyone who disobeys is promptly imprisoned (HS, 13–15).[24]

Cruikshank issued his own update of *Cinderella* in 1854 as volume 3 of the *Fairy Library*, but Dickens's attack had doomed this enterprise; a projected fourth volume never appeared. The experience of parodying *Cinderella* in "Frauds on the Fairies"—admittedly at Cruikshank's expense instead of outright—may have recurred to Dickens in 1860 as a way of satirizing Pip. Attempting to relive *Cinderella*, Pip resembles Victorian England usurping the cinder girl's story for its national myth. Similarly, Cruikshank had twisted a given tale toward his own "narrow and fanatical ends" (HS, 10) just as the pretenders in *The Tales of the Genii*, the two enchanters, placed themselves on Misnar's throne.

On 30 March 1850, Dickens had inaugurated *Household Words* with a manifesto against the Utilitarian philosophy. Challenging an increasingly fact-oriented society of commercial and industrial interests, he rejected the "iron binding of the mind to grim realities"; his periodical would rekindle "the light of Fancy which is inherent in the human breast." Skewering Cruikshank three years later was not inconsistent with this policy; his former illustrator's use of fairy tales to convey topical lessons was a crime against "the primacy of the imagination and its pleasures" (K, 275).

When *Great Expectations* commenced in *All the Year Round*, Dickens added a sobering proviso to his 1850 declaration in *Household Words*, a virtual amendment: one must also bring "grim realities" to bear on dangerous fantasies. The ever harsher social criticism in Dickens's novels of the 1850s had darkened his conception of fairy tales; he still believed that they could lift the spirit and broaden the imagination even in the hardest times. However, if overly relied upon or taken too literally, he now cautioned, fairy tales can become forms of enchantment, binding spells that one casts over oneself.

Twice when "the light of Fancy" seemed in danger of being extinguished, Dickens spoke up, first against the Utilitarian spirit of the age (*Household Words*, 30 March 1850), then in opposition to Cruikshank's redactions (*Household Words*, 1 October 1853). A decade after *Household Words* began, the problem had changed to the misuse of "Fancy" and fairy lore in favor of the very materialism that Dickens originally rekindled the imagination to offset. Surveying the nineteenth-century novel, Dickens was aghast to behold not the extermination of the fairy tale perspective that he had feared, but the adoption of *Cinderella* as a sort of communal myth extolling a snobbish expectancy in individual lives and on a national scale.

In 1853, *Cinderella* was the one tale Dickens wanted to snatch from Cruikshank's grasp. His parody of the story may be seen as a preemptive strike. In 1860 and 1861, Dickens declared that a realistic social critic could only proceed into the new decade by standing *Cinderella* on its head; that is, by countering with a tragicomic perspective the overly expectant outlook rival novelists had used it to foster. Contradictory though these actions seem, oversimplification (literalization of fairy lore) was the target both times.

Dickens rejected "iron binding" at every opportunity: he opposed restricting the mind to Utilitarian "realities," fairy tales to Cruikshank's philosophy, and *Cinderella* to a national myth for Victorians. The first two instances blatantly tampered with the imagination. Dangers in the third were the most difficult to recognize. Whenever nineteenth-century novelists relied on parallels with Cinderella's story to plot a protagonist's progress, they defrauded the fairy tale realm. Instead of kindling the fancy, which is generous and expansive, they cultivated in Victorian readers a harmful taste for an implausible expectancy as narrow as Cruikshank's demand for prohibition and as selfish as the Utilitarian emphasis on self-interest.

In a letter to Wills dated 27 July 1853, Dickens praised fairy tales as "beautiful little stories which are so tenderly and humanly useful to us in these times when the world is too much with us, early and late" (HS, 2). The adjective "useful" sounds Utilitarian, but one should stress the two adverbs immediately preceding it: "tenderly" and "humanly." Rereading or simply recalling the "little stories" allegedly proves restorative to the adult in times of pressure, just as Wordsworth, to whom Dickens alludes, found solace in recollections of nature no matter how far he removed himself from the scenes of his boyhood.[25] Fairy tales, Dickens believed, exert a softening influence even on grown-ups, to whom they promise refreshment, aesthetic pleasure and, above all, escape.[26] It was healthy—that is, amusing and harmless—for David Copperfield to impersonate his favorite characters "for a week together" (*DC*, 54), but only by impersonating Cinderella permanently can Pip be saved from dissatisfaction at the forge. Similarly, it was delusional for Victorian England to confuse its rise to power and prestige with Cinderella's. One of "the beautiful little stories" was being used to increase society's regard for a world already "too much with us"; it was the imagination that needed to be disciplined, Dickens decided in *Great Expectations*, not the heart.[27]

Still, Dickens could not lampoon *Cinderella* without promulgating his own ideas, which was Cruikshank's offense against *Hop-o'-my Thumb*. Replacing *Cinderella* with Misnar, Dickens extracted a cautionary, tragicomic paradigm from the latter, just as he accused Cruikshank of reducing the former to a moral tract. If this irony occurred to Dickens, it failed to deter him. Doubtless he considered his use of Misnar as a countertext with which to challenge *Cinderella* altruistic compared to Cruikshank's self-serving didacticism. Out of concern for the national welfare, Dickens was questioning his country's roseate view of itself and its history.

In *Great Expectations*, Dickens resolved the tug-of-war between his youthful fairy tale perspective and his mature worldview. *Oliver Twist* had accommodated both fairy tale and tragicomedy because Dickens's use of the latter was still rudimentary, hence subdominant. Utilizing the Misnar tale to negate *Cinderella* brought Dickens's "fairy-tale method" (HS, xii) into smoother alignment with his tragicomic outlook; it also finalized his antagonism to the Victorian age. He could endorse neither the prior nor the present era, neither pre–Victorian England badly in need of reformation nor England since the 1830s, in which detrimental changes—especially the blind worship of progress and materialism—had accompanied reforms. Pip's drudgery at the forge recalls Dickens's own youthful disappointments and may be said to symbolize the condition of England before the country's dramatic rise to prominence. As the collapsible pavilion in the Misnar tale replaced the cinder girl's ascent in *Cinderella*, Dickens revealed his sense of the precariousness of his own advancement and acknowledged his disdain for the nation's.

Employing the Misnar story to deflate *Cinderella* was not inconsistent with Dickens's brand of revaluative parody. Generally, he darkens the work of rivals who are allegedly too sanguine or whose parodic reworkings of his own fiction lessened its severities. Through *Cinderella*, Dickens parodied overly optimistic narrative in general: any representation of real life that enables individuals to minimize its shortcomings or downplay their own.

Given a cultural swing from disrespect for Fancy, the crisis *Hard Times* tackles, to fantasizing such as Pip's, Dickens remained true to himself in resisting both a threat to the imagination and the misuse of it. The climactic irony is that only the parodic revaluator could rescue the defender of fairy lore. To save it from Cruikshank in 1853 and England from itself in 1860, Dickens parodied *Cinderella*. When he sabotaged one of "the beautiful little stories" (HS, 2) with sterner stuff from *The Tales of the Genii,* his fairy tale perspective survived tragicomically—at the expense of a fairy tale. He preserved the paramountcy of Fancy and the value of an imagination steeped in fairy lore by authenticating one fairy tale to the discredit of another. What the Victorian era desperately needed, Dickens decided, was not less fairy lore but a more appropriate fairy tale, one with tragicomic implications. Just as Dickens stopped short of proclaiming Misnar's collapsible pavilion a satiric symbol for life, he declined to announce an end to the great age of fairy tale. Instead, *Great Expectations* should be read as its tragicomic apotheosis: nowhere else is Dickens so diligent to observe the world in light of fairy tales; nowhere else does he scrutinize more intensely the value of such a perspective.

Great Expectations is both an "inverted fairy tale" (HS, 299) and a generic culmination for the Victorian fascination with fairy lore. "Through the fairy tale" in the 1840s and 1850s, Jack Zipes has observed, "a social discourse about conditions in England took form" (VFT, xi). Fairy tales attempted "to raise social consciousness about the disparities among the different social classes and the problems faced by the oppressed" in an industrial society. Examples include John Ruskin's "The King of the Golden River" (1851), which features "a Cinderella figure" (UCK, xiii), William Makepeace Thackeray's *The Rose and the Ring* (1854), and Dickens's seminal *A Christmas Carol* (1843). These tales defended "Christian goodness" against "greed and materialism," allegedly the "most dangerous vices in English society" (VFT, xix–xx). Similarly, *Great Expectations* recommends loyalty, compassion, and forgiveness as worthwhile values in a tragicomic universe. It satirizes snobbery, revenge schemes, and the desire for money and prestige.

But literary fairy tales, Zipes adds, are social constructs; they must be revised constantly to *enforce* changes in tastes and values. Otherwise, the tales freeze into "universal absolutes"; they "assume *mythic* proportions . . . in an ideological constellation," becoming obstacles to growth and change, hence perverting the power of fairy tales in general (FT, 19; italics added). This happened to *Cinderella,* whose usefulness as a psychological boost to a financially strapped England following the Napoleonic Wars had expired long before 1860. Dickens turned to the Misnar story to *initiate* a change in attitude instead of endorsing one that had already taken place. Canceling one fairy tale with another, he expanded fairy lore's role.

One should read *Great Expectations* as a protomodern psychological tragicomedy with sensationalist trappings, a novel that is, above all, the requisite fairy tale for its time. Dickens's thirteenth novel is also a parable about the dangers of fairy tale misuse, specifically the harmful dissemination throughout

Victorian novels of Cinderella motifs. Thanks to the Misnar story, a mature social analyst with a darkening conception of life's possibilities revalued Victorian society's unrealistic image of itself by purging his own and his era's "fairy-tale focus" (HS, xi).[28] Whether Pip will turn out to be Cinderella or an enchanted usurper proves as crucial a question for *Great Expectations* as whether or not Copperfield is "the hero of [his] own life" (*DC*, 9) is to *David Copperfield*. *Great Expectations* climaxed the reliance on fairy tale in Dickens's fiction in that storybook elements "emerge out of the work's innermost design" instead of being superimposed (HS, 312). Nowhere else does Dickens rely on fairy tale so thoroughly to unify plot and theme. But the emergence and the unity involve, and much of the novel's perennial appeal stems from, parodic revaluation: Dickens rethought the success stories in *Oliver Twist* and *David Copperfield*, reviewed his own life, and exposed the smugness of a materialistic age by rewriting *Cinderella* in terms of the Misnar tale. He redefined his lifelong allegiance to fairy tale by darkening his fairy tale perspective. Like Copperfield, he never ceased to view life as "a great fairy story" (*DC*, 235). But in a world the parodic revaluator perceived as increasingly grotesque and uncertain, the Misnar story, not *Cinderella*, now had first call.

Dickens penned *Great Expectations* to promulgate an image of life in which joy and sorrow, pleasure and pain, fear one moment and amusement the next, initially seem contrapuntal but prove mutually supplemental, each ultimately blending into the other. Such is life's texture—its essence and totality. Only if life is seen as tragicomic, Dickens concluded, can one submit oneself to it. Then its many absurdities, its grotesque contrasts and contradictions, begin to make sense aesthetically if not philosophically. A lifelong reformer's final answer to life's riddle is, ironically, an aesthetic declaration, not a political manifesto or an economic program. In dubbing life a tragicomedy, however, Dickens adopted a defensible intellectual stance at the same time that he embraced a mature artistic perspective from which he could still clamor for reforms.

Tragicomedy offers a credible explanation of life's divergent tendencies. Dickens may have espoused such an outlook in response to vociferous objections to the ever bleaker vision of society in his novels of the 1850s. Complaints culminated in the famous "Remonstrance with Dickens" in which the reviewer of *Little Dorrit* exclaimed in *Blackwood's Magazine*: "[W]e sit down and weep when we remember thee, O *Pickwick*" (*B*, 497). Because it passed for a return to Dickens's "best vein,"[29] that of *Martin Chuzzlewit* and *David Copperfield*, *Great Expectations* stymied critics of *Bleak House, Hard Times,* and *Little Dorrit* who had judged a Cockney entertainer presumptuous in satirizing his country's laws, economic policies, and political institutions. Never simply an expedient or a compromise, however, Dickens's tragicomic attitude toward life was a fruitful consolidation; marshaling his forces, he made a sincere attempt to reconcile his continuing penchant for comedy with his mounting awareness of life's irresolvable insufficiencies.

In October 1860, Dickens assured his eventual biographer, John Forster, that he was treating the tragic and comic aspects of *Great Expectations* evenhandedly. For the opening number, Dickens wrote, "I have got in the pivot on which the story will turn," namely, the connection between Pip and Magwitch that leads to the novel's climax (*PL*, 9:325). Dickens refers to this as "the grotesque *tragi-comic* conception that first encouraged me [italics added]": the idea of a snob finding himself indebted to an ex-convict much as polite society depends on the labors of the poor and unfortunate. Dickens added that the "general effect" of "the opening," thanks to the "relations" between Pip and Joe, would be "exceedingly droll." Despite Pip's shameful mistreatment of Joe, theirs would be predominantly a comic relationship with tragic overtones, whereas Pip's involvement with the ex-convict would produce a tragic disaster not without comic ironies. Forster "would not have to complain of the want of humor as in the Tale of Two Cities." Instead, Dickens would maintain "a most singular and comic manner" throughout, as if in direct reply to Forster's suggestion that he "let himself loose upon some single humorous conception, in the vein of his youthful achievements" (F, 2:355).

Great Expectations crystalized Dickens's final vision of the nature of things. His timely critique of Victorian expectancy is also a timeless summation of the human condition. Neither in the works immediately preceding *Great Expectations* nor in his last two novels does Dickens exercise as expertly his gift for evoking laughter amid catastrophe. Nowhere else is the balance of ironic comedy and tragic irony—indeed, their interplay, their interdependence—quite as good.[30] Instead of alternating in crucial scenes, "the strands of comedy and tragedy are closely interwoven" (KJF, 209). This integrative feat enabled Dickens to transcend the limitations of laughter and lament without forsaking either response. *Great Expectations* continues to please different constituencies within Dickens's readership: those who perceive life as a vale of tears and others who insist that it is a titillating spectacle nevertheless.[31]

Even as a tyro, Dickens understands the mechanics of tragicomedy. At its simplest, episodes of gravity and humor alternate; serious and comic elements operate contrapuntally (MA, 100). Chapter 17 of *Oliver Twist* begins with a defense of stage melodramas that "present the tragic and the comic scenes, in as regular alteration as the layers of red and white in a side of streaky bacon" (*OT*, 118–19). "Such changes appear absurd," Dickens admitted, but "they are not so unnatural as they would seem at first sight": in one scene, the imprisoned hero collapses, "weighed down by fetters and misfortunes"; in the next, unaware of his master's plight, a squire "regales the audience with a comic song." Dickens defended "sudden shiftings" and "rapid changes" as a handy convention "sanctioned" by "long usage" (*OT*, 119). Still, *Oliver Twist* is contrapuntal mainly in a Manichean sense; it sets light against darkness, country against town, Brownlow against Fagin. Oliver's world reflects a morality play's sharply drawn opposites. In *Great Expectations,* tragicomedy's contrasts are stated, then rephrased as subtler mixtures that one is tempted to call permanent ambiguities, their poignancy the result of blending laughter with tears. Life, Dickens attests, is always funny and entertaining even when disconcertingly sad—and vice versa.

Magwitch is the tragicomic composite of Oliver's two mentors, Brownlow and Fagin, polarities who take turns governing him. More terrifying than Fagin but as paternal in the long run as Brownlow, Magwitch performs a double role as both giver and destroyer of Pip's expectations, just as Fagin deprived and Brownlow endowed. Cruelty and kindness combine in Magwitch's actions to contravene straightforward judgments. Giving Pip high hopes, Magwitch's benefaction adversely affects a young apprentice's already unsettled character; when Pip's hopes collapse upon Magwitch's return, the ex-convict actually confers a blessing disguised as a disaster.

Dickens's "grotesque tragi-comic conception" underlies the contrast between the two Christmas dinners in the second installment. In chapter 3, Pip bestows on Magwitch a makeshift feast, having stolen it from Mrs. Joe's kitchen. "Gobbling mincemeat, meat-bone, bread, cheese, and pork pie all at once," Magwitch reminds Pip of "a large dog" (*GE*, 19–20). Nevertheless, the convict's "Thankee, my boy" contradicts his ferocity; along with the tearful click in his throat as "he smeared his ragged rough sleeve over his eyes" (*GE*, 19), it expresses genuine gratitude for a charitable act suited to the season. Magwitch's humble response complicates Pip's critique of the convict's table manners; readers who share the boy's fastidiousness begin to feel like snobs. In chapter 4, no Christmas spirit shines forth around Mrs. Joe's table. "Squeezed in at an acute angle of the tablecloth," Pip seems more of a prisoner than Magwitch (*GE*, 25). Mr. Hubble calls Pip "naterally wicious," as if he were the dog that Magwitch's eating habits resemble. Mr. Wopsle pronounces "Swine" to sound like Pip's "christian name" (*GE*, 27), and Pumblechook imagines him as a "four-footed Squeaker" (young pig) having his throat cut by the butcher. Pip's share of the festivities is confined to "scaly tips of the drumsticks" and "obscure corners of pork" (*GE*, 26)—worse fare than Magwitch's.

The second installment is wonderfully tragicomic: a grave episode in chapter 3 followed by a humorous scene in chapter 4. Yet things also work the other way around. Chapter 3 is ironically heartening in that toward Magwitch, scapegoat and Christ figure, the true Christian spirit manifests itself when a seven-year-old feeds an escaped convict. As in countless fairy tales, the protagonist succors an unsavory creature who eventually returns the favor. Despite being amusing from start to close, chapter 4 is ultimately depressing; as the dinner in Mrs. Joe's kitchen becomes acutely painful to a persecuted child, one suffers a total perversion of the meaning of Christmas. Dickens intuited with relish that a "grotesque tragi-comic conception" of things best delineates the life process. Distortion, heterogeneity, incongruity, which serve the tragicomedian as first principles, are alleged to be life's key ingredients. As the grotesque does in painting and sculpture, chapters 3 and 4 combine human and animal forms in their characterizations: Magwitch as both convict and dog, Pip as boy and piglet. The combining of incongruous elements within each chapter, not just the switch from gravity in chapter 3 to humor in chapter 4, identifies Dickensian tragicomedy as the mutual—indeed, mandatory—distortion of tragedy and comedy by each other. Verisimilitude, Dickens decided, requires this. Fidelity to life presupposes an appreciation of it as unparalleled grotesquerie, the ultimate tragicomic work of art.

Although powerful, tragicomedy in *Oliver Twist* seems stark and stagey, whereas that in *Great Expectations* is timeless and up-to-date, hence its "relevance outside its own age" (QDL, 289) as a perennially pertinent reading of life. Unlike red and white layers "in a side of streaky bacon," tragedy and comedy in *Great Expectations* set each other off while also tending to become indistinguishable, if not interchangeable. In chapters 3 and 4, it seems easy at first to tell which is which; indeed, the contrast between them is the basis for Dickens's second installment. On second thought, however, one is unable to say for certain where tragedy stops and comedy starts (or vice versa), because in both chapters, each is always in part the other. In *Great Expectations*, Dickens's tragicomedy recalls Shakespeare but anticipates the modern.[32]

Tragicomedy, Robert Langbaum maintains, is "the characteristically modern style" and its source and finest exemplification can be discerned in Shakespeare's *The Tempest* (RL, 184). It follows that tragicomic vision is "the appropriate statement of age," both a reconsideration and a summation. The mature Dickens of *Great Expectations* may be likened to Langbaum's Shakespeare: a "man who having seen it all can teach us that the profoundest statement is the lightest and that life, when we see through it, is gay, is tragicomically gay—that the evil, the violence, the tragedy" fit together as if they "are all part of a providential design" (RL, 186–87).[33] Whether gayly tragic or tragically gay, paradox rather than consolation lies at the heart of Dickens's tragicomic vision. Writers who perceive the world as a contradictory totality sum up this situation but can never fully resolve it. Even though one learns from Shakespeare's last play (or Dickens's thirteenth novel) to "recognize order in disorder," to "see at work a rational and benevolent providence" (RL, 190–94), the lesson does not eradicate violence, pain, and disappointment.

Given Magwitch's years of penal servitude, Compeyson's drowning, the jilting of Miss Havisham, her incineration, Estella's married life with Drummle, and the collapse of Pip's fortunes, *Great Expectations* must conclude tragicomically, even if Pip and Estella do not meet for a final time in Piccadilly but instead discuss a permanent relationship during their reunion in the ruined garden of Satis House. In neither case can the ending nullify foregoing events or mitigate their deplorable consequences. Incorporated into a larger, comprehensive design, the negatives just enumerated—deception, betrayal, physical and mental suffering, disillusionment—become parts of a single, ever-changing force in *Great Expectations;* this force retains evil and destructive aspects no matter how just or benevolent it ultimately proves.

Perhaps "tragicomic" is the word Robert Garis sought when singling out *Great Expectations* as Dickens's most "organically imagined criticism of life" (RG, 206). It allegedly voices Dickens's "final pessimism about the possibility of human happiness" along with "his regretfully humorous acceptance of this condition." Mollified by constant bemusement, such pessimism constitutes Dickens's "deepest criticism" of earthly existence (RG, 208) but is final without being terminal.[34] Calling life a tragicomic phenomenon, Dickens registers two strikes against it, then stops short of rejection. Although life hurts, it can be excruciatingly funny even at its most disappointing. *Great Expectations* is severe in its judgments yet comic in the face of them. Dickens insists on seeing humor in Pip's predicament and in the world's inadequacies. Eschewing nostalgia and rationing Pip's tendency toward self-pity, Mr. Pirrip's voice is almost always ironic, comically self-deprecating no matter how painful the recollection. Inadequacy—the gap between expectation and fulfillment, promise and performance, ambition and ability—is often funniest, Dickens realized, when things seem at their grimmest: when, for instance, Pip's fairy godfather turns out to be a revenge-minded ex-convict, or when Pip recognizes the collapse of Misnar's pavilion, not Cinderella's rise, as the appropriate analogue for his life story.

Langbaum's concept of tragicomedy appears to operate the other way around from Garis's. Dickens's overview must be sufficiently positive to absorb but not dissolve—embrace but not disarm—life's negative factors. Is this a cut above laughingly accepting them and smiling through one's pessimism? Ultimately, one may say either that tragedy allows for comedy—at least for a comic acceptance of one's shortcomings and life's deficiencies (Garis), or that comedy allows for tragedy, incorporating negative elements it refuses to overlook yet cannot explain away (Langbaum). In either case, the tragicomic novelist's critique of life is more extensive, hence more realistic, then either tragedy or comedy by itself, so it may be described as "organically imagined" (RG, 206)—complete, integrated, sustained. *Great Expectations* remains tragicomically contrapuntal whether one accepts life's bleakest components without losing one's sense of humor or emphasizes a persistent cause for sardonic amusement running through its manifold misfortunes. Arguably, Dickens does both. Essentially Miltonic (that is, providential), Pip's downfall ultimately proves fortunate. Still, Mr. Pirrip's retrospective remains steeped in his younger self's guilty feelings, and the plot is driven by Magwitch's desire (and Miss Havisham's) to get even. Put another way, one detects Sophoclean parallels in Pip's belated discovery of Magwitch as his closest tie; when the roof falls in, however, it crushes the hopes of a ludicrous snob.

Missing from both Langbaum and Garis is Dickensian tragicomedy's protomodern tendency toward tragic farce. If *Great Expectations* relates to Dickens as *The Tempest* stands to Shakespeare, who is Prospero in the former? Presumably, Mr. Pirrip, the grown-up Pip; yet his tone of voice blends "wry" adult perceptions with those of a "scared child" (MC, 7), moving, in effect, not just back and forth from Prospero to Ferdinand but further back into childhood terrors. Another candidate might be Magwitch, who also supplies the story's Caliban. The idea of Mr. Pirrip as both Ferdinand and Prospero (namely, innocence and experience) and of Magwitch as a twofold hybridization—not just Brownlow plus Fagin but also Prospero and Caliban—adumbrates tragicomedy's shift in the less noble direction of tragic farce.

In Aldous Huxley's *Antic Hay*, Casimir Lypiatt's suicide note includes an important aesthetic observation: "Every one's a walking farce and a walking tragedy at the same time. The man who slips on a banana-skin and fractures his skull describes against the sky, as he falls, the most richly comic arabesque" (AH, 275). Just as Lypiatt fills huge canvases in a style better suited to magazine advertisements, he cloaks a profound insight within a banal example. When the man's fall results in a serious concussion, the head injury compromises one's enjoyment of a crude and embarrassing tumble that, even more surprisingly, is not unlike sophisticated ballet. In Casimir's case, although one regrets the great artist whom this insufficiently talented poet-painter struggles in vain to become, one also relishes the disdain that other characters lavish on the charlatan he actually is.

To respond fully either to Lypiatt or the "man who slips on a banana-skin," one must laugh and cry not just by turns, as in *Oliver Twist*, but simultaneously, because comedy and tragedy keep turning into each other. This reaction, dual and ambivalent, also seems called for when evaluating other modernist phenomena such as Emma Bovary's love life, Gregor Samsa's metamorphosis, or Mr. Prufrock's love song. On one hand, Emma's dreams of meeting charming men and traveling to enchanted places are ridiculous, completely unfounded;

on the other hand, her day-to-day reality, drab and dreary, is equally unacceptable: it stifles her unmercifully. One wishes to feel sorrier for Emma but cannot help laughing at her blunders. One wants to disparage her, but the quandary in which Flaubert puts her, his rendition of the human situation, excites sympathy. Inasmuch as Emma's sufferings make her too miserable simply to laugh at but are too absurd to rank with Antigone's or Clytemnestra's, she illustrates Lypiatt's idea of tragic farce.

No unqualified response settles one's attitude toward Pip's plight. To the extent that Dickens keeps it continuously funny and sad, Pip may be described as tragicomedy verging on tragic farce. Consider his strange manner of courting Biddy in chapter 17. Were it not for his infatuation with Estella and his determination "to be a gentleman on her account," says the "dazed village lad," he and Biddy might "have grown up to keep company. I should have been good enough for *you;* shouldn't I Biddy?" Pip asks (*GE*, 127). Before laughing too hard, one should realize that Pip is overlooking the story's only real Cinderella; he is also a travesty of Prince Charming in that he ignores the novel's true Sleeping Beauty. Not at all laughable is the heartbreak for Biddy, whose love for a young snob continues unabated.

Pip is more than a man slipping on a banana skin, but he does represent Pride headed for a fall. After Magwitch returns, the collapse of Pip's dreams of becoming genteel and marrying Estella culminates tragicomically with his return to the forge to propose to Biddy on what turns out to be the day of her marriage to Joe. Pip's experiences no more resemble fairy tales of expectations fulfilled than Tostes or Yonville fit into the popular romances about exotic places with which Emma Bovary filled her head at convent school.

That Pip is tragicomedy often tantamount to tragic farce becomes clearer thanks to his alter ego, the ill-fated Mr. Wopsle. The former parish clerk all but makes the transition from Shakespeare to the modern. Wopsle's performance in chapter 31—in effect, a clown playing the Prince of Denmark—is a glaring instance of tragedy being transformed into farce; it illuminates Pip's autobiography, which is a subtler, more extensive probing of the same sociopsychological phenomenon. Wopsle's Hamlet in *Great Expectations* is comparable to the play-within-a-play in *Hamlet*,[35] although Pip fails to recognize that he stands to Cinderella the way Wopsle does to Hamlet.

Wopsle is too farcical to arouse as much compassion as Pip does, just as the latter is too long-suffering to be as preposterous as Wopsle. Theirs are too sadly comic letdowns nonetheless. Through Pip and his alter ego, Dickens suggests what life is: a complication simultaneously as funny and serious as Shakespearean tragicomedy yet always in danger of shifting toward farce. That is not only how to read *Great Expectations,* says Dickens, but also how to view things in general. Pip's (and Herbert's) reaction to Mr. Wopsle's Hamlet should be ours to Pip's ups and downs in Mr. Pirrip's memoir: "[W]e had sat, feeling keenly for him," says Pip of Wopsle, "but laughing, nevertheless, from ear to ear" (*GE*, 255).

The sternest test for such a response—broad grins despite keen feelings—comes at the novel's climax: Magwitch's unwelcome reappearance. If Dickens readjusted his darker side into smoother alignment with his comic urge, it should be most evident in the chapter that has been called "one of Dickens's greatest pieces of writing" (AED, 234).[36] The scene depicting Magwitch's return runs the gamut of life's emotions: from Pip's surprise and terror, to our sense of its comic inconvenience, to gentler sentiments as a snob begins to soften toward his uncouth guest.

Chapter 39 exemplifies the mature Dickens's conviction that life is tragicomically insufficient to one's expectations, if only because the art of being properly expectant remains a mystery. Most expectation inevitably turns out to be *great*—inordinate, misguided, wrong-headed. In the novel's climactic reencounter, neither Pip nor Magwitch achieves his heart's desire. Pip is burdened with a rough ex-convict instead of a comely guardian angel. Instead of a son to resolve his cravings for filial affection, Magwitch clasps hands with a snob whom he disgusts. Although the gap that yawns between expectations and fulfillment is painful to both participants, the scene strikes the observer as a uniquely comic form of mutual embarrassment.

Pip has been chafing to learn the identity of his mysterious patron. The knowledge that it is Magwitch consternates him. First, Mr. Pirrip recalls, he "seemed to be suffocating" (*GE*, 316). Then "the room began to surge and turn"; as "the truth" of his "position came flashing on" him, he "was borne down" by a sense of disappointment and disgrace, forced "to struggle for every breath" (*GE*, 316). To suffocation Dickens adds the metaphor of drowning, which looks forward to the collision with the Hamburg steamer in chapter 54. The keynote in chapter 39 is shipwrecked expectations—reunion as dizziness, suffocation, and, potentially, fatal immersion.

Only someone whose heart is as "waterproof" as Mr. Bumble's (*OT*, 268) would laugh out loud at Pip's discomfiture. But surely there is something grotesquely comic in the unfolding contrast between the ex-convict's elation, his mounting sense of accomplishment in having returned to inspect the gentleman his money has made, and Pip's sudden deflation. Magwitch's snobbish glee at getting even with the upper classes, whom he blames for all his sufferings, comes at Pip's expense, the one person to whom the ex-convict is sincerely grateful. Yet the latter is never more of a snob than during his desperate efforts *not* to renew his relationship with Magwitch. "Stay!" Pip cries, and "Keep off!" (*GE*, 314) when Magwitch seeks to embrace him.

Magwitch's fidelity, the tireless gratitude that binds him to Pip, reminds the latter of his own truancy: "[I]t was for the convict . . . that I had deserted Joe" (*GE*, 320). At the moment that Pip feels betrayed, he realizes that he is actually the betrayer. Later, when Pip's fairy princess turns out to be the convict's daughter, the tragicomedy of expectations is complete: they are painful to forgo yet impossible to lose because, like Estella's queenliness, they were always more apparent then real.

The collapse of Pip's sense of superiority is also grotesquely comic: he discovers that his luxury has been paid for by "some terrible beast," a creature resembling Victor Frankenstein's monster (*GE*, 317). This creature not only created Pip but plans to adopt him. As Pip's self-styled "second father" (*GE*, 317), Magwitch expects to look on while his creation hobnobs with lords and ladies; he expects to be reimbursed with a son's unstinting love. His plans are as presumptuous as Pip's dreams of marrying Estella and restoring Satis House. In drawing back from them, as in grinning at Wopsle, Pip comes face-to-face with tragic farce; this time, however, he must address his own ridiculousness.

Pip is repelled when the returned transport reaches out to revive their former intimacy: "I recoiled from his touch as if he had been a snake" (*GE*, 317). The simile is tragicomic in a novel that alludes to *Paradise Lost*. In the last line of the First Stage (ch. 19), Pip observes that "the world lay spread before me,"[37] much as it awaited Adam and Eve at the conclusion of Milton's epic. When the Second Stage concludes, the world of opportunity that once beckoned an Adamic young Pip is snatched away by a reptile who behaves paternally. Instead of Pip being expelled, the serpent claims to be the garden's architect and welcomes him to stay on as his son. No wonder the rising mists of chapter 19 are replaced by the "dead" fire in Pip's grate while "the wind and rain intensified the thick black darkness" (*GE*, 321).

With a Cinderella complex, Dickens warned, comes the misconception of providence as a benevolent fairy godmother instead of a stern taskmaster. *Great Expectations* is too comical a novel of painful self-discovery to compete seriously with *Oedipus Rex*, but its comedy was shrewdly designed to puncture the false optimism Victorian readers found in *Cinderella*. Dickens considered the era's Cinderella complex a national snobbery: it was no less dangerous to the psychological well-being of the individual and society than Freud would subsequently find the complex he named after Oedipus. Perhaps Pip's sudden awareness of Magwitch as his benefactor should be compared with Oedipus's discovery that his wife and queen, Jocastâ, is also his mother. Dickens restates incestuous guilt in economic terms: just as the Haves, England's privileged minority, thrive at the expense of a hardworking, less fortunate underclass (the Have-Nots), Pip has been living off the fleshly exertions of his presumptive father; this parasitic, somewhat cannibalistic offense is made to seem as unnatural as sleeping with one's mother.[38]

Granted the king receives the more staggering blow, yet Dickens's climax has the advantage of being gruesomely funny, not just shocking. Witnessing the demise of one of Victorian society's truest monstrosities, a useless member of the leisure class, is like watching Misnar's pavilion crash down upon the usurpers of the sultan's throne in *The Tales of the Genii*, or Cinderella's carriage change into a pumpkin, or Prince Charming into a frog. Actually, it is Pip's mysterious benefactor who metamorphoses from wonder worker to "mere warmint," to use Magwitch's own words (*GE*, 316).

Oedipus is farthest from Jocastâ at the moment he discovers how closely they are related, for his discovery leads to permanent separation. Ironically, Pip is closest to Estella when the ex-convict's protegé considers himself farthest from her; that is, totally beneath her notice. Not only has she too been groomed as an instrument for revenge, but Pip's "second father" (*GE*, 317) is her real progenitor, making them figuratively brother and sister. Their marriage would not be taboo, yet Pip and Estella are never more clearly of the same caliber than at the moment when potential ties between them seem permanently severed. Grotesquely ironic, Dickens links the most coveted thing in Pip's world (Estella) with the most repellent (Magwitch), the sort of conjunction that befalls Oedipus when a natural relationship with his wife is suddenly revealed to be an unnatural liaison with his mother.

No matter how keenly one feels Pip's disappointment, multiple ironies come in rapid succession at both his and Magwitch's expense. The ex-convict claims to have "worked hard" so that Pip "should be above work" (*GE*, 317). But in the next few months, Pip exerts himself more strenuously than at any time since he left Joe's forge. First he hides and disguises Magwitch, then he barely escapes from Orlick; his scheme to get Magwitch out of England having failed, he exhausts himself attempting to have the latter's death sentence overturned. After a prolonged illness, he sentences himself to eleven years of hard work in Egypt. The result of Magwitch's repatriation is Pip's expatriation.

Pip does not invent his expectations. His sister and Pumblechook implant them; Estella's haughtiness, Magwitch's secret plans, and Miss Havisham's cruel deception aggravate the situation. Pip's hopes are also sanctioned by society in general.[39] Nevertheless, the upshot of Magwitch's return is the protagonist's downfall. Pip's life since his arrival in London has been a hoax, an absurd delusion. This abrupt reversal of fortune recalls Oedipus's but is simultaneously comic because it entails a deliberate inversion of Cinderella's story. Pip's catastrophe acquires a parodic aspect that solicits laughter amid—indeed, despite— his shock and disappointment.

Chapter 39 begins traumatically for Pip but is progressively funnier for the reader, thanks to Dickens's incessant parody of *Cinderella*. In the Grimms' fairy tale, Cinderella is transformed so resplendently in her new clothes that not even her stepmother or her two stepsisters guess her identity when she appears at the ball. Pip struggles valiantly to disguise Magwitch in *Great Expectations* lest the latter be recognized as a transported felon illegally returned. Instead of manifesting himself as a Cinderella, Pip must keep his would-be fairy godfather under wraps. On three successive evenings, a pair of pigeons bring the poor cinder girl a spectacular dress and slippers with which to captivate the prince.[40] Magnificent costuming conceals her identity and the humble station to which she has been reduced. But "the more I dressed him, and the better I dressed him," Pip moans about Magwitch (*GE*, 335), "the more he looked like the slouching figure on the marshes." *Cinderella* to the contrary, Pip's task in chapters 39 and 40 is Sisyphean: "[T]here was something that made it hopeless to attempt to disguise him" (*GE*, 335), Pip complains. Magwitch even seems to drag "one of his legs as if there were still a weight of iron on it" (*GE*, 336). Magwitch, of course, is no longer wearing a fourteen-pound anklet on his right foot; it is Pip who "slowly" begins to contemplate "what [he] was chained to, and how heavily" (*GE*, 329). As the would-be Cinderella despairs of rendering his benefactor socially presentable,[41] Mr. Pirrip creates Dickensian hyperbole out of Pip's paranoia.

"Browned and hardened by exposure to weather," with head "furrowed and bald," on which "long iron-grey hair grew only on its sides," Dickens's rendition of Frankenstein's monster is both a terrible apparition and comically intractable material. Magwitch resembles nothing but what he is: the Unvarnished Truth personified, a skeleton in Pip's closet (and society's) who insists on becoming visible to all the world. "There was Convict in the very grain of the man," Pip groans (*GE*, 336). Magwitch's resistance to disguise means that Pip can never put his past behind him any more than Dickens could, or than society can escape the consequences of an unfair social system.

Pip's difficulties in remaking Magwitch parody as overly progressive the proposition that individuals are not prisoners of original sin and the social circumstances attendant upon their upbringing. Despite Cinderella's initial demotion from beloved daughter to stepchild and servant, the rest of her story is a perfectibilitarian myth; it posits no hurdle too high, no apotheosis too forbidding. Cinderella first goes from riches to rags, but her subsequent rise, which most readers chiefly remember, epitomizes the tendency of fairy tales to foster "notions of rags to riches," of pulling oneself up by the bootstraps (*FT,* 74). Like Magwitch's raising of Pip, the latter's attempt to disguise the former calls "pullings up" into question; *Great Expectations* undermines popular belief in sweeping alterations that obliterate all traces of one's origin or humble station.

As Pip struggles to be polite—he reluctantly plays host to an unsavory visitor while becoming increasingly panic-stricken—tragedy and comedy vie for the upper hand. The next morning, the former convict's movements during breakfast are "uncouth, noisy, and greedy" (*GE*, 329). Pip deplores Magwitch's habit of turning "his head sideways to bring his strongest fangs to bear" upon his food: "[H]e looked terribly like a hungry old dog" (*GE*, 329). The incongruity of a London gentleman entertaining an "old dog" with "fangs"—dining, in effect, with Frankenstein's monster—costs Pip his appetite. The canine simile recalls the scene on the marshes in which Magwitch devours Christmas breakfast like "a large dog" (*GE*, 20). Although Cinderella becomes wife and princess once and for all, in contrast, Pip has regressed; despite fine clothes, a London address, and a mastery of foreign languages, he finds himself back in time to the point at which the novel began—he is feeding a "ravenous" man (*GE*, 329) whose indelible coarseness precludes a Cinderella-like personal transformation, the kind of change on which the former blacksmith's apprentice has staked all his hopes.

Magwitch's suggestions for a suitable disguise—wigs, hair powder, shorts—are wonderfully inept; these items went out of style nearly twenty years before, when Magwitch was last at large in England. Dressed as he proposes, the returned convict would stand out, arousing suspicion instantly. It is winter, so Magwitch's tanned, weather-beaten visage is an immediate anomaly. Everyone except lawyers, clergymen, and members of the smart set had ceased to wear wigs by 1810. Only someone very old-fashioned still used hair powder after it became taxable in 1795. Tight knee breeches (shorts) survived as ceremonial dress among the clergy—no one else wore them. Had Magwitch gotten his way, Pip concludes, his outfit "would have made him something between a dean and a dentist" (*GE*, 333). That is, he would have been doubly conspicuous as an absurd combination of church dignitary and professional man on the rise,[42] although too uncouth for the first and too old for the second. "At present," says Pip as Magwitch outlines "a dress for himself," the latter is "dressed in a seafaring slop suit, in which he looked as if he had some parrots and cigars to dispose of" (*GE*, 332). Ensconced in Pip's apartment, Magwitch resembles a wooden statue of a sailor or pirate in front of a maritime supply store.

Just as one surrenders to the comedy of the situation, however, allowing the ludicrousness of Pip's tragic predicament to develop to the full, a serious note sounds again. One may bypass the ambiguity in Magwitch's assertion that he has "come for good"; the point to emphasize is that he has risked "death by the rope" (*GE*, 331). Having been "sent for life" (transported to Australia forever), Magwitch "should of a certainty be hanged if took," as he puts it (*GE*, 319). Chapter 39 began with the collapse of Pip's expectations, a tragic downfall that turns into a comic riches-to-rags redoing of Cinderella's dealings with her fairy godmother. Broad grins revert to keen feelings in that capture might spell death for Magwitch; Pip's comic problems in disguising an illegally returned ex-convict could have deadly consequences.[43]

To Pip's horror at the moment and Mr. Pirrip's retrospective sense of the reunion's macabre comedy one must add sympathy for Magwitch. He appears largely unaware of his untimely, incongruous appearance, not to mention the unfavorable impression his boast makes on Pip: "If I ain't a gentleman, nor ain't got no learning, I'm the owner of such" (*GE,* 319). But even before Magwitch tells his life story (ch. 42) and it becomes clear that he has always been more victim than outlaw, one respects his endurance. After years of hardship in Australia, unfailing gratitude compels him to visit his "boy," to make himself "known to him on his home ground" (*GE,* 319). Magwitch looks like a cutthroat and eats like a dog, yet one notices "with amazement" that the hardened transport's eyes are "full of tears" (*GE,* 314). One is "softened by the softened aspect of the man," as is Pip. Having combined a Sophoclean surprise with tragicomic ironies, Dickens imbues both with pity and compassion for an outlandish Magwitch and a snobbish Pip. As the latter begins to warm toward his repulsive visitor, Dickens offers proof that life constantly transpires in an ever shifting mixture of modes.

Twice Mr. Pirrip instructs readers how to read his autobiography. Because Pip as Cinderella recalls Wopsle as Hamlet, one should emulate Pip's response to the former parish clerk: "I laughed in spite of myself all the time" (*GE,* 255). Involuntary laughter, pervasive if not continuous, is the reaction that *Great Expectations* seeks to elicit. But when the unconcealable Magwitch anticipates the "pleasure" it will be "to see [his] gentleman spend his money *like* a gentleman," Pip's situation impresses upon him a "sense of the grimly-ludicrous" (*GE,* 331); he is "moved . . . to a fretful laugh" (*GE,* 330). The idea of Pip appearing with Magwitch in polite society is ridiculous many times over in that Magwitch cannot show himself in public at all. Laughter that vexes or irritates the person laughing, irritation that prompts an uncomfortable laugh—such a reaction seems even closer to tragicomedy's intentional ambivalence than laughing in spite of oneself.

With the phrase "grimly-ludicrous," Dickens seesaws from Shakespearean tragicomedy to tragic farce. Mr. Pirrip reveals his sense of Pip as both the nineteenth-century Oedipus and the Victorian Cinderella, a painfully funny combination akin to seeing Magwitch as both Prospero and Caliban. Pip redoes Oedipus's self-discovery in terms of an economic downfall; as a would-be Cinderella, he never scores a lasting romantic or social success. A sense of life's grim ludicrousness (or ludicrous grimness) governs the permeation of tragic and comic sentiments by each other throughout *Great Expectations;* their interplay prompted Dickens to demolish as unrealistic any rival novel in which he alleged it was absent or inadequate.

The late 1850s were a crucial redefinition period for Dickens and the Victorian novel. At stake was the relationship of tragedy and comedy to the concept of realism. In "The Sad Fortunes of the Rev. Amos Barton" (1857), George Eliot begins chapter 5 with a short essay on the controversy; she tries to restrict tragicomedy to her emerging brand of antisensational fiction with its Wordsworthian emphasis on the "unmistakably commonplace" (*SCL*, 80). "Many remarkable novels," Eliot acknowledged, "full of striking situations, thrilling incidents, and eloquent writing have appeared only in the last season." But she suggested that readers ignore them. Instead, they will "gain unspeakably" if they "learn" from her "to see . . . the tragedy and the comedy" in the trials of a "quite ordinary" individual; namely, Amos Barton (*SCL*, 81). David Lodge has noted that Eliot's use of the term *realism* is among the earliest recorded. Reviewing Ruskin's *Modern Painters* (volume 3, 1856), she coined the term as a critical standard for judging pictures and, by implication, prose (*SCL*, 14). Going further in chapter 5 of "Amos Barton," she forged a triple alliance: if realism is preoccupied with the unexceptional, tragedy and comedy are only possible in novels not predicated on excitement and suspense (that is, "thrilling incidents," "striking situations," as in Dickens). For genuine "poetry and prose," Eliot stipulated, one "looks out," as does Amos Barton, "through dull grey eyes" and "speaks in a voice of quite ordinary tones" (*SCL*, 81).

Although Dickens admired *Scenes of Clerical Life*, he surely recognized Eliot's comments in chapter 5 of its opening story as a declaration of war.[44] She was using tragicomedy to promote an outlook on life to which he was fundamentally opposed. To repudiate Eliot's claim to a superior realism, Dickens had to file a counterclaim to tragicomedy. Contrary to Eliot, he insisted that tragicomedy and realism, his primary terms, were identical, not realism and the commonplace; the latter was a necessary ingredient for both realism and tragicomedy but merely part of each and thus synonymous with neither.

Without stinting his satire against a tale as misleading as *Cinderella*, Dickens strove to compress comedy, tragedy, and pathos into scenes such as chapter 39 of *Great Expectations*—Pip's late-night interview with his good fairy, a returned ex-convict. Realism, Dickens believed—or fidelity to life as he found it—dictated a profusion of modes in which the extraordinary and the ordinary inform each other, much as they do in Coleridge's "Christabel" or "The Rime of the Ancient Mariner"—or as Magwitch occurs in Pip's life and he in Magwitch's. In the "grotesque tragi-comic conception" (*PL*, 9:325) around which the novel coalesced in Dickens's imagination, "grotesque" borders on the redundant, for his reality is essentially so: heterogeneous, incongruous, often bizarre in its components as opposed to Eliot's obsession with the uniformly "commonplace" (*SCL*, 80). Doing "tragedy and comedy" in "ordinary tones" (*SCL*, 81) instead of counterpointing the keenest feelings and the broadest grins, Dickens replied to Eliot, was faint-hearted—an unrealistic toning down of a multifaceted phenomenon that is simultaneously hilarious and heartbreaking. "The Sad Fortunes of Mr. Philip Pirrip, Esquire" would not have been appropriate as a title for *Great Expectations*. Reductive, one-pointed, unfair to both the novel's scope and the scope of things, it tells only half the story.

In *Great Expectations,* Dickens sought to raise his brand of melodramatic realism above the sensation novels of Charles Reade, Wilkie Collins, and their Gothic predecessors (Mary Shelley, the Brontës) without ceasing to be as exciting. For the veteran comic and social critic, tragicomedy—being simultaneously funnier and grimmer than the competition—was the solution: more amusing than Lever, more incisive than Thackeray, as sensational as Collins yet a better psychologist. No one, Dickens felt, could beat him on all these fronts at once, certainly not Eliot with "ordinary" tones and incidents. Collectively his talents would exceed any rival's. Snobbish though it sounds, Dickens groomed himself to become a tragicomedian par excellence, the legitimate heir not just of Fielding and Smollett but also of Sophocles and Shakespeare.

Whether looked at psychologically, economically, or sociologically, the Pip–Magwitch relationship deserves to be ranked foremost in Dickens's fiction—ahead of his other unforgettable pairings such as Pickwick and Sam Weller, Copperfield and Mr. Micawber, or Charles Darnay and Sydney Carton. Through Pip and Magwitch, Dickens relates the story of two snobs—a condescending Pip, a grateful yet vengeful Magwitch—who grow more important to each other per se than the questionable benefits either can confer upon the other. Pip gets over his abhorrence for the ex-convict to whom he owes his rise in the world; to Magwitch, Pip becomes an adopted son or surrogate nephew, not just a proxy through whom to infiltrate the upper class and vicariously savor its privileges.

Out on the marshes for their first encounter or reunited in Pip's rooms, they seem the quintessential mismatch, the nineteenth-century novel's oddest couple. Their pairing may be called the epitome of tragicomic grotesquerie. As each other's creature, each is both the making and unmaking of the other. Magwitch's largesse raises Pip, but the transport's unwelcome return brings his protegé's prospects crashing down; elevating Pip elates Magwitch, but coming back to see firsthand the success of his project costs this representative of society's exploited classes his life. On the other hand, although Magwitch's reappearance destroys Pip's expectations, their collapse initiates the young man's moral turnaround. Similarly, despite throttling Compeyson, the harsh and hardened outcast makes a good death, having been "softened" (*GE,* 444) by Pip's attentions. The mutual regard that gradually binds Pip and Magwitch to each other is a triumph for human nature. There are no insuperable divisions, Dickens demonstrates, not even between "a brought-up London gentleman" (or stuck-up city dweller) and a self-professed "warmint," a weather-beaten, monstrous-looking ex-convict from down under (*GE*, 319, 328). Pip and Magwitch overcome contradictory worldviews; they overleap economic gaps and transcend class barriers.

No other pairing in Dickens's fifteen novels is more complicated than this psychological study that anatomizes the perils of snobbery and the compulsion it generates either to rise in the world or take revenge upon it. Yet despite the collapse of Pip's hopes and Magwitch's schemes, *Great Expectations* builds a friendship that supersedes both snobbery and revenge. At the same time that Pip and Magwitch make rubbish of Cinderella and her fairy godparent, they replace that unrealistic fairy tale with a relationship Dickens considers more imperative yet no less wonderful. Pip and Magwitch, Dickens stipulates, personify the sort of bonding that must take place between Haves and Have-Nots before England's exalted opinion of itself as destiny's darling can be justified. His pairing offers an allegedly workable model for readers to emulate. *Great Expectations* is a casebook on how to transform parasitism into partnership so that a precious few do not continue to live off the labors of the less fortunate majority.[45]

Although the gulf between Haves and Have-Nots continues to widen, not just within developed countries but also between rich and poor nations, this deplorable state of affairs is no indication of Dickens's failure. On the contrary, it makes *Great Expectations* mandatory reading and increasingly relevant outside its own age. Through Magwitch, all whom society would prefer to exploit, cast out, or marginalize ask for their due. The Pip–Magwitch relationship reveals the persistence of Dickens's satiric drive within his tragicomic worldview. Despite the temporal world's perennial inadequacy, relations between Haves and Have-Nots must be improved.

That the Pip–Magwitch connection is richly symbolic has been duly noted, never more succinctly than by T.A. Jackson:

> Self-satisfied, mid-Victorian British society buoyed itself up with as great "expectations" of future wealth and glory as did poor, deluded Pip. If it had but known, its means of ostentation came from a source (the labour of the depressed and exploited masses) to which it would have been as shocked to acknowledge indebtedness as Pip was to find he owed all his acquired gentility to the patronage of a transported felon. Magwitch differed little from the uncouth monster which respectable society envisaged to itself as the typical "labouring man." And in literal truth, good, respectable society owed as much to these working men, and was as little aware of it, as was Pip of the source of his advantages. And respectable society is as little grateful as Pip, whenever the truth is revealed (TJ, 118).

As the 1860s began, Dickens, the reformer as informer, forced careful readers of *Great Expectations* to participate in Pip's epiphany, thus to realize from whence their "advantages" derived.

Pip's "indebtedness" to an "uncouth monster" typifies a tragicomic situation: the well-off prosper at the expense of an abhorrent subclass with whom they would never accept kinship or admit interdependence any more than Cinderella's stepsisters appreciate her toiling on their behalf. Society's reliance upon the exploited, like Pip's support from Magwitch, is liable to collapse as suddenly as Misnar's pavilion, Dickens warned. Which was more accurate, he asked, Victorian England's myth of itself as a princess among nations, a country deservedly risen, or his novel's depiction of a self-deluding, self-satisfied Cinderella living off a problematic blend of drudge and fairy godparent?

Dickens's Great Expectations returns again and again to the Pip–Magwitch chapters (1, 3, 39–42, 54–56) to corroborate Dickens's use of them as his novel's germ, pivot, and core. Pip and Magwitch deflate half a dozen pairings that Dickens insisted were too unbelievable—that is, outmoded—to be paradigmatic for the 1860s: Cinderella and her fairy godparent, Potts and Whalley in *A Day's Ride,* Thackeray's Pendennis and Major Pendennis, Madonna and Mat Marksman in Collins's *Hide and Seek,* Jane and Uncle Eyre, and all of the odd relationships in *Wuthering Heights* beginning with Heathcliff's adoption by old Earnshaw.

By 1860, Dickens had been king of the hill for more than two decades. Unprecedently successful, universally admired, he had out-distanced the fictionists on the scene when he arrived in the 1830s. In *Pickwick Papers,* Dickens tailored the bawdy comedy of Fielding and Smollett to Victorian tastes. With *Oliver Twist,* he proceeded to eclipse the Newgate novels of Ainsworth and Bulwer-Lytton; in *The Old Curiosity Shop,* thanks to Little Nell, he gave the sharpest tug ever to the nation's heartstrings. In *Barnaby Rudge,* he measured himself against Scott. Health permitting, Dickens wrote John Forster once the success of *Martin Chuzzlewit* seemed assured, "I could maintain my place in the minds of thinking men, though fifty writers started up to-morrow" (*PL,* 3:590). In the late 1840s and in a widening stream throughout the 1850s, they did just that. Thackeray and Trollope found their best stride; Elizabeth Gaskell, George Eliot, Wilkie Collins, and Charles Reade appeared. The Victorian novel began to evolve in several directions at once: Collins's realism, for example, was extraordinary or melodramatic compared to Eliot's, yet both novelists coveted the top spot. Dickens had to redefine his "place" to be sure of keeping it.

Much as Dickens elbowed his way to the front a quarter of a century earlier as the premier comic novelist, he declared himself the tragicomedian for the 1860s. Whether the topic was snobbery, inheritance, revenge, or monstrosity, not to mention the arduousness of growing up, Dickens demanded recognition as the age's reigning authority. His rivals, he grumbled, had failed to perceive how interrelated these concerns are. Take snobbery and monstrosity, for example, the first a form of the second, in Dickens's view. He generates sensational suspense out of them: Magwitch's long-awaited reappearance as Pip's secret benefactor is that of both monster and snob—a more terrifying manifestation than Shelley's of a problem more threatening than Thackeray (or Lever) realized. Furthermore, Dickens's rivals' novels were seldom humorous and serious in equal amounts, much less simultaneously, whereas only a tragicomic approach could address the whole truth. Dickens charged that Thackeray in particular was too resigned, too melancholic, to be a true tragicomedian—that the more complicated artist gets angry even when laughing and cannot stop laughing no matter how angry he gets. But Thackeray's satire was neither incisive enough to inspire reforms nor comic enough to derive genuine side-splitting amusement from life's shortcomings. In Lever, unfortunately for *All the Year Round,* Thackeray's suavity degenerated into facile, irresponsible farce.

Between 1858 and 1860, Dickens reorganized his life; he separated from Catherine, his wife of twenty-two years, entangled himself with a young actress, and sold Tavistock House, his London residence. Gad's Hill near Rochester, purchased in 1856, was now the family home. Dickens ceased to be primarily a Londoner; the area in and around Rochester/Chatham became the Dickens Country. To spite Bradbury and Evans, who allegedly sympathized with Catherine, Dickens shut down *Household Words,* the weekly journal he edited for them, and began *All the Year Round.* He also commenced public readings from his own works for personal profit. The forty-eight-year-old novelist replaced older friends (John Forster, Clarkson Stanfield, Daniel Maclise) with younger ones (Wilkie Collins, Edmund Yates, Percy Fitzgerald). He dismissed Hablot K. Browne, his illustrator since the fourth number of *Pickwick Papers;* twenty-two-year-old Marcus Stone garnished the one-volume Library Edition of *Great Expectations* (1862) with eight woodcuts.

Dickens's Great Expectations contends that Dickens reconstituted his art in 1860 and 1861 just as thoroughly as he had rearranged his life. *Great Expectations* stands out in the Dickens canon as a deliberate repositioning both vis-à-vis his contemporaries and on the spectrum of nineteenth-century fiction. Consolidating his strengths as popular entertainer, creative artist, and social critic, he certified his growth into a melodramatic realist par excellence who was also a tragicomic psychological novelist; in short, a multiple preeminence for a Dickens fully mature yet rejuvenated. At issue was superiority, not just survival. Neither egotistic nor paranoid, Dickens felt that newcomers would find it harder to shove him aside if he made clearer how many prior novelists his work had out-classed. According to Phyllis Rose, Dickens's career proves that "the mode and content of the work of artistic geniuses" must "change radically at mid-life . . . if the artist is to continue to be fully creative" (PR, 167). But the midlife crisis she invents for Dickens fails to take into account the increasingly competitive atmosphere he sensed around him in the marketplace.

Victorian parody means writing what one says is the truth to expose the absurdity of the material one is rewriting. For Dickens, this involves darkening a rival's worldview, no matter if it belongs to a fellow sensationalist (Collins) or another satirist (Thackeray). Even when Dickens reached back in time to parody fiction from earlier in the century, well-known novels with which he did not want his masterwork confused, he was driven by larger concerns, not just by personal anxieties. Disdain for *Cinderella*, for example, fueled a desire to purge the bildungsroman, *David Copperfield* included, of Smilesian success stories. Had Shelley exploited the parody of *Cinderella* implicit in Frankenstein's creation of a monster, the Cinderella complex rampant in Lever and Collins might never have taken hold. Thanks to *Frankenstein*, Dickens reasoned, *Jane Eyre* was free to turn Cinderella into a cultural icon. Jane's rise from unwanted orphan to indispensable wife began the infestation of the nineteenth-century novel with Cinderella motifs.

Although *Dickens's* Great Expectations unveils a whole new dimension to Dickens's artistic genius, not even so high-powered a revaluator could rewrite half a dozen novels within a single serial. Instead, he designated Lever, a comic novelist, and Collins, a sensational realist, as primary targets—opposite ends of the spectrum on which he positioned himself as both center and apex. In addition, he reused key episodes, characters, and themes from several other novels, keeping these texts alternately in his sights and parodically redoing parts of his auxiliary targets to subvert the whole. Nevertheless, one should read *Great Expectations* several times, on each occasion but the first as a full-scale revaluation of a different rival text. This happens in chapters 2 through 8 of this book. Having been examined as a tragicomic reworking of *Cinderella* in terms of the Misnar tale, *Great Expectations* is explicated as a revision of *A Day's Ride*, a rethinking of *Pendennis*, a revaluation of *David Copperfield*, a reconsideration of Wilkie Collins, a replacement for Shelley's *Frankenstein*, and a substitute for two novels by the Brontës, Charlotte's especially.

Revaluative parodies in *Great Expectations* transpire all at once, yet one should imagine each of them as a strand or layering insinuated into the novel like a pattern of imagery or a subplot. A Victorian novel bent on revaluation of a competitor is always "double-barreled" (*HR*, 2–3), issuing its own statement by rephrasing a rival's. *Great Expectations* demonstrates that such a document can serve more than one double purpose at a time. Theoretically, there appears to be no limit to the number of rival novels with which a revaluative masterpiece can quarrel. But *Great Expectations* should be read as if it were repealing one competitor's worldview at a time. No matter how many irrelevant pairs the Pip–Magwitch pairing ultimately disqualifies, no matter how many opening scenes Dickens's first chapter eclipses, parodic revaluation is always one text subverting another, even when Dickens attacks Thackeray by disowning Lever, or when *Great Expectations* plays down *David Copperfield* by rewriting *Self-Help*.

Jerome Beaty warned that the "source" for an "interrelation of texts" could be a "convention" rather than a "particular scene in some other single work or author" (JB, 42).[46] This caveat fails to appreciate the "honeycomb of intersecting networks" (*HR*, 2) that constitutes the nineteenth-century British novel. Use of Cinderella motifs in supposedly realistic novels was a widespread practice that Dickens ridiculed in terms of several carefully selected targets that he repudiated for disseminating or furthering the era's Cinderella complex. In short, Dickens's intention was to lambaste a convention (the Cinderella story), but his strategy expanded to revile its instigator among Victorian novelists (Charlotte Brontë) not just to discredit continuators (Lever, Collins). Rivalries remain hidden (that is, undeclared); nevertheless, the modern revaluator can point to specific incidents The Inimitable was revising. Misnar's pavilion collapses—that is, supersedes, displaces, rescinds— Potts's castles in the air (Lever), Alnaschar's basket of porcelain (Thackeray), the vestry at Old Welmingham (Collins), Thornfield in *Jane Eyre,* and Heathcliff's "palace" in *Wuthering Heights* (*WH,* 111).

Great scenes proliferated in the Victorian novel because in many cases a prior novelist parodied the episode the revaluator was redoing. Twice Charlotte Brontë recasts the scene in which Victor Frankenstein's monster "forced" its way into its master's chamber (*F,* 58). First Bertha slips into Rochester's room to set his bed afire; then she enters Jane Eyre's room the night before the wedding and tears asunder the bridal veil. Arguably, Victor and Jane are both visited by their nighttime selves, but Charlotte implies that Bertha is a bigger threat than Shelley's creature. When Magwitch, just returned from Australia, invades Pip's apartment late at night in chapter 39, Dickens cancels both Frankenstein's monster and Rochester's first wife with a genuinely horrible apparition-creation, an undeterrable visitor from society's hidden underside. Magwitch's intrusion must be reread twice, as part of a rebuff to Shelley and, in a different context, as a rejection of Brontë.

The challenge facing Dickens was to interweave several revaluative parodies within a coherent novel without contradicting himself. *Great Expectations* is both an autonomous statement and a compendium of counterstatements, none of which is inconsistent with the others. Thanks to Dickens's dexterity, Miss Havisham does double duty as both a ruined Cinderella and a malevolent fairy godmother, just as Magwitch is both Pip's would-be fairy godparent and society's cinder girl. It helped that Dickens's targets have much in common: besides being riddled with Cinderella motifs, *Frankenstein, Jane Eyre,* and *Wuthering Heights* study personality development, a concern they share with *David Copperfield* and *Pendennis*. To Dickens's chagrin, *David Copperfield* had been accused of imitating Charlotte Brontë's novel and of mimicking *Pendennis* as well. *Great Expectations* was written to distance Dickens from the controversies over *David Copperfield* by discrediting Brontë and Thackeray; Dickens considered Brontë's idea of personality formation no more profound than Thackeray's conception of a snob's inner workings. Instead of comparing *David Copperfield* to *Jane Eyre*, Dickens implied, one should equate the latter with *Oliver Twist*, two novels for the 1840s, beyond which *Great Expectations*, the first post-Darwin bildungsroman, had evolved substantially.

Although *Great Expectations* can be appreciated without reference to Lever, Collins, Shelley, or the Brontës, Dickens's revaluative parodies increase his novel's authority, verifying its critique of society by savaging prior analyses. To read *Great Expectations* to the hilt, to understand it more thoroughly than all but the most perceptive first readers could or than anyone has since, one should attend to Dickens's parodic revaluations. His redefinition of temporal existence as a tragicomedy underwrites them all. Pip's dilemma—what to expect in a tragicomic world?—is still worth puzzling over. So too is the subtlety with which Dickens's satire on expectancy, Victorian and in general, retells *Cinderella* en route to telling itself. To an extent fully realizable only in conjunction with the novel's many revaluative parodies, Dickens overrules the cinder girl's story with the tale of Misnar's pavilion.

Chapter 2
Lever

Thanks to Charles Lever's unpopular serial, circulation of *All the Year Round* declined significantly for the only time during Dickens's life. His new periodical in jeopardy, the novelist had to rescue the editor by writing *Great Expectations*, which reversed the slump in sales. Consequently, *A Day's Ride: A Life's Romance* is chiefly remembered as the reason Dickens's thirteenth novel appeared in weekly installments instead of monthly parts as originally planned. But Lever's disaster sheds light on the nature of Dickens's countermeasure, not just its genesis; it helps to explain what Dickens wrote as well as when and why.

The consensus is that Dickens behaved handsomely. His "proposed remedy," inserting *Great Expectations* to accompany *A Day's Ride*, was "not drastic," Lionel Stevenson decided (*CL*, 243). Edgar Johnson went further: dreading the "blow" to Lever's self-esteem from news of negative public response, Dickens strove "generously to assuage the wound" (J, 2:965). Instead of terminating *A Day's Ride*, J.A. Sutherland commented, Dickens permitted Lever's serial to complete its run out of "a spirit of collegiality."[1]

Actually, editorial policy at *All the Year Round* prejudiced Lever's chances. When sales began falling, Dickens's decisions precluded recovery from a bad start. In addition, the novelist capitalized imaginatively on a rival's fiasco: *A Day's Ride* reminded Dickens of pitfalls to avoid and furnished a convenient target for parodic revaluation. Instead of one serial buttressing the other, a disgruntled Dickens wrote his story to cancel Lever's, in effect to repeal the latter's unrealistic worldview. *Great Expectations* is primarily a satire on Victorian expectancy, an anti–Cinderella fairy tale in which Pip's rise and fall warns an entire nation against snobbish overconfidence; but it also achieves a thoroughgoing revision of the candy-coated comedy in *A Day's Ride*. Admitting an editorial mistake, Dickens set out to prove that he was still the period's most trenchant social critic and finest serialist. Lever was forced to compensate aesthetically for the financial losses he had caused. Having been costly to Dickens, he found himself in no position to retaliate. *Great Expectations* eclipsed *A Day's Ride* so completely that the final, most interesting chapter of the Dickens-Lever rivalry has remained hidden.²

The permanent decline in Lever's reputation has obscured parallels between his younger self and the early Dickens, who were frequently regarded as contenders for preeminence. In 1830, Lever began contributing sketches of city life to *The Dublin Literary Gazette* not unlike those that Dickens, as "Boz," set in London a few years later. *Harry Lorrequer,* Lever's first novel, was serialized in the *Dublin University Magazine* (1837) shortly after Mr. Pickwick commenced his travels, then reissued in monthly parts to take advantage of Dickens's success.

Critics occasionally ranked Lever above Dickens. The popularity of *Charles O'Malley* (1841) Edgar Allan Poe wrote, "surpassed even the inimitable compositions of Mr. Dickens" (WJF, 1:274).³ One reviewer professed that he "would rather be the author of *Harry Lorrequer* than of all the 'Pickwicks' and 'Nicklebys' in the world" (*CL*, 91). When Lever's publishers advertised this comment, Dickens protested and Lever wrote an apologetic letter "to his rival" (*CL*, 95). According to W.J. Fitzpatrick, Lever in pink wrappers (installment covers), Thackeray in yellow, and Dickens in green were "the three most popular novelists of the day" (WJF, 2:185). Lever considered himself a match for Dickens; thus *Tom Burke of "Ours"* attempts a Dickensian rendition of the Paris slums and *St. Patrick's Eve* (1845) resembles a Dickens Christmas book. Dickens and Lever were frequently mentioned for the same jobs. In 1841, Richard Bentley asked Lever to edit his *Miscellany,* a post that Dickens held first. After Dickens suspended *Household Words* and commenced *All the Year Round,* Bradbury and Evans, publishers of the earlier venture, tried to persuade Lever to spearhead "a rival journal" (*CL*, 238).

Given this prolonged public competition, the invitation to contribute a serial to *All the Year Round* is puzzling. The editor surely did not plan from the outset to embarrass an old foe of the novelist. Dickens was beginning a new phase in which he reoriented his melodramatic realism toward the tragicomic and the psychological. Not so Lever, whose views on comedy and composition (that is, structure) never changed.⁴ This prolific, Dublin-born novelist's early novels vividly portrayed Irish military and fox-hunting society, but he was slipping past his prime—if not already passé. Nevertheless, Dickens courted him, as this lavish solicitation shows: "[B]elieve, my dear Lever—not only that I 'want' you now, but that I have 'wanted' such a generous spirit in a man, many a long day" (*CL*, 241). Presumably, Dickens had never heard Lever's prediction, made years earlier to Alexander Spencer, that "fast writing and careless composition" in *Dombey and Son* had "set the gravestone" on Dickens's fame (ED, 1:204). Nor did Dickens realize how jealous Lever was of his rival's ever-increasing reputation. A gambler and spendthrift, Lever envied Dickens's more secure financial position, which, ironically, he was fated to endanger.

Dickens most likely regarded Lever as a stopgap. His novel was to follow either Wilkie Collins's *The Woman in White*, or, preferably, its successor, which Dickens hoped would be a story by Elizabeth Gaskell or George Eliot. But Gaskell, who had already contributed three serials to *Household Words*, reneged and Eliot decided against what she considered the serial format's "terseness and closeness of construction" (J, 2:956). Had Lever followed Eliot or Gaskell, for whom suspenseful construction was not the sine qua non, he might have seemed more at home in Dickens's rotation. Instead, he succeeded one of the cleverest serialists the century produced. *A Day's Ride* went against the tone of the journal's previous offerings without measuring up to their excitements.

On-again, off-again negotiations may have been responsible for Lever's late start and lackadaisical approach. Discussions began in October 1859, but Dickens did not offer terms until January 1860; the starting date still depended on Eliot. Uncertain when he would be needed, Lever had no motive to work in earnest until February 1860, when Dickens requested four installments by June. Although Lever had a tentative title, his general idea, and three full months, his resolve seems to have eroded: as late as April, he was ransacking *Tales of the Trains* (1845), one of his weakest productions, "to see" if he "could steal any of the incidents" for the "new tale" he had promised Dickens (*CL*, 241).

Perhaps Lever mistook Dickens's offhand manner during the preliminaries for a nonchalance equal to his own. Perhaps Dickens underestimated the amount of strong handling the undisciplined Lever required. Dickens was not extending carte blanche in conceding that Lever could write "anything grave or gay about anything in the wide world"—as long as the material filtered through his "bright and keen eyes" (*CL*, 241). However, from the editor's manner of expressing confidence in his contributor's judgment, Lever assumed that he could rely on last-minute improvisation. He had published nineteen serials since 1837 (more than Dickens's entire output), yet he proceeded to ignore the lessons about scrupulous planning that Dickens's successes up to 1860 should have taught him. Lever may have trusted the popularity of Dickens's periodical to carry him no matter how indifferently he composed: "The *Ride* I write as carelessly as a common letter," he boasted to Spencer on 17 September 1860, "but I'd not be the least astonished to find the success in the inverse ratio to the trouble" (ED, 1:362).

As a result of so cavalier an approach, *A Day's Ride* is an episodic novel in which events succeed each other according to whatever Lever thought of next. Algernon Sydney Potts, the son of a Dublin apothecary is an upstart like Pip, discontented with his lot and anxious to appear genteel. In chapter 38, we learn that he is twenty-three years old—Pip's age by the "Third Stage." The novel chronicles Potts's ludicrous daydreams, his snobbish pretensions; it savors the embarrassments these repeatedly cause him as he travels from Ireland to London, then through parts of Belgium, Germany, Switzerland, and Austria, going as far east as Russia before returning to Great Britain (specifically, Wales) by way of Paris. These meanderings begin during the long vacation from Trinity College, Dublin, after an undistinguished first year. Armed with a small legacy from his uncle, Potts sets out as if for a ride of a day or so but is on the road approximately three years.[5]

Loosely connected mishaps, the stuff of picaresque, were foreign to the serial novel's increasing emphasis on a tight plot full of suspense and surprise. Based on Potts's itinerary, Lever's story literally rambled. Incidents were often amusing and the ne'er-do-well hero is always likeable, but Lever's casually unfolding tale could not incite readers to clamor for the next issue. One can skim chapters without losing the story line: 6, 8, 12, 14, 17, 22, and 26, all from the novel's looser first half, fall into this category. Dickens eventually said as much: in a letter for 6 October 1860, he suggested that the tale was "too detached and discursive"; it was not "strung . . . on the needful strong thread of interest" (*PL*, 9:321–22)—accurate criticisms that he would keep in mind for *Great Expectations* but ought to have leveled sooner, not after Lever's novel had been running for almost two months.

Dickens had asked Lever "to give him something lively" for his year-old journal; the editor wanted to "infuse some new blood" lest he and Collins remain its only serialists. Previously a successful contributor of shorter pieces to *Household Words,* Lever responded with a novel intended to "record the life of a fool," much as Thackeray, Fitzgerald observed, meant *Barry Lyndon* as "the autobiography of a knave" (WJF, 2:186). In Fitzpatrick's opinion, *A Day's Ride* contains "less humour and more irony than [Lever's] previous books." In other words, as it unfolded it tried to become more like *Lyndon* and less like *Pickwick,* perhaps to Dickens's dismay.[6] In August 1860, however, Potts (or Pottinger, as he restyles himself in chapter 9) was simply an anachronism.[7] The Irish equivalent of a Cockney picaro, Potts is an undergraduate version of the sporting grocer, whose disasters on horseback were ridiculed by Robert Smith Surtees in sketches collected as *Jorrocks's Jaunts and Jollities* (1838). Instead of a transfusion, Lever took the Victorian novel two decades into its past.[8]

Surprisingly, Dickens exhibited no editorial misgivings prior to publication. He assured Lever that the nondescript title was "a very good one" and warned him not to write down to a periodical audience as if it were not to be trusted "with anything good" (J, 2:956–57)—strange advice to a veteran serialist even if *All the Year Round* was several notches above the *Dublin University*

Magazine. Although Dickens recommended "condensation" as a general principle, he simply wanted assurances that Lever's hero would begin his wanderings before the end of the first installment (chs. 1–2). As of June 1860, Dickens was delighted with the "vivacity, originality, and humour" of the opening chapters, especially "the rising invention in the drunken young man" (the hero's attempts in chapter 3 to pass as someone noteworthy—the finest swordsman in Europe, a friend of the Emperor of Russia. Actually, Potts drinks too much and loses his rental horse in a backgammon game). This episode, Dickens wrote Lever, "made me laugh to an extent and with a heartiness that I should like you to have seen and heard" (J, 2:957).

For a decade, Dickens was urged to abandon social criticism for the Pickwickian manner that had made him famous. But when he reverted to something in a lighter vein, even if he did not write it himself, his audience objected. Dickens may have been drawn to *A Day's Ride*'s atavistic qualities: having pacified the Pickwickians in his readership with Lever, he would be at liberty to continue the epic critique of Victorian society that spans the 1850s from *Bleak House* through *Hard Times* and *Little Dorrit* to *A Tale of Two Cities*. For economic reasons, two novels in this Juvenalian onslaught had to be weekly serials—*Hard Times* to prop up *Household Words*, *A Tale of Two Cities* to inaugurate *All the Year Round*. With the weekly serial department entrusted to Lever, Dickens could reestablish the novel in twenty monthly parts as his primary vehicle for social analysis.

When *A Day's Ride* first appeared (18 August 1860), it was forced to compete with installment 39 of *The Woman in White*, which still had another climactic installment to go. That Lever did not capture readership from the beginning is not entirely his fault; no match for the accumulated interest in Collins's novel, his humbler fare was bound to debut inauspiciously. While Potts was renting his quadruped, Blondel, and setting out, Collins's Walter Hartright finally cornered Count Fosco. Besides Fosco's confession to the conspiracy against Laura Fairlie, the next week's final installment included Hartright's account of her vindication and his subsequent discovery of the murdered Fosco's corpse in the Paris morgue. No wonder Potts's misadventures at the "Lamb," the inn where his first and only day on horseback ends with the loss of his mount, went unnoticed.

During a previous overlap (26 November 1859), *The Woman in White* debuted on the third page of *All the Year Round* (95–104), immediately after the last installment of *A Tale of Two Cities*. It ran a mere two pages (93–95), posing little threat to Collins's suspenseful beginning (chs. 1–4). His longer installments kept Lever's tale far from the front page for *two* weeks: after opening on the ninth page on 18 August (441–47, following Collins on 433–41), *A Day's*

Ride was pushed back to the twelfth page on 25 August (469–74, following Collins on 457–68).

Distracted by Collins, few readers probably turned directly to Lever on either 18 or 25 August. Some may not have read Lever's first two installments, so the fixing power of his third installment, Potts's meeting with the Croftons (ch. 5), assumed greater importance than could have been anticipated. Reading Lever after finishing either of Collins's last two installments only served to magnify the former's deficiencies as a serialist—no economy, little suspense. Thus every conceivable course of action on the reader's part prevented *A Day's Ride* from grabbing hold. Lever's story would have begun to greater advantage had Dickens waited until September before starting its run. But it seems to have been editorial policy to launch a new serial before the old one had concluded.[9] This fostered a sense of continuity implicit in the journal's title. Instead of providing momentum for transition, however, *The Woman in White* refused to relinquish the spotlight.

On 27 October 1860, Dickens announced the December starting date for *Great Expectations*. He encouraged readers to look past Lever instead of struggling to come to terms with him. *A Day's Ride* still had five months to go. On 9 February 1861, well in advance of Lever's last installment (23 March) and with *Great Expectations* less than a third in print, Dickens announced that the end of *A Day's Ride* was in sight.[10] It was customary to reveal when one serial would end and another begin, but pointing to a conclusion *seven* weeks beforehand seems premature. Dickens timed his announcement to coincide with the "great expectations" chapter (ch. 18). The same week that Jaggers informed Pip of his improved prospects, Dickens told readers of theirs.

Dickens first mentioned *A Day's Ride* as a coming attraction on 21 July 1860, a month before its commencement. There were three reminders of its approaching inaugural: 28 July, 4 and 11 August. Thus the advent of Lever's novel and that of *Great Expectations* received similar emphasis, but the latter was promoted as an anodyne to be administered months before the former terminated. Collins's *The Woman in White* had only five more installments to go after 21 July. Readers no doubt surmised that it was nearing conclusion, but this was not made official until 18 August 1860, one week before the end.

As Lever's first two chapters appeared along with Collins's penultimate installment, Dickens included this notice: "In pursuance of the plan announced at the commencement of THE WOMAN IN WHITE, we have the pleasure of presenting to the reader a New Story by Mr. CHARLES LEVER. After the completion of The Woman in White next week, A DAY'S RIDE will occupy its place on the first page of each weekly number, and will be continued from week to week until finished." Less than four months later, *Great Expectations* appropriated the top spot that Collins had enjoyed uninterruptedly for thirty-nine weeks.

Dickens's serial automatically took precedence, banishing Lever into the recesses of *All the Year Round* for a second time: to the twelfth page again on 1 December 1860. The displacement of *A Day's Ride* has been dismissed along with Dickens's early announcement of its termination date as "minor irritations" for Lever (*CL*, 244). But his installments were soon relegated to the last pages. On 2 February 1861, for example, the issue began with chapters 16 and 17 of *Great Expectations;* then came features such as "Volunteers at Hythe," "Hard Frosts," and "In Praise of Bears." Chapter 36 of *A Day's Ride* ran last.

The "plan" divulged on 26 November 1859 did not specify Lever's novel as Collins's successor. As *A Tale of Two Cities* concluded and *The Woman in White* began, Dickens promised to reserve "the first place in these pages for a continuous original work of fiction" that he hoped would become "a part of English Literature." On 18 August, Dickens was alluding to his editorial pledge only to publish "sustained works of the imagination." The "plan" was clearly intended to mean that Dickens's periodical would never contain another of his novels after *A Tale of Two Cities.* On the other hand, it offered assurances that the inaugural serial had established the standard. By October 1860, as Lever's story foundered, Dickens must have accused himself of having broken the covenant made with his readers less than a year before. That the introduction of *Great Expectations* was a slap in the face to Lever seems not to have worried Dickens nearly as much as repairing the sacred bond he had forged with the public.

Dickens's talent as a serialist guaranteed that his troubled journal would rebound. Bolstering *All the Year Round* was impossible, however, without sinking a fellow novelist—a case of the editor deciding, in effect, to deliver the coup de grâce to a floundering contributor. Opportunities to outshine a rival proved irresistible. Lever had sealed his fate in the more than three months before *Great Expectations* was introduced. Nevertheless, it is difficult to imagine readers persisting with *A Day's Ride* during the four months the stories ran concurrently. When the opening chapters of *Great Expectations* outclassed *A Day's Ride* as unmercifully as the final episodes of *The Woman in White* had, Lever's sense of déja vu must have grown acute: first one melodramatic realist prevented his novel from catching on; then a second made certain it never did.

In a letter for 15 October 1860, Dickens lectured Lever about a serial's obligation to "fix the people in the beginning" (*PL,* 9:323-24). Two and a half months later, making his point a second time, he demonstrated how this fixing should be done. Contrary to Lever's casual opening, Dickens began *Great Expectations* with a confrontation as momentous as Walter Hartright's encounter with the ghostly Anne Catherick in Collins's initial installment. Lever's hero gets under way slowly and seems equally foolish at start and finish, but Pip's life is changed forever by an arresting apparition when Magwitch starts "up from among the graves" within seconds of the novel's beginning (*GE*, 4).

Dickens took readers' divided expectations to heart. "The opening," he insisted to John Forster in a letter for "October 1860," is "exceedingly droll" in that the "relations" between "a child and a good-natured man" (Pip and Joe) "seem to me very funny" (*PL*, 9: 325). At the same time, he had set up "the pivot on which the story will turn"—Pip's long-term affiliation with Magwitch. In the first installment, Dickens supplied Pip and Joe (ch. 2) for die-hard Pickwickians, and Pip and Magwitch (ch. 1) for sensational realists.[11] A counterpoint of comedy and terror resulted from the compression into adjoining chapters of two parallel father-son relationships sharply different in tone and significance. Outshining Lever's loosely constructed story, the first two chapters of Dickens's bildungsroman indicated that Pip's growth and development would meet the definition of tragicomedy by alternating serious and humorous episodes. Dickens's brand of melodramatic realism had tragicomic possibilities—it belonged to a higher genre than Lever's picaresque novel.

"Four weekly numbers have been ground off the wheel," and a fifth is imminent, Dickens wrote Collins on 24 October (*PL*, 9: 330). He was writing the first visit to Satis House (ch. 8) and would soon move on to Pip's exaggerated account of this event: under Pumblechook's "bullying" cross-examination, Pip describes Miss Havisham's "black velvet coach," "cakes and wine" eaten from "gold plates," dogs fighting "for veal-cutlets out of a silver basket," and the waving of flags and swords (*GE*, 68–69). After opening dramatically, Dickens rescinded the praise he had lavished on Potts's "rising invention" in chapter 3 of *A Day's Ride*. The superiority of the eight-year-old's imagination to the intoxicated undergraduate's tall tales symbolizes the relationship that Dickens quickly established between the creative faculties of their respective authors.

Closeted with distinguished company at the "Lamb," Potts feels removed "from all accidents of his situation"; that is, free to masquerade as anyone he pleases (*ADR*, 22). Soon this scion of apothecaries is bragging about estates in his family since the Magna Charta. Had Pip been quizzed further, however, there would have been no limit to his fabrications: "a balloon in the yard," "a bear in the brewery" (*GE*, 70). Both episodes use lying to expose the hero's inferiority complex, but social pressures to rise above the ordinary are harsher on Pip. Potts lies to Hammond, Oxley, Lord Keldrum, and Father Dyke to gratify an inflated sense of personal worth. Younger, poorer, and defenseless, Pip is forced to satisfy the unreasonable expectations of Pumblechook and Mrs. Joe. His subsequent desire for ascendancy, as sharp as Magwitch's, is both an internal drive and the result of exhaustive social conditioning since childhood. Potts fails to deceive his companions; Pip easily bamboozles Pumblechook and Mrs. Joe, who want their illusions confirmed. When Pip confesses his lies, even Joe seems culpable, wishing for a flag at Satis House if no coach; if no "immense" dogs to pull it, then at least a "puppy" (*GE*, 71).

In chapter 9, Dickens served notice that he intended to broaden, deepen, and above all, *darken* Lever's themes. His method of revaluing rivals was to substitute bleaker renditions that reduced to frivolity their alleged mishandling of similar materials. This process of parodic reconsideration is inherently tragicomic: no less amusing than Potts's deliberate lies, Pip's involuntary mendacity panders to society's weaknesses, endorsing the kind of harmful fairy tales that Victorian England was gullibly telling itself—lies, for example, about the unlimited privileges of affluence. No one questions Miss Havisham's right to keep a coach indoors. In a country where Magwitch grows up "a thieving turnips" for a living (*GE*, 344), she allegedly feeds her dogs veal cutlets.

Potts's temporary embarrassment in chapter 3 of *A Day's Ride* is rewritten as a formative experience for Pip in chapter 9 of *Great Expectations*, "a memorable day" that "made great changes" in him (*GE*, 73). It begins Pip's awareness of the world's fundamental "insufficiency."¹² Only eight, he already suspects that neither facing facts nor inventing fictions is satisfying. One can never remove the "accidents" (Potts's word) of one's situation; nor can one transcend them through creative fantasy. As Joe rightly warns, "lies is lies" (*GE*, 71). Yet remaining on the "level" of "common doings" will not necessarily enable one to "live well and die happy" as Joe exhorts Pip to do (*GE*, 72). Estella taunted Pip with his commonness; her insults, he realizes, "somehow" prompted the lies (*GE*, 71).

When Potts's rambles ended, Dickens had reached installment 17. Chapter 27 revolves humorously around Pip and Joe (as did chapter 2), chapter 28 indirectly around Pip and Magwitch (as chapter 1 did directly). By this point, the tension between comedy and catastrophe can be found within each chapter, not just in the contrast of each with the other. Installment 17 will be used to illustrate Dickens's revaluation strategy throughout *Great Expectations*. In chapter 27, he reemphasized his appropriation of Lever's principal theme: snobbery's perils and pitfalls. In chapter 28, he exposed the thinness of Lever's plot, prolonging Pip's uncertainties to repudiate the all-too-convenient resolution of Potts's.

Breakfasting with Pip and Joe in Barnard's Inn, Joe performs the sort of bungling that Lever reserved for Potts. In chapter 27, Dickens condemns Pip's superior attitude through the false moves it elicits from Joe. He squirms in his Sunday clothes and calls his former playfellow "sir." Yet whether fumbling with his shirt collar or spilling his food, Pip's self-styled "infant companionation" retains "a simple dignity" (*GE*, 225), whereas Pip sinks in our esteem (and his own) without actually playing the buffoon. Subtler psychologically than anything in Lever, the unsettling effects Pip has on his earliest friend and protector reveal the consequences of snobbery more incisively than Lever did by repeatedly disconcerting Potts.

The damage is self-inflicted and self-contained when Potts pretends to be a government messenger eagerly awaited at Constantinople, or when his self-importance leads Mrs. Keats to mistake him for "the young C. de P.," a count allegedly touring Germany in disguise (*ADR*, 199).[13] One smiles when Potts extols the "grand stuff" he is "made of" (*ADR*, 405), or when the "mythical narrative" of his exploits proves to be "a card edifice of greatness" (*ADR*, 82–83). But Pip's superior airs result in Joe's humiliation, which hastens his departure from London. Snobbery can be socially disruptive, Dickens lectured Lever, just like the class consciousness that causes it. Furthermore, a snobbish outlook is almost impossible to overcome; having discombobulated Joe, Pip becomes "impatient" and "out of temper," which upsets Joe even more. "If I had been easier with Joe," Pip decides in retrospect, "Joe would have been easier with me" (*GE*, 223). The episode approaches tragicomedy in that an element of cruelty seeps into Joe's plight, making readers uneasy in their laughter even when Joe's hat, a symbol of the commonness he cannot lay down in Pip's presence, keeps tumbling off the mantelpiece until its owner finally knocks it "into the slop-basin." Correcting Lever, Dickens discloses snobbery's pernicious side: not just an obstacle to the individual snob's maturation, it threatens human relationships generally.

In the second half of the installment that coincided with the resolution of *A Day's Ride*, Pip is returning to his village by coach. He recognizes one of the convicts seated behind him as the man who gave him two one-pound notes in the Three Jolly Bargemen (*GE*, 75–76). As the convicts converse, it becomes clear that the money was a gift from Magwitch, whom Pip seems fated to meet again. This prospect undermined Lever's parting view of Potts's rosy future with Kate Herbert, whose fortuitous summons brings him to her family in Wales and concludes the novel with the hero's reward. Lever's chapter 48 is later parodied extensively in Pip's flight to Egypt, his eleven-year absence from Estella, and the lingering ambiguity—will they part or not?—in the novel's last line.

For two years Potts wanders aimlessly after locating Kate's missing father, about whom more will be said later. In the final installment, he receives Kate's letter of invitation, which has been gathering dust in the Paris police department. In chapter 28, Pip reads an article in the Blue Boar's coffee room from a "dirty old copy" of the local newspaper proclaiming Pumblechook "the founder" of his fortunes (*GE*, 231). Its obvious falsity compromises the credibility of Lever's happy ending. From one document Potts learns that he has acquired a patroness whom he seems not to deserve; from another, Pip comes no closer to identifying his patron. Lever promoted Potts to wedded bliss with an ironmaster's daughter. In rebuttal, *Great Expectations* continued to build toward Magwitch's catastrophic return, which terminates Pip's social ascent, including his dream of an early marriage to Estella.

Pip's vicissitudes in chapter 29 permitted readers to consign Potts to Wales without a pang. Pip has journeyed to Rochester (ch. 28) because Joe brought him a summons from Miss Havisham (ch. 27): having completed her education, Estella wishes to see her former playmate. At their first meeting since childhood (ch. 29), Pip beholds "an elegant lady," whom Miss Havisham christens a "queen"; he feels like a "coarse and common boy again" (*GE*, 235) despite his improved manners and dress. The week after *A Day's Ride* concluded, Dickens continued to undercut its unrealistic ending by pitting Pip's summons to Rochester against Potts's to Wales. When Pip reenacts his first humiliating visit to Satis House, Potts's rise from apothecary's son to an industrialist's prospective son-in-law forfeits any remaining plausibility.

Kate's letter informs Potts that her father "loves" him and her mother "longs to know" him (*ADR*, 447). In Dickens's parody of Potts's euphoria, Pip rejoices that Estella "should be destined" for the former "blacksmith's boy" (*GE*, 244). Despite an unsatisfactory interview with Estella at Satis House and no encouragement from Miss Havisham, Pip concludes chapter 29 with a "burst of gratitude." Such a destiny occurs only in fairy tales, Dickens implied, ironically conflating *Cinderella* and *Sleeping Beauty:* unlike Potts, who has found his princess, Pip wonders when his Cinderella-like rise in the world will "awaken" Estella's "mute and sleeping" heart (*GE*, 244).

Joe's first London visit, in chapter 27, looks back to the Christmas dinner in chapter 4 and forward to Pip's breakfast with Magwitch in chapter 40, the morning after the ex-convict's unexpected return. Adults in Mrs. Joe's kitchen observe Pip "with indignation and abhorrence" (*GE*, 28), making him feel as out of place at the Christmas feast as Joe later seems in Barnard's Inn. In chapter 27, the comedy turns serious when one of nature's gentlemen, having been made ill at ease, starts to behave like a comic version of Frankenstein's monster. In chapter 40, one watches a snob forced to entertain a guest who resembles Frankenstein's creature but has actually created the snob, a tragic yet absurdly comic turn of events.

As Lever's picaresque novel ended, *Great Expectations* pointed backward and forward to show that Dickens could write about snobbery more coherently than his rival had. Readers were invited to compare varieties of snobbery, which is consistently seen as a social monstrosity: the "abhorrence" for Pip, as if all children were little monsters (ch. 4); Pip's disdain for an "utterly preposterous Joe" (*GE*, 223); and the consummation eight weeks later: Pip's "aversion" to Magwitch (*GE*, 329).

Pip's strange manner of wooing Biddy (ch. 17) should also be placed alongside his conduct toward Joe. In these scenes, snobbery takes its toll on the two people who care most about Pip. The episode is Dickens's redoing of the conversation between Potts and Kate in chapter 16 of *A Day's Ride*. Potts has been mistaken for an experienced government agent and is escorting Mrs. Keats and her companion out of the Duchy of Hesse-Kalbbratonstadt on their journey south. Having yet to divulge his real name, he tells Kate his plans to write "reviews, and histories, and stories, and short poems, and, last of all, the 'Confessions of Algernon Sydney Potts'" (*ADR*, 173). Kate immediately discerns that Potts, whom she treats as an imaginary character, should be "a creature of absurdity and folly, a pretender and a snob." He will always be "thrusting himself forward, twenty times a day, into positions he had no right to" (*ADR*, 174). Thus she describes Potts's adventures under the very sort of false pretenses that his real-life namesake is exploiting. Potts's addresses hit an unexpected snag as he becomes "a butt and a dupe," but he refuses the self-knowledge in Kate's good-natured mockery and grows angry instead.

Biddy also sees through a young man's inflated self-image, but Pip's ego is cruelly at odds with itself. The psychology of the snob is more complex than Lever realized, Dickens argues, because snobs are both pain inflicters and self-tormentors. Having bound Biddy "to secrecy," Pip confesses his dreams much as Potts confides in Kate: "I want to be a gentleman," he says (*GE*, 126). "Oh, I wouldn't, if I was you!" Biddy advises, "don't you think you are happier as you are?" Kate disarms a simple snob, but Biddy recognizes Pip as both criminal and victim—unfair to her and cruel to himself. Debunking Potts's harmless deceptions, Dickens has Pip unwittingly demonstrate snobbery's heartlessness: "If only I could get myself to fall in love with you," he complains, tantalizing Biddy, who also wishes it (*GE*, 130). Conceived in contrast to Potts, Pip is the product of Dickens's determination to reveal the snob as he looks *from inside* (that is, to himself): a bundle of guilt and insecurity, not merely a figure of fun to be lampooned.

When Orlick, yet another version of Frankenstein's monster, intrudes upon Pip's walk with Biddy, she stammers "I—I am afraid he likes me" and Pip interprets the journeyman's "daring to admire her" as a personal insult, "an outrage to myself" (*GE*, 131). Dickens carries snobbery well beyond the one-pointed satire in Lever's chapter 16: although Orlick's aspiring to Biddy is as presumptuous as Pip's claim to Estella, Pip considers himself so far above Orlick that the latter's interest in a woman supposedly inferior to Pip nevertheless injures his self-esteem. Ironically, Pip behaves contemptuously toward a projection of his baser self even when it wisely prefers Biddy to Estella.

In *A Day's Ride,* Potts is the only case presented in detail, but in-depth studies of snobs abound in *Great Expectations.* According to Humphry House, "the snob problem was not acute before the forties" (H, 153), so in 1860 and 1861, Dickens was assessing twenty years of its ravages. He claimed to understand snobbery better than Lever did because *Great Expectations* sees the epidemic beginning in the late twenties, when the London stages of the novel transpire. Supplanting *A Day's Ride, Great Expectations* proclaimed itself a virtual primer on the subject of snobbery, hence the real textbook on "the great Snob world."[14]

Some form of snobbery taints nearly everyone in *Great Expectations,* including Joe, whose awkwardness in front of Pip and Herbert (ch. 27) is not unlike self-abasement before an alleged superior.[15] Characters in *Great Expectations* are either undeservedly pleased with themselves and contemptuous of others, or they become snobs from a sense of inferiority, having been slighted by the superior sort of snob or by an uncaring society. Snobbery afflicts a regal Estella, who makes young Pip feel common; it prompts Pumblechook and Mrs. Joe to take credit for Pip's good fortune; and it drives Wopsle to disgrace himself on the London stage and Orlick to attempt murder twice. Jaggers scraping a case from under his nails with his penknife is like Pip dreading to be seen with the soot of the forge upon him. Wemmick believes that "Walworth sentiments" make him more humane than the Londoners in Little Britain. Herbert calls Pip "Handel" out of dislike for the name "Philip," but the substitution is a highbrow allusion to the German-born composer's "The Harmonious Blacksmith" (*GE,* 177). Herbert's mother pities herself for not having married "a title" (*GE,* 188). The Pockets consider the loutish Bentley Drummle "one of the elect" because he is "the next heir but one to a baronetcy" (*GE,* 191); that is, next to being next in line.

Snobbery does not produce a new kind of fool in *A Day's Ride,* Dickens scowled, but it creates a new sort of criminal in *Great Expectations.* Compeyson uses society's respect for outward respectability to break Miss Havisham's heart (although well-dressed, he is not the brewer's daughter's genteel suitor); later it allows him to shift the blame for money laundering to the uncouth Magwitch. Using Compeyson to extend Lever, Dickens showed another of snobbery's darker sides: it compels those who have been made to feel inadequate to punish their so-called betters. Both Magwitch and Miss Havisham, arguably the story's most desperate snobs, prosecute vendettas against gentlemen. They crave recognition through retribution—Magwitch by seizing pleasure through Pip, Miss Havisham by disseminating pain through Estella. Caught in networks of snobbery that seem coterminous with society itself, Pip changes from the second variety of snob to the first—from an inferiority revealed by Estella to a false sense of superiority in patronizing Biddy and Joe.

Dickens presented himself, not Lever, as an expert on snobbery's punishment and cure. Twice Potts's snobbish conduct nearly involves him in a duel (chs. 38, 47). He narrowly escapes a beating from the jealous husband whose wife he pursues by mistake for Kate (ch. 11). In contrast, Mrs. Joe is clubbed almost to death by Orlick, who later attempts to strangle Pip. Estella's spirit is "bent and broken" by Drummle (*GE,* 480), who meets a violent end. Wopsle is lambasted by London's theatergoers; Pumblechook is shamefully mishandled by Orlick's gang. Miss Havisham dies of burns after accidentally setting herself afire. Magwitch is condemned to hang but expires beforehand from injuries sustained in an escape attempt, during which Compeyson is drowned. The wages of snobbery, Dickens decreed, are higher than Lever's comic novel had admitted.

Denigrating "this boasted civilization of ours" as nothing but "snobbery," Potts resolves "to overthrow the mean and unjust prejudices, the miserable class distinctions" standing between an apothecary's son and greatness (*ADR,* 127, 246). That the novel's primary example of snobbery rails against it did not impress Dickens as a blistering indictment; he presents snobbery as the product of social injustice, a consequence of life's basic unfairness. At the heart of *Great Expectations* lie four cases of snobbish exaltation of self: Miss Havisham, Magwitch, Pip, and Estella. She is Miss Havisham's adopted child; Pip is Magwitch's "dear boy" (*GE,* 317) and Miss Havisham's protégé, which initially makes him more brother to Estella than suitor. To minimize Lever's single snob, Dickens shows snobbery infecting society's key roles and relationships.

In Magwitch, Dickens consolidates all the individuals toward whom society has behaved unjustly, while Pip, the beneficiary of Magwitch's labors, personifies the faults of everyone in the system who profits from its fundamental unscrupulousness. For Pip, unlike Potts, there can be no redemption unless he atones for the snobbery of society-at-large. Pip rises above himself in the best sense—above Selfishness, not merely above his station; he rectifies the social injustice in class distinctions not by scrambling up the social ladder to marry a wealthy man's daughter, as Potts does, but by bending toward Magwitch with compassion instead of condescension.

Pip's gradual acceptance of Magwitch as a fellow creature effects a cure for the snobbery in them both. It reverses the self-serving affection with which Compeyson deceived Miss Havisham. In addition, Pip eventually seeks to make the convict's daughter his wife, even when she is no longer a fairy princess. These actions ameliorate the consequences of Compeyson's pseudo-genteel criminality. Potts is repeatedly humiliated, Dickens contended, but Pip learns humility by seeking and extending forgiveness—absolving Miss Havisham, embracing Magwitch, asking pardon of Biddy and Joe. He breaks the cycle whereby the snubbed become revenge-seeking snobs.

Yet Pip's encounter with Trabb's boy is surely a humiliating experience, more devastating than Lever's upendings of Potts. Three chapters after Joe's visit to London, Dickens replays the blacksmith's embarrassment when another former equal pretends to be disoriented by Pip's new splendor. Trabb's boy, says Pip, "feigned to be in a paroxym of terror and contrition, occasioned by the dignity of my appearance" (*GE,* 245). But humiliation, Dickens reminded Lever, is the risk that snobs run, not a cure for snobbery. Pip's subsequent humility, in contrast, is a virtue.

Trabb's boy atones for his effrontery when he helps Herbert and Startop save Pip from being murdered by Orlick (ch. 53). Recalling his humiliation in Rochester's High Street, Pip concedes that he would gladly have "taken the life of Trabb's boy on that occasion" (*GE,* 245–46). When Pip recovers consciousness in the old sluice house and realizes that he has not been killed, the first thing he recognizes with gratitude is "the face of Trabb's boy!" (*GE,* 426) His participation in Pip's rescue is one of several turnabouts that make conspicuous the absence of similar cure scenes in *A Day's Ride.* Joe's nursing Pip back to health in chapter 57, for example, reverses the blacksmith's self-abasement in chapter 27 and neatly complements Pip's unselfish attendance on the dying Magwitch (ch. 56).

"Throughout this true history," Potts exclaims, "I have candidly revealed the inmost traits of my nature." He hopes to "make some compensation to the world by an honest exposure of his motives, his weaknesses, and his struggles" (*ADR,* 329). Unfortunately, Potts is an insouciant faker willing to live on credit from deeds as yet undone. He has found it "easy" to "eke out life with a forgery" (*ADR,* 416). For Pip, forgery is a serious issue, whether it connotes working at Joe's forge, life in London as a counterfeit gentleman, or the chain forged between himself and Magwitch. No matter how disastrously Potts is outwitted or discredited, his voice remains the picaro's. *A Day's Ride* derives little benefit from its hero's afterthoughts, but Pip wrests from Potts the idea of chronicling a young snob's doings from the perspective of his older, wiser self. Pip, not Potts, reexamines his youthful adventures with a mixture of self-deprecating irony and genuine remorse, of humorous recollection tinged with self-recrimination.

George Bernard Shaw attributed the failure of *A Day's Ride* to Lever's incisiveness: forever daydreaming, his self-deceived hero was allegedly too close to real life and smote readers "full in the conscience" (*CL,* 243). Potts, however, is hardly a Browningesque case study. Shaw overrated the young Dubliner as an "utterly original contribution to the study of character," a compliment better suited to Dickens's revaluation of Lever's protagonist.[16] Grey Buller, a minor British diplomat who arranges Potts's release from the Ambras Schloss, describes the hero as "the most sublime snob I have ever met" (*ADR,* 430). The charge exonerates not just Buller but anyone intelligent enough to credit his observation. Pip, Dickens countered, is both the epitome of snobbery and no exception to the rule; his attitude reflects and enlarges upon the community's failings. Snobbery furnishes clues to life in Pip's village and in London as well. Dickens contended that Father Dyke's epithet for Potts—a "great psychological phenomenon" (*ADR,* 65)—was self-congratulatory on Lever's part; it was also more appropriate for a blacksmith's boy turned gentleman than for an Irish apothecary's shiftless son on vacation from university.

Mistaking incessant self-pity for a rich interiority, Edgar Rosenberg lauded Potts's uncanny ability to diagnose his own delusional disorders, but Pip, not Potts, is the timelier psychological portrait of a self-scrutinizing snob. Potts, Rosenberg admits, is "clinically autistic." Such self-absorption deserves to be called "Potts's disease" (N*GE,* 419, 418). Although Dickens blames Lever for making Potts a Cinderella, he also argues that Pip better personifies the overexpectancy of his age; unlike Potts, he suffers the consequences of its Cinderella complex. "The very character of snobbishness in Pip and Potts," Rosenberg has stated, "is so different as to make comparison itself all but meaningless" (N*GE,* 419).[17] Nevertheless, Dickens exploits the contrasts. Pip's malady is the manifestation of a distinctly Victorian sociological complaint, admittedly comic to watch but whose seriousness Lever misunderstands. Thanks to parodic revaluation, a complex case history (Pip's) pushes aside a supposedly ridiculous one (Potts's).

G.K. Chesterton viewed *Great Expectations* as a "Thackerayan" tale that showed "how easily a free lad of fresh and decent instincts can be made to care more for rank and pride and the degrees of our stratified society than for old affection and for honour" (GKC, 197). Actually, Dickens took deadlier aim through Lever at Thackeray's *Pendennis;* he urged readers to believe that Pip—not Pen or Potts—is the *locus classicus* for snobbery in the Victorian novel. Through a devaluation of Lever's even lighter touch, Dickens abused Thackeray's urbane satire, which he considered too lenient. He branded snobbism a tragicomic disease, a national calamity too widespread for rivals to scoff at. Dickens put Snobbery on an equal footing with his conception of Selfishness in *Martin Chuzzlewit,* or Pride in *Dombey and Son;* it was one of several interrelated deficiencies in human nature, especially virulent since the 1840s, that struck at the foundations of Victorian society. The era's snobbish pretensions, its self-delusions—twin prerequisites, Dickens maintained, for the all-out pursuit of wealth and position during the 1850s—were not a foolish throwback as were Potts's; presented accurately, they were extensive, continuing to spread, and as detrimental as Pip's.

In both *A Day's Ride* and *Great Expectations,* a social outcast holds the key to the protagonist's future. He crosses the hero's path several times before their climactic confrontation. In each case, the hero falls in love with a bewitching girl without suspecting that she is the daughter of the figure repeatedly crossing his path. Dickens refashioned Lever's main ingredients——outlawed father, beautiful daughter, unsuitable suitor—into a suspenseful anti–fairy tale. One of his letters criticized Lever for not devising a "needful strong thread of interest" on which to string his story (*PL,* 9:321-22), but that did not prevent Dickens from strengthening what "thread" there was for his own purposes.

Through the first eight chapters of *A Day's Ride,* Potts's efforts to recover his rental horse supply a pretext for his wanderings. He sets out on foot after Father Dyke, who has ridden off on Blondel (ch. 4); then he enjoys the company of Edward and Mary Crofton, brother and sister. They befriend him at their cottage until Dyke's letter to Crofton tells about winning a horse from a fool (ch. 5–7). Dyke also reports having sold Blondel to his former owner at a handsome price. Apparently, Blondel, who is named for King Richard the Lionhearted's favorite minstrel, is still fit to be the circus star he once was in *Timour the Tartar* (*ADR,* 13); the owner, who trained the animal years ago, considers him a good luck charm. Ironically, Blondel will prove the making of everyone who rides him *except* Potts.

Embarrassed by Dyke's letter, Potts flees by boat to Wales (ch. 8) and to London by train, hoping to overtake Blondel, whose new owner has sailed for Ostend. In the train depot, Potts meets Kate Herbert and is instantly smitten. She, too, is traveling to the Continent, reduced circumstances having forced her to become a lady's companion. Although they travel in different compartments, the conversation in Potts's reveals two things: a fugitive named Samuel Whalley is at large, and Kate is his younger daughter. When Pip overhears the two convicts discussing Magwitch, Dickens redoes more dramatically the discussion of Whalley that Potts overhears in chapter 9. Potts immediately associates Kate with Whalley's daughter because "Herbert," which Dickens reuses for Pip's roommate's Christian name, was Lady Whalley's maiden name; presumably, Kate has adopted it to escape notoriety.

Dickens recasts the Potts–Whalley connection as the grotesquely pivotal Pip–Magwitch relationship. The latter's crucial irony—Pip's discovery that he has betrayed his better self and best friends for genteel privileges financed by an ex-convict whose reappearance in effect cancels them—reversed Lever, who overcompensates Potts for less-than-spectacular exertions on Whalley's behalf. When the convict tells about executing Magwitch's errand, Pip feels the speaker's breath "on the back of [his] head" and "all along [his] spine," unlike Potts who is half asleep when he hears the story of Sir Samuel Whalley's fall from ironmaster to bankrupt fugitive. Potts has yet to see Whalley, so Lever generates none of the suspense that Dickens derived from beginning with a face-to-face meeting between Pip and Magwitch, then rekindling the excitement when the "secret-looking man" appears in the Three Jolly Bargemen as Magwitch's agent nine chapters later (*GE*, 75–76).

Whalley has been disowned by his partner-patron, Sir Elkanah Crofton, malevolent uncle of the kindly Croftons. A passenger in Potts's carriage remembers that Crofton "first established Whalley in the iron trade" when the latter entered Milford, his worldly possessions tied up in a handkerchief (*ADR*, 93). Dickens revised this bland report: Magwitch was just out of Kingston Jail "on vagrancy committal" when Compeyson "took [him] on to be his man and pardner" (*GE*, 346). The Crofton-Whalley partnership is reworked as a parable in which the better-educated live comfortably off the less fortunate. Crofton's unfairness to Whalley, a malignity insufficiently explained as a snob's quarrel over Whalley's right to a knighthood (that is, has Whalley or Crofton been more useful to the other; *ADR*, 94–95), is replayed as Compeyson's exploitation of Magwitch, a criminal who is nonetheless a victim of snobbish prejudice against the lower orders.

Lever immediately discloses the pertinent facts about Whalley, including a hint that he has not committed suicide as rumored but will turn up again in some unlikely place—"smelting metals in Africa," cutting a canal through an isthmus, or being "prime minister" to an Indian rajah (*ADR*, 93). Dickens withholds full particulars of Magwitch's criminal career for twenty-six weeks until the returned transport relates his life story to Pip and Herbert (ch. 42). In addition to increasing the suspense, Dickens indicated how difficult it was for someone like Magwitch to obtain a sympathetic hearing. He also replaced Whalley's exotic options with Magwitch's hard-earned success in Australia, a more believable location to readers of *All the Year Round*. For a moment, one suspects that the speaker prophesying Whalley's resurgence "in a tone of confidence" might be the missing person incognito. But another passenger describes him as an eyewitness to the quarrel between Whalley and Crofton. So Potts's informant does not rival Dickens's ominous improvement: the stranger who stirs his rum-and-water "with a file" in chapter 10, then sits behind Pip on the stagecoach (ch. 28).

After escorting Kate and Mrs. Keats part way to Lake Como (chs. 13–27), Potts has several run-ins with his future father-in-law, never suspecting that "Harpar the Englishman" is Whalley in disguise. In chapter 33, Potts is taken to the police station following a brawl at the "Balance" hotel in Constance; Thomas Harpar is there, embroiled in passport problems. Having invited Potts to breakfast, Harpar offends him by attempting to borrow ten pounds. Surprisingly, Potts regrets quarreling and follows Harpar to Lindau in Austria. When he comes upon Harpar experimenting with two model ships, causing each to sink slowly to the lake bottom, the latter "sneers" at Potts "for making nothing of the experiment" (*ADR,* 333), calling him "just the stamp of man for an apothecary" (*ADR,* 339). This random insult hits home, though not as subtly as the London rowing coach's observation that Pip has "the arm of a blacksmith" (*GE,* 195). Nevertheless, in chapter 36, Potts invites Harpar to dine and loans him ten pounds. Their relationship remains cooler and more coincidental than Pip's with Magwitch; upon separating, Potts and Harpar shake hands "not very warmly or cordially either" (*ADR,* 342).

Four chapters later, Potts is arrested by mistake for Harpar. Curiously, he allows himself to be incarcerated for what seems nearly a year, first at Innsbruck, then in the Ambras Schloss, so that Harpar can effect his escape. From his cell at Innsbruck, he sees Blondel performing in a circus in the center of town (*ADR,* 392). The horse is being ridden by Catinka, one of two circus people who were Potts's traveling companions from the time he was dismissed by Mrs. Keats to his meeting with Harpar. Later, at Odessa, Potts will hear of a beautiful circus girl having eloped with a Bavarian prince who bought Blondel for thirty thousand piasters (ch. 48). Thus the horse that Potts never regains transforms Catinka into a princess while enriching his owner.

Harpar has been accused of assaulting a certain Rigges, his former associate and traveling companion, who ran off with their money. By chapter 41, the disguised bankrupt has been officially outlawed. Rigges constitutes one of Lever's missed opportunities: scheduled to identify Potts as Harpar (ch. 43), he never materializes. Then he drops all charges (ch. 44); finally, one learns that he has died (ch. 48). According to the warrant describing Rigges's tussle with Harpar, they fell into a stream and "both went down beneath the water" (*ADR,* 388). This may have given Dickens a clue for Magwitch's final struggle with Compeyson, Rigges's more integral counterpart. Pulled from the Thames, Magwitch whispers to Pip that he and Compeyson went overboard together: "[T]hey had gone down, fiercely locked in each other's arms, and . . . there had been a struggle under water" (*GE,* 442).

At Lindau, the Croftons, also on Whalley's trail, inform Potts that their uncle died repentant; to compensate for mistreating his former partner, Sir Elkanah has named Whalley's alleged widow his legatee (ch. 35). In the next chapter, therefore, Potts dines with the object of the Croftons' search. In chapter 39, having joined their hunt for Whalley, Potts is traveling in the Upper Rhine valley with an explanatory letter for Kate from Mary Crofton; his arrest in chapter 40 curtails his activities. By going to prison in Harpar's stead, Potts liberates the person he should have had detained. After being released, Potts visits Kate on Malta (ch. 45) to divulge his humble origins and declare his love; he accepts Kate's commission to locate her father.

Surely Lever's original readers suspected that Harpar is Whalley sooner than Dickens's equated Magwitch with Pip's benefactor. Otherwise they would have missed the joke: Potts is seeking someone he has already found *twice;* he will continue to look for him for another three chapters without realizing that he has already met Whalley repeatedly as Harpar.

Whalley wanders in and out of the later chapters without supplying the kind of stitching that Dickens prized. According to Crofton, the fugitive has been spotted at Riga, a Latvian seaport (ch. 35), or on the Rhine (ch. 45) according to Kate, a sighting that Potts fails to connect with the assault on Rigges and his own arrest. Presumably, Whalley is the Englishman mentioned in the *Levant Herald* who has left Musted Pasha's service for employment in Russia (ch. 45). Nevertheless, Whalley appears to exert little direct influence on *A Day's Ride* between chapters 9 and 33. Dickens's convict is away much longer (after chapter 5 until chapter 39—in short, for about sixteen years), but he always seems close at hand. Whalley has vanished only recently in chapter 9, and the meeting between Potts and Harpar at the "Balance" probably occurs not too long thereafter. For more than twenty chapters, Potts never seriously contemplates how important his association with Whalley will be, whereas Magwitch is rarely absent from Pip's consciousness.

Magwitch's interventions are Dickens's redoing of Harpar/Whalley's less impressive reappearances. These interventions have greater impact because, paradoxically, they are clearer to Pip, although less direct than Harpar's to Potts, and seem more ominous than literal recrossings of Pip's path would have been. Magwitch resurfaces more pointedly through emissaries than Whalley does as Harpar: the man with the file for example (ch. 10), or Jaggers announcing Pip's "great expectations" eight chapters later. Reminders of Magwitch include the discarded leg iron with which Orlick fells Mrs. Joe (ch. 15), "my convict's iron," says a guilty Pip (*GE*, 120). A visit to Newgate reminds Pip of the novel's opening scene, convincing him that the "taint of prison" has "encompassed" him ever since his "childhood out on [the] lonely marshes" (*GE*, 263). Magwitch thus intervenes in chapters 10, 15, 18, 28, and 32, before returning in 39. The novel's pivotal relationship provides much of its spine. Pip's coach ride with the convicts occurs just eleven chapters before the transported felon's reappearance; the visit to Newgate only seven chapters prior to it. Dickens not only made the Pip–Magwitch relationship more representative of social problems than the Potts–Whalley connection that it parodically revalues; the former also functions more efficaciously for unity and suspense.

Potts finally overtakes Kate's father, whom he still knows only as Harpar, in Sebastopol (ch. 48). He puts his know-how as an apothecary's son to use in repairing a seriously injured American contractor—Harpar's latest impersonation. The immediate result for Potts is seven weeks of fever, beginning just after Harpar, battered and feverish, passes the crisis point. While Potts is out of action, Harpar/Whalley recovers financially as well as physically; the former industrialist recoups his fortune by raising sunken ships, the project for which he was rehearsing with toy models (ch. 36). In addition, his English creditors, having been appeased, want him to "recommence business." News of his rehabilitation, he informs Potts, is "well known in England now" (*ADR*, 443); ironically, the last person to learn of it is Whalley's designated rescuer. In Dickens's reworking, Magwitch is the only person never to learn that as an illegally returned transport, he cannot keep his fortune, much less bestow it on Pip.

Anxious to give Potts the brush-off, Whalley calls him "not much of a doctor . . . nor . . . very remarkable as a man of genius" (*ADR*, 444). Before departing, he offers Potts "a capital travelling-cloak," but no capital. Having posed as a man of leisure, Potts must decline a monetary reward, a decision Whalley hastens to accept but that Potts styles "the coup de grâce of my misery" (*ADR*, 444). Permanent frustration of Potts's expectations is out of the question, however. Inasmuch as Kate's letter recalls Potts to her side, Whalley either only pretends to gruffness in order to test his daughter's admirer, or else he has revised his belittling assessment of Lever's hero and is willing to play fairy godfather after all. Whalley's transformation is never convincingly explained. Potts's good luck is the novel's ultimate non sequitur in a picaresque world predicated on discontinuity.

Once Pip reencounters Magwitch, everything goes awry. Dickens's revaluation unravels Lever's happily-ever-after conclusion and the cheerful view of expectancy it conveys. Pip can neither keep Magwitch alive nor retain the ex-convict's money. Unlike the exonerated Whalley, Magwitch returns to England uninvited, becoming a criminal again in doing so. No one is pleased to see him; his old nemesis is not only still alive but also eager to testify against him. In addition, Pip's bout with fever, the result of Herculean efforts to save Magwitch, proves costlier than Potts's: Biddy marries Joe before Pip recovers sufficiently to propose.

To substitute a mature tragicomic perspective for Lever's overly simply comic conception of things, Dickens reduced the latter to the unreality of a Cinderella-like fairy tale. *Great Expectations* parodies stories in which the hero-suitor, having faithfully served the father-king, perhaps by releasing him from enchantment, is amply rewarded with the ruler's daughter for his bride. In Lever's father-daughter-suitor triangle, society reinstates Whalley, whose daughter then embraces Potts. In contrast, Magwitch's return disenchants Pip, opening his eyes to his real situation. Magwitch is incriminated over again because the outcast, Dickens maintained, can never be incorporated until society undergoes extensive transformation. Instead of Potts catching up with Whalley, Magwitch comes back to haunt Pip because, like Frankenstein's monster, the wrongs a society condones never go away.

Dickens pulverized the unexamined optimism inherent in the picaresque format. Potts's ability to rebound from every setback, not to mention his Cinderella-like elevation in the final chapter, posed no threat to society's conception of itself as a steadily improving phenomenon. Through Pip's inability to save Magwitch (that is, to obtain justice) and win Estella (earn love), Dickens combined a cheerless social prognosis with the suggestion that life itself, no matter how droll, is inevitably full of disappointment.

Magwitch's determination to clasp Pip is more upsetting than Whalley's eagerness to be rid of Potts. But the deceptive contrast between the latter's bad luck and the former's apparent good fortune adds a comic twist to Dickens's bitter ironies. Much to his regret, Pip acquires the benefactor that Potts wants. The ex-convict disconcerts Pip not with the revelation of himself as the father of the latter's beloved—which of course it will turn out that he is—but as the benefactor who Whalley, having acknowledged himself as Kate's father, refuses to become. When Potts perceives that Harpar is Whalley, he clutches his arm "with amazement" (*ADR*, 443). When Magwitch kisses Pip's hands and prepares to "embrace" him, signs of gratitude that Potts would have welcomed, a horrified Pip cries "Keep off!" (*GE*, 314)

Magwitch's consanguinary salutation is more chilling for Pip then Whalley's coldness is to Potts. "Look'ee here, Pip, I'm your second father. You're my son," Magwitch exclaims (*GE*, 317), having filled Pip with "abhorrence" and "repugnance." "But didn't you never think it might be me?" Magwitch then asks (*GE*, 318). Pip's reply is a multiple negative followed by a double disclaimer: "O no, no, no, . . . Never, never!" Pip cries. This painful outburst is also comically hyperbolic, more protest than denial. Pip's excessive rejection of Magwitch as his benefactor parodies Potts's belated discovery that Harpar is Whalley.[18] It is Lever's worldview and his unrealistic final chapter that Dickens, through Pip, is repeatedly negating—not to mention that he is also ruling out the individual's ability to suppress the past or society's to exclude undesirables.

The recuperating industrialist tries to repay the ten pounds that Harpar borrowed from Potts. In Dickens's revision, Magwitch refuses to be reimbursed for the two one-pound notes he sent Pip, setting fire to them instead. Dickens connects repayment to his novel's revenge theme: Magwitch cannot be bought off cheaply. There is comedy in Pip's anxiety to cancel a debt that is only a fraction of what he actually owes, but one also detects a hint of menace when Pip describes how Magwitch "gave [the notes] a twist, set fire to them at the lamp, and dropped the ashes into the tray" (*GE*, 315).

Magwitch's munificence is more problematic than Whalley's rudeness. The latter acts brusquely but is ultimately and inexplicably kind, a comic reversal that one finds confusing psychologically. Magwitch's ostensible generosity contains an insidious mixture of cruelty in that Pip has been groomed to be the exconvict's instrument for revenge. Dickens rewrites Whalley's attempt at loan repayment more believably (and more frighteningly) as Magwitch's long-term project to force society to make restitution to him through Pip.

Lever's fugitive ironmaster would prefer not to have been rescued by an idler with a "dreamy mode of life," a boulevardier proud of his freedom from manual labor (*ADE*, 442). Ironically, Potts would have been more acceptable as the son of an apothecary. Dickens complained that Lever, facile as usual, ignored the gravity of the situation to obtain an easy laugh. Whalley's desire for a blue-collar rescuer is a snobbishness so unreal that Dickens contested it twice: in Magwitch's desperation to fashion his protegé into a gentleman even other gentlemen will envy, and in Pip's refusal to be made genteel by someone he is ashamed to be seen with publicly. Nothing could illustrate the width of the gap between the Haves and Have-Nots more poignantly, Dickens countered, than Magwitch's lifelong obsession with crossing it, even vicariously, and Pip's realization that, given his ties to Magwitch, he has not really crossed it after all.

Whalley's rehabilitation is depicted chiefly in financial terms; his ordeal seems not to have furthered his moral advancement or Potts's. Dickens's reworking emphasizes the intricate mutual improvement that Pip and Magwitch work upon each other despite the forfeiture of the latter's fortune. Having bound Pip to Magwitch, Dickens separates money from redemption. Potts's father dies offstage during the hero's wanderings after succoring Whalley, so Potts inherits enough to get by on; Pip must be rescued from debt by Joe. Dickens dramatically resolves Pip's relationships with *both* of his fathers. Despite this double reconciliation, however, Pip cannot have two fathers any more than Potts can, but Pip's conduct during the loss of one father (Magwitch) entitles him to regain the other (Joe).

As to Potts's "reasons" for helping someone with whom, as a gentleman, he could not expect to "hit if off" (*ADR*, 442), Whalley remains puzzled. This "piece of devotion," Potts says, "I really did not understand myself." The answer is all too simple: their class origin not dissimilar, identification is from like to like. More newsworthy, Magwitch and Pip get along because Dickens insisted that differences in age, class, and outward appearance need not erect insuperable barriers. The Pip–Magwitch connection exudes an affirmative (that is, comic) afterglow within a tragic framework in that although society remains divided into Haves and Have-Nots, the bonds between one of each become like those between father and son.[19] From the Potts–Whalley encounter, Dickens charged, readers with a complacent view of themselves as a progressive society would learn nothing, but the Pip–Magwitch association offers an instructive paradigm.

Whalley conceals his interest when Potts recounts his search for Kate's father. But when Potts displays Kate's "old seal-ring," Whalley declares that he gave it to her when she was sixteen; "I am her father," the missing parent asserts (*ADR*, 443). In Dickens's revision, Magwitch's disclosure—"I'm your second father. You're my son" (*GE*, 317)—causes a bigger sensation and, one must repeat, has more social ramifications. Once Pip has figured out Estella's parentage, it is he who tells Magwitch about his daughter instead of being apprised of her by him. Dickens preserves the secret of Estella's parentage even longer than he withholds the identity of Pip's benefactor. Pip makes his discoveries about a benefactor and his daughter in reverse order to Potts and in a manner that confirms life's tragicomic complexities.

Seventeen chapters after learning of Magwitch as his patron, Pip breaks the news to him about Estella. Dickens's timing gives each revelation its due. When Pip tells the ex-convict that his daughter is alive, "a lady and very beautiful" (*GE*, 456), his kindness surpasses Potts's to Whalley. In Dickensian tragicomedy, simultaneously a refutation of Lever's outlook and an explanation of the nature of things, positive events never obliterate negatives; instead they tone down life's disappointments in a manner loosely parallel to the way an ex-convict and a snob soften as they draw closer together. The reader balances Pip's loss of expectations—he is literally penniless at Magwitch's death—against the latter's regaining of a daughter. After telling the expiring father about Estella, however, Pip loses his benefactor more decisively than Potts appears to when Kate's father tells him about her.

At roughly the midpoint of *A Day's Ride,* Potts confesses that he likes to build "castles in Spain"—"architectural extravaganzas" that he eagerly decorates and inhabits. "I built my castle to live in it," he claims; "from foundation to rooftree, I planned every detail of it to suit my own taste, and all my study was to make it as habitable and comfortable as I could." Usually, Potts admits, his "tenure was a brief one," ending suddenly while he was "breaking" an egg "at breakfast" or putting on his gloves "to walk out." Yet "no terror of a short lease ever deterred" him "from finishing the edifice in the most expensive manner." He "gilded" his "architraves" and "frescoed" his ceilings as though they were to endure for centuries (*ADR*, 194).

Pip likens the loss of his unearned gentility and the consequent breakdown of his plans to marry Estella to the collapse of Misnar's pavilion. He develops this comparison in the last two paragraphs of chapter 38, just before the novel's turning point. Constructed by Horam, the sultan's vizier, Misnar's pavilion is engineered to cave in upon usurpers. In the best-known story from *The Tales of the Genii,* Horam returns Misnar to power by directing him to sever the rope that releases a stone slab over the royal divan, crushing the two enchanters who have seized control of his sultanate.[20] In chapter 39, Magwitch's disclosure of himself as Pip's secret benefactor deals Pip's prospects a blow similar to the one Misnar's axe dealt the usurpers.

Retelling "the Eastern story," Pip describes how "the heavy slab . . . was slowly wrought out of the quarry . . . and fitted in the roof," while the "rope was . . . slowly taken through the miles of hollow [tunnel] to the great iron ring." Then, "all being made ready with much labour, and the hour come," the rope was cut "and the ceiling fell. So, in my case," Pip asserts, "all the work, near and afar, that tended to the end had been accomplished, and in an instant . . . my stronghold dropped upon me" (*GE*, 309–10). Instead of Potts's ephemeral "ceilings," built one after another as if "for centuries" but actually no more than harmless repetitions of human folly, Pip recounts a painstaking process of self-deception, after which, at the appointed time, only one "ceiling" falls, but it permanently destroys unwarranted expectations.

Dickens revalued Lever's architectural symbol; in its stead, Pip invokes a deadly version of Potts's Spanish castles: Misnar's pavilion. It signifies Dickens's recognition of a purposive world in which the life process achieves long-term objectives by twists and turns, dramatic surprises that seem logical in retrospect, perhaps providential. Misnar's pavilion is also a stark reminder of the precariousness of self-serving schemes, if not of daydreaming in general; it reinstates a tragicomic idea of expectancy—not as wishful thinking, but in terms of a retributive universe, a place wherein consequences can be traced to their causes and accounts are settled eventually, although the tragicomedy never ends.

By novel's end, Bert Hornback has argued, Pip and Magwitch embody Dickens's ideal of true friendship (BH, 65); through Pip's disappointments, Dickens expressed reservations about Cinderella stories, of which Potts's is a blatant example. Snubbed by Catinka, herself a Cinderella who rises from gypsy circus performer to Parisian lady, Potts is nevertheless summoned by Kate to marital bliss and financial security. Unlike the Potts–Whalley association or Potts's success with Kate, Pip's tragicomic connections to Magwitch, Miss Havisham, and Estella emerge in the same way Horam built his sultan's palace: with a remorselessness akin to fate. Contrary to Potts's comedic world, which promotes unaccountability, Pip's relationships intensify into patterns requiring not just hindsight to be understood, but moral interpretation as well.[21]

A Day's Ride, Dickens maintained, is built flimsily, like Potts's Spanish castles. The novel's specious symmetry results from a facile economy of characterization, an artificial compactness at odds with the hero's rambles. Catinka's Bavarian prince is presumably Max of Swabia, with whom Potts quarrels in the hotel at Constance. Grey Buller, who arranges Potts's release from prison, is the minor diplomat whose despatches Potts carried off by mistake from the Dover train. George Buller, with whom Potts almost duels on Malta, is Grey's brother; George reads Grey's letter about a snob named Potts to their cousin Kate. Bob Rogers, who captains Potts's ship from Malta to Odessa, is brother to the skipper who ferried Potts from Ireland to Wales. When the first Rogers gives Potts a letter of introduction to his brother (ch. 8), Lever either foresaw Bob's appearance in chapter 46 or resolved to implicate him later. Lever probably began with a general idea for the Harpar-Whalley interchange and some notion of how to resolve Potts's search for Blondel, but as was noted earlier, many of the intervening incidents, the novel's midsection, lack a sense of urgency and seem extemporized. In short, Lever did just enough planning to foster the impression that his picaresque comedy critiqued a world of whose interlockings its author had full knowledge and control.

Dickens parodied Lever's meretricious designs by underlining profounder coincidences that he considered truer to life's tragicomic texture, its subtly interwoven threads. Jaggers defends Estella's mother and helps Miss Havisham to adopt Estella; he also defends Estella's father. Financially, he is equally useful to Pip's surrogate parents; besides handling Miss Havisham's estate, he administers Magwitch's fortune, including Pip's benefaction. Compeyson not only deceives Miss Havisham but also forsakes Magwitch twice: when they are partners, and by betraying the returned transport. Estella proves to be Pip's only legacy from both his false fairy godmother and would-be fairy godfather. Having annihilated Pip socially, Trabb's boy later rescues him from Orlick.

Instead of the Buller brothers, fraternal sea captains, and Whalley doubling as Harpar, Dickens fashioned Orlick as a projection of Pip's darker self. He reserved one side of Wemmick for Walworth, another for London; he paired the gentleman Magwitch creates (Pip) with the lady Miss Havisham has made (Estella). Magwitch's return is pivotal for Pip's life, but Dickens deemed Whalley's reappearances no thicker a story thread than Blondel's. Although Dickens reused Lever's structural devices—reappearance, doubling, and coincidence—he probed them for psychological complexity and social relevance while exposing Lever's enslavement to comic convenience.

Lever's picaresque universe unfolds as a comedy of errors: Potts mistakes a married woman for Kate; he is mistaken for a government messenger, a nobleman in disguise, a gypsy. The German authorities imprison him, mistaking him for Harpar. Such mistakes, Dickens opined, resemble Potts's castles; they arise rapidly from the narrative, then dissolve without a trace. In *Great Expectations,* when Dickens rethinks Lever's overemphasis on the comic, mistakes darken into tragicomedy and have far-reaching consequences more indicative,

Dickens contended, of what life is. Pip mistakes Miss Havisham for his benefactor; he pursues Estella instead of Biddy for his marriage partner. He confuses his life story with Cinderella's when the tale of Misnar's pavilion is a more accurate paradigm for his rise and fall.

Just as the crash of Pip's expectations recalls the collapse of Misnar's pavilion, Dickens's collapsing of Lever's novel has reverberations for Thackeray; his fiction is often under attack directly in *Great Expectations* and by proxy whenever Dickens denigrates *A Day's Ride*. Whether or not Lever believed he was writing a Thackerayan novel, Dickens treats *A Day's Ride* as an unfortunate consequence of the Thackerayan mode. He accuses both of his rivals of a similar misconstruction of the human condition. His revaluation of Lever amounts to a clarification of his doubts about Thackeray. That neither had been vigorous enough in satirizing snobbery, Dickens argues, puts them ultimately on a par.

"I have no use for out and out comedy writing or out and out tragedy writing," Christopher Isherwood declared; "I think both pictures that they give of life are false in the most heartless way. I don't know which is worse—the triviality of the total comedian or the superficiality of the total tragedian" (DG, 154). Dickens's reaction to Lever and, by extension, to Thackeray anticipates Isherwood's sentiments.

Dickens rejected Lever as the "total comedian," an oversimplified version of the early Dickens himself. Throughout *A Day's Ride,* Potts's misfortunes invariably have comic consequences as one Spanish castle after another collapses. Lever's worldview deceives by ignoring the presence of pain and sorrow. Although hardly the work of a "total tragedian," Thackeray's Horatian satire was just as superficial, an alternative that the increasingly angry Dickens of the 1850s refused to countenance. Implicit in his world's *vanitas,* its fickleness or emptiness, Thackeray's resignation precludes a Juvenalian indignation in the face of life's deficiencies; it also tends too much toward melancholy, thus falling short of the tragicomedian's healthier response: an ability to accept such deficiencies humorously. To both reactions—indignation and comic acceptance, especially the latter—Dickens now laid claim.

That both Lever and Thackeray are ultimately unreliable—"false" in heartless ways—could be demonstrated, Dickens believed, without denying the latter's superior skills. Their different but equally incomplete perspectives cause both to deal too kindly with snobs. Endlessly amusing, they are funny but harmless in Lever's comic world, absurd and pointless in Thackeray's fruitless one, but never as tragicomic as Pip is or a national disaster as they are in Dickens's overview, which he strove to keep both funny and serious.

Had Thackeray addressed snobbery adamantly in *The Book of Snobs* (1846–

1847), *Vanity Fair* (1848), and especially *Pendennis* (1850), he might have prevented the "out and out comedy" of *A Day's Ride,* no substitute, Dickens belatedly realized, for the scourge that Thackeray should have wielded. When "the snob problem" (H, 153) approached crisis proportions in the 1840s, he neglected to quash it, the urbanity of his critique in effect paving the way for the innocuousness of Lever's.

Compared to Potts's castles in Spain, Misnar's pavilion is the more complex symbol, subtler and centralized. Besides connoting a tragicomic world, it furnishes the superior model for a well-constructed novel that crushes snobs and rival novelists simultaneously. Multifaceted, it stands for collapse as well as craft or craftiness. Misnar's pavilion is both a rejection of Potts's (and Lever's) airy fabrications and a stronger admonishment than Thackeray's for the individual's extravagant hopes and the nation's. Which edifice, Dickens asks, does society's overestimate of its progress and potential resemble, Potts's castles or Pip's pavilion?

Dickens may have been reminded of the Misnar story from *The Tales of the Genii* when Lever's serial caused the circulation of *All the Year Round* to plummet. The collapse of Pip's plans—"my stronghold dropped upon me" (*GE*, 310)—is latent in Dickens's complaint to Lever that sales of the new periodical "drop rapidly" due to *A Day's Ride* (*PL,* 9:321–22), one drop suggesting the other.

Besides prompting Dickens to compare the snob's delusions to a collapsible edifice, Lever helped give *Great Expectations* its title. One should not overlook sonnet 21 of Sir Philip Sidney's *Astrophel and Stella,* lines 7 and 8 of which culminate with a reference to "that friendly foe, Great Expectations" (AE, 158–59). If Pip (that is, Philip) Pirrip is the Victorian version of Sir Philip's Petrarchian lover, his expectations are actually his worst enemy. But Lever's *A Day's Ride* supplies a more likely inspiration. About to be identified as the fool who lost his horse to Father Dyke, Potts invents a dying uncle to justify his hasty departure from the Croftons' country retreat: "I vaguely hinted at great expectations," he says (*ADR,* 86). In contrast, when Pip's Uncle Provis (Magwitch) dies, he leaves his nephew destitute, "in debt," with "scarcely any money" (*GE,* 457).

The expression "great expectations" was not uncommon in the 1850s. In chapter 17 of Charles Kingsley's *Yeast* (1851), for example, one finds "the characteristic" of the country identified as "a yearning, . . . an expectation." Dickens capitalized upon the expression himself as early as 1843, when Martin Chuzzlewit used it in chapter 6 of the novel that bears his name (and his grandfather's) for its title: "I have been bred up from childhood with great expectations," the recently disinherited young hero declares, "and have always been taught to believe that I should be, one day, very rich." The phrase's titular potential as a euphemism for overexpectancy, false hopes and their inevitable collapse, seems implicit in Martin's remarks about his upbringing and subsequent letdown.

Chapter 9 of Lever's novel appeared in *All the Year Round* on 29 September 1860, although Dickens had surely seen proofs and the manuscript earlier than that. He may have begun composing what became *Great Expectations* sometime between 24 to 28 September; if so, it was an untitled short piece that he expected to finish in a day. On 2 October, he held the famous "council of war" at the headquarters of *All the Year Round* and decided to rush in with a weekly serial of his own to rescue his periodical from Lever's unpopular tale. Two days later, only five days after publishing Lever's ninth chapter, he first mentioned the title of this new serial in a letter to John Forster (*PL*, 9:319–20).

Ironically, Dickens's immediate inspiration for his title may have come from the novelist whose solicited contribution to *All the Year Round* had disappointed Dickens's expectations and frustrated its author's own. The title may also refer to Dickens's high hopes for the safety of his journal, his confidence that he could instigate a turnaround from the slumping sales he blamed on Lever. Conceivably, Dickens repaid Lever doubly for disappointing him: first, he borrowed a phrase from his contributor and made it one of his most memorable titles; second, he showed Lever how to fashion this title's ironic possibilities into an aesthetically pleasing, sociologically important, economic success.[22]

No one gave Lever's title a second thought, but Dickens's reverberated throughout the Victorian period and beyond. Writing in 1882, Frederic Harrison summed up the nineteenth century by epitomizing its perfectibilitarian outlook: "It is *not* the age of money-bags and cant, soot, hubbub, and ugliness. It is the age of great expectation and unwearied striving after better things." Unwilling testimony to Dickens's impact, this passage from an essay titled "A Few Words about the Nineteenth Century" can be read as a belated attempt to turn the satire in *Great Expectations* inside out, as if one could offset Pip's collapsible pavilion by rebuilding Potts's castles in Spain.

In a chapter on "Victorian Optimism," Walter Houghton, besides quoting Harrison, pinpointed 1830 as the rising date for "an atmosphere of supreme optimism about the present and future" (WH, 33). Thus Dickens's title, excerpted from Lever, had a double-barreled effect in 1860: it criticized a perennially unrealistic attitude, an unhealthy state of mind, and it attacked a peculiarly nineteenth-century variation of it that may be called the era's Cinderella complex. It had manifested itself in two waves: first in the 1830s (the decade by which events in *Great Expectations* have reached their unhappy climax), and again, more insistently, throughout the 1850s. In the later decade, an increasingly disillusioned Dickens capped off his social criticism with *Great Expectations;* this anti–Cinderella tale became the fifth novel, starting with *Bleak House*, in his series of checks to what Houghton called "the note of ecstatic anticipation which marked the period after 1850" (WH, 33).

Shaw opined that Dickens listened to Bulwer-Lytton and revised the original conclusion because the latter showed him how closely it resembled Lever's in *A Day's Ride*. "Note, by the way," Shaw wrote, "that the passing carriage in the Piccadilly ending was unconsciously borrowed from A Day's Ride: A Life's Romance... but in Lever's story it is the man who stops the carriage, only to be cut dead by the lady. That also, was the happiest ending both for Potts and Katinka, though the humiliation of Potts makes it painful for the moment. Lever was showing Dickens the way; and Dickens instinctively took it until Lytton moidered [that is, worried] him from fear for its effects on the sales" ("P," xviii).[23]

Shaw's comments are provocative but badly skewed. Bulwer would not have been concerned about the impact on sales from the thirty-sixth of thirty-six installments. Nor can one argue that Dickens was unaware that the Piccadilly ending resembled a scene in Lever. He blamed *A Day's Ride* for lowering the circulation of his new periodical and had introduced *Great Expectations* to counteract the drop in sales, so he would never have copied a resounding failure. Shaw was wrong to raise the specter of unconscious plagiarism from a novel that Dickens had kept an eye on constantly, hoping for its popularity to improve. Instead, one ought to credit Dickens with a deliberate redoing of Lever, a satiric reworking or revaluative parody. Dickens's first ending was designed to invalidate Lever's carriage scene, but the second, he must have decided, works even better to expose a rival's unrealistic conception of character growth and plot resolution.

In the original ending, Dickens changed the tone of Lever's carriage scene to suit his novel's tragicomic treatment of snobbery and its consequences, subjects he implied *A Day's Ride* had trivialized. A Pip and Estella who gaze "sadly enough on one another" must savor the bitter results of their snobbishness— his has left him expatriated and alone; she has suffered "outrageous treatment" from Bentley Drummle (*GE,* 481). Unlike the saddened Piccadilly Pip, the Potts whom Catinka cuts "dead" seems terribly shallow, not much different from the foolish young man in Lever's opening chapters; nor is he seriously stunned by Catinka's disregard. In short, the Piccadilly encounter made the carriage scene in Lever's comic novel seem frivolous. Dickens exhibited a regenerate hero (and heroine) whose forté is now humility, not being humiliated, which is the upstart Potts's fate from start to finish.

But Lever's novel does not actually conclude with the scene Shaw described. Instead, *A Day's Ride* may be said to end twice. First, Potts receives his comeuppance from Catinka. He was ashamed of his attraction to this untutored gypsy child, a laid-off circus performer, when they were both vagabonds in Germany; now, having eloped with a Bavarian prince, Catinka travels the Parisian boulevards in style and awards Potts the snub he deserves when he attempts to renew their acquaintance. Then comes, as it were, a revised or happier ending. At the police department, Potts finds a letter that has been waiting for him for over a year from Kate Whalley, whom he has not seen since he set off to locate her outlawed father. A grateful Kate requests the hero's presence in Wales. The novel's one-sentence final paragraph foreshadows Pip's ban on future partings: "I set off for England that night—I left for Wales the next morning—and I have never quitted it since that day" (*ADR,* 447).

In the original ending, Dickens stopped his novel at the point where he implied Lever's should have (namely, Potts's encounter with Catinka). In the second ending, he parodied the gloating in Potts's final paragraph with Pip's calm hope confidently expressed. Pip's ambiguity sounds genuine and appropriate; it replaces Potts's disingenuous ambiguity, which is really facile certainty in disguise. Potts is recalled to Kate after a separation of a year or two and immediately following the snub he receives for presuming to address a prince's lady. In contrast, eleven years are required to reunite Pip and Estella, Pip must press his suit, and it remains uncertain if he has succeeded.

Perhaps Bulwer, like Shaw, mistook the original ending for a straightforward "borrowing" from Lever. More likely, Dickens felt that the original revaluation was insufficient; thanks to the auxiliary ending in which Potts tells of hastening to Wales, *A Day's Ride* appears to survive Dickens's Piccadilly put-down. Lever's second ending, the summons from Kate and her father, is the real false note—a deus ex machina, as Dickens probably realized upon reflection. In addition to rewarding an unchanged Potts unduly, it guaranteed him a lifetime of artificial uneventfulness. Shaw was right to see Lever's carriage scene as "the happiest possible ending both for Potts and Katinka" but not just because they are as ill-suited to each other on a Paris boulevard as they were in a German forest; a stronger reason for calling this the "happiest" eventuality (and also the least credible) is that Catinka's triumph over Potts leads, illogically and unfairly, to his Cinderella-like apotheosis.

Dickens's letter to Lever for "Sixth October" 1860 supposedly "tried to break the news . . . gently" (J, 2:965). Edgar Rosenberg praised Dickens's "immaculate tact and sympathy" (N*GE,* 396). But the editor's ominous opening must have caused Lever to gasp: "I have a business report to make, that I fear I can hardly render agreeable to you" (*PL,* 9:321–22): "We drop rapidly and continuously with The Day's Ride." If one compares this letter from the offices of *All the Year Round* with one written the same day to John Forster from Gad's Hill, conflicts appear. In the former, Dickens reluctantly discloses plans for intervention. He depicts himself waiting "week after week" for "the least sign" that *A Day's Ride* was about to "take hold." Reporting the plunge in sales was "disagreeable," he admitted, but he felt "no other uneasiness or regret" (*PL*, 9:321–22). In the latter, Dickens revealed his displeasure with the "considerable advance" of Lever's novel in hand; he foresaw "no vitality" in upcoming installments (*PL*, 9:320). Either Dickens's original estimate was euphoric, or he felt that the promise of the opening chapters had not been kept. Perhaps Dickens no longer saw Lever's increasingly Thackerayan novel as the revitalization of the Pickwickian mode for which he at first mistook it. An unflattering fourth possibility is that the editor had allowed the public's indifference to reverse his opinion.

Lest *All the Year Round* be "much endangered," Dickens told Forster, he had resolved on "dashing in now" with *Great Expectations* (*PL*, 9:320). On "Fourth October," Dickens had written Forster about a "council of war" at the offices of *All the Year Round*. During this meeting, it became "perfectly clear that the one thing to be done was, for me to strike in" (*PL*, 9:319–20). So the letter for 6 October confirmed decisions already brewing several days earlier, decisions outlined to Forster on 4 October but not to Lever. Dickens also informed Forster of the "thousand pounds" he would receive "for early proofs" of *Great Expectations* to America (he had granted the transatlantic serial rights to *Harper's*).

"Dashing in now" was Dickens's flamboyant phrase for a business decision that he had mulled over for several days, then began to implement with characteristic thoroughness. This was hardly another charge of the Light Brigade. The editor carefully mapped out a course that he felt confident would enable the novelist to redeem *All the Year Round* before irreparable damage was done. Dickens's sureness in settling on a plan of action in the first week of October suggests that he may have given the situation considerable attention even earlier. His last step was to inform Lever. The letter of 6 October outlined a rescue mission for which the practical details had already been hammered out; in effect, Dickens notified Lever of a fait accompli. When the crestfallen contributor volunteered to conclude *A Day's Ride* quickly, Dickens's follow-up letter of 15 October appeared to leave such decisions to Lever's discretion (*PL*, 9:323–24). Once Dickens resolved to transform *Great Expectations* into a weekly serial, chose 1 December as its starting date, and arranged for American serialization, however, Lever's actions scarcely mattered; the fate of *All the Year Round* was out of his hands and back in Dickens's.

When the "business report" for 6 October insisted that "There is but one thing to be done," it ruled out alternatives. "One thing to be done" is a phrase carried over from the "council of war." In the second paragraph, only five sentences long, "must" is used four times to create the requisite sense of necessity: Dickens "must get into" the pages of *All the Year Round* "as soon as possible";

otherwise, the triple adverb in the final paragraph stresses, it will be "very, very, very difficult" to halt the journal's decline. Dickens clearly fostered an atmosphere of emergency to prevent additional deliberations and justify his proposal.

On 15 October, replying to a mea culpa letter from Lever that morning, the editor waxed hyperbolic in "most earnestly" professing to have "not the slightest atom of reservation" about *A Day's Ride*. Not only was it the "best" novel Lever "ever wrote," but Dickens was as "proud and glad to have it" now as he had been the previous June. Unfortunately, "it does not do what you and I would have it do," Dickens added, as though the work itself were delinquent independently of its author (*PL*, 9:323–24). The blame, Dickens decided, should fall on the serial format, which became a convenient scapegoat. *A Day's Ride* failed to catch on because "it does not lay some one strong ground of suspended interest." Many of "the best books ever written would not bear the [serial] mode of publication," Dickens continued, because—and this is "one of its most remarkable and aggravating features"—the serialist must "fix the people in the beginning," or else it is "almost impossible to fix them afterwards."

Dickens found a way to associate Lever's "best" book with "the best books ever written" without actually specifying it as one of them. He identified a strong opening and a suspenseful proposition as hallmarks of the weekly serial. These attributes are preeminent in *Great Expectations*, put there no doubt to correct Lever's oversights, while demonstrating Dickens's mastery of serialization's peculiar demands. To elevate Lever's spirits, Dickens sent him an essay on the serialist's art. Describing it as "a strange knack," he laid bare serious weaknesses in Lever's composition that he then turned into his own serial's major strengths. Dickens pretended that the veteran serialist was a victim of serial publication when even George Eliot, as yet a non-serialist, could readily identify its distinctive requirements.

"For as long as you continue afterwards," Dickens declared on 6 October with reference to the starting date for *Great Expectations*, "we must go on together" (*PL*, 9:321–22). This mixture of resolution with regret suggests that he felt yoked to his less talented contributor. Having finally separated from his wife in 1858, he now saw himself trapped in a bad marriage of another sort. This letter-writer deserves some sympathy: his daunting assignment was to exculpate a novel that the editor had lauded initially but now considered a liability.

Circulation of *All the Year Round* allegedly rose quickly due to *Great Expectations*, but clear-cut evidence of dramatic recovery is difficult to find. "No sooner had [Dickens] stepped in with his new story," Anny Sadrin asserted, "than the sales of *All the Year Round* rose gratifyingly" (AS, 14). Her authority for this statement, Robert L. Patten, estimated the eventual readership of *Great Expec-*

tations at one hundred thousand weekly. Nevertheless, Patten's chart of Dickens's income from *All the Year Round* indicates no immediate rebound in early 1861.[24] On 31 October 1859, Dickens realized £469 in profits from the periodical's first six months; by 30 April 1860, his income from the new venture had risen dramatically to £1,246 and rose again to £1,365 by 31 October 1860. At that time, *A Day's Ride* had been running for two and a half months and Dickens had already written Lever the two letters. The next six-month dividend on 30 April 1861, at which point *Great Expectations* had just passed weekly installment 22 with fourteen to go, dropped to £509, not much higher than the figure for the journal's first six months; the dividend of £310 for 31 October 1861, nearly three months after *Great Expectations* had concluded, hit an all-time low. A full recovery did not take place until 30 April 1862, when Bulwer-Lytton's *A Strange Story* had completed its run; Dickens netted £1,320, almost exactly his earnings a year and a half earlier for the six months ending 31 October 1860.

Small balances for 1861 presumably reflect the fall-off in sales caused by Lever's unpopularity, a decline already evident in September 1860 but not felt in the pocketbook for several months—not until booksellers returned unsold copies of *All the Year Round* and began reducing their orders. The 31 October 1860 balance included the early Lever issues, but profits remained high due to record sales for installments 24 through 40 of *The Woman in White*. Sales were in fact dropping despite the high balance. Contrary to appearances, they were steadily rising between then and 31 October 1861, when the consequences of Lever's failure showed up as low profits for that April and October. The £856 decline in Dickens's earnings between 31 October 1860 and 30 April 1861 was nearly twice as large as his profits from *All the Year Round* during the journal's first six months. Had Lever done his duty by simply maintaining the circulation of *All the Year Round,* Dickens stood to realize another £2,000 between 31 October 1860 and the same date a year later.

If not exactly a financial disaster, inclusion of *A Day's Ride* was certainly expensive. Dickens sold the American serial rights to *Great Expectations* for £1,000, half the price tag for Lever's debacle. Two thousand pounds was equivalent to the profit Dickens could expect from twenty-five public readings in England.[25] If the fall from £1,365 to £509 to £310 had continued for another period, Dickens's journal would have fizzled into the red. On 1 February, Dickens told William de Cerjat that although Lever's story "had been a deadweight," things were better now.[26] Yet it took from 31 October 1860 until 30 April 1862 before Dickens's account books confirmed that his "dash" into *All the Year Round* had been in time to rally his journal.

Dickens paid Lever £750 for the serial version of *A Day's Ride,* a princely sum for a circulation depressant (J, 2:966).[27] The payment brought the overall cost of dealing with Lever to £2,750. What cannot be calculated, however, is

Lever's target value. Without stimulus from *A Day's Ride*, would *Great Expectations* be as incisive a social satire, as compact a masterpiece of shock and suspense? Would it be as grotesquely funny, as tragicomic? Would it ponder the definition of gentility so deeply, or the problem of snobbery so extensively?

After 1860, Dickens the editor planned further ahead, relying on proven crowd-pleasers instead of courting reluctant serialists such as George Eliot. On 6 October, Dickens announced to Forster that Charles Reade and Wilkie Collins would follow *Great Expectations*. "Our course," Dickens boasted, "will be shaped out handsomely and hopefully for between two and three years" (*PL*, 9:320). As things turned out, Bulwer-Lytton's *A Strange Story* preceded Collins's *No Name* and Reade's *Hard Cash*. Dickens abolished the overlap policy: *Great Expectations* ended on 3 August 1861 and *A Strange Story* began on 10 August; although Bulwer concluded on 8 March 1862, *No Name* did not start until 15 March. When Dickens accepted Bulwer's story on 23 January 1861, he envisioned prosperity ahead for thirty-six months—all the way to 26 December 1863 when Reade's novel concluded. Dickens's "dash" into the pages of *All the Year Round* was actually the first leg of a four-serial run, an impressive marathon.[28]

"The difficulties and discouragements" of serial publication "are enormous," Dickens consoled Lever (6 October 1860); "the man who surmounts them today may be beaten by them tomorrow" (*PL*, 9:321–22).[29] Dickens, however, would not be "beaten" again. The invincible lineup of Bulwer, Collins, and Reade, sensational realists all, would see to that. For Lever, tomorrow never came. "It was clear to both men," Fred Kaplan has stated, that Lever "would not have a second chance" (K, 432).[30] Despite avowals on 15 October that Lever continue to regard him as his "other self" (*PL*, 9:323–24), Dickens had done all he could—as editor of *All the Year Round* and parodic revaluator of *A Day's Ride*—to liberate himself from a burdensome contribution. In his remaining nine years as the journal's conductor, he never asked Lever for another serial.[31]

Chapter 3
Thackeray

G.K. Chesterton mistook *Great Expectations* for a paean to Thackeray: "Thackerayan" throughout, it should be read as "an extra chapter to *The Book of Snobs*" (GKC, 197). Dickens, Chesterton maintained, tried to become Thackeray—"a quiet, a detached, even a cynical observer of human life" (GKC, 201). *Great Expectations* impressed Chesterton as the only "one of [Dickens's] works in which he understands Thackeray" (GKC, 200).

Were this estimation acceptable, Dickens's thirteenth novel would offer the curious spectacle of the era's foremost novelist attempting to emulate his closest rival: "After 1847," Sutherland has noted, Thackeray "was, simply, the second greatest novelist in England" (*BS*, 12).[1] Once Thackeray had chastised snobbery in fifty-two weekly installments of *The Snobs of England* (not to mention twenty-four monthly numbers of *Pendennis*),[2] Dickens would not have devoted thirty-six weekly installments of *Great Expectations* to reiterate Thackeray's views. Such a prolonged act of homage makes little sense aesthetically or commercially, but parodic revaluation explains Dickens's conduct perfectly.

Lever's floundering serial recalled England's snobbery to Dickens's attention. *A Day's Ride* not only depressed the circulation of *All the Year Round,* but Lever's superficial analysis of Algernon Sydney Potts, his novel's "sublime snob" (*ADR*, 430), also made light of snobbery's perils and pitfalls. Dickens held Thackeray responsible for such shallow analysis. In the 1840s, Thackeray had underestimated—hence, failed to forestall—an outbreak of snobbery that by 1860 had reached epidemic proportions.[3] Had Thackeray's satire done its job, Dickens implied, *A Day's Ride* would not have had to confront the snobbery problem. Unfortunately, Lever compounded Thackeray's mistakes: he aimed for a comic portrait of a "fool" much as Thackeray, in *Barry Lyndon,* had painted one of a "knave" (WJF, 2:186). In both cases, the joke lay in watching an Irish adventurer continually give himself away in the course of a narrative supposedly bent on self-justification. Some readers, however, found Lyndon likeable and Potts yet another loveable rogue.[4]

Where snobs were concerned, Dickens called for harsher measures. The interplay between Pip's older and younger selves is designed to be consistently more incriminating for Pip and more critical of the values he imbibes from his society than the contrast between Potts's intentions, or Lyndon's, and the embarrassing results each achieves. Thirty-six installments of *Great Expectations*—"That Pip nonsense," as Carlyle, roaring with laughter, called each new installment (J, 2:970)—had to undo eight months of Lever's serial, thirty-six, all told, of Thackeray's if one adds the weekly installments of *The Book of Snobs* to the monthly numbers of *Pendennis*.

Lever's Potts supplies the missing link between Thackeray's Pen and Dickens's Pip. In replacing Potts with Pip as the archetypal anatomy of a snob, the classic case history, Dickens also parodied Pen through Potts. He designated Pip, not Potts or Pen, the compleat snob and *Great Expectations*, not *The Book of Snobs* or *Pendennis*, much less *A Day's Ride*, the Victorian handbook on snobbery. Thackeray considered his fiction "true" and Dickens's not so,[5] but the latter novelist grouped *Pendennis* with *A Day's Ride* as still another Cinderella story for Pip's misfortunes to correct. Critics who ten years earlier had lumped together *Pendennis* and *David Copperfield* were admonished to separate *Great Expectations* from both.

Repeatedly, Dickens embarrasses Lever and Thackeray by having things both ways: there are too many snobs in *The Book of Snobs*, as Dickens's intensive treatment of one snob in *Great Expectations* implies, yet not nearly enough, because all of Thackeray's specimens are handled alike, chiefly from the outside. Dickens dismissed Thackeray's exhaustive catalogue for being neither truly panoramic nor genuinely psychological. If there are clerical snobs, banking snobs, city snobs, country snobs, military snobs, political snobs, university snobs, conservative snobs, Radical snobs, and literary snobs, to run through a handful of Thackeray's categories, targets become increasingly indistinguishable from each other. Their proliferation results in a watering down of the crisis. Once snobbery has become "universal," to use Sutherland's adjective (*BS*, 3), rather than epidemic, once "the great Snob world" (*BS*, 45) and the external world perfectly coincide, Thackeray cannot stigmatize it, the way Dickens does, as a growing threat to the national character.

On the other hand, Dickens devalued Lever for not concentrating in detail on more than one example of snobbery. *Great Expectations* contains four in-depth studies: Pip, Estella, Magwitch, and Miss Havisham, not to mention Orlick and Wopsle. Ironically, Thackeray's superabundance dilutes a phenomenon, whereas the egregiousness of Lever's major instance isolates it. Both amount to the same thing: underestimation of the scope and gravity of a national calamity.

Detecting snobs everywhere, a cynical Thackeray becomes resigned, even tolerant; insufficiently critical of Potts, a lighthearted Lever remains frivolous, unalarmed. Neither manages to be simultaneously severe and amused to the right extent of both. Using what Thackeray called "the Great Subject" of snobbery (*BS*, 114), Dickens accused both of his rivals of a failure in tone that compromises their respective philosophies: in different ways, each had neglected to cultivate the ideal mix of comic recognition despite indignant disappointment that only tragicomedy can provide.

For fifty-two consecutive issues of *Punch*, Thackeray hammered away at England's snobs before giving up in mock despair. In "Chapter Last," he regrets that "the enormous theme of Snobs" demands "endless" labor (*BS*, 203); he is compelled to stop with "but fifty-two bricks" when he could have built "a pyramid." In effect, says Dickens, Thackeray surrendered, leaving the job unfinished, the field to the enemy, and both eventually to an incompetent like Lever.

Titling his opus *The Book of Snobs*, Thackeray sounded biblical for the hardcover edition but flirted with the charge of having written a bible for snobs, a guide to acquiring the very vice he allegedly found reprehensible. Having located the category of snobbishness to which he or she belongs (or aspires), the reader identifies with a species or joins a club—neither of which is a particularly painful act of self-recognition. Dickens designed *Great Expectations* as the opposite kind of handbook—part exposé, part warning. Ostensibly from the pen of Mr. Pirrip, a former snob, this confessional memoir serves first as an eye-opener, then as a self-help manual for the recovering, repentant snob.

Thackeray's serial title was even more counterproductive: *The Snobs of England, By One of Themselves.* Such an admission of complicity, no matter how slyly sophisticated its irony, seemed unrealistic if not morally irresponsible; in effect, disarming in the worst way for a would-be satirist. Among its many advantages, the second ending of *Great Expectations* numbers a greater opportunity to emphasize that its central figures, Pip and Estella, unlike both the author of *The Book of Snobs* and Lever's Potts, have been severely chastened; they are snobs no longer.

Great Expectations, one must reiterate, is about snobbery and infested with snobs but decidedly not written by one. In the original conclusion, this was not as clear. Ensconced in her equipage and with "personal fortune" intact (*GE*, 481), Estella appears affluent and unperturbed, not "bent" and "broken" as she describes herself in the second ending (*GE*, 480). She can only assure Pip—she will not have to demonstrate—that she has learned about his heartbreak through her own sufferings.

Dickens's first final scene ends with Pip declaring, "I was very glad afterwards to have had the interview" (*GE*, 482). This nicely subverted the ending of *A Day's Ride*, in which Catinka, once a gypsy circus performer but now a Parisian lady, deigns not to recognize Potts when he accosts her carriage. Instead of Lever's trivial comedy, one snob snubbed by another whom he patronized before her rise, Dickens's first ending strove for a mutually sobering encounter. In the second ending, however, it became evident that two cases of snobbishness—Pip's expectations of gentility fostered by Magwitch, and Estella's heartless haughtiness inculcated by Miss Havisham—have both been frustrated, indeed, cured. Gone forever is the tone of genial complicity in both Thackeray's title and throughout his pseudobiblical tome; in its place, a semi-Miltonic tragicomedian expels Pip and Estella from a false realm that includes Thackeray's snobbery handbook and Lever's picaresque novel, both of which *Great Expectations* falls upon as judiciously as Misnar's pavilion crushes Ahaback and Desra.

Thackeray claimed to "have ... an eye for a Snob"; he was allegedly mining "rich veins of Snob-ore" (*BS*, 5). Dickens disagreed. The "Snob test" (*BS*, 205) that Thackeray had invented and applied failed miserably thanks to his lessening of the snobbery phenomenon by overextension and self-implication. By the end of *The Book of Snobs*, the snobs of England have become the English themselves; "I myself," Thackeray confessed, "have been taken for one" (*BS*, 5). He cautioned the reader not to "judge hastily or vulgarly of Snobs" lest he or she be numbered among them (*BS*, 5). Such clever ironies prevented Thackeray from empowering himself as the snob crusher whom Dickens thought society needed.[6]

They also stopped Thackeray from rendering the snob's offensiveness sufficiently complex. Thackeray correctly perceived England's curse as the "mammoniacal superstition" (*BS*, 205): sneaking, bowing, cringing on one hand, bullying on the other, from lowest to highest, all because of the "diabolical invention of gentility which killed natural kindliness and honest friendship" (*BS*, 205). But it is Pip, Dickens insisted, more illustrative than all of Thackeray's snobs from *The Book of Snobs* put together and a darkening of Potts as well, who best demonstrates the snob's unique psychological predicament: he suffers equally and continuously from both an inferiority complex and a superiority complex, as if he were switching back and forth from cinder girl to Cinderella.[7] Oafish and abject in Estella's presence, a conceited Pip lords it over lesser lights such as Orlick and Trabb's boy. In looking down on Biddy and Joe, the only persons in *Great Expectations* who love him for himself, Pip deals "kindliness" and "friendship" deadlier blows than any administered by Thackeray's entire collection of snobs.

In Dickens's opinion, gentility is not an invention of the devil (not "diabolical") but a harmful social construct wrongly equated with having money or the status it can buy. Yet Pip's patent, not Potts's or Pen's, is truly devil-sent, having been funded down under by Magwitch so that the diabolical ex-convict can revenge himself upon the society that cast him out. Not only does Pip's unmerited gentility rest upon the exertions of an unfortunate the way Haves in general thrive at the expense of Have-Nots; it also certifies both Haves and Have-Nots—the genteel snob, no matter how polished, and the uncouth class that slaves to maintain him—as equally appalling social monstrosities.

Emphasis on the monstrosity and revenge concomitant with snobbery is missing from Lever and Thackeray. Throughout *Great Expectations*, characters who have been snubbed become the worst snobs; they seem desperate to get even in order to repay an affront, thereby proving themselves good enough. Viewed in this light, Magwitch must be judged as big a snob as Pip; so too Orlick, who resents Biddy's preference for Pip and the latter's superior position at the forge. Even Trabb's boy exacts revenge for the abuse he bore from his employer on Pip's account when the newly enriched former apprentice buys clothes for London. Elements of monstrosity and revenge make snobbery grotesquely tragicomic, Dickens instructed Thackeray. The author of *Great Expectations* felt compelled to study it psychologically—from the inside out as well as from the outside in.

Yes, Pip is a perpetual source of amusement, as Thackeray suggests all snobs are. But, Dickens adds, he is also a painful embarrassment to his closest associates, a bane to social relationships in general, and above all, a constant burden to himself. In excruciating detail, Mr. Pirrip reveals his younger self's anxiety, insecurity, and self-recrimination. Dickens enunciates all of these to underscore the unrealistic shortsightedness of what Chesterton called Thackeray's "quiet," "detached," "even ... cynical" observations (GKC, 201). Such a dispassionate, one-pointed stance, Dickens alleged, makes a curiosity out of a monstrosity and is no match for the spirited tragicomedian's multidimensional analysis.

Like Thackeray scrutinizing snobs, Dickens observes Pip from the outside; so does Mr. Pirrip, Pip's unsparing grown-up self. But Mr. Pirrip works harder than Thackeray or Lever to present snobbery from the inside as well—from young Pip's perspective as a self-tormentor: a "poor dazed village lad" (*GE*, 128) whose snobbery makes him miserable; he is enchanted—indeed, self-divided—by his growing admiration for Biddy despite his recurrent cravings for Estella. One is never asked to accept snobs in *The Book of Snobs* or Pen or even Potts at face value, but neither Lever nor Thackeray, Dickens demonstrates, explores snobbery in all its tragicomic splendor—in terms of the snob's difficulties, pathetic as well as ironic, in taking himself at his own evaluation.

When the newly elevated Pip resolves to bestow a "gallon of condescension" (*GE*, 145) on everyone in his village, Mr. Pirrip's phrase, coined in retrospect, suits Pip's feelings perfectly; it allows us to laugh at the young snob's absurd largesse even as his predicament becomes clearer. Eleven chapters later, Pip revisits his village without looking in on Joe. Upon returning to London, he sends "a penitential codfish and barrel of oysters" instead (*GE,* 246). As "gallon" becomes "barrel," Mr. Pirrip's mixture of pity and contempt for his misguided younger self nicely captures the guilty discomfort behind such munificence.⁸ This is a snob, Mr. Pirrip shows us, who realized that his conduct, no matter how amusing we find it, was making himself and others unhappy, yet could not stop.

Through Pip and from Mr. Pirrip one learns not just what the Victorian snob looks like, how differently he behaves to superiors as opposed to inferiors, and what detrimental effects his preoccupation with distinctions based solely on rank and wealth has upon society, but also how awful it felt to be one. There was nothing as psychologically subtle or as critically severe in Thackeray or Lever, Dickens believed. Sutherland's praises to the contrary, Thackeray's one-dimensional caricatures—Sir George Tufto, Major Ponto et alia—did not lay down "drills for disinfection" (*BS,* 14). A truly introspective exposition of the snob's sufferings and dilemmas, *Great Expectations* supplied the more reliable guide not just to self-recognition but also to a cure for the individual snob.⁹

Great Expectations ought to be read as an extensive rebuttal to *The Book of Snobs,* not an additional chapter of it, much less a "Thackerayan" novel. That Dickens "understands Thackeray" in 1860 and 1861 (GKC, 200) is only correct ironically: Dickens made a monumental effort at such understanding in order to parody Thackeray in addition to dismantling Lever, two rivals with an insufficiently tragicomic worldview.

While *The Snobs of England* was running in *Punch,* Thackeray had a run-in with Douglas Jerrold, the magazine's principal political commentator. Jerrold urged upon Thackeray the more severe tone of radicals like himself in place of the latter's calmer satire based on caution, coaxing, and compromise. According to Sutherland, Jerrold's "dictatorial personality" broke out at weekly staff meetings (*BS,* 15), but on this occasion, Thackeray's views prevailed with *Punch*'s editorial board and are reiterated in "Chapter Last" of his text: "You cannot alter the nature of men and Snobs by any force of nature; as, by laying ever so many stripes on a donkey's back you can't turn him into a zebra" (*BS,* 204–5). In effect, Thackeray disenfranchised radical humorists like Dickens, who take themselves too seriously as reformers and confuse novels with forums for social theory.

Thackeray considered it sufficient to poke fun at "the disease" of snobbery, to awaken the nation's mind on the subject, then to let others discover the remedy (*BS,* 22). Having applied "the Snob test" to several hundred suspected snobs, Thackeray stepped aside, hoping "some great marshall," a champion of "Equality," would rush forward to reorganize society (*BS,* 205). Throughout *Great*

Expectations, Dickens replies that Thackeray withdrew because he had no solution or was too pessimistic to believe in one. Consequently, society had to make do with Lever, whose satire was even less curative than Thackeray's.

What Thackeray calls his "Punchine wrath" (*BS*, 90) fell short of the magazine's customary asperities. For the hardcover edition, he toned down *The Book of Snobs* even further: he "removed" several of the more "satirical" chapters, as Sutherland pointed out (*BS*, 21), including chapter 17, the more acerbic of two attacks on Literary Snobs.[10] By 1847, Sutherland maintains, Thackeray "wanted to leave the savage satires of his youth behind him" (*BS*, 21). Throughout *The Book of Snobs,* Gordon N. Ray argued, the satire exhibits a certain "gentlemanliness," a critical impulse that is essentially conciliatory.[11]

Sutherland suggests that Thackeray excised chapter 17 to placate his fellow authors, Dickens especially, who had deplored *Novels by Eminent Hands,* originally titled *Punch's Prize Novelists* (*Punch,* April–October 1847), as a betrayal of the literary profession. Thackeray had ludicrously mimicked the style and concerns of several novelists he considered undeservedly successful, among them Bulwer, Disraeli, and the ever vulnerable Lever.[12] How, then, could Dickens parodically revalue *The Book of Snobs* in *Great Expectations* without being hypocritical?

One answer is that parodic revaluation is substantially different from Thackeray's burlesque of the day's popular novelists. The latter form of attack is eighteenth-century in style and purpose; it recalls Fielding's writing *Shamela* to laugh at Richardson's *Pamela,* whose absurdities Fielding exaggerated. Unlike the more earnest, if not deadlier, Victorian variety, such parody ridicules without substituting truth for falsity as the parodic revaluator does: an allegedly more realistic character, scene, or point of view for the one that his (or her) revaluation dismisses as preposterous by reconfiguring aright.

Deposing Bulwer, Disraeli, and their ilk was similar to enthroning Colley Cibber and the poets of "Dullness," as Alexander Pope did in *The Dunciad.* Such actions discredited literature, exposing cardinal instances of its falseness and fatuity. To Dickens, such behavior seemed to lower literature itself and was typical of Thackeray's irresponsible, nonreformist temperament. In contrast, Dickens's reconsideration of Potts and Pen as Pip, admittedly a purging, also rehabilitated literary endeavor by accurately redoing two supposedly unreliable case studies of a snob instead of merely scoffing at them.

Writing to Dickens shortly after the row with Thackeray, Jerrold complained of the latter's "eternal guffaw at all things"—a comic perspective rendered ineffective by its cynicism, which paradoxically made Thackeray sound "quiet," "detached" (*GKC*, 201), and precluded spirited calls for sweeping change. For any "comic history of humanity" that lacked "occasional gravities," Jerrold expressed unbridled contempt: "After all, life has something serious in it," he protested to Dickens (*DJ*, 445).

"Anent the Comic History of England and similar comicalities (Snobs in general included) I feel exactly as you do," Dickens replied (*L*, 1:804). Clearly, he favored laying on "stripes" (lashes). He was not simply consoling Jerrold, whose viewpoint Thackeray's had routed. If Thackeray's concluding remarks in *The Book of Snobs* struck at Dickens through Jerrold, Dickens got even with Thackeray by upending his would-be imitator, the Lever who wrote *A Day's Ride*.[13]

In effect, Dickens announced the basis not just for his reworking of snobbery in Thackeray but also for the concomitant parody of Lever's even feebler guffaws. No "comicalities" without "gravities," and vice versa; in this informal exchange between Dickens and Jerrold, one finds the formula that foreshadows and encapsulates Dickens's scorn for rivals who fail to grow angry enough when dealing with inadequacies in human nature and the nature of things. Like Lever, they generally underestimate the darker side; or like Thackeray, lenient because fatalistic, they appear resigned to it. In place of Thackeray's "eternal guffaw," an overemphasis on *vanitas* to the exclusion of *gravitas*, Dickens proposed Pip's "fretful laugh" when he discovers his "grimly ludicrous" ties to Magwitch (*GE*, 330).[14]

In chapter 39 of *Great Expectations*, Magwitch confounds Pip with the revelation that he is the young man's benefactor. This deservedly famous climactic scene, which parodies Cinderella's rewarding interviews with her fairy godmother, should also be read as a satiric redoing of Major Pendennis's surprise visit to Pen's London apartments in chapter 28 of *Pendennis*. The darker Dickens's reconsideration of the Major's social call becomes, the closer the latter's connection to the unrealistic fairy tale being parodically revised as Pip's rise and fall.

Dickens wanted Thackeray implicated in promoting the Victorian era's Cinderella complex. Rewriting an uncle/mentor's visit to his nephew/protegé in order to disclose its resemblance to an improbable fairy tale, Dickens refused a rival's claims to have captured "the sentiment of reality."[15] To peruse Thackeray's account of Pen's growth and development was to swallow yet another unbelievable success story, Dickens alleged; *Pendennis* corroborates the Victorian era's snobbish view of itself as a Cinderella.

Pen shares rooms with George Warrington in the Upper Temple's Lamb Court. Arriving by omnibus, Major Pendennis reaches Pen's "dingy portal" at midday; nevertheless, this dandy must stumble up three flights of "abominable black stairs" whose bannisters "contributed their damp exudations to his gloves" because the "feeble and filthy oil-lamps" have yet to be lit (*Pen*, 1:289). Pip and Herbert Pocket inhabit apartments in the Temple's Garden Court. "Dressed... roughly... and hardened by exposure to weather" (*GE*, 312), Magwitch returns from Australia to behold the young man he considers both nephew and son. Pip hears Magwitch's "footsteps on the stair" late on a night "stormy and wet," when the wind howls "like discharges of canon" (*GE*, 311). The staircase oil lamps have all been "blown out." Dickens begins by coarsening the uncle figure and substituting a gloomy night for a grey afternoon.

Despite damp railings, the visit goes well in Major Pendennis's estimation. Having dropped in unexpectedly after a period of coolness, the Major resumes avuncular responsibilities. "I shall be on the watch for you," he reassures his nephew, "and I shall die content, my boy, if I can see you with a good ladylike wife and a good carriage, and a good pair of horses, living in society, and seeing your friends, like a gentleman (*Pen*, 1:292). As the Major subsequently reiterates, Arthur, thanks to his "person and *expectations* . . . ought to make a good *coup* in marriage" (*Pen*, 1:384; first italics added).

Having devised a program for Pip, Magwitch too plays a supervisory role. For years as a "hired-out shepherd in a solitary hut,"[16] he kept Pip's image before him: "If I gets liberty and money," Magwitch resolves, "I'll make that boy a gentleman!" (*GE*, 317). "Yes, Pip, dear boy," he returns to exclaim, "I've made a gentleman on you! It's me wot has done it!" The ex-convict promises that Pip will "show money with lords"; if there are "bright eyes somewheres, wot you love the thoughts on," Magwitch adds, "they shall be yourn, dear boy, if money can buy 'em" (*GE*, 318).

Magwitch has made personal sacrifices beyond the Major's ken: "I lived rough, that you should live smooth" (*GE*, 317), he boasts. But Dickens's intent in reissuing the Major's worldview coarsely from Magwitch's mouth is to uncover the former's true sentiments, thereby defusing Thackeray's satire. Dickens reduces the realization of "expectations" and the scoring of a marital "*coup*" to outspending nobles and purchasing a woman's "bright eyes," a franker if grosser statement of the crass snobbery in both situations, Pen's as well as Pip's.

Surely Dickens recalled Thackeray's "expectations" passage prior to composing chapter 39. Magwitch's "dear boy" echoes the Major's "my boy." Rewritten as an ex-convict's unwelcome return, the visit from patron to beneficiary proves an unmitigated disaster. Magwitch's reappearance crushes Pip's monetary hopes from Miss Havisham along with the prospect of wedding Estella. An "affectionate uncle" speaks his "simple philosophy"—such is Thackeray's ironic summary of the Major's materialistic prognostications. Pen is bemused by the discrepancy between his mother's morals and the worldly Major's; Pip, on the other hand, is traumatized. "That's it, dear boy! Call me uncle," insists Magwitch, soon to be Uncle Provis (*GE*, 328). "All the truth of my position came flashing on me," Pip relates, "a multitude" of "disappointments, dangers, disgraces, consequences of all kinds" (*GE*, 316).

If the Dickens–Thackeray antithesis translates into truth versus falsity, Pip's situation, not Pen's, delivers a flash of insight about the perversity of the Victorian social system, Dickens argues. Pen is merely the Victorian gentleman as an insufficiently industrious young man whose worldly-wise uncle gives him unsound advice, with which, however, many Victorian uncles doubtless agreed. Pip suddenly comprehends that he is a parasite, an encumbrance on society, and a victim of its twisted values just as his would-be uncle is. "I worked hard, that you should be above work" is how Magwitch phrases it (*GE*, 317). Ironically, he sanctions society's division into Haves and Have-Nots even as he boasts of having subverted the system by converting one of the latter into one of the former.

What Thackeray misplayed as a comic visit on an otherwise unexceptional afternoon, Dickens reshapes into a frightening visitation, his novel's climactic day of reckoning. He transforms an amusing episode into a tragicomic masterpiece. As Pip's false hopes fall apart, his autobiography turns from a Cinderella story into one that recalls the collapse of Misnar's pavilion. However, unlike Pen and Major Pendennis, who remain to novel's end as they appear in chapter 28, Pip and Magwitch develop a mutually beneficial relationship that cures the snobbery in both the would-be uncle and his hesitant nephew.

Major Pendennis cannot literally bestow fortune and position on Pen the way Cinderella's fairy godmother's gifts of dresses and shoes elevate her to princesshood. But taking credit in advance, he claims to foresee Pen's attainment of wealth and rank. In Dickens's parody, where entertaining such expectations amounts to snobbish overvaluation of the self, none of Magwitch's promises to Pip is fulfilled; the returned transport may be said to deprive Pip of the magnificent future he returns to announce and that the Major envisions for Pen.

Yet Magwitch opens Pip's eyes to his actual situation and to society's, a priceless adjustment. In contrast, Pen's visit from his uncle illustrates a general lack of severity that Thackeray's urbane satire transmitted to feeble imitators such as Lever. Which fairy godfather's program, Dickens asks, more tellingly reveals the self-serving materialism underlying the Victorian era's view of itself as fortune's child—the Major's fond hopes of Pen's promotion to an enviable wife and carriage, or Magwitch's perverse scheme for Pip's (and his own) triumph over lords and ladies? A mildly satirical scene, the Major's visit recalls rather than rescinds Cinderella's meetings with her fairy godmother. As Dickens saw things, this similarity compromises Thackeray's estimate of himself as the superior social realist and heralds the Potts–Whalley encounter—the meeting of Cinderella figure and fairy godfather at the conclusion of *A Day's Ride*.

By 1860, Dickens's bid to remain the age's premier social realist hinged on his insistence that his rivals wrote Cinderella stories. In doing so, they flattered nineteenth-century England's snobbish perception of itself as a chosen people who had surmounted numerous difficulties earlier in the century in order to rise to prominence by the 1850s as a jewel among nations. Reduced from riches to rags upon Magwitch's return and capture, all hope blasted of early marriage to Estella, Pip tells his tragicomic life story to countermand Potts's good fortune with Kate Whalley, which confirmed Pen's with Laura Bell, not to mention Copperfield's with Agnes Wickfield. Dickens burdens Pip with *two* parodic benefactors, each with a sadistic streak: Miss Havisham, who cruelly misleads him into thinking of her as his patroness, and Magwitch, whose benevolence toward Pip doubles as an act of revenge upon society. Similarly, reconsidering *Pendennis,* he saw at its core not one but *two* Cinderella stories for Pip's to revalue: Arthur's and Laura's.

Especially reprehensible, Dickens emphasized, was his rivals' willingness to create Cinderella-like heroes who also marry a Cinderella, thereby reinforcing their own Cinderella-ness and corroborating further the national myth of unstinting expectancy and ascent. Lever does not reward Potts with Kate Whalley until she has gone from riches to rags and then back to riches as her father loses, then regains, wealth and respect. Even *David Copperfield* perpetuated the general enchantment when David finally recognizes his soulmate in Agnes, whose father is nearly ruined by Uriah Heep. "I have loved you all my life!" she confesses when Copperfield finally proposes (*DC*, 725).

By novel's end, Thackeray celebrates the "happiness" of Pen's marriage, his successes as an author, and especially "the [good] fortune of Laura" (*Pen*, 2:394). The plot of *Pendennis,* Dickens mocked, turns on preventing a young snob from throwing himself away on no less than three unqualified Cinderellas: "the Fotheringay," as Foker phrases Miss Emily Costigan's stage name (*Pen*, 1:37), Fanny Bolton, and Blanche Amory. In contrast, Pip is never good enough—not for Estella, not for Biddy. He hungers after a false Cinderella (Estella), thereby overlooking the true one (Biddy) until too late.

Having been freed from three successive enchantments, Pen finally comes to appreciate Laura Bell, a parallel for Copperfield's Agnes and the novel's only plausible female Cinderella. Laura is a hearth child, a poor dependent never looked upon with "favorable eyes" by Pen's snobbish father and uncle (*Pen*,

1:80). In effect, she is raised for Pen in his own home by his mother. Helen Pendennis doubles as her son's good fairy in this respect: at Fairoaks, she does for Pen with her ward what Pip's "fairy godmother" (*GE,* 155), Miss Havisham, deceives him into thinking she intends to accomplish for him at Satis House with her ward, Estella. Dickens parodically revalues the threesome of Helen Pendennis, Laura, and Pen as Miss Havisham, Estella, and Pip. As Pip's hopes of winning Estella and inheriting Satis House collapse, so too, Dickens implied, should the fairy tale basis for Pen's triumphant marriage in Thackeray's supposedly realistic novel.

When Foker takes Pen to the play, the latter finds Miss Fotheringay's sandals, actually "of rather a large size," as "ravishing as the slippers of Cinderella" (*Pen,* 1:39). Besides being poor, this Irish actress is already twenty-six and not very intelligent. "A woman who spells affection with one f," as Major Pendennis snobbishly puts it (and Thackeray evidently agrees), will never entrap a Pendennis (*Pen,* 1:125). Having failed with Pen, however, she enters society as the wife of Sir Charles Mirabel, G.C.B. (*Pen,* 1:286). Her successor is Potts's Catinka, the circus performer in Lever's *A Day's Ride* who marries wealthy Prince Max and becomes a Parisian lady.

Fanny Bolton shares a bed "in a cupboard" with her two little sisters. When Arthur Pendennis notices her in Vauxhall Gardens and becomes her escort for the evening, it was, Thackeray writes, as if "the Prince had appeared and subjugated the poor little handmaid" (*Pen,* 2:97). Although Fanny later nurses Pen through a serious fever, Helen Pendennis and Laura Bell rout her from his sickroom; in their snobbish opinion, she is beneath a gentleman's station. Indeed, Fanny stands to Pen not as Cinderella to the Prince or even as Biddy to Pip; instead, she embodies the sort of temptation Emily poses to Steerforth, or Clarissa to Lovelace.[17]

Thackeray certifies Pen as the novel's Cinderella by overruling Blanche Amory's claims. This near-marriage reminds us that all three protagonists—Thackeray's Pen, Lever's Potts, and Dickens's Pip—contemplate union with a woman who turns out to be an outlaw's daughter. Only *Great Expectations,* Dickens argued, confronts this crisis for the purpose of serious social criticism. Unlike Pen, who is eager to discard Miss Amory once her parentage is revealed, Pip remains infatuated with Estella, from whom *his* ties to Magwitch (not hers) appear to separate him forever. Potts's good fortune with Kate Whalley and her exonerated father to the contrary, Pip's devotion to Magwitch is not richly rewarded.

In chapters 37 and 38 of *Pendennis,* several personages important to the story arrive in London: Blanche Amory; her mother (Lady Clavering) who is fabulously rich thanks to her father's success as an indigo smuggler in India; Sir Francis Clavering, Lady Clavering's second husband and Blanche's stepfather; and the alleged "envoy from an Indian Prince, a Colonel Altamont, the Nawaub of Lucknow's prime favourite" (*Pen,* 1:376–77). Although Altamont insists he is a "gentleman," he knows a "secret" regarding Sir Francis and is blackmailing him.

That Altamont is actually John Amory, Blanche's "outlawed" real father (*Pen,* 2:238), was surely clear to careful readers as early as chapter 26: Altamont is delighted to hail "Betsy Amory" at the Baymouth ball (*Pen,* 1:267). Who else would know Blanche was "christened Betsy" but had "crowned" herself with a more romantic name (*Pen,* 1:229)? Nevertheless, in chapter 42 and again at the end of 43, Thackeray tries to generate suspense as Captain Strong ponders "the secret tie between Altamont and Clavering" (*Pen,* 2:41).

Dickens twice revaluates this "secret tie": once as the bond between Magwitch and Pip, and again as the link between Compeyson and Magwitch. In the latter, the so-called gentleman has the returned ex-convict in his power, not vice versa. Realistically, Dickens pointed out to Thackeray, the Victorian upper class possessed so many advantages of money and position that any member of it was bound to enjoy the upper hand. Altamont has Clavering shaking in his boots; Dickens knows that Magwitch stands no chance against Compeyson.

Should Altamont reveal himself as Amory—the legal husband of Clavering's wife—her marriage to Clavering would be nullified and the income he depends on from it would disappear. Ironically, Magwitch's return ruins Pip's chances of marrying Estella and impoverishes him besides. Mere connection with someone of Magwitch's caliber, Dickens informed Thackeray, is enough to destroy one socially in the real world. That Clavering could retain a tie with Amory so as not to break the tie with Lady Clavering struck Dickens as absurd.

Altamont/Amory's reappearance, Dickens protested, holds no more social significance than Samuel Whalley's return to prosperity does in *A Day's Ride.* Each is extraordinary, one of a kind, hence without symbolic power. In *Great Expectations,* society's sins come home to roost in the person of Magwitch. Pip has an epiphany; only he, not Potts or Pen, learns where money comes from: lower-class drudges like Magwitch, the perennial cinder girl, who toils so Pip can be genteel. Surely, Dickens intimated, it is more important, not just more difficult, to identify Magwitch as both Pip's secret benefactor and Estella's father than to guess that Harpar is Whalley (Kate's father) or that Altamont is Amory (Blanche's parent). Which return exposes the criminality not of the returning transport but of society generally? Which, Dickens asked, unravels the social fabric—Magwitch's, or Altamont/Amory's?

Before long, several characters besides Clavering—namely, Major Pendennis, Morgan (his servant), and Arthur himself—realize that Altamont is John Amory, a "fugitive convict" from Australia; he "had cut down the officer in charge of him," Thackeray explains, so "a rope would be inevitably his end, if he came again under British authorities" (*Pen*, 2:252). "Death is probably over him if he discovers himself," Pen says, "return to transportation certainly" (*Pen*, 2:332). Oddly, Altamont/Amory cannot expose Sir Francis without doing greater harm to himself, yet unlike Magwitch, who faces a similar penalty, he seems unconcerned for his personal safety. Magwitch twice underlines the threat hanging over him: "I was sent for life. It's death to come back . . . I should of a certainty be hanged if took"; later, he anticipates "death by the rope, in the open street" (*GE*, 319, 331). This double declaration is more chilling than Thackeray's explanation of Altamont's possible fate; Dickens parodied the enforced seriousness, the artificial danger, imposed upon Thackeray's comedy, replacing it with the true *gravitas* allegedly underlying his own.[18]

Finding his daughter is not prominent among Amory's reasons for returning to England, whereas the chance to see Pip has drawn Magwitch. "Pip, I'm here," Magwitch exclaims, "because I've meant it by you, years and years" (*GE*, 332). Instead of Altamont's return to blackmail Clavering, Dickens offers Magwitch's tragicomic blend of gratitude toward Pip and revenge upon society. Compelling it to accept Pip is a subtler form of blackmail than Altamont's threat to have society disown Clavering.

In chapter 65, Blanche and Mrs. Bonner go "up the stairs" to visit Captain Strong, Altamont's roommate (*Pen*, 2:289). Mrs. Bonner, Blanche's nurse in India, screams in recognition of Altamont as Amory; she has told Blanche he "was drowned in New South Wales" (*Pen*, 2:332). "I'm dead, though I'm your father," Altamont/Amory informs Blanche (*Pen*, 2:291), who then screams too. Dickens rewrote this farcical scene as his novel's tragicomic climax. The goal was to demote *Pendennis* to silliness and raise *Great Expectations* in the direction of tragicomedy. When Pip hears "a footstep on the stair" (*GE*, 311), it belongs to an ex-convict who shortly declares: "Look'ee here, Pip. I'm your second father" (*GE*, 317), confounding Pip and triggering a sensation for Mr. Pirrip's readers that silenced any gasps caused by Altamont/Amory's announcement.

In Dickens's revision, inconveniences of an ex-convict's return from Australia fall directly on Pip, the personification of society's Cinderella complex; in *Pendennis*, they descend upon Blanche, exploding her marriageability while enhancing prospects for Pen's union with Laura. Dickens transfers the shock of recognition and the consequent loss of social standing to Pip in order to fault Thackeray for keeping his story's male Cinderella unmarked. Magwitch proves a better father to Pip then Altamont/Amory has been to Blanche, yet a more severe liability; her father's return discounts her socially but leaves her financially intact as "her grandfather's heir" (*Pen*, 2:332). Magwitch's money is forfeited to the Crown. Blanche simply screams; crushed to learn that he is Magwitch's dependent, Pip is speechless: "[M]y lips had parted, and had shaped some words that were without sound" (*GE*, 316).

Magwitch returns "dressed ... roughly, like a voyager" (*GE*, 312); similarly, Altamont/Amory's occupation is that of merchant seaman. Amory's disguise consists primarily of an unconvincing wig,[19] the source presumably for Magwitch's naive faith in "disguising wigs" that "can be bought for money" (*GE*, 331). Warrington snobbishly insists that "Arthur Pendennis can't marry a convict's daughter; and sit in Parliament as Member for the hulks" (*Pen*, 2:333). Whether or not Thackeray concurred, Pip not only regrets the loss of someone who turns out to be a convict's daughter ("O Estella, Estella!" [*GE*, 318]) but the even greater loss of his first "second father," Joe, whom in effect he "deserted" for Magwitch (*GE*, 320).

Between Blanche's superficial scream and Pip's genuine terror ("my blood ran cold within me" [*GE*, 318]), Dickens contended, stretched a decade of artistic maturation—his. Just as Estella is the archetypal femme fatale and Blanche psychologically less interesting, a mere coquette, Dickens hoped that *Great Expectations* would tower over *Pendennis* the way Shakespearean tragicomedy overshadows Restoration farce. Thanks to the vigor of Dickens's parodic revaluations, any painfulness in Pen's snobbish confession simply evaporates: "It is not a very pleasant thought to me that I am engaged to a convict's daughter," Pen laments (*Pen*, 2:336). When Magwitch appoints himself Pip's "second father" (*GE*, 317), Dickens simultaneously sabotaged Harpar/Whalley's disclosure of himself to Potts as Kate's father and Altamont/Amory's manifestation of himself to Blanche.

Pip hides Magwitch in hopes of saving his life, never telling Estella about him; Blanche conceals her knowledge that Altamont is Amory in hopes that she can still have her choice of Pen or Foker. As things turn out, she bypasses the former only to be rejected by the latter, which makes her the story's principal loser. Pen, Foker, Lady Clavering—all benefit from her downfall. Lady Clavering remains legally married, because her alleged first husband, Altamont (real name Johnny Armstrong), was already married to Mrs. Frisby.

Altamont is merely a comic antecedent for the more complicated villainy Dickens creates with Compeyson. Bigamist and blackmailer though he is, Altamont/Amory/Armstrong cannot err grievously enough to produce a tragicomic masterpiece like Miss Havisham. Neither Mrs. Frisby nor Lady Clavering comes close. Similarly, Lady Clavering's accusation, "You've no heart" (*Pen*, 2:387), seems wasted on the shallow, conniving Blanche. Darkening the charge as he reinstates it, Dickens transfers Lady Clavering's outburst to Miss Havisham, who directs it against Estella, where Dickens felt confident it belongs: "'You stock and stone!' exclaimed Miss Havisham. 'You cold, cold heart!'" (*GE*, 302)

At the Clavering Arms, Morgan corners Altamont/Amory/Armstrong, but Mr. and Mrs. Lightfoot overcome the Major's former servant. The "fugitive convict" (*Pen*, 2:252) escapes *to* London in yet another farcical mix-up that Dickens redid at length as Magwitch's attempt to escape *from* London, the more plausible direction for an illegally returned convict and with graver consequences: immediately fatal for Compeyson, eventually so for Pip's fairy godfather.

Just as Dickens criticized *A Day's Ride* for not being "strung . . . on the needful strong thread of interest" (*PL*, 9:321–22), he deplored *Pendennis*'s inferior sense of the pivotal. If readers wished to learn how the life process operates—what sort of threads run through it connecting events and holding things together, and how to locate the cardinal, crucial factor around which all else turns—they should study *Great Expectations*, Dickens asserted, and ignore *A Day's Ride* and *Pendennis*. Only a tragicomic, sensational realist, not a picaresque novelist like Lever or the cynical proprietor of *Vanity Fair*, could demonstrate simultaneously the importance of both thread and pivot (life's warp and woof).

Throughout *Great Expectations*, Pip's unfinished relationship with Magwitch supplies the suspenseful thread on which the former's life story is "strung." One senses the inevitability of the latter's reappearance, which could happen at any moment. Suspensefully yet satirically, Dickens rewrote the farcical resurfacing of Altamont/Amory as Magwitch's tragicomic return. The Altamont/Amory affair, Dickens demonstrated, was too thin a thread on which to string a novel whose monthly installments ran for over two years. In Dickens's estimation, this affair supplied an even weaker pivot. Admittedly, monthly installment 12 (chapters 36–38) was exactly the midpoint of Thackeray's seventy-five chapter novel. But not until chapters 37 and 38, the last two in volume 1, did Thackeray begin to develop his plans for discovering Altamont/Amory as Blanche's father. By January 1850, *Pendennis* was more than a year old.

One is introduced to Colonel Altamont at length in chapter 37; in the succeeding chapter, he crashes a party at the Claverings' London residence, having threatened to "burst" Sir Francis "all to atoms" (*Pen*, 1:378). A revenant like Magwitch, Altamont is also a recidivist who seems incapable of moral improvement no matter how many times he reappears. A novel's midpoint and pivot, Dickens instructed Thackeray, are not synonymous. Unlike *Pendennis*, *Great Expectations* has a working pivot from its outset. Around Pip and Magwitch, Dickens boasted, everything of consequence in *Great Expectations* may be said to revolve. So central is Dickens's pivot that he equated it with his novel's catalyst, calling it "the grotesque tragi-comic conception that first encouraged" him to undertake the novel (*PL*, 9:325). Dickens challenged readers to discern Thackeray's original creative impulse in the Altamont/Amory plot thread. Was it not closer to the improvisations of a picaresque novelist such as Lever? Magwitch's return, which triggers the collapse of Pip's expectations, grows directly out of the novel's first scene, a clear-cut case of lifelike, long-term cause and effect.

Chapters 42 and 43 of *Pendennis* end almost identically: in the former, Captain Strong wonders "what was the secret tie between Altamont and Clavering" (*Pen*, 2:41); in the latter, he resolves to learn "the nature of the tie which bound the two men together" (*Pen*, 2:53). Because Strong has no great personal stake in the matter, his surmises do not increase what little suspense there is. When Pip comprehends the nature of his connection to an ex-convict, he does so in imagery stronger than Thackeray's and, Dickens added, more appropriate; "tie" becomes chain: "What I was chained to," says Pip, "and how heavily, became intelligible to me" (*GE*, 329–30).

Dickens wanted his complex revaluation of *Pendennis* to be structural as well as thematic. Magwitch reveals himself at the two-thirds mark; then the final third of the novel works out the aftermath of Pip's new self-awareness. To this crucial aspect of the critical event in their respective novels, Thackeray and Lever give short shrift. Neither Harpar/Whalley nor Altamont/Amory has symbolic significance as an authorial reflection on social injustice. So Lever discloses that Harpar is Whalley and Thackeray reveals that Altamont is Amory as close to the ending as possible, Dickens objected. The Pip–Magwitch pivot continues to turn for fifteen chapters after the latter manifests himself as Pip's benefactor. Dickens substantiated his brand of extraordinary realism, at once melodramatic and tragicomic, by ridiculing his rivals' joint failure to fashion a socially significant sensation that was truly pivotal.

Thackeray urged the middle class not to imitate aristocratic models, Sutherland has argued (*BS*, 14). Heeding such advice supposedly would have put an end to the snobbery syndrome. In response, Dickens utilized the undeserved advantages that Drummle enjoys over Pip to show how ineffectual, if not unrealistic, he considered Thackeray's admonishment. Given social pressures and personal ambition, it is impossible for Pip not to try to emulate his so-called betters. At their trial, where a well-groomed Compeyson gets off lightly compared to the uncouth Magwitch, Dickens demonstrates that being unable to emulate can be disastrous.

Pendennis and *Great Expectations* are both well stocked with negative variations on the gentility theme, the ideal Victorian gentleman emerging as none of the following: not Sir Francis Clavering, or Major Pendennis, or the Marquis of Steyne (the epitome of "an English gentleman" in the Major's opinion [*Pen*, 2:184]); not Compeyson or Drummle, two even harsher critiques of the genteel. The only true paradigm, Dickens insisted, is Joe Gargery. Unlike his rivals, Pip has for a model the quintessential gentle man. Pip's superiority to Potts and Pen rests to a large extent on his eventual similarity to Joe.

Great Expectations concludes with a flurry of paternal-avuncular activity on Pip's part. In imitating the finer actions of his surrogate fathers, Joe and Magwitch, Pip starts to become the moral center absent from *A Day's Ride* and *Pendennis* that neither Potts nor Pen seems likely to provide. Like *David Copperfield, Pendennis* features a protagonist who "does not claim to be a hero" (*Pen*, 2:394). Neither does Pip, but by novel's end he could file a modest claim. Having learned to imitate Joe, Pip stands out in sharp contrast to Potts and Pen as a commendable portrait of a Victorian gentleman.

To "little Pip," Pip relates as both guardian and benefactor: no longer averse to the cinder girl's humble circumstances, he takes a stool "by the child's side" in the kitchen firelight just as Joe used to sit beside him (*GE*, 476). "Next morning," Pip escorts his namesake "to the churchyard" and sets him "on a certain tombstone," symbolically assuming responsibility for "little Pip" on the spot where he was seized by Magwitch (*GE*, 477). In the original ending, we last see Pip "walking along Piccadilly with little Pip" (*GE*, 481), so he introduces the child to London as well. In the revised ending, Pip will protect the widow of a wife beater just as Joe, whose father regularly "hammered" him (*GE*, 47), not only married Mrs. Joe but did all he could to shelter Pip from her heavy hand. Potts and Pen end in triumph comparable to Cinderella's. They also marry Cinderellas. In contrast, the parodic revaluator noted, Pip matures into a modest facsimile of a fairy godmother, the role that Magwitch and Miss Havisham botch and that Major Pendennis and Sir Samuel Whalley try to reprise—the former incompetently in Thackeray's novel, the latter implausibly in Lever's.

Speaking ironically, Thackeray regretted that everyone was not brought up to respect the Peerage "as the Englishman's second Bibie" (*BS*, 17). Major Pendennis knows the "name and pedigree of everybody in the Peerage"; "I wish to heaven you would read in Debrett every day," he counsels his nephew (*Pen*, 1:88). Yet it is Dickens, not Thackeray, who dramatizes the domestic consequences of such a curriculum and finds them tragicomic. While Mrs. Pocket reads a book "all about titles" (*GE*, 191) and regrets not having married one,[20] chaos reigns throughout her establishment: "six little Pockets . . . tumbling up" to adulthood without decent supervision. One laughs uneasily when Dickens dramatizes the plight of her financially strapped husband; Mr. Pocket's life exemplifies such quiet desperation that he attempts "to lift himself up" by his hair "with both hands" (*GE*, 191). If readers wish to witness the damage done within English households by Peerage worship, Dickens suggested, they should read about Pip and the Pockets and forget Major Pendennis's instructions to Pen.

In *Pendennis*, Mr. John Pendennis, Pen's father, is afflicted with "the secret ambition . . . to be a gentleman" (*Pen*, 1:9–10). Dickens loads such snobbish desires squarely on Pip: "I admire [Estella] dreadfully," he confesses to Biddy, "and I want to be a gentleman on her account" (*GE*, 128). Thus it is not Pen, a second-generation snob, but Pip who Dickens felt better exhibits the origins and development of the snobbery disease. House's point that "the sexual element in snobbery" has seldom been "emphasized enough" (HH, 67) makes John Pendennis's aspirations simplistic. In Pip's desire to become genteel on Estella's "account," Dickens parodies the lack of frankness in Lever's characterization of Potts and Thackeray's of Pen and his father; both neglect the sexual side of snobbery even more completely than they overlooked its revenge aspect.

Purportedly a burgeoning realist, Pen warns of contradiction and comeuppance if one "indulges in happy day-dreams, or building of air-castles" as he has done in contemplating marriage with Blanche (*Pen*, 2:343). Lever's Potts also claims to know how to build "castles in Spain" (*ADR*, 194), a weakness he never ceases to indulge. In Dickens's revaluative opinion, only Pip knows what it feels like to have such an edifice cave in upon one's unsuspecting self.

Having learned that Blanche is a "convict's daughter" (*Pen*, 2:333), Pen writes her a strange letter. Although it expresses his willingness to stand by his marriage proposal, he pleads between the lines to be let off. Pen informs Blanche that he has learned an "awful secret," one that has "changed all [his] prospects" and cancelled his "vain and ambitious hopes" (*Pen*, 2:348–49). "Our fine daydreams are gone," Pen writes; "Our carriage has whirled out of sight like Cinderella's" (*Pen*, 2:348). But the embarrassing "secret" is Blanche's, not Pen's, Dickens's revision points out; only her coach turns into a pumpkin. Far from a demoted Cinderella, Pen is still princely, free now to wed Laura, the novel's undiscovered princess. When Dickens redid this episode, Pip is revealed as the unfrocked Cinderella, his the shameful secret and crushed hopes. Thanks to Magwitch, Pip learns that he has never been a real Cinderella and that Estella, whom he still mistakes for that personage, is not reserved for him.

That Pip, a cured snob, evinces moral growth beyond the grasp of Potts and Pen is nowhere clearer than in the final paragraphs of chapter 56, in which Magwitch expires (*GE*, 456–57). On prior visits during Magwitch's imprisonment between trial and sentencing, Pip has been reading from the Bible: "[I]t became the first duty of my life to . . . read to him, what I knew he ought to hear," says Pip (*GE*, 452). How the former snob became an accomplished exegete is uncertain, but not his choice of texts. Magwitch having drawn his last breath, Pip, "mindful, then, of what [they] had read together," quotes from the parable of the Pharisee and the publican. Of "the two men who went up into the Temple to pray," Pip recalls (*GE*, 457), the Pharisee thanks God that he is "not like the rest of men," robbers and cheaters, and not "like this publican" who cannot "pay tithes" such as the Pharisee can afford (Luke 18:9–14). In contrast, the publican prays by "striking his breast, saying 'O Lord, be merciful to me the sinner!'" It is the publican's prayer that Pip repeats over Magwitch: "O Lord, be merciful to him a sinner!" (*GE*, 457).

In changing "me" to "him," neither Pip nor Dickens misquotes scripture.

Pip is not identifying with the Pharisee. Instead, he utters a prayer for Magwitch in which he impersonates the publican on Magwitch's behalf. "I knew that there were no better words that I could say beside his bed," Pip declares (*GE*, 457).[21] Christ's parable contrasts the Pharisee's snobbish exaltation of self with the publican's humility. Putting himself in Magwitch's place and praying humbly as his proxy, Pip reveals a sound understanding of Christ's teachings; he also shows empathy with the lowly—with an ex-convict in *Great Expectations* and with the publican, the victim of snobbery in Luke's gospel. Compared to the hints about her parentage in Pen's self-serving letter to Blanche, the information Pip confides to Magwitch regarding Estella relieves a dying man's anxiety by assuaging a lingering guilt. In no way does it preclude Pip from reciting over Magwitch a prayer that signifies the new humility in them both. Pip administers not the coup de grâce that Pen's letter to Blanche resembles, but "a sort of viaticum" (HH, 67–68).

Pen's letter to Blanche refers to his discovery of her closest relationship as "a painful circumstance" that "having once befallen" is "as fatal and irreparable as that shock which overset honest Alnaschar's porcelain and shattered all his hopes beyond the power of mending" (*Pen*, 2:348–49). Pen alludes to "The Tale of the [Barber's] Fifth Brother," Shéhérazade's yarn for the one-hundred-sixty-second night of *The Arabian Nights*. With his meager inheritance of "a hundred dirhams," Alnaschar buys a large basket of glass to resell "at a profit." Putting his wares on display, he daydreams of buying ever larger quantities, reselling them also until he has enough money for a fine house, slaves, and horses. Once rich, he expects to marry the vizier's daughter, schooling his regal bride to accept him as "her master." Should she offer him a cup of wine without being duly obsequious, he will "'kick her with [his] foot like that.' So saying, he kicked with his foot and knocked over the basket of glass, . . . and everything in it was broken" (*AN*, 282–84).[22]

Dickens parodied Pen's reference to the breakage of Alnaschar's porcelain from *The Arabian Nights* as Pip's allusion to the collapse of Misnar's pavilion in *The Tales of the Genii*. Only the latter story, as a paradigm for Pip's career, supplied a true antithesis to the enchantments of *Cinderella*. Indeed, Dickens retorted, Alnaschar's story serves as Pen's analogue for the ruination of Blanche's prospects rather than his own. Pen's disappointments with Blanche and Altamont are merely so much broken glass compared to Pip's with Estella and Magwitch; the latter recall the sudden caving in of a sultan's palace. Pip's is the more cautionary tale by the same amount that the collapse of a royal pavilion exceeds the overturning of a basket of glassware.

Thackeray saw himself as "the Historian of Snobs," his country's greatest "Snobographer" (*BS*, 134), but Dickens thrust himself into this role in place of his allegedly less qualified rival. *Great Expectations,* Dickens proposed, was the realistic history of snobbery: in terms of Pip alone—that is, leaving aside Magwitch, Estella, and Miss Havisham—it depicted snobbery's beginnings, growth, consequences, and, above all, cure. Mr. Pirrup's self-lacerating autobiography was the superior snobography, the true inside story, not the omniscient narrator's satiric yet forgiving biography of Arthur Pendennis. Which is more reliable, Dickens asked, Mr. Pirrip's damaging disclosures, or Thackeray's awkward pretense at internal veracity: "As all this is taken from Pen's own confessions, . . . the reader may be assured of the truth of every word of it" (*Pen,* 1:189)?[23] For history and biography, Dickens advised, readers should peruse *Great Expectations,* not *The Book of Snobs* for one and *Pendennis* (or *A Day's Ride*) for the other.

Pendennis is steeped in nostalgia for one's younger self. Because neither the tragic nor comic in Thackeray's fiction is virile enough, Dickens contended, each vitiates the other. Having expatiated, for example, on Pen's idleness, pleasure seeking, and indifferent study of the law, Thackeray marvels at his alter ego's "condescension" and "impertinence" yet typically remarks: "[T]here is something almost touching in that early exhibition of simplicity and folly" (*Pen,* 1:304). Pen's is forever the arrogance of "a young prince in disguise" (*Pen,* 1:304), the role Potts is eager to play for Mrs. Keats (*ADR,* 199). But when Mr. Pirrup recalls how Pip told Biddy he was "good enough" for her if not for Estella (*GE,* 127), the retrospective is painfully funny, not "touching." Pip's arrogance, hardly princely, belongs to an upstart for whom life is preparing a comedown.

"Knowing how mean the best of us is," Thackeray says in conclusion, "let us give a hand of charity to Arthur Pendennis, with all his faults and shortcomings" (*Pen,* 2:394). To Pen a helping hand is extended; in Dickens's parody, Pip extends one to Estella. "I took her hand in mine," Pip ends his story, "and we went out of the ruined place" (*GE,* 480). Pen needs guidance, but a truly matured Pip appoints himself Estella's guide to a fallen world. One admirer likens Thackeray's narrative tone in the final lines to "the mellow wisdom of the Old Fogy,"[24] but the impression created, laughs Dickens, is one of facile homecoming. A failed tragicomedian whose social criticism lacks gravity but whose comedy is too melancholic, Thackeray, says Dickens, welcomes Pen to the club of human frailty where all is forgiven, just as Potts, Pen's feebler clone yet again in this regard, is summoned to permanent domestic bliss in Wales.

Chapter 4
David Copperfield

Like *Pendennis,* Michael Lund has noted, *David Copperfield* is a lengthy bildungsroman whose hero survives youthful infatuation to become a successful writer with an angelic wife (ML, 77). Both novels, Carol Hanberry MacKay agrees, "detail the growth into maturity of young men who become writers"; they "'develop' through a series of romantic interests, and each finally gets a second chance at marital happiness with a sister-figure" (CHM, 242).

In Victorian fictions, however, apparent similarity can mask revaluations that reach to the core. Mark Cronin has argued that *David Copperfield* is a "response" to *Pendennis* in which Dickens "corrects" Thackeray's portrait of the developing artist (MCr, 216). As a burgeoning author, Copperfield exemplifies diligence; contrary to Pen and by implication, Thackeray, Copperfield is never arrogant or half-hearted. Lever, it follows, depressed Dickens as an egregious ramification of Thackeray's poor authorial attitude. Neither rival, Dickens complained, took the artist's vocation seriously or sufficiently appreciated art's capacity to stimulate reform.

In 1860 and 1861, Dickens capitalized on similarities between *David Copperfield* and *Pendennis.* He updated his life story to render both novels obsolete. Thanks to the many parallels between his bildungsroman and Thackeray's, Dickens enjoyed the luxury of parodically revising the former at the expense of the latter.[1] The more he toned down his earlier stocktaking, the more he also subtracted from Thackeray's autobiographical novel. In effect, he questioned the very idea of presenting one's life as a success story. Without seeming to renege, Dickens distanced himself from an increasingly visible rival by firmly separating himself from his earlier fictional incarnation.

For instance, Dickens initially rewrote the Pendennis–Mrs. Pendennis–Laura triangle as the less pleasant threesome of Steerforth–Mrs. Steerforth–Rosa Dartle; then he redid both trios as Pip–Miss Havisham–Estella, thereby also darkening the fairy tale relationship of David to Aunt Betsey and Agnes. In *Great Expectations,* Dickens finally hit upon the definitive parody for the configuration in both *David Copperfield* and *Pendennis* of Cinderella-like hero, fairy godmother, and Cinderella-like heroine. He hoped that he had sabotaged this Cinderella motif permanently.

Thackeray contrasted Pen with Warrington and Foker, who are drawn respectively to Laura and Blanche. Dickens provided David Copperfield with less appealing "shadow selves" (CHM, 245): James Steerforth and Uriah Heep, who are attracted to Emily and Agnes. More beleaguered than either Pendennis or Copperfield, Pip must deal with Orlick and Drummle, who pursue Biddy and Estella. Thackeray's contrasts remain straightforwardly Fieldingesque, but in *Great Expectations* Dickens invented a protomodern set of foils; variants of Frankenstein's monster, Pip's alter egos are Mr. Hyde-like projections of his inner self.

Pendennis is the story of Thackeray's younger self as told by a friendly biographer who resembles his older self. Thackeray subdivided himself into Pen and Warrington: portraits of the artist as a young man and as a not-so-young man (*TW*, 45, 51); he was able to depute his own unfortunate marriage to Warrington, thus procuring a happy ending for Pen.[2] Like Thackeray's kindly disposed biographer, a nostalgic Copperfield reviews his life and career with "only a modicum of self-mockery" (CHM, 245). Throughout *David Copperfield,* "fantasy elements pervade the very infrastructure" (CHM, 243); Copperfield may smile at his younger self for comparing life to "a great fairy story" (*DC*, 235), but the eponymous author "playfully indulges in self-conscious fairy tale ascriptions and openly invokes the 'enchantments' that captivated him" (CHM, 245).

Instead of Warrington's unhappiness assuring Pen's good fortune, instead of Agnes to compensate David for Dora, a not-so-young Pip is offered a second chance with a faded femme fatale. Dickens darkens the mood of an entire mode—he questions the way of the world as it is presented in earlier bildungsromans, his own and Thackeray's especially. Copperfield is still a more commendable portrait of an artist than Pendennis; besides reexamining the efficacy of Copperfield's goals and stamina, however, *Great Expectations* repudiates the Cinderella motifs that *Copperfield* and *Pendennis* share with so many reputedly realistic fictions of the age.

In *Great Expectations,* Dickens revokes the cordiality that pervades Thackeray's retrospective by overruling a similar attitude in Copperfield's. Incessant self-scrutiny replaces David's willingness to review his life in pleasant fairy tale terms. Mr. Pirrip's autobiography transforms the bildungsroman into an unsparing revaluation of one's past that is judgmental, therefore true. Pip's autobiography is as much a "fairy story" as David's, but it comes to resemble the Misnar tale, not *Cinderella.* Pip's false hopes, delusional aspirations symbolic of society's in general, collapse upon him as suddenly as the sultan's deadly ceiling crushes the usurpers who personify inordinate expectation.

David Copperfield and *Pendennis,* Pip's memoir objects, gratify too readily the expectancy of positive resolution indigenous to the bildungsroman, but not to life itself. They reveal the genre's fundamental resemblance to a Cinderella story in which the protagonist, aged twenty-something, does one or more of the following: achieves total self-awareness, discovers a satisfying vocation, comfortably inherits, consummates a felicitous marriage.[3] In contrast, Pip's sudden realization that he is a forgery converts an idle Londoner contemplating marriage into a celibate clerk self-exiled to Egypt. Unlike Copperfield's, the bildungsroman that Pip writes revaluates the genre's essentially benevolent (that is, comic) orientation.

It also follows the protagonist well into his thirties. Copperfield reaches twenty-one in chapter 43 when his story is two-thirds over; he is twenty-six or -seven at its close and only thirty-seven when he writes. Pip is twenty-three when Magwitch reappears, already thirty-four in the revised ending, and in his fifties when Mr. Pirrip publishes.[4] *Great Expectations* is the only bildungsroman of its day that one may call a tragicomedy; it goes on long enough (and is written with sufficient retrospective) for Pip to learn that life is one too.

Pen and Copperfield acquire circumspection, as did their antecedents such as Tom Jones. Pip achieves a superior maturity, Dickens argues, because through failure he also learns humility. To be truly mature, Dickens insisted, one must expect losses and disappointments to outnumber successes, invariably precluding or tempering them. Pip copes with this fact of life. *Pendennis,* Dickens charged, borders on vindication (Pen's), just as *A Day's Ride* opts for Potts's exoneration. Fundamentally different from these apologias and more scrupulous than Copperfield's, Pip's bildungsroman qualifies as a record of self-reclamation. Writing it, a therapeutic act as well as a service to society, indicates that Pip's recovery from his era's Cinderella complex has been thorough and lasting.[5]

Great Expectations should not be read as *Copperfield*'s companion piece but as its replacement, Dickens's "mature revision of the progress of a young man in the world" (HH, 64). Until that "young man" grows old enough to realize how illusory advancement can be in a tragicomic world of ups and downs wherein joy and sorrow tread upon each other's heels, he remains unformed. Indeed, largely because the once-heartless Estella has also learned what it means to be "bent and broken ... into a better shape" (*GE,* 520–21), Pip recognizes his destined counterpart in ways that Agnes, a guardian angel above life's fray, can never stand to David.

David Copperfield expresses Dickens's self-confidence as a novelist just coming into full possession of his powers. Yet once Dickens had written *Bleak House, Hard Times, Little Dorrit,* and *A Tale of Two Cities, Great Expectations* voiced the successful artist's "anguished perplexity" (EM, 245). Discontented personally at decade's end, he had grown increasingly pessimistic about social and historical process. Using Mr. Pirrip's review of his younger self's mistakes as the new paradigm for what bildungsromans should do, Dickens substantially lowered Copperfield's sense of arrival and accomplishment.

Dickens's second first-person narrative may be read as "a brutal self-appraisal" of his own passion for status, money, and Ellen Ternan (N, 10). Still uneasy about his lower-middle-class origins, Dickens doubted whether writing successful fiction had made him a gentleman. Upon reinspection, he concluded that an all-out drive for rank, wealth, and success—on his part and his country's—was not inherently worthwhile. To this revaluing of his age's expectations, especially its beliefs in romantic love and upward social mobility, indispensable to both the Cinderella complex and the Victorian bildungsroman, Dickens brought an intense personal involvement foreign to Lever and Thackeray.

George Bernard Shaw emphasized the increasingly "black" background against which Dickens set his novels after his "ignorant middle class optimism" collapsed. When he "lost his belief in bourgeois society and with it his lightness of heart he had neither an economic Utopia nor a credible religion to hitch on to," Shaw concluded; unable to endorse Christ or Marx, "his world became a world of great expectations cruelly disappointed" ("P," xxi).[6] Actually, Dickens found his most fruitful subject after his optimism collapsed: a sense of life as a tragicomic phenomenon in which most outlooks, his own as well as those of rival novelists, needed revising.

Dickens informed John Forster that he had "read *David Copperfield* again the other day ... to be quite sure [he] had fallen into no unconscious repetitions" (*PL*, 9:325). Margaret Cardwell thinks this refresher worked: "There are no repetitions of *David Copperfield* in Pip's story" (*GE*, xx). But the operative word is surely "unconscious"; *Great Expectations* coruscates with premeditated revaluations of themes, scenes, and characters from *Copperfield*.

If Dickens desired to expunge "unconscious repetitions," he did a sloppy job. Both novels allude to rope-walks, fetters, Quintus Roscius Gallus, the battery, busy bees, and the Piazza Hotel in Covent Garden, to name just a few overlaps. When David enters Rochester/Chatham in search of Aunt Betsey's house, he observes that the mastless hulks in the "muddy river" are "like Noah's arks" (*DC*, 160); a similar comparison occurs to Pip at the end of chapter 5 when Magwitch is returned to an offshore prison that looks "like a wicked Noah's ark" (*GE*, 41).

Only the reviewer for *The Saturday Review* (20 July 1861) opined that *Great Expectations* presents "an entirely different set of incidents" from those in *David*

Copperfield: "[T]he power of novel creation which Mr. Dickens possesses is shown in nothing more than that he should have succeeded in keeping two stories of a boy's childhood so wholly distinct." Otherwise, the consensus runs against Cardwell. Shaw acknowledged Dickens's intent to revise "the favorite child David" as both "a work of art" and "a vehicle of experience" ("P," v-vi).[7] Fred Kaplan called *Great Expectations* Dickens's "ultimate reworking of the story of his own life" (K, 432). Unless a bildungsroman presented growth and development tragicomically, Dickens came to doubt its veracity as an art work and a "vehicle of experience" (that is, a realistic text).

The parodic revisions of *David Copperfield* carried out within *Great Expectations* are typical of hidden rivalries permeating nineteenth-century fictions: a counterstatement within every major statement, a rebuttal in every assertion. *Great Expectations* is unusual in that much of the recrimination it contains is self-inflicted by a novelist who claimed not to be repeating himself; one listens not just to Mr. Pirrip reconsidering Pip but also, through a redoing of himself as Pip, to Dickens's reservations about his self-portrait as Copperfield.

Both novels open with what Harry Stone considers "a fairy-tale visitation" ("FTO," 324), but Magwitch proves a more terrifying fairy godmother than David's formidable great-aunt. His apparition is a comment on her manifestation as well as a parody of Cinderella's fairy godmother's. Only *Copperfield* expressly alludes to Shakespeare's play, but both visitors—aunt and convict—recall "the ghost in Hamlet" (*DC,* 16). Like David, Pip is fascinated by his father's grave, abused as an orphan, and presented with two women to choose from. One may also parallel Aunt Betsey with Miss Havisham, Traddles with Herbert, Micawber's Australia with Magwitch's,[8] the butcher boy whom David fights with Trabb's boy, Barkis and Peggotty with Wemmick and Miss Skiffins, Mr. Murdstone's math problems with the sums Pumblechook imposes on Pip, Biddy with Agnes, and David's mother with Mrs. Pocket, until the list of repetitions and variations threatens to overflow the page. Dickens's title may be a byproduct of rereading *David Copperfield:* having become Mr. Wickfield's partner, Uriah Heep asks if David has heard "of a change in my expectations" (*DC,* 322).

Revaluations of *Copperfield* in *Great Expectations* outnumber "precise parallels"; the latter alert readers to the former and often turn into them, bringing about a "change in perspective" that makes *Great Expectations* "the mirror image of *Copperfield*" (ME, 146–47). Thus *David Copperfield* explores the consequences of unwise marital choices—Aunt Betsey's, David's mother's to Murdstone, David's to Dora. In *Great Expectations,* Joe, Mr. Pocket, Estella, and Miss Havisham have unhappy marriage experiences, but Pip's history, a sociologically pertinent critique of mid-nineteenth-century England's entire value system, transforms a bittersweet memoir into a satire on expectancy in general, not just in marriage.

Having been married to "a husband younger than herself" who was "strongly suspected of having beaten" her (*DC,* 10–11), Aunt Betsey envisions the establishment of a female protectorate. She not only expects David's mother to give birth to a girl but also plans to be the child's "godmother." "There must be no trifling with *her* affections," Aunt Betsey declares: her niece "must be well brought up, and well guarded from reposing any foolish confidences"; "I must make that *my* care," she vows (*DC,* 14). But Aunt Betsey's expectations are foiled almost immediately when David's mother delivers a nephew instead of a niece.

Aunt Betsey recast as a vengeance-seeking snob, Miss Havisham is also disappointed twice on widely separated occasions: not just by Compeyson, who swindled and jilted her, but cruelly by Estella, who cannot love her. The owner of Satis House is a darker, psychologically more complicated study of baffled hopes than David's aunt, who is merely the victim of her own "undisciplined heart" (*DC,* 558). She overcomes marital disaster to become David's "second mother" (*DC,* 297), an appellation chillingly revisited when the newly returned Magwitch declares to Pip, "I'm your second father" (*GE,* 317).

Using Estella, Miss Havisham will trample men. To repay a man-made society she considers a heartless monstrosity, Miss Havisham creates a heartless monster. Ironically, the young woman's ingratitude includes Miss Havisham, much as a refined Pip finds Magwitch repulsive. David's regard for Aunt Betsey never wavers, but in Pip's autobiography, giving and taking have been perverted; instead of a protective fairy godmother and the thankful recipient of her kindness, vengeful benefactors victimize ungrateful Cinderellas.

"You would like to be a lady?" David asks; "Em'ly looked at me, and laughed and nodded 'yes.'" Young David considers her elevation "not at all improbable" (*DC,* 38). Emily's ambition to be genteel leads to her downfall yet is only indirectly tragic for David and without any saving comic grace. Steerforth's betrayal of Copperfield's childhood sweetheart seems Byronic, not Victorian. When the above conversation is replayed in *Great Expectations,* with Pip confiding his hopes to Biddy, the young snob has contracted the social virus of the day: he personifies the era's Cinderella complex, which Dickens condemns as self-promotion through self-deception. In effect, David condones Emily's fantasies, but Pip is pulled up short by Biddy's friendly admonitions. To his avowal, "I want to be a gentleman," she replies, "Oh, I wouldn't, if I was you!" (*GE,* 126). Although Biddy gives Pip the good advice that David should have imparted to Emily, Pip's Cinderella-like aspirations, more consequential than Emily's, reverberate nationally as a satiric commentary on unrealistic cultural myths that glorify rising.

Repetition becomes revaluation when Dickens redoes David's stint with Murdstone and Grinby in terms of Pip's apprenticeship at the forge. In the warehouse, Copperfield sinks to labeling, corking, and packing wine bottles; he experiences a "sense of unmerited degradation" that rivals Cinderella's (*DC*, 148). David's "hopes of growing up to be a learned and distinguished man" are "crushed" (*DC*, 137). Similarly, Pip, "restlessly aspiring discontented," toils "against the grain" (*GE*, 107). The difference is that Copperfield, like Dickens in Warren's Blacking Warehouse, knows that he is below his station, hence translatable to higher ground, whereas the maturer Dickens is suspicious of the phenomenon of rising itself; through Pip, he expresses doubts about the merit, permanence, and above all, satisfaction to be found therein, individually or nationally. Realizing that the "influence" of his expectations on his character "was not all good," Pip ruefully concludes: "I should have been happier and better if I had never seen Miss Havisham's face, and had risen to manhood content to be partners with Joe in the honest old forge" (*GE*, 271).

Products of "chronic uneasiness," reflections such as this keep Pip awake in London in the middle of the night. Obviously, he cannot return to being a cinder girl. Being unable to go back, Dickens realizes, adds to the riser's discomfort. Pip is impressed, albeit belatedly, with the honesty of his former lot and asserts that he could have "risen" satisfactorily in it, "to manhood" that is, rather than gentility. That he might have been not only "happier" but "better," Mr. Pirrip has Pip recognize, is the final rub. Unlike Copperfield's, Pip's bygone days as a cinder girl take on a modicum of nostalgic appeal.

When young Dickens worked in the window of the Blacking Warehouse, the real-life experience behind Copperfield's assignment at Murdstone and Grinby's, he was ashamed to be seen by his father.[9] Pip's greatest dread is to be seen by Estella at his "grimiest and commonest"—with "black face and hands" from "doing the coarsest part" of his job (*GE*, 108). Having misconstrued Estella for a genuine princess, Pip fears that her gaze through "one of the wooden windows" (*GE*, 108) at the forge will expose him as a hopeless pretender, a cinder girl in perpetuity. In 1850, *Cinderella* is a viable analogue for Copperfield's plight; ten years later, the imagined presence of Estella, herself a pseudo-Cinderella, reduces Pip to a grimy imposture in his own eyes.

Pip's fear of being discovered at manual labor seems irrational inasmuch as Estella never exhibits the slightest inclination to visit the forge. But it reveals that Pip, unlike young Dickens and Copperfield previously, is plagued by a fundamental sense of unworthiness; like a dirtier, secret self, it must be kept hidden. Cinderella is relegated to servant's duties by a stepmother determined to conceal her stepdaughter's superior qualities. In contrast, the parodic revaluator puts the situation the other way around: although a Cinderella lies concealed within the fairy tale's cinder girl, Pip's anxieties suggest that an ineradicable cinder girl lurks within every person or society masquerading as a Cinderella.

Unable any longer to tolerate Murdstone and Grinby's, Copperfield goes in search of a fairy godmother. He arrives at Dover looking every inch the cinder girl: "from head to foot . . . [he is] powdered . . . with chalk and dust" (*DC,* 167). Like Cinderella, he is tattered, dirty, without a pallet; but Aunt Betsey, acting on Mr. Dick's advice, has her nephew washed, freshly clothed, and put to bed.

Having taken "a look at Newgate" with Wemmick while awaiting Estella's London visit (*GE,* 259), Pip feels "contaminated," as dirty as David was upon reaching Aunt Betsey's. Stained by a "soiling consciousness," he tries to "beat the prison *dust* off his clothes and feet (*GE,* 263; italics added). This dust, one feels, is a reminder of the forge as well as of Magwitch. Pip cannot shake off either. Origins and formative experiences abide with Pip regardless of his upward movement, which, in consequence, seems superficial and contradicts David's fumigation at Aunt Betsey's.

Copperfield falls from bliss. Deprived of his mother and Peggoty, he is sentenced to cinder girl drudgery at Murdstone and Grinby's but finds a fairy godmother in Aunt Betsey. Pip is cursed with *two* fairy godmothers; although he escapes from a soiling servitude at the forge, he discovers that he has been misled by Miss Havisham and misused by Magwitch, both of whom seem as interested in revenge as in benefaction.[10] In *David Copperfield,* Harry Stone has argued, Dickens's "own life becomes a fairy tale" ("FTO," 324); the novel "is really a rags-to-riches story" in Monroe Engel's opinion (ME, 151). But from Aunt Betsey to Miss Havisham, from Emily's desire to be a lady to Pip's craving for gentility, from Copperfield's career as a vindication of the success story to Pip's as a parody of it—the direction in all instances is the same: through conscious, parodic repetition toward tragicomic instances of foiled expectation; these downgrade Dickens's previous bildungsroman by subverting Victorian society's infatuation with *Cinderella.*

Jerome Buckley has argued that *David Copperfield* established the rules for the nineteenth-century bildungsroman in English (*DC,* x).[11] One must add that *Great Expectations* systematically reconsiders them. It is as if Mr. Pirrip were impressing upon Copperfield that the format itself is presumptuous; even when a bildungsroman offers "four splendid 'retrospects'" (*DC,* viii), its pontificatings on *love, maturity,* and above all, *success* are likely to sound naive to the author's fully matured self. As has been implied throughout this chapter, Dickens's anti-*Copperfield* axioms are: 1) failure is a better teacher than success; 2) age is a better judge than youth; 3) friendship is a more reliable bond than passionate love.

The "broad outlines of a typical Bildungsroman" (JHB, 17) are not unlike a Cinderella story. A child of sensibility, either orphaned or alienated from the father, escapes the social and intellectual constraints of a provincial environment; in the big city, he survives a debasing love affair, replacing it with an exalting one. Despite much struggle and misdirection, he acquires a vocation and formulates a philosophy of life. Copperfield, for example, becomes his own narrative's hero because he discovers his identity as man and artist; he learns to discipline his emotional and moral life. His is the story of spiritual integrity achieved—in short, "the making of a gentleman" (JHB, 20).[12]

In Pip's bildungsroman, the hero's rise and fall recalls the tale of Misnar's pavilion, a story about ambition building toward collapse, not apotheosis. Pip alienates himself from Joe, his surrogate father, only to be horrified when a returned transport declares himself the young man's benefactor or "second father" (*GE,* 317); not only does the orphan have *two* substitute fathers but he abandons the truly gentle and benevolent one for a vengeful, violence-prone ex-convict who resembles Frankenstein's monster. Pip ends up departing the big city (London) for a decade of humble clerking in Egypt, the biblical country symbolic of exile. Instead of moving from a debasing love affair with Estella to an exalting one with Biddy, Pip allows the first to rule out the second. Eventually, he attempts to redeem the debasing affair by converting it into something more creditable.

Great Expectations chronicles both the making and unmaking of a gentleman. Fortunately, the latter event, a climactic catastrophe, is followed by Pip's remaking of himself on sounder principles. His is ultimately a tale of moral and emotional rehabilitation; nevertheless, the bulk of it remains something no bildungsroman ever professes to be: the diary of a failure, an ex-snob's account of expectations that turned sour.

Dickens expands the "darker space" that *David Copperfield* located between boyhood and maturity (JHB, 29), repositioning the crucial phase between the attainment of one's majority (the conventional idea of adulthood) and full-bodied maturity, which arrives later for Pip. His reformation takes place mostly in the novel's "Third Stage"—*after* his twenty-first birthday, when thanks to Magwitch's return and recapture, everything collapses: instead of promotion, inheritance, marriage, Pip must forego Estella and renounce life as a London gentleman, losing Biddy too in the process.

Mr. Pirrip lectures practitioners of the bildungsroman that to be truly useful, novels about one's growth and development should be composed by writers closer in age to Prospero than to Romeo. The novel of a young person's maturation need not presume a youthful progenitor. Its author, unheroic and deromanticized, should eschew self-glorification; he should pen an anatomy, not an advertisement, much less an apologia. Most important, it must be a sociological document that relates the hero's shortcomings to society's, examining each in light of the other as both cause and effect: Pip's autobiography as a case history of the era's Cinderella complex, for example.

A policy statement underlies Dickens's uniqueness in having fathered a second bildungsroman. After setting the conditions for the format, he felt compelled by experience to revaluate them ten years later. Combined with a rereading of *David Copperfield*, novels such as *Pendennis* and *A Day's Ride* convinced him that the fictionalization of one's "season of youth" (Goethe's term) should be delayed until it can be entrusted to one's older self—someone like Mr. Pirrip rather than David Copperfield—and told from a tragicomic perspective as a realistic work of social criticism.

"David's progress," John P. McGowan has written, "leads him from a childhood 'romanticism' toward a staunch reliance on and, at times, stoical acceptance of 'the reality principle,' a movement thematized as the maturation of an 'undisciplined heart'" (JPM, 3). True enough, yet David's is always a success story, "pointing upward" from start to final line (*DC*, 737). Pip learns harder lessons in an ironic progress that actually consists of a series of setbacks: by the penultimate paragraph in chapter 58, he is thoroughly bankrupt—no money, no girl, no patent of gentility, no country. Having "sold" his remaining possessions to appease creditors, Pip states, he "quitted England" (*GE*, 475).

Great Expectations, one decides, is an "adult" bildungsroman, Dickens's parodic "correction to the conventional optimism" (ME, 168) that Copperfield's autobiography, despite its hero's toil and tribulations, never seriously interrogates. "As Dickens' life of outward success in the fifties turned more to ashes in his mouth," Angus Wilson has speculated, "he must have come to a profound disgust with David's self-satisfaction and snobbery if not with his own" (AW, 528). Pip's life expresses Dickens's discovery of reality's principles: fortune is not the way to happiness; no princess awaits. Moreover, romantic love is an even greater disappointment than money and success, twin vacuities, which Pip, like the younger Dickens and the country at large, foolishly deifies.

In *Great Expectations*, Dickens all but replaces romantic love—the prize that is awarded to heroes in conventional bildungsromans—with the ideal of friendship, a bond that may include physical passion but is more dependable than one reliant chiefly upon it. Pip and Estella are to continue as "friends," whether together or "apart" (*GE*, 480). That is the smartest way to continue, Dickens insists. In the revised ending, when Estella coaxes Pip to tell her that they "are friends," she completes his education, espousing the liberating superiority of friendship between man and woman as opposed to passionate longing, which can be both obsessive and possessive.

As a necessary corollary to the paramountcy of friendship, *Great Expectations* urges forgiveness. Dickens substitutes change of heart for the disciplining of that organ so important in *David Copperfield*. Pip, Magwitch, Miss Havisham, and even Estella soften—indeed, melt—contrary to David, who takes Annie Strong's advice to get tougher emotionally (*DC*, 577–78). Most heroes in bildungsromans must toughen in order to succeed. Put simply, *David Copperfield* advocates hardening, disciplining, strengthening; as its parodic revaluation,

Great Expectations champions softening for its hero and his associates. Mr. Pirrip does not relent toward snobbish characters; Thackeray and Lever were said to be guilty of that. But a softening by the characters themselves is hailed as a prerequisite for a world with fewer snobs and closer friends.

Just as Miss Havisham begs Pip to forgive her, he pleads with Biddy and Joe: "[P]ray tell me, both, that you forgive me!" (*GE*, 475).[13] Like Miss Havisham, who has not been Pip's true friend, he has been disloyal to Joe. In the revised ending, Pip is struck by "the saddened softened light" in Estella's "once proud eyes" (*GE*, 478). A plea for mercy is implicit in her declaration that she has given "the remembrance" of Pip's love "a place in [her] heart" (*GE*, 479). Presumably, she will also weaken in her resolve to "take leave" of him, for weakening on such matters is positive.

The most impressive softenings involve a hardened ex-convict and a supercilious snob. As Pip offers the newly returned Magwitch a drink, he observes "with amazement" that his unwelcome visitor's eyes "were full of tears" and reports himself "softened by the softened aspect of the man" (*GE*, 314). In a novel that features revenge but favors relenting, only Orlick and Drummle, Pip's foils, never weaken; the latter, who abuses Estella, dies "from an accident consequent on ill-treatment of a horse" (*GE*, 477), whereas we last see the former attempting to throttle Pip.[14]

Going further, one may assert that Pip, prompted by Estella, signals his maturity by proposing marriage but calling it uninterrupted friendship—one to be enjoyed without partings. The novel's "best relationships," according to Bert Hornback, "are those between Pip and Joe, Pip and Herbert, Joe and Biddy, and finally Pip and Estella"; upon relationships such as these, Dickens "proposed that we should build our lives" (BH, 135). Strangely, the Pip–Magwitch friendship, arguably the most important bonding in the novel, is absent from Hornback's list. But Pip triumphs in our esteem because ultimately he manages to model his relationship with Magwitch on his friendship with Joe; he suggests for himself and Estella something similar to the tie between Biddy and Joe or between himself and Herbert: not an exalting love in place of an earlier, debasing one but a partnership based on kindness and mutual support.

Asked by Estella in the second ending if he does well living abroad, Pip responds: "I work pretty hard for a sufficient living, and therefore—Yes, I do well!" (*GE*, 479) The dash after "therefore" is intriguing. Either Pip was about to regret not being as affluent as his expectations once promised, or else, in an epiphanic moment, he equates "hard" work for "sufficient" profit with doing well. That he gets along, accepts his humble lot, and does all the good he can without daydreaming of anything more is a third possibility. Whichever the case, the dash sharply redirects Pip's response, negating remorse and regret in favor of facing things as they are, while looking to the future without undue expectancy. Compared to Copperfield, Pip seems older, chastened, more experienced; nevertheless, he is looking forward instead of back.

In the "Last Retrospect," Copperfield writes "far into the night" (*DC*, 737) but does so indoors, where he seems cozily content, perhaps complacent. Mr. Pirrip's finale takes place outside with the moon on the rise: two greatly disappointed individuals, each a failed Cinderella, meet again in the ruins of Satis House and find in each other encouragement and support to make another start. The earlier bildungsroman ends comically—that is, happily, all of a piece; the later, revaluative one concludes tragicomically with mixed feelings. The "broad expanse of tranquil light" (*GE*, 480) is not uninviting, but the sense of uncertainty is stronger outdoors. This is a fallen world in which the future holds more challenges, fewer assurances, than the domestic haven that David has regained inside with Agnes.

Having entertained Mr. Peggoty throughout his visit from Australia, David and Agnes part "from him aboardship" when he sails for home; "and we shall never part from him more, on earth," Copperfield adds as the penultimate chapter ends (*DC*, 734). In the last chapter, David dismisses—in effect, parts from—the rest of "the shadows" (characters, scenes, memories) from which he has fashioned his novel. Pip's concluding line, "I saw no shadow of another parting" from Estella, (*GE*, 480), conflates and revalues key elements—partings, shadows—from the last two chapters of *David Copperfield*.

David is definitive regarding Mr. Peggoty and dismissive of his memories; less certain about Estella, Pip is nevertheless prognosticative rather than elegiac. He has learned a cautious expectancy. Consequently, although *Great Expectations* darkens *David Copperfield*, the later bildungsroman dispels shadows instead of dismissing them. Imagining himself on his deathbed, Copperfield expresses confidence in Agnes's salvific attendance at that parting moment. *Great Expectations* acknowledges that life is "ever so many partings welded together" (*GE*, 224), as Joe defined it, but concludes with Pip's hope that at least one of them can be deferred indefinitely.

Copperfield's life story could have been included among the hymns to self-advancement in Samuel Smiles's *Self-Help* (1859). Smiles declared that he wrote this manual for getting on "principally to illustrate and enforce the power of George Stephenson's great word—PERSEVERANCE" (*SS*, 222). With Dickens's approval, Copperfield "uses his native talents with earnest, *persevering* industry to win economic success and literary fame" (GBN, 796; italics added). Ten years later, for a society even more obsessed with getting ahead, an era overly inclined to equate material prosperity with salvation, Dickens corrected *David Copperfield* with *Great Expectations* by penning the autobiography of a failure.[15]

In the preface to the 1866 edition of *Self-Help*, Smiles would deny that "Failure" needs "its Plutarch as well as Success"[16]: "a record of mere failure . . . excessively depressing as well as uninstructive . . . ought [not] to be set before youth." People, Smiles insisted, "do not care to know about the general who lost his battles, the engineer whose engines blew up . . . the painter who never got beyond daubs . . ." (*SH*, vi–vii), or, one presumes, the London gentleman whose fortunes collapse after a Cinderella-like rise from apprenticeship in a village forge.

But the real need, as Dickens diagnosed it in 1860, was for an anti-Cinderella story. Mr. Pirrup's book about dealing with life's tragicomic disappointments is funny and "depressing" simultaneously, never "uninstructive." Not averse to being failure's Plutarch, Dickens scowled at Smiles's pernicious belief that one should only acknowledge popular, remunerative success. The more pressing assignment was to describe how one recovers moral balance after errant dreams collapse as suddenly as Misnar's pavilion in "the Eastern story" that Pip, a would-be Cinderella, belatedly recognizes as a truer analogue for his career (*GE*, 309).

Great Expectations replaced self-help stories about perseverance inevitably leading to wealth and titles with one that chronicled a young snob's defeat and self-reclamation. Pip's is a purely private victory yet a cultural imperative, Dickens insisted, in a country that wrongly considered its rise in the world on a par with Cinderella's, as if England's fortunes, like David's Agnes, were always "pointing upward" (*DC*, 737). Dickens alleged that Smiles and his ilk encouraged people to ignore the possibility of failing—indeed, to deny the existence of their own shortcomings—and to calculate self-worth chiefly in light of how far they had risen.[17]

Great Expectations should be read as Dickens's reconsideration of himself, an attempt to separate his second bildungsroman from his first and from bildungsromans it allegedly resembles, such as *Pendennis*. But Dickens camouflaged this parodic deflation by frowning on Smiles—by toning down the importance of "self-advancement popularized so effectively by men . . . such as Samuel Smiles" (DW, 200). Shrewdly, Dickens deflected onto *Self-Help* much of the embarrassing revaluation involved in redoing his "favourite child."[18]

Just as Dickens distanced himself from *David Copperfield* by rewriting *Pendennis*, he further reduced his earlier bildungsroman by disabling *Self-Help*. Through Pip's story, Dickens admitted that money, position, and success had proven less satisfying upon attainment than as Copperfield's goals. But he accomplished this self-disclosure by satirizing the materialistic "life objectives" (DA, 125) that *David Copperfield* shares with *Self-Help* and that both hold in common with *Cinderella*. Dickens darkens *Copperfield,* upends *Self-Help,* and contradicts *Cinderella* for being naive and unrealistic. Never the principal target, Smiles falls victim to an undeclared animus within a hidden rivalry; he is used to make Dickens's markdown of Copperfield's bildungsroman appear less self-incriminating. Whenever Smiles's text is mentioned over the next several pages, in one's mind the full inscription should read: *Self-Help* as stand-in for the rise of David Copperfield.

By Smilesian standards, Pip is definitely no success. Starting with nothing, Smiles's heroes build railroads, invent labor-saving machines, earn knighthoods, and above all, amass millions. Most of Pip's monies, technically Magwitch's, never reach his pockets; upon the ex-convict's capture, they are forfeited to the Crown. Pip also loses the two women in his life, so he leaves England emotionally impoverished as well as financially broke. In chapter 58, he winds up his affairs rapidly, as do countless failures in Victorian fiction, before fleeing to less expensive places:[19] "I sold all I had and put aside as much as I could, for a composition with my creditors," says Pip, "and I went out and joined Herbert" (*GE*, 475).

As "clerk to Clarriker & Co." (*GE*, 475), he begins to apply himself strenuously, although never with the results Copperfield enjoys or the Smilesian self-helper expects. His climb to a modest competency—"third in the Firm" (*GE*, 476)—is tedious rather than phenomenal; Mr. Pirrip awards it a one-paragraph summary. Whether a would-be Cinderella or the subject for a Smilesian anecdote promoting self-advancement, Pip cuts a sorry figure compared to Copperfield.

Replacing Copperfield's fall and rise with Pip's rise and fall, Dickens dismissed *Self-Help* as a collection of fairy tales; it had no more probity as a cultural commodity, he implied, than the *Cinderella*-driven fictions of the age, *Copperfield* included, for all of which *Great Expectations* serves as a parodic riposte. Dickens insulted Smiles by ridiculing *Self-Help*, a documentary of examples from real life, alongside Lever's *A Day's Ride* and Thackeray's *Pendennis*. Theirs are only two of many Victorian novels suffused with unrealistic Cinderella motifs whereby the protagonist rises like a Cinderella or marries a Cinderella-like heroine, sometimes both. To such motifs, Dickens insinuated, Smiles's sequence of unvarying success stories lent credence.

Born in Scotland the same year as Dickens, Dr. Samuel Smiles (1812–1904), despite a medical degree, spent his career as a railroad man—first as secretary to the Leeds and Thrisk Railway (1845), then in London in a similar capacity for the South-Eastern Railway (1854).[20] In 1859, he created a new genre: the self-help book, modern examples of which include Dale Carnegie's *How to Win Friends and Influence People* (1936) and Norman Vincent Peale's *The Power of Positive Thinking* (1955). *Self-Help* sold 20,000 copies within a year of publication and 160,000 in Smile's lifetime (*SS*, 223). In comparison, the first edition of *Great Expectations* (1,000 copies on 6 July 1861) was quickly followed by "four more impressions, called 'editions'": 750 copies on 5 and 17 August, 500 on 21 September, and another 750 on 30 October (*GE*, xiv), for a total of 3,750. In hardback, Smiles's sales outdistanced Dickens's.

Self-Help "voiced the dominant philosophy" of the prosperous mid-Victorian years between the bleak 1840s and the conflicted 1880s (AB, 15). These were the years of Dickens's harshest social critiques, especially the 1850s, which he greeted with the Smilesian *David Copperfield,* then satirized repeatedly in *Bleak House, Hard Times, Little Dorrit,* and *A Tale of Two Cities* prior to *Great Expectations.* In 1859, Smiles threatened to rival the greatest Victorian novelist, as if the former's uplifting anecdotes, not the latter's Juvenalian satires, were moral necessities for the age—a cheerleader, in short, instead of Cassandra.

Smiles became the "pious chronicler" of the men responsible for England's industrial greatness (*SS*, vii). In one anecdote after another— "busts" he called them, brief lives "rather than full-length portraits"—their stories pointed to "lessons" in "industry, perseverance, and self-culture" (*SH*, xi). Sir Richard Arkwright, for example, sprang "from the ranks" of laborers to invent the spinning machine for cotton (*SH*, 3); Josiah Wedgwood, inventor of Wedgwood ware, had barely learned to read and write when he was removed from school to begin life "as a 'thrower' in a small pottery" (*SH*, 105). These success stories proved to Smiles that individuals make their own destiny—everyone can "employ his life nobly" (*SH*, 396). "Impediments thrown in the way of human advancement," Smiles promised, "may for the most part be overcome by steady good conduct, honest zeal, activity, perseverance, and above all by a determined resolution to surmount difficulties, and stand up manfully against misfortune" (*SH*, 402).

Skillfully melding precepts and anecdotes, Smiles issued a rallying cry, a call to rise in the world. He reiterated his insistence that achievements must come to the deserving; that hard work will always be rewarded; that success does not demand genius or extraordinary powers but results from the determined use of ordinary capabilities[21]; that life, especially in Great Britain over the past century, should be read in terms of success stories, of which the country was a virtual compendium, saturated with foolproof strategies for readers to use in getting on. The effort to promulgate all this required nearly five hundred pages. By the time Smiles finished, he had added successful self-helpers from politics and the arts (Sir Robert Peel, Lord Brougham, Lytton, Disraeli) to his examples from industry and engineering (Watt, Arkwright, Heathcoat, and Stephenson).

Phenomenally influential as a social document, *Self-Help* inculcated the qualities Smiles considered keys to greatness; it set the age's social requirements for success: with cheerful prudence, one should exude energy and steadfast determination.[22] Given these attributes, Smiles pontificated, "adverse circumstances—even the barrenest poverty—cannot repress the human intellect and character, if it be determined to rise" (*SS*, x). In short, everyone can rise from cinder girl to princess. Contrary to the mature Dickens's tragicomic perspective, his indignant yet humorous acceptance of this world's shortcomings, the guru of self-help raised false expectations; he told readers they would never have to compromise, never have to settle for less, never be forced to come to terms with life's inadequacies or their own.

Beginning with his novel's second paragraph, Dickens parodically revalues self-help as an impractical philosophy whose essential heartlessness exceeds the Utilitarian's resolve to look out for number one; that is, enlightened self-interest. Self-help, Mr. Pirrip has Pip imply, is similar to survival of the fittest.

Pip refers to his "five little brothers . . . who gave up trying to get a living, exceedingly early in that universal struggle" (*GE*, 3). Doubtless this alludes to Darwin's theory of natural selection.[23] But contained in Mr. Pirrip's phrasing of Pip's childhood fantasy is a modest proposal that infant mortality be attributed to children's failure to persevere. "Trying to get a living" can simply mean trying to stay alive. Pip's siblings did not try hard enough to rise; hence Pip's peculiar impression that they "had all been born on their backs" and, being incurably lazy, "had never taken" their hands out of "their trousers-pockets" (*GE*, 3).

To debunk Smiles several times over, Dickens based *Great Expectations* on parodic variations of the popular psychologist's success stories. Three interwoven anti-Smilesian anecdotes, each allegedly truer to life, provide sly commentary on Smiles's simplistic panacea: Pip's undeserved rise and sudden comedown, Joe's refusal to raise himself or to be raised by Pip, and Magwitch's unsettling transformation from powerless convict to vengeful Croesus.

Riches furnish "no proof whatever of moral worth," Smiles frequently cautions (*SS*, 364), but Dickens considered such protestations disingenuous. Readers who expressed gratitude for *Self-Help* generally credited its precepts for their financial upswing: "I rose to be a partner," one wrote (*SS*, 226); "I became prosperous," reported another (*SS*, 228). To move up in the world, Pip is taught by society, means to improve one's social standing, augment one's income, and leave behind the less upwardly mobile (Joe, Biddy, Trabb's boy).

Pip's dramatic ascent, Dickens scoffed, is what most readers of *Self-Help* hoped would happen to them, with or without a strong effort on their part. Despite Smiles's disclaimers that "there is no royal road" to success and that "the True Gentleman" can be recognized by his "personal qualities," not by his "personal possessions" (*SH*, 345, 467), Dickens alleged that the stories in *Self-Help* were written to fuel extravagant hopes. The emphasis in Smilesian anecdotes on humble starts and exalted conclusions overshadowed the hard work in between by guaranteeing its efficacy, by normalizing apotheosis.

That large "numbers" of working-class people were "continually advancing and bettering themselves" (*SH*, 345)—an endless procession of "illustrious Commoners raised from humble to exalted positions by the power of application and industry" (*SH*, 238)—was not true, Dickens complained. Pretending that it *was* true only encouraged would-be Cinderellas such as Pip to expect miracles. Algernon Sydney Potts, Lever's picaresque hero, condemned "the stern discipline of an age" in which one "could only rise by successive steps" (*ADR*, 5–6). Dickens's superior parody of the self-helper as impatient overleaper, Pip expects to go directly from blacksmith's apprentice to master of Satis House, just as Cinderella went from drudge to princess in just a few days.

Throughout *Great Expectations,* Dickens equates the impulse toward self-improvement with base cravings for social and material advance. The idea is to become better off, not a better person. Although many of Smiles's heroes helped themselves by helping society, Pip is motivated by pure selfishness, a hunger for worldly success. His career exposes *Self-Help*'s underlying perversity: if real success and true gentility are not to be equated with riches and rank, Dickens asked, why exhort readers to persevere in order to rise in the world and become affluent? Given this internal inconsistency, Dickens dismissed Smiles's success manual's lip service to "Gentleness" and "self-respect" as a feeble afterthought (*SH*, 467, 478).[24]

To selfish individualism within a mechanical, material world, Dickens charged, Smiles had imparted a specious spiritual aura, as if getting ahead were the same as doing the Lord's work. Consequently, when Pip learns of his "great expectations" from Jaggers,[25] "the confidential agent of another" (*GE*, 137, 136), his Cinderella-like elevation has the combined force of an annunciation (a call from God) and an ascension into the heavens. By a hidden benefactor's grace, Pip is "immediately removed from his present sphere" (*GE*, 137) in order to pursue his true vocation: being genteel.

"The very endeavor to gain a firmer position in the world," Smiles maintained, "has a certain dignity in it, and tends to make a man stronger and better" (*SH*, 347). Yet in his saner moments, Pip, the self-tormenting would-be gentleman, considers himself a "lunatic" for wanting to rise in the world on Estella's account (*GE*, 128). He admits he "patronized" Biddy, his "first teacher" (*GE*, 142). Once he learns of his improved prospects, he finds his old room at the forge "mean" and "little," and rejoices that he will soon be "raised above [it] for ever" (*GE*, 144). In short, Dickens retaliated by portraying the Smilesian self-helper as the grandest snob in the nineteenth-century novel, a bigger instance of snobbery than Lever's Potts or Thackeray's Pen. *Self-Help, Cinderella,* and the unmerited self-satisfaction known as snobbery form a three-part nexus in Pip, with each incriminating the other two by association.[26]

"The spirit of self-help," Smiles asserted, is not only "the root of all genuine growth in the individual"; it also promotes "national vigour and strength" (*SH*, 1). From Smiles's perspective, rousing people to better themselves is the "highest patriotism and philanthropy" (*SH*, 3) because the entire nation benefits from "the personal improvement" of the men, women, and children composing it. In Dickens's counterstroke, the true patriot is the parodic revaluator, not Smiles, who is his country's snobbish celebrator. For the good of all parties, *Great Expectations* reveals that England is Pip writ large, just as Pip's aspirations epitomize the national failing (snobbery). A country of self-helpers, Dickens lashed out, is actually a nation of materialistic snobs. In the guise of self-help, Utilitarian self-interest holds sway, and the Cinderella-complex of deluded individuals like Pip abets and reflects a larger mania: the communal myth of Victorian England as modern history's greatest success story, a rise of unprecedented importance that made self-satisfaction irresistible and self-scrutiny unpatriotic.

The second ending, one concludes, better accords with Dickens's parody of Smiles. Judged by his criteria, Pip is insignificant, a small businessman home from Egypt on furlough. Gone in the revision is Estella's "personal fortune" (*GE*, 481), on which she and her Shropshire doctor live comfortably in the original conclusion. In the first ending, Pip and Estella go separate ways. When Dickens entertains second thoughts, however, they must help each other; friendship and forgiveness, cooperation and unselfishness, become more imperative than self-help, which is made to appear self-centered, as if one could improve one's character without relating to the needs of others.

Smiles conceded there was "no reason why the condition of the average workman should not be a useful, honourable, respectable, and happy one" (*SH*, 345); "nor is a life of manual employment . . . incompatible with high mental culture," he stipulated (*SH*, 33). Nevertheless, the implication throughout *Self-Help* is that higher is always better. Failure to rise, in short, is failure. More sanguine than Marx, Smiles foresaw "the healthy spirit of self-help" serving "to raise" workers "as a class . . . levelling them up to a higher and still advancing standard of religion, intelligence, and virtue" (*SH*, 346). Dickens ridiculed this pie-in-the-sky notion—an entire class emulating Cinderella—by having Joe Gargery, illiterate but a realist compared to Smiles, reject such nonsense, proving deaf to its meretricious allure.

When Pip proposes to teach Joe to read, the latter, contrary to Smilesian expectations, is reluctant: "Mrs. Joe mustn't see too much of what we're up to,"

Joe warns. "It must be done, as I may say, on the sly" (*GE*, 49). Mrs. Joe, says her husband, "would not be over partial to my being a scholar, for fear as I might rise. Like a sort of rebel" (*GE*, 50).

Absurd though it sounds, Joe rightly perceives self-help posing a threat to the community it supposedly invigorates. Predicated on rivalry and competition, self-help is inimical to friendships and a potential blow to Joe's conjugal bliss, such as it is. A society full of husbands striving to rise, Joe intuits, would be analogous to revolution, a widespread uprising that would introduce inequality and imbalance into countless marriages. Preferring self-sacrifice to self-help, Joe is a parody of the Smilesian hero: a good man of strong character who elects to stay put. He is never more eloquent than in response to the Smilesian query, "Why don't I rise?" (*GE*, 50)

Pip hopes "to do something for Joe" after he comes fully into his expectations, but the young snob fears his best friend may be intractable material: "[I]t would have been much more agreeable if [Joe] had been better qualified for a rise in station" (*GE*, 146). To Biddy he complains that the blacksmith's "manners" will make it difficult "to remove Joe into a higher sphere" (*GE*, 147). Snobbish though Pip's misgivings are, they seem real enough. Dickens parodies Smiles's naivete, the unrealistic assumption that self-made men become polished as they persevere, acquiring sophistication automatically as a byproduct of success.

Biddy objects that Joe "may be too proud to let any one take him out of a place that he is competent to fill, and fills well and with respect" (*GE*, 147).[27] In effect, Joe does not want to be Cinderella. Any individual with a true sense of pride, Dickens told Smiles, will imitate Joe and not the heroes in *Self-Help*. The justifiably proud individual takes pleasure in the place he or she occupies, instead of making his sense of self-worth dependent on reaching an allegedly higher plane. Ironically, only such an individual—a person like Joe—is worth raising, Dickens was convinced. Even more ironically, Pip never heeds Biddy's caution or applies Joe's refusal to outstrip Mrs. Joe to himself and Biddy. Rising above Biddy, at least in his own estimation, Pip loses her forever.

Joe's refusal to rise or be raised, Dickens's revaluative parody demonstrates, is commendable, nobler than Smiles's self-help ideal. Yet such is the force of Pip's ascent, such the respect it commands in society, that even right-hearted Joe is almost cowed by it. During the disastrous breakfast at Barnard's Inn, Joe is hopelessly out of his element; flustered at the sight of a socially improved Pip, the blacksmith cuts a clownish figure in his "holiday clothes," forever losing control of his hat and addressing Pip as "sir" (*GE*, 223).

But Joe regains his standing with his parting speech. Besides the poetic, forge-inspired definition of life as "ever so many partings welded together," it contains Joe's assertion that "Diwisions . . . must come," not just departures

(*GE*, 224). "You and me is not two figures to be together in London," Joe declares, firmly separating himself from the risen Pip. "I'm wrong in these clothes," Joe continues; "I'm wrong out of the forge, the kitchen, or off th' meshes" (*GE*, 225). Should Pip wish to see him in the future, Joe decrees, he will have to step down in the world and "put [his] head in at the forge winder" (*GE*, 225). It is as if Cinderella, coming to her senses, went back to the hearth and resumed her chores. Joe forever disassociates himself not just from his ill-fitting "holiday clothes" but from Pip and Cinderella, for both of whom a rise in the world immediately demands a new wardrobe. Thus when Jaggers tells Pip of his good fortune and upcoming transfer to London, he immediately adds, "you should have some new clothes" (*GE*, 139).

Unlike Magwitch, who intrudes upon Pip twelve chapters later, Joe refuses to partake of Pip's rise, even to share in it vicariously as a visitor. Pip detects "a simple dignity in him" (*GE*, 225), something Dickens implied his readers would not find as readily in Smiles's numerous examples of successful self-helpers, each more Cinderella-like than the others. Joe's self-respect is not an outward accoutrement but an internal reality. Unlike the cinder girl's sense of self-worth or that of Pip himself, whose "thick boots" expose him to Estella's scorn (*GE*, 61), Joe's dignity is such that "the fashion of his dress could no more come in its way when he spoke these words [about abandoning London], than it could come in its way in Heaven" (*GE*, 225), the ultimate in rising.

Dickens has things both ways. On one hand, although Joe Gargery embodies the "inbred politeness which springs from rightheartedness and kindly feelings" and that Smiles insisted "is of no exclusive rank or station" (*SH*, 369), he is made to appear sheepish, out of place, when he comes to London. His discomfort suggests that Smiles's dismissal of rank and station as criteria for gentility is unfounded, false to society as Dickens knew it, and probably insincere.

On the other hand, Joe supplies evidence for Smiles's contention that a real gentleman is always "the lord of a great heart," whether it beats under a peasant's coat or beneath "the laced coat of a noble" (*SH*, 369). But for a credible example of such genteel great-heartedness in humble attire, Dickens chided Smiles, one must refer to Joe Gargery in *Great Expectations*, not to the endless parade of success stories in *Self-Help*, where greatness invariably means getting on, moving up, winning out.

Through Pip, Dickens satirized *Self-Help* as a reflection of—and a stimulus to—every daydreamer's desire to rise like a Cinderella. With Joe's reservations about raising himself, Dickens parodied the reigning definition of improvement: Joe's case proved that real goodness, true value to one's society, has no obligatory relation to bettering one's worldly standing. But the severest caricature of a self-helper in *Great Expectations* is not a would-be Cinderella or a reluctant riser; that distinction belongs to a ruthless adherent to Smilesian principles: Abel Magwitch. Taken literally, Dickens jeered, the self-help ideal was more likely to unleash a Magwitch than to produce another Stephenson.

Self-Help, Dickens implied, is capable of creating a social enormity as unnatural as Frankenstein's monster yet more determined to lodge its claims. Magwitch possesses all the Smilesian virtues in abundance, especially perseverance and endurance, Copperfield's hallmarks. But thanks to a system that neglected, then punished him, Magwitch lacks a lofty ideal, a worthier goal than revenge; he misdirects his Smilesian energies toward perverse ends, namely, the settling of his long-standing grudge against society.

In the preface to the 1866 edition of *Self-Help,* Smiles rebutted criticism that he worried insufficiently about the relation of means to ends. He tried to defend self-help as a process that not only would generate worthwhile goals but that is praiseworthy per se: "It is not the result . . . that is to be regarded so much as the aim and the effort, the patience, the courage, and the endeavour with which desirable and worthy objects are pursued" (*SH,* vii).

Through Magwitch, Dickens objected that to some extent all risings, even his own, occur at society's expense, instead of for its benefit as Smiles maintained. There is an element of snobbery and revenge, a sense of getting even, in every success story, Cinderella's included. Someone is telling society that he or she is better, stronger, or smarter than it thought. Magwitch succeeds in spite of society, not in order to advance the common good. Even when colonists in New South Wales look down on the prospering ex-convict as a former criminal who got lucky, Magwitch, feeling superior, can gloat: "If I ain't a gentleman, nor yet ain't got no learning, I'm the owner of such"; "I'm making a better gentleman nor ever *you'*ll be!" (*GE,* 318–19).

Magwitch's rationale for self-improvement—one rises not in order to get ahead but to get even—imparts a vengeful, antisocial twist to Smiles's idea, revealing its implicit aggressiveness more frighteningly than did Joe's fears of appearing rebellious. "Blast you every one," the returned ex-convict exclaims in Pip's rooms, "every one, from the judge in his wig [who sentenced Magwitch], to the colonist a stirring up the dust," presumably on horseback while Magwitch walked (*GE,* 330). A dangerous travesty of the rags to riches story, Magwitch's grotesquely Cinderella-like progress from transported felon to entrepreneur and gentleman-maker is no invigoration for Victorian England, but an outsider's challenge to the system. With Magwitch, Dickens expressed abhorrence for both the system and the sort of threats he imagined it provoking.

"I am not a going fur to tell you my life, like a song or a story-book," Magwitch promises Pip and Herbert as chapter 42 begins (*GE,* 344). Nevertheless, his recital, added to information he gave Pip in chapters 39 and 40, completes an excellent parody of a Smilesian anecdote; it should be read as a rewriting of one, an irreverent addition to *Self-Help*. Ironically, transportation to New South Wales as a violent, hardened criminal is the only good thing that England's social system ever does for Magwitch. Before that, he was a cold, hungry child whom nobody pitied and who "got to be a man" by either sitting in jail or doing a profusion of odd jobs "that don't pay" (*GE*, 345). In Botany Bay, however, having been left money by his master, Magwitch redoubled his efforts; thanks to a rigorous regimen, to use his own words, he "prospered wonderful" (*GE*, 318).

"I've been a sheep-farmer, stock-breeder, other trades besides," Magwitch recollects. Yet even in bondage as "a hired-out shepherd in a solitary hut," he kept Pip's face before him (*GE*, 317), having resolved to earn enough money to make the boy a gentleman. A lifelong drudge or cinder girl, Magwitch vows to create a genteel Pip in order to achieve through him a vicarious transformation as splendid as Cinderella's. Note the ultra-Smilesian perseverance in Magwitch's declaration: "[T]he harder it was, the stronger I held, for I was determined" (*GE*, 319). Imagining himself funding Pip's Cinderella-like rise and thereby triumphing over the society that transported him, Magwitch confesses, was the goad to extra effort, the "way I kep myself a going"; such was the purpose "I held steady afore my mind" (*GE*, 319).

"Real honour," Smiles wrote, "is due to the man who honestly carves out for himself by his own native energy a name and a fortune, diligently exercising the powers and faculties which belong to him as a man." Dickens did not live to read this passage from Smiles's *Life and Labour* (1887; quoted in B-C, 73), but similar sentiments pervade *Self-Help*. Nowhere in this success manual's brief biographies, however, will one find a stronger champion of willpower and natural energy, a clearer example of the outer-directed person carving his way, than Abel Magwitch. Compared to him, Dickens sneered, Stephenson, Wedgwood, and Arkwright had easy lives. An ex-convict reveals Smiles's formula's limitations by exceeding its requirements. Magwitch is at once the epitome of self-help and its terrifying incarnation, a wicked parody of a shallow idea that damns it by darkening it to bring out its hideousness.

Pip's efforts "to struggle out of brutality and ignorance into the light of decency and self-respect," Robin Gilmour has argued, is an "essentially moral struggle" until perverted by Miss Havisham and Estella (B-C, 96). One should add that Pumblechook and Mrs. Joe become willing accomplices, and that Magwitch's struggles, more desperate than Pip's, are equally twisted. Dickens's point—in opposition to Smiles and Gilmour both—is that thanks to a general aura of exorbitant expectancy (that is, the Cinderella complex), and thanks also to fantasy-producing tomes like *Self-Help*, Victorian England had lost sight of true decency and genuine self-respect. Nowhere is this clearer than in the wonderful coincidence of a young boy's dreams of rising and an ex-convict's schemes to create "a brought-up London gentleman" (*GE*, 319), two affronts to socially useful moral struggle that seem made for each other.

Loss of true decency and self-respect goes far to explain Magwitch's misconception that his expression of gratitude toward Pip is a priceless boon: "I lived rough, that you should live smooth," the returned ex-convict boasts; "I worked hard, that you should be above work" (*GE*, 317). In effect, says Magwitch, he has persevered so that Pip need not; he has been the cinder girl so that Pip can become a Cinderella. Magwitch accomplishes for Pip a grotesque parody of the economic situation that too many Victorians enjoyed and that many, Dickens charged, considered ideal: being above certain kinds of work (that is, like Cinderella) due to someone else's labors (the cinder girl's equivalents).

Admittedly, Pip's epiphanic discovery of the sordid basis for his high expectations—and for society's as well—crushes those expectations once and for all. He realizes that he owes his gentility to a creature who is the very obverse of the refinements he craves. But Dickens subverts Cinderella's transformation from servant to princess by positing a cinder girl (a drudge like Magwitch) for every affluent person (a Cinderella like Pip). Although Pip is horrified, Dickens sees a concomitant irony of tragicomic proportions: such is the split between Haves and Have-Nots, such is the stranglehold the Cinderella complex has exerted on the popular mind, that Magwitch cannot imagine conferring on Pip a greater benefit than doing the latter's dirty work for him; this, Dickens wants readers to realize, is not self-help for either party after all.

"And do well, I am sure?" Estella asks Pip after he has told her that he still resides abroad (*GE*, 479). Acquiescing, Pip nevertheless stipulates that he must "work hard for a sufficient living." He has fallen far short of Copperfield's professional success and domestic happiness, even if at the last he personifies a scaled-down version of Smilesian precepts. That Pip's un-Cinderella-like clerkship in Egypt may be said ultimately to result from Magwitch's fortune-making in Australia discredits Magwitch twice over: as both Pip's cinder girl or surrogate worker, and as his would-be fairy godmother. No system predicated on Cinderellas and drudges (Haves and Have-Nots) should be allowed to continue, Dickens wanted readers to conclude, no matter how many individuals managed to rise from its ranks.

But the final scene between Pip and Estella also replays ironically Pip's conversation with the just-returned transport. Magwitch having listed his numerous New World occupations, Pip says: "I hope you have done well" (*GE*, 315). "I've done wonderfully well," Magwitch replies; "no man" who went to Australia under similar conditions "has done nigh as well as me. I'm famous for it."[28] As these conversations make clear, Pip's story, compared to Magwitch's, is no Smilesian anecdote, whereas the ex-convict's is one only in a perverse way. Through Pip and Magwitch, the Plutarch of Failure proscribes Smilesian success stories, using *Self-Help* as *David Copperfield*'s proxy. Insufficiently critical of the prevailing economic system, they are detrimental to society's moral well-being.

The Reform Bill of 1832 ushered in an era of unprecedented expectancy in which progress and prosperity were to go hand-in-hand. Although Dickens acknowledged numerous improvements, he soon ceased to subscribe to this prognosis. It was, he suggested, a snobbish lie. Setting Pip's autobiography, a tale of frustrated hopes, in the London of his own childhood, Dickens made his disbelief in the Victorian era's cultural myth retroactive to the 1820s; the country's exalted view of itself as a civilization continuously in the ascent—in effect, a Cinderella—had been unbelievable from the start.

Stagnant old England—rotten boroughs, unearned privilege, callousness toward the poor—had simply been replaced by a brave new world of bankers, bureaucrats, scientists, and industrialists, a confederacy with a Utilitarian bias that Dickens mistrusted but Smiles idolized. Money, not good breeding, became the prerequisite for power and automatic prestige, as Pip, poor as well as coarse in the early 1800s, already realizes. Widespread veneration for material success, Dickens complained, threatened to preclude any serious critique of Victorian society on terms other than its own.

Yet in 1859, regardless of Dickens's mounting personal and social dissatisfaction throughout the decade, Smiles's self-improvement manual fostered the impression that life in Victorian England was one success after another; according to Smiles, upward mobility continued to propel an entire nation toward unparalleled ascendancy. Indeed, the opening section of *Self-Help*, titled "National Progress," purports to be a contribution toward the country's advancement: Smiles assists England to rise by exhorting her citizens to raise themselves.

Consequently, *Self-Help* posed a unique challenge to Dickens's idea of himself as the era's premier social realist. Even if he vanquished rival novelists such as Lever and Thackeray, he still had to undercut Smiles. Otherwise, he might be superseded as society's principal critic and setter of values by a philosopher of popular culture, a biographer telling supposedly verifiable Cinderella stories. *Great Expectations* suggests that even nonfiction success stories, the Cinderella-like mini-biographies in Smiles's best-seller, be scorned as harmful fairy tales. Smiles's confused power to idealize material success and ennoble its pursuers, said Dickens, is a truly perverse enchantment whose spell must be broken.

Never before Smiles had a writer invested such unequivocal faith in the procreative power of biography; a book containing the life of a true man, he maintained, bursts with "precious seed" (AB, 11). Its "chief use . . . consists in the noble models of character in which it abounds" (*SH,* 436), models that spawn countless imitations. Unlike his first autobiographical novel, Dickens's second parodied the Plutarchian assumption that only great men's lives produce additional great men. In offering a humbler, more useful role model, *Great Expectations* met a greater need: it provided warnings, guidance, and encouragement to materialists and success worshippers, insisting they take note of Pip and be such snobs no longer.

"The literature of How to Get Ahead," it is worth reiterating, "typified by Samuel Smiles's best-selling *Self-Help* (1859), had an incalculable effect on the ordinary Victorian's value system and moral orientation" (RA, 170). In Dickens's opinion, such literature also had a deleterious impact on supposedly realistic Victorian novels, whose appropriation of Cinderella motifs it corroborated. Smiles's popularity depressed Dickens as both a manifestation of the period's view of itself as a fortunate princess—England, the epitome of rising—and a likely exacerbation of that complex.

Self-Help disowned failure, but *Great Expectations* is preoccupied with the subject. Dickens peoples his cast with failures such as Pip, Wopsle, and Mr. Pocket. Just as Pip fails to realize his prospects, Wopsle is unable to revive the drama; Mr. Pocket will never secure the title his wife thinks he deserves. Similarly, Magwitch's schemes for Pip go awry, as do the latter's efforts to smuggle Magwitch out of England, Miss Havisham's plans for Estella, the latter's marriage, and, fortunately, Orlick's plot to murder Pip.

Not even Herbert rises by his own exertions. He would never have become "a capitalist—an Insurer of Ships" (*GE*, 181) without Magwitch's capital, which Pip uses as down payment for his roommate's partnership, not to mention the nine hundred pounds Pip borrows from Miss Havisham to complete the purchase.[29] In short, Dickens was eager to be the Plutarch of Failure if only to demonstrate that Smiles was an unrealistic optimist, not a serious philosopher, hence no Plutarch at all.

Without an understanding of failure, Dickens warned, it was impossible to view life whole. More so than Plutarch's *Lives*, *Self-Help* distorted life's essentially tragicomic nature. No individual's life can be an undifferentiated success; it was even less plausible for life after life to follow a similar pattern, moving from hardship, past seemingly insurmountable obstacles, to unqualified triumph. The sultan's collapsible palace in *The Tales of the Genii* furnishes a more accurate analogue; although fabulous in appearance, its ceiling is liable to cave in at a moment's notice, particularly upon the presumptuous and overconfident, among whom Dickens included Smiles and self-helpers.

Each parody of the self-help idea augments the others: the embodiment of his era's inordinate expectancy sees his Cinderella-like rise abruptly halted by the most bitterly perseverant self-helper Dickens could imagine—a Have-Not determined to penetrate society's upper reaches. For so unsavory a self-helper (Magwitch), an aspirant Cinderella (Pip) has "deserted Joe" (*GE*, 320), the most deserving to rise of the three. When the Plutarch of Failure rewrites *Self-Help*, it spawns a would-be Cinderella and a Frankenstein's monster, putting the former in the latter's grip.

Dickens was not obliged to sell Gad's Hill, break with Ellen Ternan, and return to Warren's Blacking. Nor does logic demand that Pip go back to the forge. In dismissing Copperfield with Pip, Dickens enjoyed the luxury of remaining Dickens while overhauling the value system in his earlier autobiographical novel. Without forfeiting preeminence, he could explore his misgivings about all risings, Victorian England's and his own included. Pip's autobiography is both an admonition, obliquely delivered, and an equally indirect, acutely painful personal confession. Dickens's second stocktaking in ten years announced that his previous self-appraisal had been premature. Still confident that he could outrun his rivals, he nevertheless revealed that he was several removes from his former, happier self.

The final irony is that Mr. Pirrip wrests artistic success from his younger self's personal failure. Pip is neither first nor second at Clarriker's, but Mr. Pirrip has written the century's finest bildungsroman, a replacement for *David Copperfield* that can also be read as a repudiation of *Pendennis,* a reformation of the entire genre, and a genuinely useful self-help manual: a guidebook for the self-reclamation of overly expectant snobs.

Chapter 5
Collins

"Undermining the traditional bourgeois ethic of self-help," it has been argued, was Wilkie Collins's goal in *The Woman in White* (NR, 47).[1] Actually, this was Dickens's job, and he accused Collins of complicating it. In Dickens's opinion, his younger rival sensationalized *Cinderella,* devising plots to steepen her fall and intensify her sufferings in order to accentuate each step of her arduous, often vengeful, recovery. Madonna's loss of hearing (*Hide and Seek*), Laura Fairlie's of identity (*The Woman in White*), Magdalen Vanstone's of legitimacy (*No Name*)—these are just three instances of sudden misfortunes that exacerbate Cinderella's tumble from father's darling to stepmother's cinder girl.

In addition, Collins invariably endows one or more of his characters—the Cinderella figure, her princely champion, or the fairy godmother's equivalent—with unusual tenacity, the perseverance that Smiles judged undefeatable. Although merely a drawing teacher, Walter Hartright restores Laura Fairlie's identity and recovers her estate; first he outwits the unscrupulous Sir Percival Glyde, then he corners the even wilier Count Fosco. Not surprisingly, the preamble to *The Woman in White* characterizes it in Smilesian terms: "the story of what a Woman's patience can endure, and what a Man's resolution can achieve" (*WW*, 33).

Similarly, Mat Marksman returns to England in order to right the wrongs done twenty years before to Mary Grice, his sister, who was also Madonna's unwed mother.[2] He has the stubbornness of an avenging angel. After "penetrating the mystery of Madonna's parentage by the mother's side," he forms "the strongest of all resolutions—a vindictive resolution" to discover "the villain who had been Mary's ruin" (*H&S*, 353).

Collins was an indispensable ally in the "realism wars" that broke out all over the Victorian novel during the 1850s (*HR*, 2). Like Dickens, he repudiated tamer productions by more sanguine social critics—novelists who were more tolerant of, perhaps more resigned to, the status quo or who put too much trust in the world's gradual betterment. Insofar as Collins strove to appease the public's appetite for Cinderella stories, however, Dickens's confederate let down the side.

The Woman in White is built around Walter Hartright's spectacular ascent from drawing master to master of Limmeridge House, thanks to Laura Fairlie's climactic reinstatement as its mistress. Collins's novel, Dickens objected, was a Cinderella story twice over. No matter how suspensefully deployed, Collins's Cinderella motifs lighten the text, which exudes a fairy tale meliorism. When Walter's rise and Laura's recovery validate *Cinderella,* Collins allegedly compromises the high-powered melodrama that he and Dickens relied upon to subvert less trenchant critiques of society in novelists as different from each other as Anthony Trollope, Elizabeth Gaskell, and George Eliot.

To Dickens's increasing annoyance, Collins held fast to the basic Cinderella motif: the protagonist's shift from riches to rags to riches again. This unfailingly positive cycle contradicted Dickens's tragicomic conception of life's incessant ups and downs. He and Collins both believed in providential supervision whereby, at intervals, things set themselves to rights, even if it takes a natural or political upheaval of catastrophic proportions. But stunning rebuke and providential reward do not always occur in that order, Dickens decided; neither is ever conclusive or even exclusively one or the other, as Pip's unfortunate elevation and the collapse of his expectations, which is salvationary, both demonstrate.

In *Great Expectations,* Dickens parodies Collins for the latter's refusal to revalue *Cinderella* parodically—his reluctance to deny its truthfulness to life, his failure to question its efficacy as a cultural myth. Walter Hartright and Laura Fairlie experience greater difficulties than Potts did; they inhabit a darker world of graver challenges than Pen's. Nevertheless, Dickens maintained, Collins's hero and heroine are ultimately just as Cinderella-like as protagonists in Lever and Thackeray.

Collins's complicity in furthering the era's Cinderella complex, his willingness to supply success stories, made him a twofold rival; while trying to outdo Dickens's sensational realism, he prevented his fellow novelist from undoing the nation's fascination with *Cinderella* as a paradigm for its own rise and a guarantee of continuing ascendancy. Dickens felt that his integrity as a social critic, psychological novelist, and above all, as a tragicomedian, compelled him to disassociate *Great Expectations* from *The Woman in White*. That Collins's *Hide and Seek* had been received as "a Dickensian novel" (*H&S,* ix) made such disassociation seem even more imperative.

One may certify summer 1854 as the beginning of the Dickens–Collins rivalry. Before Dickens's major assault on *The Woman in White,* he and Collins sparred in *Hard Times* and *Hide and Seek*. Their opening scenes correct each other's view of circus life, although it is not always clear who is parodying whom. Consequently, Dickens's revisions of *The Woman in White* include a further debunking of *Hide and Seek*: in particular, the parodic substitution of Magwitch, Pip's problematic patron, for Matthew Marksman, the second of Madonna's two genuinely protective fairy godfathers.

Dickens wrote *Hard Times* between 23 January and 18 July 1854; he serialized it in *Household Words* from April to August of that year. Collins began *Hide and Seek* in April 1853, finishing it on 17 May 1854; Bentley published it less than a month later on 6 June. So Collins had completed the circus episodes in Book One before Dickens put pen to paper. Although they saw each other regularly in 1853 and 1854, neither Dickens nor Collins had the other's printed text to revise.[3]

Conceivably, Dickens and Collins went to the same circus, one that featured equestrians and clowns.[4] Each then depicted the experience oppositely from the other and for different purposes, so that Collins's novel, applied to Dickens's, acquires the force of conscious parodic revision. The misfortunes of Sissy Jupe and Louisa Gradgrind to the contrary, Madonna blossoms into a full-blown Cinderella once she gets away from Jubber's circus; it is as if *Hide and Seek* came hot off the press in pursuit of Dickens's misrepresentations of circus life in *Hard Times*.

On the other hand, Dickens may have seen *Hide and Seek* in manuscript form before beginning to write; he appears to be mocking Collins's *Cinderella* fixation even though he published most of *Hard Times* before *Hide and Seek* was issued. Mrs. Sparsit is a comically wicked stepmother who nearly accomplishes Louisa's ruin. Sissy's prince arrives—she has "happy children" (*HT*, 219)—but her savior remains unseen and unnamed. Louisa's only options, unfortunately, are Josiah Bounderby and James Harthouse, an ogre and an antiprince.

Bounderby's claims to have experienced hard times exceed those of the cinder girl's.[5] After being "born in a ditch," Coketown's industrial magnate reputedly was deserted by his mother, spent nights "in a pigsty," had to teach himself to read, but "pulled through," rising in the world to become "banker, merchant, manufacturer" (*HT*, 16–17). Actually, the caring parents of this self-professed Cinderella scrimped to afford him a good start. Bounderby is a wealthy factory owner who manufactures the "facts of his life" (*HT*, 18); when his doting mother appears, his falsehoods take their rightful place among "the popular fictions of Coketown" (*HT*, 138). Denying Mrs. Pegler, Bounderby literally insists on being self-made (*HT*, 192), hence without obligation to others. Dickens's champion of laissez-faire is both a fraudulent Cinderella and the novelist's most effective caricature, prior to *Great Expectations*, of the self-help idea.

"Routinely described" as a case of "undue . . . influence," *Hide and Seek* is considered so feeble a facsimile that one commentator called it "Dickens-and-water" (*H&S*, ix, xiii; *WC*, 9). Yet Collins insists that he, not Dickens, gives a realistic picture of the typical Victorian circus. The harshness of its performers' lives turns Jubber's circus, falsely billed as "the Eighth Wonder of the World" (*H&S*, 55), into a travesty of "Sleary's Horse-riding." The depiction of Jubber's is the sort of darkening of another novelist's bright spot that Dickens normally indulged in.

Collins seems to be saying that Dickens lied. The circus is a nasty place that sensible people run away *from*. Mr. Gradgrind catches Tom and Louisa peeping through a loophole at the "graceful" Miss Josephine Sleary on horseback and the "trained performing dog Merrylegs" (*HT*, 14). In Collins's opinion, Sleary's establishment provides no creditable escape from an oppressive childhood. No proponent of reliable solutions to society's ills, it follows, would romanticize a sordid reality into an exciting alternative.

Thanks to Sleary's intercession, Sissy Jupe is received into Mr. Gradgrind's household. In contrast, Jubber tries to prevent Valentine Blythe from adopting Madonna, the infant phenomenon who is his circus's main attraction. Which is more believable, Collins seems to ask, a benevolent proprietor who finds a foster home for a clown's deserted child, or a selfish promoter holding fast to his meal ticket? A cowardly abuser of women and children, Jubber performs professionally as a clown, Sissy's father's occupation, but is actually a "most atrocious looking stage vagabond" (*H&S*, 59), a malicious parody of Sleary, Dickens's imperfect yet commendable spokesperson for popular amusements.

To expose the arid rationality of the "hard fact fellows" who ignore the wisdom of the heart and make the head "all-sufficient" (*HT*, 95, 166), Dickens transfers Sissy from the vitality of Sleary's circus to Gradgrind's cold domicile and M'Choakumchild's colorless schoolroom. The switch, Collins's novel implies, is from a phony ideal (Sleary's circus) to its negation, the stifling of "imaginative graces and delights" (*HT*, 219) that Dickens's ideal could never encompass in the first place. Sissy becomes the cinder girl of Gradgrind's household, constantly persecuted for the sincerity of her direct, emotional responses. In Blythe's bohemian establishment, a genuine sanctuary, Mary develops into a full-fledged Cinderella; renamed Madonna, she is the most beautiful treasure on display in the artist's studio, a virtual incarnation of a canvas by Raphael.

Master Kidderminster relishes being held by one of Sleary's galloping equestrians, "the wild Huntsman of the North American Prairies"; the little man is "carried upside down over [the rider's] shoulder, by one foot, and held by the crown of his head, heels upwards, in the palm of [the rider's] hand" (*HT*, 27). Preposterous, Collins seems to reply. While impersonating "The Hurricane Child of the Desert," Madonna "slipped" from Mulley Ben Hassan's hand and was "struck stone deaf by the shock" of her fall (*H&S*, 56–57). She is meant to appear a more glaring victim of social neglect than the more spectacular, comparatively well-adjusted Kidderminster. Although deaf and dumb from her riding accident, a stricken Madonna voices the allure of an aesthetic outlook on life, beauty's siren call, more expressively than the outspoken Sissy or a lisping Sleary.

It is as if a painter's son were ridiculing the grandson of servants for positing a rundown circus as the antidote for Victorian society's ever increasing preoccupation with "facts and calculations" (*HT*, 8). Collins had no love for sworn enemies of "the robber Fancy," M'Choakumchild's vicious epithet for the creative imagination (*HT*, 12). But to emblematize humanitarian impulses and the softening influence of arts and entertainment, Collins replaced the orphaned daughter of a runaway clown with a Cinderella figure whom he compared to a living painting; he also chose a practicing artist to be her rescuer and preserver, the first of the novel's two highly proficient fairy godfathers.

Having saved Madonna from Jubber, Blythe enshrines her in a living work of art; after luncheon at Doctor Joyce's, she is the "centre figure" in a painterly composition, flanked by "the rector's eldest daughter, who was sitting at her right hand on a stool" and a second daughter kneeling "on the other side, with both her arms round" a large dog (*H&S*, 75). As if critiquing a group portrait, Collins emphasizes "the varying expressions of the three; the difference in their positions; the charming contrast between their light, graceful figures and the bulky strength and grand solidity of form in the noble Newfoundland dog," not to mention the "lustrous" lawn, flowers, trees, "seen through the open window."

To Dickens's surprise, Collins appeared to be proclaiming himself the superior realist: he, not Dickens, knew the truth about circuses. Yet *Hide and Seek* also laid claim to sounder, more sophisticated conceptions of art's powers and the nature of the creative life. Because Collins fashioned Madonna and Valentine Blythe into more pliable symbols for art and the aesthetic imagination than Dickens's Sissy and Sleary, the younger novelist seemed to be crowning himself the more redoubtable artist, Fancy's stauncher champion.

In suffusing *Hide and Seek* with Cinderella motifs—imagining Art or Beauty as a Cinderella whom the artist as fairy godfather must snatch from sordid circumstances—Collins thought he was adopting a fairy tale perspective to rival Dickens's. Unfortunately, too many nineteenth-century novels, in Dickens's estimation, were already based on *Cinderella*. Madonna falls from Mulley Ben Hassan's hands, but one fairy godfather rescues her and a second dotes on her, a progress from rags to riches that Dickens rewrote by burdening Pip with Miss Havisham and Magwitch while patterning Pip's rise and fall after that of Misnar's pavilion.[6]

Three years into their friendship, Collins dedicated *Hide and Seek* to Dickens "as a token of admiration and friendship." This may explain his admirers' hesitation to declare all-out war between their man and his ostensible mentor. Instead, recent editors of Collins's novels flirt with the possibility that Collins continually rewrites Dickens. Says Virginia Blain of *No Name:* "It is almost as though Collins wanted to conduct a literary debate with Dickens, begun in *Hide and Seek* (1854)" (*NN,* xix).[7] Similarly, Catherine Peters has observed that in *Hide and Seek,* Collins "seems to be deliberately inverting, or adopting, Dickensian themes for his own quite different purposes" (*H&S,* xiii),[8] which is parodic revaluation in a nutshell. Conducting a debate with Dickens is how many of the major Victorian novelists got their start as social critics.

Instead of trying to establish Madonna's parentage, for example, as Mr. Brownlow seeks to do for Oliver Twist, Blythe hopes to hide his adopted daughter's origins lest someone from the past claim her. Of the two strategies, Collins implies, Blythe's is more sensible even though the painter must keep secrets, questionable behavior that Dickens and Collins usually deplore. Better than Brownlow, Blythe understands that danger lurks in the recoverable past, not just in the unpredictable future.

Luckily, Matthew Marksman uncovers the secret of Madonna's parentage. The discoverer could have been a devilish Fagin or a rogue like Monks. As Blythe hides the truth and Mat sees it, everyday domestic life becomes more intense than most melodramas. Observed realistically, Collins showed Dickens, the familiar exhibits a romantic side exciting enough for any sensationalist. Mat is an agent of providence, a sort of avenging angel, yet unlike the contest between Brownlow and Fagin, the struggle between Marksman and Blythe need not pit the forces of light against those of darkness. Ultimately, the exertions of Madonna's second fairy godfather safeguard the efforts of her first.

Zack Thorpe, of whom Madonna seems enamored, turns out to be her half brother. Collins reverses the transition from brotherly love to a suitor's passion that Copperfield makes with Agnes. Initially feckless, Zack improves from jobless pub crawler to fraternal prince.[9] Collins may also be commenting on Tom Gradgrind's multiple failures as Louisa's brother. Incredibly, Tom hands over his sister to the sexually impotent Bounderby, then robs his new brother-in-law's bank.[10] Collins chips away at Dickens's credibility throughout *Hide and Seek:* Jubber in place of Sleary, Madonna for Kidderminster, Marksman versus Blythe instead of Fagin against Brownlow, brotherly love for Zack and Madonna rather than marital bliss for Copperfield and Agnes.

No glass slipper leads Zack to his future bride. Instead, a hair bracelet supplies the vital clue to Cinderella's identity. Marksman notices a similarity between Zack's hair and several strands woven into a hair bracelet that once belonged to Mary Grice, Madonna's unwed mother. Thus it becomes clear that

Zack's puritanical father, formerly known as Arthur Carr, is Madonna's progenitor as well.

Despite the substitution of bracelet for slipper, Cinderella still rises providentially—like the cinder girl, Madonna recovers from a fall. Inasmuch as she is deaf and dumb, however, she symbolizes society's helpless victims who must be protected—indeed, hidden—from further harm (Blyth's job) until justice seekers, veritable agents of providence such as Marksman, eradicate social ills. England could resolve its problems, *Hide and Seek* suggests, by regarding them as cinder girls in need of redress. When Pip's expectations collapse like the sultan's deadly palace, however, so does the ameliorant expectancy preserved in Collins's Cinderella motifs.

Unlike twentieth-century editors, Dickens had no difficulty recognizing his younger colleague as a serious threat to his supremacy. In July 1854, Dickens wrote to Georgina Hogarth: "I think [*Hide and Seek* is] far away the cleverest novel I have ever seen written by a new hand. It is much beyond Mrs. Gaskell" (*L*, 2:570), whose *North and South* may also be read as a negative response to *Hard Times*.[11] Nevertheless, Dickens sounds caught off guard, as if he had underestimated Collins. He reported himself "very much surprised" by *Hide and Seek*'s "great merit." Overnight, Collins had changed from youthful admirer into major competitor.

From *Hide and Seek* Dickens singled out "Old Mat," whom he considered "admirably done," as "the thing in which I observe myself to be most reflected" (*L*, 2:570). Catherine Peters likens Marksman to Dickens personally on the basis of their common "restlessness," their appetite for "taking long walks, especially at night." Mat's "sailor-like appearance and protective friendship for a younger man," she added, "could all be taken from Dickens himself" (*H&S*, xi). But Dickens did not think his person and habits had supplied Collins with Mat's original. More likely, he meant that Madonna's self-anointed guardian angel was Collins's novel's most insidious usurpation of the Dickensian mode for purposes antithetical to Dickens's own.

Marksman is a splendid grotesque: clad entirely in black, including "a black velvet skull-cap" because he was scalped in South America (*H&S*, 182).[12] Nevertheless, this benevolent semisavage returns from "lonesome places" (*H&S*, 191) to prove more competent as a rescuer than Nell's single gentleman (*The Old Curiosity Shop*) and just as useful as Sol Gills to Walter Gay (*Dombey and Son*) or Emily's Mr. Peggotty (*David Copperfield*). Richer than Old Chuzzlewit and a better investigator, Mat ferrets out his enemies' secrets more determinedly than Tulkinghorn.

Unfortunately, Collins put Mat to work as fairy godfather in the very sort of Cinderella story Dickens increasingly desired to expunge from the nineteenth-century novel. Coarser, more complicated than Marksman, Magwitch is also more ferocious, more vengeful, more dangerous socially. Indeed, he seems grotesquely tragicomic in sincerely desiring to repay both Pip and Compeyson; that is, in wanting to serve as Pip's fairy godfather while getting even with polite society. Pip's perversely benevolent "uncle" (*GE*, 325) should be read as a deliberate darkening of Madonna's single-minded Uncle Mat. It was not enough to replace Collins's women in white (Anne Catherick, Laura Fairlie) with the more memorable Miss Havisham, herself a parodic fairy godparent. Dickens also redid Mat parodically as Magwitch.

The nineteenth-century novel's most unforgettable fairy godfather, Dickens hoped, would be Magwitch, not Marksman. As a result, all fictions seriously predicated on Cinderella motifs, not just *Hide and Seek*, would be discarded as unbelievable. Parentless Pip is removed from Joe's forge more miraculously than Blythe retrieves Madonna from Jubber's circus. But Magwitch's ultimately disastrous efforts on Pip's behalf amount to a retraction of Matthew Marksman's services to Zack and Madonna.

Dickens mercilessly parodies Collins's fairy tale story line. Blythe rescues Madonna and adopts her; her uncle returns from South America to protect and provide for her. In contrast, Pip is deceived into believing Miss Havisham is his benefactress; his prospects collapse when an ex-convict returns from Australia intent on being his uncle. Miss Havisham misleads Pip, using Estella to break his heart. Magwitch wants to endow Pip with money and a wife but effectively deprives him of both, nearly getting him killed twice, first in the Thames and a second time from fever and exhaustion.

Undercut *Hide and Seek*'s dependence on the fairy godfather device, Dickens decided, and one deals the era's Cinderella complex a deadly blow. Collapse the absurd notion of providence as a benign fairy godparent, as Dickens does with both Magwitch and Miss Havisham, and no novel indebted to *Cinderella*, no fairy tale vision of England itself as Cinderella, can survive.

That Dickens created Magwitch with the idea of spiking Marksman seems clear from their physical resemblance and the rough dialect each speaks. Magwitch looks uncannily like Mat. Hale and hearty with "a splendid muscular development" (*H&S*, 306), Mat is readily identified as a merchant seaman who has circumnavigated the globe; "tanned to a perfectly Moorish brown" during twenty years abroad, his face is "overgrown by coarse, iron-grey whiskers" (*H&S*, 181). Upon entering Pip's apartments some sixteen years after their encounter on the marshes, Magwitch is "dressed ... roughly; like a voyager by sea." "A muscular man, strong on his legs," "browned and hardened by exposure to weather," Magwitch has "long iron grey hair" (*GE*, 312). Besides repeating the brownness, Dickens transfers "iron grey" from Mat's whiskers to

Magwitch's hair. The hardening Magwitch acquired outdoors echoes the "twenty years of hardening" that Mat has undergone in North and South America (*H&S*, 209). But although Mat and Magwitch are both returners, only the latter is actually reappearing in the text.

Mat enters Collins's novel already affluent from "digging gold in California" (*H&S*, 189). Dickens thought readers would find Magwitch's good fortune in Australia more plausible than Mat's success as a miner. He sits at his ease in "the Snuggery," drinking and smoking. Our first sight of Magwitch is of a "fearful man, all in coarse grey . . . with broken shoes, and with an old rag tied round his head" (*GE*, 4). He threatens to cut Pip's throat and eat his "fat cheeks" (*GE*, 4–5). Mat "bolts his dinner like the lion in the Zoological Gardens," Zack observes in awed amusement (*H&S*, 303). Just as "ravenous" at breakfast the morning after his reappearance as he was on Christmas Day in 1812, Magwitch nauseates Pip: "[A]s he turned his food in his mouth, and turned his head sideways to bring his strongest fangs to bear upon it, he looked terribly like a hungry old dog" (*GE*, 329). Of the two, Dickens insisted, Magwitch is the real bogy.

"I'm a rough 'un, I know," Mat tells Valentine Blythe, "but I hav'nt broke out of prison, or cheated the gallows" (*H&S*, 326). Magwitch has done both. He claims to have risked "Death by the rope" for returning to England illegally (*GE*, 331). Mat has milder qualms; having departed as "a tidy lad aboard ship," presumably in the Royal Navy, he is not likely to "be shot as a deserter" two decades later (*H&S*, 189, 374). "Give us your hand, young 'un!" Mat implores Zack after the latter has "stood by" him in a tavern brawl (*H&S*, 187). But Pip shudders when Magwitch grasps his hands; "for anything I knew," he explains, "his hand might be stained with blood" (*GE*, 319).

Mat's avuncularity oversimplifies providence's complicated superintendence. Only in a fairy tale, Dickens charged, would justice come so unerringly, its beneficiary a Cinderella as totally deserving as Madonna. Despite his gruff exterior, Mat, nicknamed "old Rough and Tough" (*H&S*, 228), smoothes everything out. In Book Two, he clears up the mystery of Madonna's parentage, thereby solidifying her place in Blythe's household. He revenges Mary Grice, exposes Mr. Thorpe, makes a more dependable person of Zack, then returns to the wilds, having succeeded in all his endeavors as if prodigal son and fairy godfather were realistic variations on deus ex machina. In contrast, Magwitch is no prodigal son but society's sins come home to roost, a genuine outcast as unwelcome to the country that expelled him as Frankenstein's monster to its creator.

Through Magwitch, Dickens undoes Mat's successes. Marksman finds his sister's illegitimate daughter (his niece), but Magwitch never sees his child. Having observed Madonna, Mat tells Zack: "Mary's child has lived to grow up, and that's her" (*H&S*, 378). Only on his deathbed does Magwitch learn that Estella, whom he presumed dead, "is living now . . . a lady and very beautiful"

(*GE*, 456). One presumes Mat will bequeath the bulk of his fortune to Madonna; Magwitch can give Estella nothing. In having Pip, not Magwitch, learn the secret of Estella's parentage, Dickens humbles Pip for having expected to rise by marrying an ex-convict's daughter whose regality is a sham.

Mat is confounded by Madonna's resemblance to his sister; "it was a'most as awful as seeing the dead come to life again" (*H&S*, 253). "She had Mary's turn with her head," Mat reflects. Pip puts two and two together for a less welcome realization: Estella's gestures in chapters 29 and 32, especially "her hand waving" to him from a coach window (*GE*, 263), remind him of Molly's powerful hands at Jaggers's dinner party in chapter 26. Madonna's resemblance to Mary mitigates the loss of a sister; Pip becomes painfully cognizant that his Cinderella's mother has been acquitted of murder.

Marksman's investigations strengthen Madonna's privileged position in Blythe's establishment. No one is likely to challenge the painter's right to have adopted her. In contrast, Magwitch's return ruins Pip's prospects at Satis House. The ex-convict's reappearance puts an end to daydreams of adoption: Miss Havisham "had adopted Estella," Pip muses; "she had as good as adopted me, and it could not fail to be her intention to bring us together" (*GE*, 232). The more negatively Magwitch's intervention restates Mat's, the more the latter seems too good to be true and the more improbable *Hide and Seek* becomes, *Cinderella* and England's snobbish conception of itself collapsing along with it.

Besides safeguarding Madonna, Mat declares himself father and uncle to Zack (*H&S*, 192), who improves under his tutelage from scapegrace to responsible citizen. Unselfishly, Mat makes a better man of Zack. Magwitch tries to create a gentleman in order to infiltrate society vicariously, thus outsmarting the system that excludes unfortunates like himself. Yet Zack's friendship with Mat, Dickens argued, does not broaden the scope of human relationships as dramatically as the bond that develops between Pip and Magwitch does. Despite less auspicious beginnings, the latter turns out to be the more instructive civics lesson.

Having confronted Thorpe and secured his confession, Mat burns the old man's letter to his son: "'For your sake, Zack,' he said, and dropped the letter into the fire" (*H&S*, 417). Mat declines to make public Thorpe's relationship to Mary Grice and Madonna. In Dickens's parody, we watch Magwitch "set fire" to the one-pound notes that Pip attempts to repay (*GE*, 315); the ex-convict refuses to have his connection with Pip and polite society dismissed so easily. Nor does Magwitch ever relent toward Compeyson, a greater blackguard than Arthur Carr.[13] Drowning Compeyson, however, he signs his own death warrant, breaking "two ribs," which "wounded one of his lungs" (*GE*, 451). Unlike Mat, who can return to South America after helping Madonna and Zack, Magwitch fails to escape from England despite Pip's assistance.

When Mat first appears in Book Two, he is about to be overpowered in a tavern brawl. Zack comes to his rescue. They fight "back to back" (*H&S*, 184), holding off a score of patrons. Pip's pivotal encounter with Magwitch makes Zack's first meeting with Mat seem belated, almost accidental. In Dickens's redoing, the story's critical confrontation opens the novel: Pip succors a desperate escaper whose gratitude proves a mixed blessing. After Mat and Zack escape, the latter decides to pursue his acquaintance with this "odd fellow" because "something may come of it" (*H&S*, 193). Pip has no desire to see Magwitch again.

For a society that identified with Cinderella, Dickens asks, which is more disturbing sociologically—which more traumatic—Zack's discovery that his puritanical father seduced Mat's sister, or Pip's realization that the convict he once assisted is his fairy godfather? Pip's truly frightening predicament in chapters 39 and 40—his epiphanic discovery of a violence-prone ex-convict for a patron—is also grotesquely comic as a parodic complication of Zack's situation in Collins.

Zack and Mat room together after the former falls into disfavor at home. In contrast, Pip is appalled when Magwitch enters his apartments, eager to settle in. "Where will you put me?" Magwitch asks; "I must be put somewheres, dear boy" (*GE*, 319). From the menace in Magwitch's statement, one detects his sense of himself as a problem society has yet to resolve. Pip is understandably "afraid to go to bed" (*GE*, 320), even after he transfers the key "to the outside" of Magwitch's bedroom door and locks him in (*GE*, 321).[14]

Mat lays "a goodly collection of bank-notes" on the table and exhorts Zack, "Take what you want." The young man helps himself to "two ten-pound notes as a loan" (*H&S*, 219–20). In Dickens's ominous revision, Magwitch's emissary, the man with "a handkerchief tied over his head" who stirs his drink with a file,[15] slips Pip "two fat sweltering one-pound notes" (*GE*, 79). Mat's casual generosity has no strings attached, no long-term consequences; Magwitch's gift is part of a plan to repay the entire social system.

Instead of Mat drinking and smoking in the tavern, his scalped pate in a skullcap, or offering Zack a loan, Dickens presents Magwitch's fateful messenger: the "cunning," "secret-looking man" in the Three Jolly Bargemen, probably a recently released convict, with a "handkerchief tied over his head in the manner of a cap, so that he showed no hair" (*GE*, 87). Then, replacing Mat with Magwitch upon the latter's return (ch. 39), Dickens shows what it would really be like to have a desperado as one's benefactor.

Hide and Seek, it has been argued, "fiercely castigated" snobbery (*H&S*, xiii), the unlikely bond between a maritime Mat and Zack Thorpe, gentleman's son, serving as prime instance of the novel's antipathy to class distinctions. Granted, neither Mat nor Zack behaves snobbishly toward the other, despite the former's wealth and the latter's breeding. But Dickens objected that Zack and Mat, unlike Pip and Magwitch, hit it off immediately; their domestic arrangements spring to life as if there were no serious differences in rank or age to overcome. Pip declares himself "softened by the softened aspect of the man"—the snob even feels "a touch of reproach"—when he notices that his "hardened" visitor's "eyes were full of tears" (*GE*, 314).[16] Yet it takes several chapters and quite a few weeks after Magwitch's unwelcome return before Pip's terror and revulsion cease. Only gradually does the tie between them mature into the mutual love and respect one might ascribe to father and son. Nothing in the Mat–Zack relationship rivals Pip's snobbishness, his air of dismissal, when he attempts to repay Magwitch's one-pound notes and rid himself of an unpleasant visitor: "You can put them to some other poor boy's use," he suggests (*GE*, 315).

How can *Hide and Seek* castigate snobbery, Dickens asked, when it repeatedly fails to dramatize it as strikingly as *Great Expectations* does? Not even the central transgression in Collins's novel smacks of class prejudice. Arthur Carr is genteel and cosmopolitan, while Mary Grice is a Dibbledean hosier's daughter, but Mat's desire for revenge on his sister's false lover remains fraternal. It is unmarked by the snobbish hatred a "common sort of wretch" like Magwitch feels for Compeyson, whom he calls "a dab [an expert] at the ways of gentlefolks" (*GE*, 349, 345).

In Dickens's opinion, Collins struck no telling blows against snobbery, certainly not by having Mat challenge Zack to "a turn-to at Beggar-my-Neighbour. Sixpence a time" (*H&S*, 289). They play for over an hour with "a greasy pack of cards" that anticipates Magwitch's "ragged pack" (*GE*, 337), but Collins does not present the contest as a painful eye-opener for either player. "Zack won," he declares (*H&S*, 290). In Dickens's retelling, Pip plays "beggar my neighbour," the only card game he knows, with Estella, who wins both hands (*GE*, 61–62). The contest supplies an early instance of the misery Miss Havisham has trained Estella to inflict on men. "Beggar him," she commands Estella as the game begins.

In both name and outcome, "beggar my neighbour" seems designed to humiliate Pip; instead of winning, as Zack does, he is deprived of his self-esteem. "What coarse hands he has!" Estella exclaims. When Pip misdeals, he is "denounced . . . for a stupid, clumsy labouring-boy." The second hand ends as did the first: "[S]he beggared me," Pip reports; "she threw the cards down on the table when she had won them all" (*GE*, 62). Since winning this game is entirely a matter of luck,[17] Estella's consecutive victories indicate how thoroughly Pip has been overwhelmed by snobbish disdain. "Her contempt" for me "was so strong," Pip confesses, "that it became infectious, and I caught it" (*GE*, 61).

Dickens refashions Zack's seemingly incidental card game with Mat into a probing psychological portrait of *three* snobs. Estella scorns the ineptitude one might expect from a blacksmith's helper accustomed to handling heavier, thicker objects. Ironically, Estella too is a victim of a snob's disdain; she has been warped by Miss Havisham's hatred for all males because one spurned her. Miss Havisham vents her feelings by using Estella as a tool to crush a young boy's ego. Pip's defeat is epiphanic. He realizes how inferior Estella's class considers him. But the "contempt" he catches from her marks the beginning of his snobbery, his yearning to join those lofty enough to look down on him. He begins to despise coarse hands and clumsy behavior, which explains his willingness to desert Joe in chapter 19 and why in chapter 39 he finds the returned transport more repulsive than Marksman ever seems to Zack. He gambles with a fairy godfather who uses the game to slip him sixpences. In Dickens's reconsideration, Pip plays with a heartless Cinderella whom their fairy godmother encourages to degrade him.

Like *Great Expectations, Hide and Seek* features a revised ending. In the first edition, Zack spends an adventurous year traveling with Mat in South America, where they part forever just as Pip and Estella separate permanently in Piccadilly in Dickens's original ending. While abroad, Zack learns by letter of his father's death; he is told his family's "dreadful secret"; namely, that Thorpe, as Carr, fathered an illegitimate daughter, Madonna, who is thus Zack's half sister (*H&S*, 426).[18]

In his preface to the 1861 edition, Collins announced that he had "altered the termination of the story." After an interval of "eighteen months," Zack goes back to South America; this time, he persuades Mat to return to England with him, "and the Man of many Wanderings rested at last among the friends who loved him, to wander no more" (*H&S*, 430).

Collins could no more assign Mat to Brazil than Dickens could leave Pip in Egypt. Compared to Collins's revised and indisputably happier ending, however, Dickens's revision seems ambiguous. Although Pip returns to reconcile with Estella, theirs is a somber reunion; Magwitch and Miss Havisham are dead (not to mention Compeyson and Drummle), Satis House is in ruins, and it remains unclear whether Pip is home for good even if he and Estella resolve never to part. When Estella asks, "you live abroad still," Pip replies, "Still" (*GE*, 479).

Dickens considered Mat's reintegration less plausible than some critics find Pip's reunion with Estella in the second ending. Marksman is gone twenty years before reappearing to locate his sister's child. Self-exiled again, this time for less than three years, he is "welcomed" back with a kiss from his niece (*H&S*, 430). But the failure of Magwitch's first return precludes any repetition of it. Greeted coldly by Pip, the illegally returned ex-convict is captured, imprisoned, and sentenced to death.

Yet one cannot maintain that Dickens rewrote both of Mat's successful returns as Magwitch's single but fatal reappearance. The 1861 version of *Hide and Seek* was published in September, a month after the final installment of *Great Expectations.* As with *Hard Times* and *Hide and Seek,* it is difficult to say who is having the final word; that is, which ending, *Hide and Seek*'s or that of *Great Expectations,* parodies the other.

Arguably, Collins rewrote his conclusion because Dickens had revised *Great Expectations.*[19] If Dickens could restore Pip to Joe, Biddy, and Estella, Collins felt he ought to reclaim Mat for Madonna, Zack, and the Blythes. In doing so, he repaired some of the damage Dickens had done to Cinderella motifs in the 1854 *Hide and Seek* by sabotaging the fairy godfather device. In the 1861 *Hide and Seek,* the fairy godfather reappears triumphantly to enjoy the results of his earlier visit. Mat returns after only about two and a half years, not the eleven Dickens needed for Pip's return.

Nevertheless, it strikes the modern revaluator as if Dickens's revised ending redoes Collins's, if only because one tends to associate *Hide and Seek* with 1854. Ironically, *Hide and Seek* seems to be reworking circus episodes in *Hard Times* but was actually written first; similarly, Dickens's second ending for *Great Expectations* comments shrewdly on *Hide and Seek*'s revised conclusion despite being in print before Collins altered his final paragraphs.[20]

Zack brings back Mat but can never marry Madonna; as her fairy godfather, Mat has procured a half brother for her, not a husband. On the other hand, Pip may marry Estella but must do so without Magwitch's assistance. The crucial issue, Dickens tells Collins, is not whether hero and heroine remain brother and sister or become husband and wife; what matters is whether or not outcasts can be reincorporated into society. *Great Expectations* appears to take a hard look at sentimental improbabilities that allegedly soften Collins's sensationalism. In a roundabout way, his disposition of Mat's case flatters the nation's Cinderella complex. Putting one's faith in society's reabsorptive power, its ability to reinstate outlaws and outcasts, Dickens argued, was no more realistic than believing in Cinderella's inevitable recovery from cinder girl to princess. If Mat's reincorporation is a variation on Cinderella's rebound, *Hide and Seek* emphasizes both: Madonna's apotheosis as Cinderella and the civilizing repatriation of her "grim, scarred face" fairy godfather (*H&S*, 430). Indeed, Mat's initial repatriation solves the mystery of Madonna's parentage and assures her ascendancy in Blythe's household. Its domestic virtues, in turn, draw Mat home for good.

When Marksman first learns his sister's cruel fate, he nearly faints. "Over twenty years of hardening," he exclaims, "don't seem to have hardened me yet!" (*H&S*, 209). Toward Arthur Carr, Mary's seducer, Mat conceives an enmity that Dickens replays as Magwitch's bitter hatred for Compeyson. "By God, I'll be even with him!" Mat swears (*H&S*, 372). Yet toward Madonna, his niece, Mat's eyes "grow clearer and softer" (*H&S*, 397). Finally, having confronted Carr in the person of Mr. Thorpe, Mat moderates his revenge; he burns Thorpe's confession, sparing "Zack's father for Zack's sake" (*H&S,* 419).

Dickens complicates the conflict in Marksman between hardness and softness (revenge and forgiveness). Every time Pip notices that the "hardened" ex-convict has "softened" and responds to his unconventional fairy godfather in kind (*GE,* 375), Dickens makes Collins's thematic conflict his own. Softenings within Marksman alone become the softenings of Pip and Magwitch toward each other. Electing forgiveness over revenge is said to be both more difficult and more imperative in *Great Expectations;* a snob and a social outcast become like father and son, a breakthrough more restorative for society than a vengeful brother's decision not to expose the man who ruined his sister lest such disclosure pain the seducer's legitimate son.

In the revised ending, Collins tried to regain control of the revenge versus reconciliation theme. The "once hardened" Mat Marksman is "softened" by Zack's pleas and returns to England with him (*H&S,* 430). The new conclusion is in fuller accord with the rest of the novel, Collins decided. But in Dickens's allegedly more truthful version, mutual softening between Pip and Magwitch has no power to make society relent. Instead of softening toward Magwitch, it exacts full penalties. When to soften the individual, when to deplore the unlikelihood of this phenomenon becoming official policy—*Great Expectations* understands these distinctions, but *Hide and Seek,* Dickens protested, does not. The later novel should supersede the earlier as the superior example of psychologically realistic social criticism.

Reincorporation of the outcast stands for the rehabilitation of unfortunates generally, all whom society neglects or misuses; it is analogous to the cinder girl's rebound from rags to riches. Unfortunately, the reincorporation theme must be numbered among the Victorian novel's unrealistic Cinderella motifs, Dickens declared. Pip's filial bond with Magwitch constitutes a softening of greater magnitude and significance than Mat's toward Mr. Thorpe. But the system that casts out Magwitch, *Great Expectations* fears, will never soften sufficiently to take back the monsters it has created.

Regrettably for Collins, the Pip–Magwitch relationship is more memorable. Mat and Zack may be "two comrades . . . in years so far apart, in sympathies so close together" (*H&S,* 430), but Dickens parodied their closeness, implying that it prospers too easily. In contrast, Magwitch expires; Pip, left destitute, nearly dies of fever. The parody only grew stronger after Collins's revision added permanent physical proximity for Mat and Zack to their temperamental affinities. Collins may have been showing Dickens how to reintegrate the outcast, but it seems as if Dickens had already told his rival that this is more difficult than he thinks.

As Mat uncovers his sister's fate and finds his niece, he "reawakens feelings that link him to society" (*PT,* 31). Consequently, he returns for good. Collins's agents of providence may step outside the lines, taking justice and revenge into their own hands; ultimately, however, they reaffirm their ties to society by doing so. The decision to rejoin the community, Dickens countered, is never chiefly the outlaw's. Collins's revised ending "actually improves the novel" (PT, 35) only if one assumes that society and its outcasts both desire rapprochement.

Lever brings home the outlawed Samuel Whalley to end *A Day's Ride;* having regained solvency plus reputation, he recommences doing business in his native Wales. Collins permits Mat to return twice, and Dickens has Pip come back from Egypt. But despite all the softening reconciliations that conclude *Great Expectations*—Pip with Miss Havisham, Pip with Magwitch, Pip with Estella—Dickens's revaluative parody wants things both ways. Even with the prospect of a marriage in the revised ending, Dickens darkens the optimism he judged facile in novelists as different from each other as Collins and Lever. Pip's return from Egypt should not be confused with Cinderella's resumption of former status. Unlike Whalley and Marksman, Magwitch can never be repatriated; his attempt to repatriate himself remains a criminal act.

From one point of view, the primary one, friendship between Pip and Magwitch symbolically heals the split between Haves and Have-Nots—or at least it recommends that the split be healed and offers a paradigm. Viewed from another, secondary perspective, however, Magwitch is driven to kill Compeyson, then society kills Magwitch. Enmity between Magwitch and the social system burns as brightly as the hatred between Magwitch and Compeyson, each of these antagonisms a refutation of improbable softenings in Lever and Collins as well as a gloss upon the other. When Magwitch returns, Pip's expectations of maintaining genteel status and marrying Estella collapse like Misnar's pavilion. *Great Expectations* revokes the favorable impact of Marksman's reappearances so that *Hide and Seek* falls apart along with Pip's unfounded hopes.

Magwitch is a sustained parody of Mat Marksman, whom Dickens wants to cancel. Similarly, Miss Havisham eclipsed both Anne Catherick and Laura Fairlie to emerge as the best-known "woman in white" (*WW,* 55) in nineteenth-century fiction. Dickens's reclusive madwoman epitomizes the consequences of overexpectancy; in his estimation, that was the real problem for Victorians, more so than the stifling proprieties symbolized by the whiteness of Anne Catherick's attire, to which Laura's "plain white muslin" bears an "ominous likeness" (*WW,* 86, 80). Miss Havisham is a "withered," lusterless Cinderella, clad in yellowing bridal clothes for a wedding never to be (*GE,* 59); she struck Dickens as the perfect tragicomic image—ghastly yet absurd—for expectations cut short.[21]

Through Miss Havisham, Dickens parodically revalued Cinderella and her fairy godmother simultaneously, for his woman in white is both a failed Cinderella and a deceitful fairy godparent. Collapsing in one personage two key elements in the cinder girl's story reversed the double success that Cinderella figures enjoy in *The Woman in White:* Walter Hartright rises from drawing master to marry an heiress and sire a gentleman, "the Heir of Limmeridge" (*WW*, 645); stripped of wealth, status, and identity by Sir Percival and Count Fosco, Laura Fairlie regains all three, thanks to Walter, her prince, and acquires a husband besides.

Competing sensational realists since the mid-1850s, Dickens and Collins intensified their competition in 1860 to determine who was the superior psychological novelist. A tug-of-war over *Cinderella,* namely, how to use this popular fairy tale, became crucial to the outcome of a rivalry that was friendly but incessant. In *The Woman in White,* Collins invokes Cinderella's story, her downfall from beloved daughter to persecuted drudge, as his analogue for what happens to individuals wrongfully confined as mental patients. Dickens retorted that a novelist's efforts to appear more psychological should not rely on the inept psychologizing of unrealistic fairy tale motifs.

If victims of society's failings are portrayed as variations on the cinder girl, redemption of the social process takes on the simplicity of fairy lore; it hinges on nothing more than the individual's physical rescue and financial recovery. It is sheer madness, Dickens fumed, to correlate the cinder girl's dilemma with the unfairly confined lunatic's when more credible metaphors were available for society's determination to conceal its problems rather than solve them—deportation of convicts like Magwitch to Australia, for example.

In Dickens's revaluative parody of *The Woman in White,* Cinderella gives her name to a snobbish misconception of self grave enough to be considered a mental disorder: the Cinderella complex as a manifestation of mass lunacy. Collins's comparison of the unjustly institutionalized mental patient to the cinder girl is said to make martyrdom out of mania. Dickens denigrates exorbitant expectancy—Pip's, Miss Havisham's, even Magwitch's—as a pervasive imbalance. Throughout *Great Expectations,* the craving to rise in the world, the lust to attain (or regain) wealth, rank, and power is both a private and a social pathology. It is treated as a personal failing that is also a national one, each more reprehensible than society's mistreatment of lunatics.

In both *Hide and Seek* and *The Woman in White,* Collins brands the proprieties a collective madness, a self-inflicted confinement. As a public spectacle in Jubber's circus, Madonna not only emblematizes "the deafness of early Victorian society" to the unfortunates on its margins (*H&S*, viii); she also pays for her mother's sexual transgression. When Sir Percival conspires to reduce Laura Fairlie to servile status, his new wife symbolizes the defenselessness of married women under Victorian law. Obedience to her father's wishes puts Laura in Sir

Percival's power; her reluctance to disobey him costs this Cinderella figure as dearly as not having a husband penalizes Mary Grice. Confined to an asylum, unable to prove her identity as Lady Glyde, Laura is worse off than Madonna.

Collins campaigned for a franker, less straitlaced society, a less hypocritical community that offered better protection for all. In such a world, individuals would not have to pretend to be "spotlessly pure," like a woman in white (*WW*, 80); nor would they be as vulnerable. But Dickens construed Cinderella motifs in Collins's novels as obstacles to liberalization—they implied that the key to salvation lies in the acquisition (or reattainment) of material comfort, not in the readjustment of snobbish attitudes or the rethinking of personal and national priorities, which Dickens called for.

Dickens objected that the Cinderella complex, not subservience to propriety, should be denounced as the era's truly collective madness. Using Cinderella as a victim, it followed, only abetted the complex. As Collins's Cinderellas escape "cinderhood" or are rescued from it, tragedy is avoided; their recoveries reaffirm the era's belief in upward mobility and England's ascendancy instead of psychoanalyzing such overconfidence, indeed, bemoaning the insanity of it.

In Dickens's opinion, Collins's overreliance upon Cinderella motifs carries him dangerously close to the prevailing psychosis that quantified gentility in terms of money and privilege. Despite blending Gothic realism with pressing social concerns, *The Woman in White* rested squarely upon Cinderella's story. Like Madonna's rescue from the circus, Laura's restoration—from asylum inmate to mistress of Limmeridge House—simply replays *Cinderella*. Laura's reinvestiture in an elaborate public ceremony (*WW*, 637–38), the novel's climax, outdoes Cinderella's wedding.

Neither of Collins's white-clad Cinderellas—Anne Catherick, Laura Fairlie—is ever rightfully institutionalized; on the contrary, the plot turns on Sir Percival's attempt to substitute Laura for Anne; that is, to put an unjustifiably confined woman in place of one whose need for confinement is debatable. Miss Havisham, one should remember, is crazy, a casualty of her disappointed expectations and thus appropriately self-confined, having converted Satis House into her private asylum.

The challenge for the psychological realist, Dickens twitted Collins, went beyond deciding who should be locked up and who should not. Which psychological novelist could restore the country's mental health—that was the real issue. *Great Expectations* certifies the Cinderella complex, not observance of the proprieties, as the national mania and suggests that few are exempt. Obedience to the proprieties is relegated to a minor aberration, more nuisance than neurosis.

Guilty as well as guiltless, victim then victimizer, Dickens's woman in white reminds us that Pip too, more so than Laura or Anne, is far from blameless; a dupe of society's obsession with money and position, he is also a cardinal illustration of such cravings. A jilted Miss Havisham behaves vindictively as Pip's presumed fairy godmother because of her un-Cinderella-like misfortune. But Pip's expectations collapse like Misnar's pavilion because the blacksmith's apprentice embraces the general delusion of his age; as mad in his way as Miss Havisham in her personal asylum, he builds himself an imaginary palace of false hopes. As did Victorian England, Pip thinks himself a Cinderella. He imagines providential superintendence as a fairy godparent devoted to him personally, much as Collins commissions Marksman to supervise Madonna.

Pip's complicity in furthering the Cinderella complex of his time marks him as both victim and perpetrator. Rehabilitating him poses a thornier psychological problem than Hartright encounters in reinvesting Laura. Unlike Laura's reinstallation, Pip's recovery is mostly internal; it does not entail a dramatic material comeback. On the contrary, the unhealthy frame of mind that society fosters in Pip and that he consequently personifies must be discarded—that is, cast out—by individuals and country alike, as Pip seems to realize in exiling himself to Egypt.

To obtain redress, protagonists in *The Woman in White* must violate the proprieties; they overstep the boundaries to which an initial conformity created their predicament. Had Laura not kept her promise to her father, had social pressure not prevented a drawing teacher from proposing to an heiress, the plot to defraud Laura of her identity and usurp her possessions never could have crystalized. Hartright would not have had to take the law into his own hands and, acting as providence's deputy, pursue Sir Percival and Count Fosco to their deaths.

But consequences of the age's Cinderella complex, Dickens demonstrated, overshadow the disasters caused by adherence to propriety. Hartright's ethically problematic conduct does not result in multiplication of the original evil. Collins's protagonists grow stronger as they transgress, and society improves. The era's Cinderella complex, on the other hand, perpetuates itself. Perennial cinder persons, such as Magwitch, and frustrated Cinderellas like Miss Havisham cannot withhold fealty to the age's most influential fairy tale. Miss Havisham eagerly plays fairy godmother, deceptively for Pip and perversely in raising Estella; expulsion from society drives Magwitch to install Pip as snugly among the Haves as an ex-convict's money will allow.

Spurred by Dickens's desire to become a more psychological social critic, Collins hoped to complicate his fiction beyond his rival's by capitalizing on contemporary psychiatric theory. This he could have learned through John Forster, secretary to the Lunacy Commission in 1859 and 1860.[22] Collins also knew the available texts, such as Dr. John Conolly's *Indications of Insanity,* and was conversant with the ongoing controversies regarding mental illness that had been raging since 1854. As *The Woman in White* was being serialized, Parliament was deliberating the treatment of lunatics, including the disposition of their property.

For *The Woman in White,* Collins drew heavily on a French case: Mme. de Douhault's brother had her incarcerated in the Salpetrière under a false name in order to assume control of her inheritance. Sir Percival Glyde has similar designs on Laura's twenty thousand pounds. Through Glyde's nearly successful attempt to institutionalize one stepsister in place of the other, Collins decried Victorian society's lack of a viable definition of insanity. Uncertainty regarding proofs of mental illness, he warned, endangered sane and insane alike; it led to mistreatment of the latter and facilitated wrongful confinement of the former, twin abuses that *The Woman in White* dramatizes in the cases of Anne Catherick and Laura Fairlie.[23]

To underline the wrong done to Anne and Laura, Collins adopted "a mythical approach . . . to *Cinderella.*" He encouraged readers to sympathize with the mental patient as society's victim, "a kind of Cinderella, deprived of a life of privilege and thrust into an existence of privation, misery, and drudgery" (BFL, 92, 114). In an age obsessed with upward mobility, such "deprivation," it has been suggested, may even be characterized as "the failure of *great expectations*" (BFL, 116; italics added). Collins showed how easily Anne's retardation could be used to confine her unnecessarily and then be used again as the guise for Laura's confinement in her look-alike's place; he equated the predicament of both women with Cinderella's when she is reduced to a cinder girl.[24]

Does the mentally ill person's sudden fall from affluence (freedom) into drudgery (confinement) best illustrate the way social ills originate, grow, and finally burst forth? Dickens thought not. Magwitch is a social problem longer in the making than any mental breakdown. He resembles the cinder girl from the start: abandoned by a tinker who "took the fire with him, and left [young Magwitch] wery cold" (*GE,* 344), with no cinders to huddle next to. In Dickens's opinion, a transported felon, not an asylum-bound heiress, better symbolized society's penchant for concealing its deficiencies, for banishing victims of unfairness and neglect.[25] Instead of beginning with a mental patient escaping "on a close and sultry night" (*WW,* 46), Dickens's parodic revaluation commences "on a memorable raw afternoon" (*GE,* 3) with a prisoner fleeing the hulks, an escape not just from harsher confinement but one that poses greater danger to social stability.

Collins believed that he had exposed a major social failing—his era's laxity in defining and scrutinizing mental problems. Fashioning "a psychological study for his time," he had certified himself a novelist "skilled in psychological analysis," especially in depicting Anne Catherick (BFL, 121, 135). Pip, Dickens countered, was the psychological study the times required; he suffers the real loss of "great expectations" (*GE*, 137), a more significant setback than either Anne's loss of freedom or Laura's deprivations, because Pip's false hopes are indicative of a general lunacy. Collins was right to link Cinderella and mental patients, Dickens snickered, but chiefly because the expectancy that her rise (or recovery) supposedly justified could be seen as the equivalent of a psychological disorder.

In short, Dickens worried about the psychological well-being of the individual who aspires to emulate Cinderella and the sanity of a nation that identified its rise with hers.[26] *Great Expectations,* not *The Woman in White,* supplied the era's missing definition of madness: a capacity for inordinate expectations, as seen many times over in Pip's plans for himself, Magwitch's for Pip, Miss Havisham's for Estella, even Wopsle's for English drama, all of which go awry. Instead of Cinderella serving Collins as a symbol for society's victims, its mental patients especially, a series of parodic Cinderellas epitomizes a communal madness worse than slavish observance of the proprieties.[27] Pip and Miss Havisham signify the general mental malady, sad yet ridiculous, of being overly—indeed, madly—expectant.

According to Sir Henry Dickens, the woman in white's appearance to Walter Hartright in the Hampstead Road was one of the two scenes in literature that his father regarded as being "the most dramatic descriptions he could recall" (HD, 54).[28] When Dickens opens *Great Expectations* with the sudden eruption of an escaped convict—"a fearful man, all in coarse grey," Pip's impression is that Magwitch "started up from among the graves at the side of the church porch." This horrific resurrection supersedes Hartright's notion that the woman in white "had that moment sprung out of the earth" (*GE*, 4; *WW*, 47).[29] Instead of "a hand laid lightly" on Walter's shoulder, Pip exclaims that the convict "seized me by the chin" (*GE*, 4–5).

Collins's white-clad Cinderella figure is fleeing not from a ball at the stroke of midnight "because it is so late" (*WW*, 53), but from unmerited imprisonment in a nearby madhouse. "She has escaped from my Asylum," one of her pursuers cries (*WW*, 55). Yet *The Woman in White* still culminates with Walter's Cinderella-like ascent and Laura's Cinderella-like recovery, both of which Walter's rescue of Anne, herself a variation on the cinder girl, nicely prefigures. The difference, Dickens insisted, is between complicity (*The Woman in White*) and subversion (*Great Expectations*). Collins's sensational opening only looks like revaluation. Ultimately, it substantiates *Cinderella.*

Readers perusing the first chapter of *Great Expectations* should realize they are reading an irreverent redoing of *Cinderella*—the novel's fairy godmother demanding succor from its cinder girl. The assistance Pip gives Magwitch— "wittles" and "a file" (*GE*, 5)—surpasses Walter's service to Anne, for whom he merely summons a cab. Thanks to this opening scene, Magwitch resolves to punish society by making a Cinderella for himself since he cannot make one of himself. In short, both novelists begin with a pivotal incident that alludes to *Cinderella*, but Dickens's pivot is also a stake.

Dickens proposed Pip, not Anne Catherick, as the obligatory mental case, the figure around whom a first-rate psychological novel should turn. Collins may have thought he had done "a study of an aberrant Victorian adolescent" (BFL, 123), but Pip fits this description better than Anne, whose internal state is never explored. Dickens protested that his extended analysis of Pip's mental condition addresses the nation's even as it punctures the very fairy tale Collins uses to give *The Woman in White* its psychological dimension.

Pip's outing with Biddy on a lovely summer Sunday may be read as a parodic revaluation of Anne's eerie midnight escape from the asylum. Chapter 17 of *Great Expectations* is not just a parody of Potts courting Kate in chapter 16 of *A Day's Ride;* to savor fully the tragicomedy in Pip's ridiculously self-destructive behavior, the modern revaluator should explicate chapter 17 a second time as the exploration of a would-be Cinderella's unsettled mental state, hence a further deflation of the Cinderella motifs in Collins's melodrama.[30]

Biddy is Dickens's novel's only reasonable facsimile for Cinderella, but Pip's Estella fixation prevents him from recognizing her until too late.[31] Although chapter 17 commences with an account of Biddy's "extraordinary" improvement in appearance and temperament, Pip continues to think of her as "common" (that is, a cinder girl); she "could not be like Estella," the "beautiful young lady at Miss Havisham's" (*GE*, 124). Consequently, when Pip walks out with Biddy, an ostensible act of courtship, the would-be escapee from life at the forge comes to resemble a bedlamite being given an airing by his attendant.

Throughout chapter 17, Mr. Pirrip presents his younger self not just as someone desperate to be genteel, but also, and in consequence, as a person with a socially significant mental disturbance. "I want to be a gentleman," he informs Biddy in what he himself calls "a *lunatic* confession" (*GE*, 126, 128; italics added). Biddy shakes her head "with a sorrowful air" to hear such craziness. At one point, as Pip's desires pull him in one direction (Estella's) while common sense points to Biddy, he seems schizophrenic; he experiences a recurrence of "the singular kind of quarrel with myself which," he complains, "I was always carrying on" (*GE*, 127).

As Pip and Biddy sit side-by-side in the grass by the river, she tries to "put [him] right" by pointing out that Estella is "not worth gaining over" if she makes him miserable (*GE*, 128). Stung by this rebuke, Pip behaves like a madman: "I turned over on my face . . . and got a good grasp of the hair on each side of my head, and wrenched it well. All the while knowing the *madness* of my heart to be so very *mad* and misplaced that . . . it would have served my face right if I had lifted it up by my hair, and knocked it against the pebbles as a punishment for belonging to such an *idiot*" (*GE*, 128; italics added). Carefully, Biddy recovers her patient; she removes Pip's hands "one after another" from his hair, "soothing" him until his fit dissolves in tears.

Whenever Pip appears on the verge of reconciling himself to life at the forge with Biddy and Joe, his Cinderella complex deranges him. "Some confounding remembrance" of Estella and Satis House ("the Havisham days") "would fall upon me," he confesses, "and scatter my wits again" (*GE*, 131). Mr. Pirrip repeatedly describes his younger self "picking up" his "scattered wits," vainly attempting to collect himself mentally. "And often, before I had got them well together," Pip laments, they "would be dispersed in all directions" a second time "by one stray thought" of Estella (*GE*, 132). That such thoughts are most unsettling, tantamount to a serious mental breakdown, is evident from Pip's virtual reuse of the phrase "fall upon me" for the sudden collapse of his expectations when Magwitch returns: "in an instant . . . the roof of my stronghold dropped upon me" (*GE*, 310).

Dickens uses Orlick to connect chapter 17 with the redoing of Collins's dramatic opening in chapter 1 of *Great Expectations*. By the time Biddy and Pip return from their excursion, it is evening. At the sluice gate near the churchyard, Pip recalls, Orlick "started up . . . from the ooze" (*GE*, 130), much like Magwitch "started up from among the graves." More so than Pip, for whom he serves as a darker second self, Orlick behaves like an escaped lunatic, not only "dancing at Biddy" but "with a yell of laughter . . . slouching after" them all the way home (*GE*, 130). Orlick's antics choreograph Pip's internal disorder. Instead of a single escapee, "a solitary Woman" all "in white" (*WW*, 47), Dickens supplies Magwitch, Pip, and Orlick—the first a more dangerous fugitive for society to deal with, the latter pair more indicative of its unstable mental condition.

Hartright obeys his instincts and rescues Anne despite an "uneasy sense of having done wrong" (*WW*, 54).[32] As Walter hesitates to intervene, Collins fires his opening salvo against propriety's restrictive influence. Besides the impropriety of meddling in matters unclear to him, Walter experiences moral uncertainty: an unattended woman on a lonely road late at night is possibly a prostitute whose request for help may be solicitation. In contrast, chapter 17 of *Great Expectations* amounts to a tragicomic dilemma, an impasse neither Pip nor Biddy resolves to the other's satisfaction. Pip remains the prisoner not just of menial existence at the forge but also of daydreams even more painful. Although

Biddy considers Pip's hopes "absurd," she despairs of rescuing a young fool whom she loves despite his increasingly snobbish attitude. The frustrations of a "poor dazed village lad," as he styles himself (*GE*, 128), reduce Biddy to tears.

Still confused at chapter's end, the village blacksmith's apprentice is a self-tormenting snob, whose mental turmoil is designed to make Walter's struggles look easy, if not unreal. The unsuccessful outing from the forge in chapter 17 makes Anne Catherick's liberation from the asylum inconsequential compared to Magwitch's escape and facile in light of Pip's continuing predicament. "Perhaps after all," Pip muses, invoking the wrong person as his liberator, "Miss Havisham was going to make my fortune when my time was out" (*GE*, 132). Implying that his apprenticeship is a term of confinement, a sentence being served, Pip cannot stop daydreaming of an alternative future he has done little to earn.

In Pip's twilight encounter with Estella in "the old garden" near the ruins of Satis House (*GE*, 478), Dickens redoes Collins's spectacular opening yet again. The opportunity to parody Collins coming and going, at start and finish, was a factor, one presumes, in Dickens's decision to revise his original ending. Miss Havisham's private asylum no longer stands, but Pip and Estella are both drawn to the spot; they "meet again," Pip marvels, "where our first meeting was!" Estella has never been back since marrying Drummle. That she returns on the evening Pip chooses to "revisit the sight of the old house" after an eleven-year absence (*GE*, 478) seems more providential than Walter's being on the road to London at the late hour when Anne eludes her captors.

Looking down "the desolate garden-walk," Pip beholds "a solitary figure" (*GE*, 478). Suspense builds as he realizes, in rapid succession, that it is "the figure of a woman" not a ghost, that the figure recognizes him and has "uttered [his] name" while approaching, that it is Estella. Dickens's closing scene emphasizes return, not escape. Unlike Walter, who facilitates Anne's flight, Pip detains Estella, proposing in effect to do so permanently. He exceeds Walter's role as rescuer in *The Woman in White* by combining it with Biddy's as Pip's caregiver in chapter 17. In short, Pip volunteers himself as Estella's keeper, offering to relieve and maintain her, not to restore her to former glory as Walter does with Laura. Pip takes Estella's hand in his, contrary to Walter, who removes from his bosom the woman in white's unwanted—indeed, improperly placed—"thin . . . cold hand" (*WW*, 50).

Unlike both Walter and Anne in Collins's opening and Walter and Laura at the close, Pip and Estella have put the Victorian novel's nonsense about Cinderella and her prince behind them. The second ending should be read as both the close and beginning of a crucial rescue mission. Once Pip liberates himself and Estella from a troublesome past, he insists they take care of each other. His final remarks sound like a prognosis for the recovery not of fortune or position as in *Cinderella* but of perspective or sanity. Pip and Estella have both come down in the world but seem to have regained their moral and mental balance.

Sir Percival Glyde enjoys considerable success turning first Anne, then Laura into cinder girls (asylum inmates), but Walter Hartright emerges as the novel's true maker and breaker of Cinderellas. He discovers that the spare copy of the marriage register for Welmingham Parish Church contains no record of Sir Percival's parents' marriage; so the entry in the vestry copy at Old Welmingham is a forgery. Walter is stunned to learn of Sir Percival's illegitimacy; he is "not Sir Percival at all, . . . he had no more claim to the baronetcy and to Blackwater Park than the poorest labourer who worked on the estate" (*WW*, 529).

Walter, Sir Percival realizes, can turn him from baronet to cinder girl: disclosure of his secret "would deprive him at one blow of the name, the rank, the estate, the whole social existence that he had usurped" (*WW*, 530). That Sir Percival's identity, his Cinderella-hood, is less substantial than his principal victim's (Laura's) is one of Collins's finest ironies; it drives the false baronet to his death in the vestry fire he accidentally sets while trying to eradicate his forgery before Walter exposes it.[33]

In Dickens's parodic revision, Pip is the greater pretender; he, not Sir Percival, epitomizes the illegitimate gentleman, not just the falseness of the commonly accepted idea of gentility, but also the venality of an elaborate socioeconomic system designed to elevate and protect a worthless ideal. The secret origin of Pip's status, his dependence for rank and fortune on Magwitch's years of hard labor, is an uglier fact of life, Dickens's revaluation claims, than Glyde's family "secret" (*WW*, 301).

Sir Percival has defrauded the legitimate heir, a distant relative of his father's. In England's fraudulent social system, those in positions of affluence and authority, Dickens argued, are seldom entitled to—indeed, rarely have earned—their wealth. Moreover, they seem unaware of its sources: the blood and sweat of Have-Nots, which Magwitch's exertions symbolize. Thus the world's Haves, Dickens lectures Collins, are often no more legitimate than Sir Percival, as Magwitch demonstrates by making Pip a "London gentleman" (*GE*, 319) and Pip illustrates in temporarily becoming one.

Sir Percival is exposed as a false Cinderella, a cinder girl in baronet's clothing; through Pip's downfall, wanting to rise like Cinderella is exposed as a more serious miscalculation, worse then Sir Percival's forgery. Just as the unfairly confined lunatic is not really a cinder girl, the technically illegitimate gentleman, Dickens objected, cannot be considered the falsest version of Cinderella. Better to substitute Pip in both cases: a tragicomically disturbed person instead of the undeservedly institutionalized Anne, an idle Londoner supported by a corrupt economic system rather than a literal bastard like Sir Percival. Having lived high on the labor of a Have-Not like Magwitch, the wrong sort of "second father" (*GE*, 317) every Have depends upon, is more shameful, Dickens maintains, than having no legal father at all.

Wiped out financially when Magwitch returns, Pip ends his London life abruptly. "In an instant the blow was struck," Pip reports, and his gentility, an imaginary edifice wrongly called his "stronghold" (*GE*, 310), collapses. In the termination "at one blow" of the "whole social existence" that Sir Percival "had usurped" (*WW*, 530), Dickens found the catastrophe that *Great Expectations* would outdo. Pip's downfall exceeds Sir Percival's, rivaling the terrible fate of the usurpers in the Misnar tale. For the flaming vestry in which the baronet perishes, Dickens substitutes the sultan's traplike pavilion; it crushes inordinate expectations generally. Only "one blow" is needed to destroy Sir Percival, yet the "blow" that levels Pip's "stronghold," falling "in an instant," does more extensive damage. An entire social framework comes crashing down; a class of usurpers, the Haves, is exposed instead of a single illegitimate inheritor.

Clothes chiefly make or disenfranchise Cinderella. Dressed raggedly as a cinder girl, she commands little respect; outfitted for the ball in resplendent gowns by her fairy godmother, she captivates a prince. Collins took liberties with *Cinderella*, as happens when Laura's half sister is forced to take her place,[34] but relies heavily on the clothing motif. It proves essential to the substitution of one half sister for the other. Collins's dependence on this motif gave Dickens an excellent opportunity to diminish the credibility of *Cinderella* and *The Woman in White* simultaneously.

To strip the era's Cinderella complex of its luster, to cancel Cinderella's rise as a paradigm for England's, Dickens derides the snobbish notion that dress determines destiny. In *The Woman in White*, he mocked, upward mobility requires no more than an improved wardrobe; conversely, removal of a person's clothes means loss of identity. No one in *Great Expectations* gains a firmer sense of self simply by donning new clothes. Tragicomically, Pip's sartorial improvements impress everyone except himself and Trabb's boy. Collins's shallowness as a psychological realist, Dickens alleged, stems in large part from his subscription to an unrealistic clothes philosophy borrowed from *Cinderella*.

Mrs. Fairlie's decision to dress Anne "all in white" (*WW*, 84) has been compared to the fairy godmother's gifts of new dresses to Cinderella (BFL, 119). The bestowal proves disastrous in the short run but is ultimately providential; the "violent fancy" (*WW*, 84) that Mrs. Fairlie takes toward Mrs. Catherick's daughter seems tamer than Magwitch's toward Pip, yet it triggers a general sorting out. Besides giving Anne a sense of identity, it leads to the discovery of her paternity as Mr. Fairlie's daughter.

More important, Anne's interchangeability with Laura might have gone unnoticed had the former not resolved to "wear white as long as I live" (*WW*, 84). Fosco could not have formulated the fatal plan whose backfire destroys Sir Percival and himself. Similar costuming reveals physical similarities. Only when Laura, "dressed in plain white muslin," stands "alone in the moonlight" does Walter connect her with the "solitary Woman" he encountered two nights before (*WW*, 86, 47). The plot that turns Laura into a cinder girl may be said to thicken rapidly from that moment.

In *The Woman in White,* garments that connect the look-alike half sisters with Cinderella and each other not only confer power and self-esteem; they also dictate the outcome of pivotal events. White clothes signify recovered freedom for Anne, who uses the magic in them to extricate herself from unjust confinement. When Laura's clothing is taken away, however, she forfeits all proof of her identity; she ceases to be Lady Glyde as suddenly as Cinderella changed from her father's darling into an ill-used kitchen maid once her stepsisters "took away her beautiful clothes" (*BG*, 87). No longer a baronet's wife, Laura becomes Anne Catherick instead, friendless and supposedly retarded.

Having procured a cab for Anne, who quickly drives away, Walter is overtaken by two men in a carriage. He overhears one of the asylum keepers tell a policeman that they are pursuing "a woman in a lavender-coloured gown." No, the other pursuer insists, "In white, policeman. A woman in white" (*WW*, 55). "The clothes we gave her were found on her bed. She must have gone away in the clothes she wore when she came to us." Repossessed of her prized outfit, Anne can escape, elude pursuit, solicit Walter's help, and thus regain not just her freedom but also her sense of self as the Cinderella whom Mrs. Fairlie draped in white.

Transformation of Laura Fairlie into the lowly Anne Catherick is accomplished through a simple change of costume. "Her own clothes were taken from her at night," Fosco later confesses to Hartright, "and Anne Catherick's were put on her in the morning" (*WW*, 630). Brought to the asylum that Anne escaped from at the beginning of the story, Laura is confined as Anne not just because of "the likeness" she bears her but also due "to the clothes" (*WW*, 631).

Having been drugged by Fosco, Laura recovers her senses in the asylum to find herself dressed and addressed as Anne Catherick. Walter narrates: Laura "heard herself called by Anne Catherick's name, . . . her own eyes informed her that she had Anne Catherick's clothes on" (*WW*, 448). "Each article of her underclothing" bears Anne's name. "Look at your own name on your own clothes," a nurse admonishes Laura, "and don't worry us all any more about being Lady

Glyde" (*WW,* 448). Were it not for her other half sister, Marian, who facilitates her escape, Laura might have had to become Anne permanently.

The Woman in White cannot be considered a good example of psychological realism, Dickens protested, when its plot pivots exclusively on externals, namely, clothes. Whoever is dressed like Laura, be it she or Anne, is accepted as Lady Glyde. In Dickens's anti-Cinderella parody, change of costume accompanies Pip's rise in the world but fails to strengthen his sense of identity or improve his self-worth. Pip finds no comfort in a new wardrobe; its tragicomic failure to generate sufficient internal reassurance—that is, to convert him from cinder person to Cinderella in his own estimation—is a bad omen. Dickens parodies *Cinderella* and *The Woman in White* at what he regards as their weakest point: the psychologically shallow illusion both encourage that appearances control reality, that a splendid outfit, as opposed to a grimy exterior, can produce internal improvement as well. In chapter 18, a village blacksmith's apprentice is advised to capitalize on his "great expectations" by dressing up (*GE,* 137), but can never do so impressively enough to suit himself.

Having adjourned from the Three Jolly Bargemen to Mrs. Joe's parlor, Jaggers, as Magwitch's deputy or stand-in fairy godfather, astounds Pip by proposing the young beneficiary's removal to London, where he can acquire a gentleman's education. But "first," stipulates Jaggers, "you should have some new clothes to come in, and they should not be working clothes" (*GE,* 139). Pip asks Mr. Trabb to make him "a fashionable suit of clothes," as if the tailor, acting the fairy godparent's part, could transform a blacksmith's apprentice into a cosmopolite. Between them, however, Jaggers and Mr. Trabb cannot do for Pip the miracle that Mrs. Fairlie works for Anne. Pip's transformation never convinces Pip. Despite a new suit, he remains unable to disguise his inner uneasiness, the suspicion that Joe's friendship and Biddy's love may be worth more than an apparently providential stroke of good fortune. Pip fails to experience his elevation internally; unlike Cinderella, he proceeds to exhibit his newly outfitted self in all the wrong places.

"New clothes" cause Pip un-Cinderella-like problems from the minute he orders them. He wants his selections "sent to Mr. Pumblechook's," where he intends to don them before leaving for London. "It would be very disagreeable to be stared at by all the people here," Pip confides to Joe (*GE,* 143). The budding snob turns a deaf ear when his best friend and protector points out that the Hubbles would like to see Pip in his new finery and that "the Jolly Bargemen might take it as a compliment" (*GE,* 143). "You'll show yourself to us, won't you?" entreats Biddy on behalf of Joe and herself.

Although Pip condescendingly complies with Biddy's request, he dresses up in his new clothes for the first time under the auspices of two false patrons, Mr. Pumblechook and Miss Havisham. "On Friday morning," nearly a week after Jagger's announcement, Pip goes to Pumblechook's "to put on [his] new clothes and pay [his] visit to Miss Havisham" (*GE*, 154). Neither of these phony fairy godparents has brought about Pip's alteration, even though the former takes credit for it and the latter, a malign rendition of Mrs. Fairlie, cruelly nurtures Pip's suspicions that she is responsible.

Both scenes—Pip's getting dressed at Pumblechook's and his farewell to Miss Havisham, whom he mistakes for his benefactor—parodically revalue Cinderella's triumphant changes of costume and Collins's reliance on the transformation motif. New clothes translate Cinderella from cinder girl to princess, just as Anne's white costume facilitates her escape and the loss of her ladyship's clothes relegates Laura to the asylum in Anne's place. Outwardly substantially enhanced, Pip finds his sense of having undergone a genuine alteration increasingly problematic in that he begins to change inwardly for the worse.

"My clothes were rather a disappointment, of course," Pip confesses. To rationalize this letdown, which the phrase "of course" starts to do, he adds his opinion that "probably every new and eagerly expected garment ever put on since clothes came in, fell a trifle short of the wearer's expectation" (*GE*, 154). Not so with Cinderella's ball gowns or Anne Catherick's white dresses. Each of the former's new outfits exceeds its predecessor: from one of gold and silver to "one even more splendid" to one "more magnificent and radiant than all the others" (*BG*, 90). Unlike Cinderella's new clothes, Pip's symbolize life's shortfalls, the tragicomic gap between materialistic expectancy and its insufficient gratification. Victorian society, in Dickens's opinion, was bound to experience similar disappointment; misled by its new-found prosperity after the bleak 1840s, it was basking in the comparatively good times of the 1850s rather than acknowledging fundamental inequalities in its socioeconomic system.

Ill at ease, Pip walks from Mr. Pumblechook's to Miss Havisham's "by all the back ways"; he feels "at a personal disadvantage, something like Joe's in his Sunday suit" (*GE*, 155).[35] Instead of waxing glorious as does Cinderella or boldly escaping like Anne Catherick, Pip skulks in his new outfit, feeling awkward and insecure, a usurper or impostor.

Miss Havisham encourages Pip to think his new clothes are of her providing. "'This is a gay figure, Pip,' said she, making her crutch-stick play round me, as if she, the fairy godmother who had changed me, were bestowing the finishing gift" (*GE*, 155). Pip's farewell visit to Miss Havisham is the most tragicomic in a crescendo of scenes from chapters 18 and 19 that depict his transformation from village lad to London-bound gentleman as a parody of Cinderella's metamorphosis from kitchen servant to prince's bride, a metamorphosis England liked to think was analogous to its own. Of such nonsense, Dickens implied, mid-Victorian society's Cinderella complex was made.

"The finishing gift," as Pip calls Miss Havisham's cruel imitation of a fairy godmother's kindness, counts as a euphemism within a euphemism: a non-gift that anglicizes the coup de grâce. When Miss Havisham plays along with Pip's insinuations that she is his mysterious patron—"my fairy godmother," he says aloud (*GE*, 155)—the enchantress seals his fate, corroborating his misconceptions about the source of his illusions for the next twenty chapters until Magwitch returns. "Good-bye, Pip!—You will always keep the name of Pip, you know" (*GE*, 156), declares Miss Havisham. Echoing Jaggers's stipulation, actually Magwitch's, Miss Havisham imposes a condition that Pip believes only his benefactor would know. Her parting words, part prophecy, part command, parody Anne Catherick's promise to Mrs. Fairlie: "I will always wear white as long as I live" (*WW*, 84).

Mrs. Fairlie resolves to "have a stock of white frocks, made with good deep tucks, to let out for [Anne] as she grows" (*WW*, 85). Anne's outburst comes in response to Mrs. Fairlie's genuine generosity: a lifetime supply of gowns and the sense of identity they confer are real gifts. The "deep tucks" promise healthy growth. But Miss Havisham has not bought Pip's clothes; nor will he grow into the expectations she cruelly raises to enchant him and punish her overly expectant heirs. Anne's gratitude is childish but sincere, Pip's uncalled for. She is simple—indeed, retarded—but he behaves more foolishly.

When Miss Havisham "stretched out her hand," Pip reports, "I went down on my knee and put it to my lips" (*GE*, 156). The scene is painful to witness yet profoundly ludicrous; instead of a knight or a lover pledging fealty to his lady, a village blacksmith's apprentice pays undeserved homage to a dotty but spiteful recluse. To the extent that Pip's expectations represent those of his deluded society, Dickens portrays Victorian England as a would-be Cinderella kneeling in reverential acknowledgement of its good fortune, which is personified as a bitch goddess whom it has mistaken for its fairy godmother.

Before leaving for London, Pip treats Joe and Biddy to proof of his transformation from cinder girl to Cinderella: "On this last evening," Pip writes, "I dressed myself out in my new clothes, for their delight, and sat in my splendour until bedtime" (*GE*, 156). The phrase "for their delight" is Mr. Pirrip's satiric description of his younger self's ridiculous attempt at selfless magnanimity. Full of misgivings, Pip makes an uneasy Cinderella, a snob on the verge of self-contempt. His "splendour" suggests an Eastern potentate, an incongruity in Mrs. Joe's kitchen yet with powers lasting only "until bedtime," which sounds more provisional than Cinderella's transformation, if not banal as well. Not surprisingly, Pip's sleep consists of bad dreams.

The next morning, having taken his leave, Pip turns to see "Joe throwing an old shoe after [him] and Biddy throwing another" (*GE*, 157). Presumably as a good-luck gesture, shoes are normally tossed at departing newlyweds. Here they complete Dickens's parody, throughout chapters 18 and 19, of the clothes motif from *The Woman in White*. Inordinate expectations are Pip's bride: a guaranteed income and the status it confers. Although he is being celebrated, shoe tossings make it look as if he were being driven away. Bombarded, Pip is clearly a phony Cinderella, who leaves no glass slipper in his wake.³⁶

To pay the former's mounting debts and finance the latter's intrigues, Sir Percival and Count Fosco compel the look-alike half sisters to change places: Lady Glyde is to be institutionalized as Anne, while the latter is forced to give Sir Percival the money he would receive in the event of his wife's death. Unfortunately, Anne dies of heart failure the day before Sir Percival brings Laura to St. John's Wood to make the switch.

Nevertheless, Laura is confined to an asylum as Anne Catherick, Anne is buried as Lady Glyde, and Sir Percival inherits. After Marian Halcombe secures Laura's release, she is rejected by all, including her uncle, as an impostor to "the name, the place, and the living personality of dead Lady Glyde" (*WW*, 434). Ironically, Laura is dismissed as a would-be usurper, falsely claiming to be Cinderella when actually she is an heiress trapped in the identity of a cinder girl.

Bent on "restoring [Laura] to her place in the world," determined "to win the way back for her" to her name and inheritance" (*WW*, 581, 434), Hartright gradually nurses a cinder girl back into the princess she was. Once Sir Percival is dead, Laura "sometimes looked and spoke like the Laura of old times" (*WW*, 577).³⁷ "The worn and wasted look which had prematurely aged her face was fast leaving it," Walter observes, "and the expression which had been the first of its charms in past days was the first of its beauties that now returned" (*WW*, 576); indeed, the "golden days of our first companionship seemed to be revived . . . as if Time had drifted us back on the wreck of our early hopes to the old familiar shore!" (*WW*, 577). Walter is able "to restore" Laura's good looks along with "her station" (*WW*, 435). Reversing time's passage, Collins's hero puts everything back the way it was before Laura accepted Glyde.

In Dickens's parodic darkening of these allegedly unrealistic developments, shipwreck is irreversible.³⁸ Pip cannot restore Estella or times past. He cannot restart Miss Havisham's clocks or rebuild Satis House. Unlike Laura's returning charms, "the freshness of [Estella's] beauty was indeed gone," Pip admits (*GE*, 478). When Dickens parodies Walter's restorative efforts on Laura's behalf, Pip's detective work, his research into Estella's parentage, turns up an ex-convict and a murderess.³⁹ The precariousness of ascendancy, Dickens maintained, not the fragility of identity, is what *Cinderella* should be revamped to illustrate.

Replacing *The Woman in White* with *Great Expectations* was not usurpation, Dickens believed, but analogous to reinstalling Laura Fairlie or removing Sir Percival in favor of the legitimate heir. Pushing aside Collins as the expert on sanity, the superior melodramatic realist crowned himself the decade's up-and-coming psychological novelist. He examined the Cinderella complex as a widespread psychosis, a personal and communal illusion that, in Pip's case, has neurotic side effects (guilt, anxiety). Pip's snobbish desire to rise like a Cinderella makes his "state of mind" (*GE*, 42), arguably the novel's main concern, not just more distracted than poor Anne Catherick's or more frantic than Sir Percival's, but more indicative than either of the national craziness.

Chapter 6
Mary Shelley

Besides trying to obliterate Walter Hartright's encounter with the woman in white, Dickens's sensational opening aimed to discredit chapter 16 of *Frankenstein,* in which the creature tells his creator how he strangled the latter's younger brother. *Great Expectations* commences by reworking Mary Shelley's child-snatching scene. When Magwitch grabs Pip, Dickens seizes control of Shelley's novel, promoting a fleeting incident into a seminal one. Incompetent as a monster-maker, the implied argument goes, Shelley could hardly be expected to foresee a social system that regularly turns people from all classes into monstrosities.

Time and place matter little in chapter 16, Dickens complained. William Frankenstein meets his doom under idyllic conditions; as monster stifles boy, "gentle breezes" accompany a brilliant sunset "behind the stupendous mountains of Jura" (*F,* 122). In contrast, Dickens's thoroughly English monster freezes in a country churchyard composed from two churches just outside Rochester.[1] Mixing resurrection with nativity, Magwitch rises "from among the graves" (*GE,* 4) on a cold Christmas Eve. Little William taunts Shelley's monster, rashly calling it "an ogre" who wishes to "eat" him (*F,* 123). When the starving Magwitch contemplates Pip's "fat cheeks" (*GE,* 5), Dickens's darker, cannibalistic world displaces Shelley's sunlit Switzerland; ironically, it is Pip who will live off Magwitch.

Frankenstein's monster relates William's demise in a few words: "I grasped [the child's] throat . . . and in a moment he lay dead at my feet" (*F,* 123). Dickens prolongs and later repeats the Pip–Magwitch encounter. True monstrosity, he demonstrates, is not displayed in Shelley's sixteenth chapter but throughout his thirteenth novel. *Great Expectations,* not *Frankenstein,* tells the true story of how a child, snatched from his surroundings, becomes the instrument for a complicated revenge. "I have sworn eternal revenge" against "all mankind," Frankenstein's monster exclaims, but William's homicide, swift and uncompromising, cannot rival the grotesque mixture of cruelty and benevolence in Magwitch's long-term plans for Pip. To parody Shelley's much-too-abbreviated child-snatching scene, *Great Expectations* replaces obnoxious child and simplistic creature with a profounder study not only of revenge's social causes but also of its psychological consequences for victim and perpetrator alike.

In the ever-widening case of *Great Expectations* versus the Victorian era's Cinderella complex, novels could be considered enemies of realism if they were imbued with Cinderella motifs or facilitated another novelist's use of them. Shelley was vulnerable in the latter regard; having ignored the parody of Cinderella and her fairy godparent latent in the creator–creature relationship, she left the way open for *Jane Eyre* to install the Cinderella figure as a cultural heroine.

Great Expectations is an up-to-date monster story that dismisses Shelley's as a ludicrous fairy tale. A fairy godparent making a Cinderella, Dickens insinuated, is just as unnatural as Shelley's misguided scientist creating his creature. To undermine *Cinderella* and *Frankenstein* simultaneously, Dickens insists on fundamental resemblances between them. In Dickens's tragicomic grotesquerie, both Magwitch and Miss Havisham, fairy godparents to Pip and Estella respectively, are also monster-shapers.[2]

In other words, Dickens sought to dismiss *Frankenstein* as a bizarre fairy tale; he wanted to designate *Cinderella*, as well as nineteenth-century novels reliant upon Cinderella motifs—novels such as *Jane Eyre*—the real horror stories. Pip's autobiography combines yet subverts both. Pip is seized by a monster who turns out to be his fairy godparent; a would-be Cinderella discovers he is the creature of a Frankenstein-like monster.

Great Expectations should be read as an anti-Cinderella story in which Magwitch's efforts to raise Pip socially recall Frankenstein's to impart life to his creature. Ironically, Magwitch physically resembles the monster, whereas his creation passes for respectable urban gentility. Dickens finds truly monstrous the clamorous overexpectancy that Cinderella's story inspires not only in Pip but also in creatures like Jane Eyre, in Dickens's eyes a little monster who never outgrows her Cinderella complex. Deflating *Frankenstein* as a twisted fairy tale while designating *Cinderella* and novels based on it the stuff of horror stories, Dickens elicits smiles and gasps simultaneously, making *Great Expectations* all the more tragicomic.

The challenge was to write a monster story more pertinent than *Frankenstein*—more intense psychologically, timelier—without interfering with a would-be Cinderella's realization that he has been reliving the story of Misnar's pavilion. Magwitch's return supplies the catalyst: a monsterlike ex-convict manifests himself as Pip's maker (that is, fairy godfather). His reappearance triggers the traumatic epiphany that collapses the protagonist's expectations as if they were the sultan's fabled pavilion and Pip one of the usurpers therein. Pip discovers that he is as much Magwitch's creature as the ex-convict he succored is his, the ultimate horror story being that society's Haves and Have-Nots create each other. Dickens reprimands Shelley for missing the parody of *Cinderella* implicit in the relationship of monster to maker, then blames her again for writing a monster story no longer cautionary for the 1860s.

George Levine called *Frankenstein* one of realism's "central myths" and yet "an antimyth" (GL, 25, 27). Dickens's response to Shelley's story is much clearer: *Cinderella,* he opines, became the Victorian era's key myth because *Frankenstein* was not the antimyth it ought to have been.

Frankenstein, one admirer of Shelley's novel maintained, "is absolutely obsessed with how a Monster is made and in the making of the Monster Mary Shelley has depicted with disturbing effectiveness just what 'monstrosity' is" (DM, 52). Monsters can be produced, Shelley warned, by "uninhibited scientific and technological development, without a sense of moral responsibility" (AM, 114).[3] Dickens disagrees on both counts. The entire social system is implicated in the making of psychologically misshapen creatures such as Magwitch and Miss Havisham, not just the scientists at work within its technological community. Dickens's parodic reassessment of Shelley's novel redefines monstrosity. How society creates outcasts such as Magwitch, how money creates gentlemen like Pip—these variations on the theme of monster-making are the new horror stories for the times; instead of Shelley's *Frankenstein,* old-fashioned and irrelevant in Dickens's opinion, they should be required reading for all Victorians.

Shelley, says Dickens, understands less about monsters than Thackeray or Lever knew about snobs; none of these three novelists anticipated that snobs would overrun England by 1860 or that snob and monster frequently would be the same person. If the truth were shown, Dickens told Shelley and Thackeray both, Pip's snobbish cravings for wealth and gentility would be recognized for the society-wrecking monstrosities they are.

Both monster and monster-maker, Magwitch exhibits a capacity for monstrosity beyond Shelley's comprehension. Yet the monsterlike Miss Havisham is nearly his equal as a monster-shaper. Thanks to this pair of snobs—an ex-convict and a jilted bride each anxious to get even for being overlooked and undervalued—the pursuit of revenge pervades *Great Expectations* where it is revealed as a supremely grotesque form of monstrous (snobbish) behavior.

Dickens insisted that he, not Shelley, shows how monsters are made—not just Magwitch and Miss Havisham, but also how Magwitch makes Pip and Miss Havisham makes Estella. Compeyson, who represents the gentleman class, has a hand in creating both Magwitch and Miss Havisham. Wemmick may be seen as Jaggers's creature, if not his creation, just as Mr. Trabb has his boy. Pip is stalked, or at least plagued, by a small army of monsters: Magwitch, Orlick, Drummle, the "avenging phantom,"[4] even by Joe who descends on Barnard's Inn in chapter 27 like a comic Frankenstein's monster.

The situation becomes complicated when Trabb's boy, "attended by a company of delighted young friends" (*GE*, 245–46), accosts Pip three times in rapid succession. On each occasion, "that unlimited miscreant" ridicules Pip's Cinderella-like transformation from blacksmith's apprentice to urban gentleman; twice he affects to be dazzled by Pip, then mimics the latter's snobbish haughtiness. His "dignity" in tatters, Pip flees "across the bridge . . . into open country" (*GE*, 246), feeling he has been "ejected" from town in "disgrace."

Dickens rewrites as tragicomedy the incident in which Frankenstein's monster is "attacked" by villagers; "grievously bruised by stones," the creature is forced to escape into "open country" (*F*, 95). As with the child-snatching scene, Dickens elaborates a situation whose convolutions Shelley underestimated. It is creatures like Pip, not Frankenstein's monster, whom society would be well advised to drive from its midst, Dickens tells Shelley, and derision makes a more powerful weapon than stones.

When Pip buys his London clothes at Trabb's, he causes the tailor's boy much misery. Already a snob, Pip is overjoyed to see "the most audacious boy in all that country-side" literally "collapse" when the unctuous tailor ushers his "distinguished" customer out the door (*GE*, 149–50). The bigger the gap between himself and Trabb's boy, the better Pip's newfound self-importance feels. Disgruntled, without expectations, destined always to be a cinder girl, Trabb's boy nevertheless considers himself on terms of "equality with any blacksmith" (*GE*, 149), so his triple assault on Pip in the High Street is a snob's revenge upon a snob.

Thanks to Trabb's boy, Pip is stalked by a ruthless caricature of himself, a projection as painfully humorous as Orlick's will be morose and deadly. But it is Cinderella—the gentleman Pip has become—who is effectively exposed as a social enormity, not Trabb's boy or Orlick. Expulsion of Frankenstein's monster seems easy and obvious in comparison.

One marvels at the conflation of *Frankenstein* and *Cinderella* in Dickens's redoing of the monster's expulsion as the Trabb's boy episode, Dickens's point being to suggest interchangeability, just as he later makes Pip and Magwitch each other's creature. Trabb's boy is both a non-Cinderella and Pip's harasser, whereas Pip's embattled Cinderella-hood comes to seem a monstrous creation. In other words, a monster who will never be Cinderella stalks a Cinderella whose elevation has made him monstrous, a creature to be ostracized. Thanks to Pip's Cinderella-like rise, both he and Trabb's boy have become uniquely Victorian monsters: snobs.

Pip and Trabb's boy, Pip and the "avenging phantom," Pip and Orlick, Pip and Drummle, even Pip and Joe—Dickens multiplies parallels to Frankenstein and his creature; the more variations he introduces, the more limited Shelley is made to appear. But Pip and Magwitch constitute the main parodic revaluation, a systematic deepening and darkening of Shelley's basic situation. *Great Expectations* is crammed with monsters and monster-makers because, to Dickens's horror, monstrosity has become the social norm. Tragicomic developments from Cinderella-like expectations, developments seldom unrelated to the snobbery and desire for revenge born of socioeconomic inequities—that, said Dickens, is what monstrosity really is. Enumerating its mid-century variations, he reduced Shelley's novel to a one-pointed, outdated exploration of what had become a widespread phenomenon. From top to bottom, Dickens scowled, society was monster-ridden, more grotesque than any Gothic novel.

As Pip reads to Magwitch in a "Foreign language," the latter surveys him "with the air of an Exhibitor." Pip resembles a scholar being presented for public examination or, less flatteringly, the trained animal of a carnival showman. "The imaginary student pursued by the misshapen creature he had impiously made," Pip despairs, "was not more wretched than I, pursued by the creature who had made me, and recoiling from him with a stronger repulsion, the more he admired me and the fonder he was of me" (*GE,* 337).

Parodic reversals abound. A creature whom the indifference of society has created now creates a creature all his own. But creation is an act of piety for Magwitch, expressive of his regard for Pip and reverence for gentility; he can imagine no greater gift. Pip's creator loves his creature, who abhors his creator, unlike Frankenstein, who dreads and dislikes his monster. Yet Pip rightly claims his predicament is worse than Frankenstein's. His consternation becomes increasingly plausible if one recognizes the conflation of *Frankenstein* and *Cinderella:* as a would-be Cinderella performs for a grotesque fairy godparent who reminds him of Frankenstein's monster, Pip learns that he too is a hapless creature; his social position, financial well-being, and marital hopes originate from, and depend upon, an uncouth ex-convict.

Pip makes a damaging sociological discovery, Dickens insisted, more pertinent than anything in *Frankenstein:* the nefarious gap between Haves and Have-Nots in nineteenth-century England only makes sense if each is seen as a monstrosity that the other continually creates. Pip's epiphany to this effect is more immediate and nearly as terrifying as the realization that his career parallels the usurpers' in the Misnar tale. The parallel with *Frankenstein* occurs to Pip on the spur of the moment, while he is actually reading to Magwitch; the reference to Misnar's pavilion is Mr. Pirrip's afterthought; it clarifies Pip's life story, not just his relation to Magwitch from chapter 39 onward, and thus remains the novel's controlling analogue.

Comforts enjoyed by England's more fortunate classes depend on the toil and hardship of the disadvantaged. Inequalities in the economic system create nothing but parasites and slaves—monsters on both sides. Inasmuch as Pip is Magwitch's creation and the latter is polite society's, Victor Frankenstein and his creature belong on the dustheap, Dickens implied; they no longer represent the current state of affairs. Dickens substitutes the complicated, highly ironic Pip–Magwitch connection for Shelley's no-longer-relevant creator–creature relationship. Shelley's protagonist is called "imaginary" (*GE*, 337), whereas Pip's sufferings, Mr. Pirrip maintains, are not. Having Pip allude to Shelley's novel suggests that he is real and *Frankenstein* just a story. Similarly, the socioeconomic system of Victorian England at mid-century is a more heinous offense against nature than the atrocious creature Frankenstein assembled.

Unlike Victor, who loathes his creation instantly, Magwitch grows "fonder" of his every second, but the more he admires Pip, the greater the latter's revulsion. Magwitch's snobbish regard for the gentleman he has created intensifies Pip's snobbish disdain for the monster who created him. Rescinding *Frankenstein*, *Great Expectations* defined a more perplexing bind: although Pip overcomes his disdain, no amount of misplaced pride that Have-Nots take in their handiwork can of itself bridge the gap between them and the Haves whom they benefit. Their helplessness to inspire regard exceeds that of Shelley's monster. All too eager to move from creature to creature-maker, Magwitch never perceives the extent of his failure in the latter role because Pip conceals the fact that the illegally returned transport's fortune has been confiscated. Transformation from cinder girl to Cinderella becomes horrible when the relationship of each to the other is revealed to be that of monster to monster-maker.

"I was the slave of my creature," Victor Frankenstein laments (*F*, 133) when asked to provide his monster a female companion. In great distress, he utters the words that presumably gave Dickens the idea for making Pip and Magwitch not just each other's creator but also each other's creature.[5] Both could utter Frankenstein's outburst with greater justification than Frankenstein, Dickens responded. In his parodic reworking of Victor's plight, the idea of being slave to one's creature becomes full-fledged; it furnishes a better analogy for the relation, under capitalism, of upper class to lower (and vice versa) than of scientist to science. Dismissing Frankenstein's protest as a one-dimensional role reversal, Dickens showed the truly horrifying state of affairs in Victorian society. Each half of an adversarial pair—privileged and disenfranchised (that is, victimizer and victim)—is as far from the other as Cinderella is from cinder girl; yet, paradoxically, they remain inseparable in that each is both the other's creator and sustainer.

Dickens claims to know better than Shelley what an abomination it is to create a monster and how awful it feels to be another's creature. Moreover, he depicts the inevitability with which the creator turns into the creature's slave, for power results in dependency. Frankenstein seems genuinely surprised by such a turn of events, but Pip's comments indicate that Dickens foresaw this phenomenon whenever an unnatural inequality prevails.

Magwitch is turned into a criminal outcast by society's neglect; to retaliate, he creates a gentleman, the epitome of an insider, but fails to anticipate his creature's revulsion at so unsightly a benefactor. Like Magwitch, Miss Havisham has been made into a monster by Compeyson's perfidy. Having created a heartless Estella to break men's hearts, she is reduced to futile pleading for her adopted daughter's affection. Estella and Miss Havisham, Pip and Magwitch, Magwitch and Compeyson—at some point, each member of each pair loses the upper hand and is at the other's mercy, even if only Pip declares himself "more wretched" than Frankenstein when faced with his "misshapen creature" (*GE*, 337).

Viewing himself "in a transparent pool," Frankenstein's monster confesses, "I became fully convinced that I was in reality the monster that I am" (*F*, 101). In Dickens's redoing, the parody of narcissism is tragicomic. Under Magwitch's scrutiny, Pip begins to perceive his absurd "condition" as an ex-convict's idea of a privileged person. "It does me good for to look at you, Pip. All I stip'late is, to stand by and look at you, dear boy!" (*GE*, 329) Pip sees his monstrousness through the eyes of a Frankenstein's monster who is inordinately thrilled with the useless creature he has made. Pip is what Magwitch would like to see if he were to stare at himself in a pool. But Pip takes little pleasure in the sight of Magwitch or in the latter's delight at seeing him, both of which involve intimations of monstrosity. In a moment of self-recognition, Pip regards himself not as a comfortable member of the well-to-do class but as a creature's creature, Dickens's harshest definition of a Victorian gentleman.

In other words, were it Pip gazing into the pool, he would not want to see either Magwitch, who calls himself a "dunghill dog" (*GE*, 317), or the unwholesome creation Magwitch calls "my gentleman" (*GE*, 330). Which is more disheartening, Dickens asks, the disgusting reflection of himself that Shelley's monster sees, or the commodity that Pip beholds? Through the eyes of its unsavory "owner" (*GE*, 319), Pip sees the artificial life-form (namely, a gentleman) that owner owns.

Regardless of books in foreign languages and fine clothes, each member of the privileged class, Dickens remarks, should be seen the way Pip sees himself when being seen by Magwitch: as a monstrosity made by monsters whom the privileged class has created. As Magwitch scrutinizes his "brought-up London gentleman" (*GE*, 319) with immense self-satisfaction, Pip acknowledges that his monstrosity is internal, not visible like the outwardly "misshapen" creature's in Shelley; it consists of all the foolish expectations that he "deserted Joe" (*GE*, 320)—that is, behaved monstrously—in order to gratify.

Frankenstein's monster's discovery of his ugliness is followed by an even uglier disclosure; from lessons Felix gives Safie, the monster concludes that "the possessions most esteemed" by society "were high and unsullied descent united with riches" (*F*, 106).[6] *Great Expectations,* Dickens contended, drives this lesson home more effectively; it specifies rank and wealth as hollow ideals that nevertheless enjoy higher esteem in Dickens's day than in Shelley's—proof that her monster's revelations changed nothing. As in the child-snatching scene, Shelley's touch is deemed superficial. Pip's life story dramatizes the scramble for money and position that Shelley's monster simply mentions; Dickens also explores the unhappy consequences of the scramble, which Shelley did not.

Frankenstein's creature classifies himself as "a monster, a blot upon the earth" when he fails to meet either of society's criteria for acceptance (*F*, 106). Still "absolutely ignorant" at this point of his "creation and creator," he lacks money, friends, property; to make matters worse, he is "endued with a figure hideously deformed and loathsome." Without the advantages of either wealth or birth, the monster concludes that he is "doomed to waste his powers for the profits of the chosen few" (*F*, 106).

To eclipse Shelley, Dickens converts the monster's discoveries into one devastating epiphany for Pip. Upon Magwitch's return, Pip sees himself as a monstrous creation; but he does so because his creation by a creature such as Magwitch obliges him suddenly to admit the monstrosity of the entire social system in which he and his maker are caught up. It dooms thousands like Magwitch to waste their energies in support of parasites such as himself. Not just the exploited worker is repugnant, Dickens corrects Shelley's monster, but also "the chosen few" who derive their "profits" from him. In Dickens's revision, Pip's knowing who made him, not ignorance of his maker, bars him from participation in a privileged class that refuses to admit its sustainers. Pip sees himself to be monstrous expressly because he has acquired the money and position Frankenstein's creature will never possess.

Compelling Pip and Magwitch to play both monster and monster-maker, Dickens complicated the creator–creature opposition in *Frankenstein* and made nonsense of Cinderella, for whom the roles of cinder girl and princess remain distinct; for her, going from the former to the latter is an unqualified improvement. *Great Expectations* fuses monster story and bildungsroman in that Mr. Pirrip equates his younger self's coming of age with making monstrous discoveries that Shelley's monster is incapable of.[7]

Dickens's parodic revaluation of *Frankenstein* updates Shelley's monster story for a Victorian audience. Easily as sensational as *Frankenstein, Great Expectations* claims to be more realistic, psychologically more complex, and of greater sociological relevance, three criteria that are the parodic revaluator's hallmarks. In Magwitch, John Forster observed, one beholds "a sort of upside down and altogether human Frankenstein monster,"[8] a more interesting sociological phenomenon than Shelley's incredibly single-minded fiend. In Pip's recognition of himself as his creature's creature, a monster made by the monster whom Pip and his ilk have made, Dickens locates the ultimate in tragicomic reversals.[9] In comparison, Frankenstein's monster's attempts to join the human race are deemed not merely pathetic and improbable in 1860 but also unimportant.

Victor Frankenstein creates a single monster. Unfairness and inequalities in Victorian society, Dickens jeered, create them by the score. The misguided scientist unwittingly parodies Cinderella's fairy godmother once, creating a repulsive Cinderella; but in thriving at the expense of the overworked and undervalued, Dickens charged, beneficiaries of England's class-driven, privilege-oriented economic system parody Cinderella's fairy godparent over and over with each new Have-Not produced. *Great Expectations* maintains that Magwitch stands for society's downtrodden proletariat more effectively than Frankenstein's monster. One thinks of Magwitch as an ex-felon who strikes it rich, yet he works harder in Australia than Frankenstein's creature does for old man De Lacey. For Frankenstein himself, the monster never lifts a finger. In Dickens's revision, a hard-working ex-convict represents the nineteenth-century's mistreated laboring class. Magwitch challenges a social system that not only created and exploited him but also treats his kind as outcasts if they object.[10]

Ironically, Frankenstein gets into greater difficulty by refusing to fashion a second creature than he did by making the first. His refusal of the creature's request for a mate—"You must create a female for me" (*F*, 124)—infuriates the monster, who immediately strangles Henry Clerval, Victor's best friend. On Frankenstein's wedding night, the creature renders his creator mateless by crushing the throat of Elizabeth Lavenza, Frankenstein's bride. In Scotland, Frankenstein actually begins to provide a companion for the creature but destroys it "half-finished"; "I had resolved in my own mind," Frankenstein confesses, "that to create another like the fiend I had first made would be an act of the basest and most atrocious selfishness" (*F*, 144). He wishes to prevent creatures like the monster from propagating "a race of devils" that might endanger "the existence of the whole human race" (*F*, 140).[11]

Dickens found Frankenstein's altruistic self-restraint absurdly belated. In *Great Expectations*, society's selfishness knows no limit; it does not care how many unfortunates the socioeconomic system spews forth even if they constitute a threat to its survival. Just as snobs create more snobs throughout Dickens's novel, monsters create other monsters; Magwitch is society's creation and Pip is Magwitch's, just as Estella is Miss Havisham's while Miss Havisham is Compeyson's handiwork. Such feats of propagation, Dickens informs Shelley, are virtually unstoppable in a materialistic culture obsessed with using everything, including other people, to obtain money and position or to get revenge for being denied them. *Frankenstein* misrepresented a widespread socioeconomic crisis as a biological one. Monstrosity is not a laboratory product, Dickens insisted, but a social construct. Erect a set of barriers separating classes—Haves from Have-Nots, for example—and you render them horrible in each other's eyes, the way Magwitch despises Compeyson and Compeyson fears Magwitch.

Having completed his "creature" in the lab at "one in the morning" on "a dreary night of November," Frankenstein is overcome by disgust (*F*, 57). But his attempt to hide in his room fails: the monster "forced its way through the window shutters"; it "held up the curtain of the bed" with "one hand stretched out" toward its maker (*F*, 58). In Dickens's parodic rewriting, Pip hears "a footstep on the stair" at "eleven o'clock" on a "wretched" night, "stormy and wet" (*GE*, 310–11). He is surprised, he says, to see his unexpected visitor "holding out both his hands to me" (*GE*, 312).

As Magwitch repeatedly tries to clasp Pip, Dickens does more than revise the monster's intrusion into Frankenstein's bedroom; he also replays his own opening chapter and Shelley's child-snatching scene a second time. Unlike Frankenstein's importuning monster, who whines and threatens, Magwitch exudes self-confidence, having come to collect dividends on his investment. Instead of a newly made monster plaguing his creator with complaints and demands, Magwitch returns from penal servitude, followed by years of unstinting self-sacrifice, to behold the fruits of his labor: to savor vicariously through Pip the pleasures and privileges of a system that individuals such as himself toil to uphold.

Magwitch's proffered embrace of the privileged class that Pip represents is tragicomic in its ambivalence; paternal yet potentially violent, it implies an arrangement that may have to be imposed upon the fortunate few by the slaves they decline to recognize, much less salute. One of the countless outcasts whose welfare Victorian England has ruthlessly neglected, having expelled him from its midst, Magwitch assumes a proprietary air both humorous and ominous, looking about him in Pip's apartments "as if he had some part in the things he admired" (*GE*, 312).

"You are my creator," Frankenstein's monster shouts at Victor, "but I am your master,—obey!" (*F*, 142) Compared to Magwitch's assumption of part ownership, this demand is mostly bluster. Frankenstein ignores it just as he rebuffs the creature itself the night of its creation. Realistically, Dickens countered, the monsters that society creates will assert rightful ownership even as they appear to be intruding. One minute Magwitch addresses Pip as "Master"; the next, he cannot resist taking credit for his unsuspecting dependent's prosperous circumstances: "I've made a gentleman on you! It's me wot has done it!" (*GE,* 312, 317)

Magwitch's unwelcome return, Dickens's second redoing of Shelley's child-snatching scene, also revises her account of Frankenstein's wedding night, when the monster intrudes to strangle his creator's bride. "O Estella, Estella!" Pip cries internally when he learns of his ties to Magwitch (*GE,* 318). Once the ex-convict has revealed himself as a most unsuitable benefactor, there can be no wedding night for his unhappy protegé. Unlike Victor and Elizabeth, Pip and Estella never reach the altar. Ironically, Pip's monster promises to find him a bride at the very moment he crushes all hopes for one: "There's bright eyes somewhere—eh?" beams Magwitch. "They shall be yourn, dear boy, if money can buy 'em" (*GE,* 318). The Pip–Magwitch interdependency is a bigger barrier to fruitful human relationships, *Great Expectations* argues, than is the Frankenstein–monster connection.

As in Shelley's child-snatching scene, Dickens complained, no correlation exists on Victor's wedding night between a gruesome murder and its pictorial setting: a "fair" day, a sighting of "beautiful Mont Blanc" enroute to the honeymoon villa, a gorgeous twilight and sunset (*F,* 166–67). In contrast, Magwitch manifests himself on a night appropriately apocalyptic: "mud, deep in all the streets" after days of rain, "furious" gusts of wind tearing off roofs, the bridge and shore near the Temple "shuddering" in wind and rain (*GE,* 310–11).

Whose obtuseness is more dangerous for society, Dickens asks, Frankenstein's or Pip's? The former never imagines that his creature's threats apply to Elizabeth; gentleman like the latter never suspect where their money actually comes from. "But didn't you never think it might be me?" Magwitch inquires. Pip's cry—"Oh, no, no, no, . . . Never, never!" (*GE,* 318)—precedes "O Estella, Estella!" by just a few paragraphs and is meant to sound more anguished than Elizabeth's scream.

The monster's every act of violence is directed against Victor's relatives and friends, yet he takes the creature's ominous declaration—"I shall be with you on your wedding-night" (*F,* 142)—personally. Even though all clues point to Magwitch, Pip persists in considering Miss Havisham his fairy godmother; he expects her to confer on him Estella and Satis House. Elizabeth's murder may seem a greater disaster than Pip's disappointment, but only the latter, Dickens implies, symbolizes the false hopes of an entire nation, what Walter Houghton, as if describing a wedding night, called "the note of ecstatic anticipation which marked the period after 1850" (WH, 33).

"As if possessed of magic powers," Frankenstein maintains, "the monster had blinded me to his real intentions" (*F*, 160). Excusing his own stupidity, Victor blames everything on the creature. Pip never thinks of Magwitch for a benefactor, because he is misled by Miss Havisham. When Pip accuses her of "humouring his mistake," she retorts: "You made your own snares. *I* never made them" (*GE*, 358). This is surely disingenuous, but Pip, unlike Frankenstein, is not allowed to excuse monstrous behavior. Foolishly, Victor neglects to tell Elizabeth about the monster; he promises to confide a "dreadful secret" on the "day after" their marriage (*F*, 159). To Pip's credit, he never informs Estella that her adopted mother deceived him or that her real father is a monsterlike former convict. So who is truly the victim of "magic powers" (that is, spells or enchantments), Dickens demands, Frankenstein or Pip? In identifying his secret patron, the latter's choice lies between a witchlike Miss Havisham and an ex-felon whose name combines "witch" with "Mag," probably short for "magus" or magician.

Armed for his wedding night, Victor appears ridiculous: "I carried pistols and a dagger constantly about me" (*F*, 161). But these are useless precautions it turns out; having brought Elizabeth to a remote villa, he leaves her for "some time" to search for the monster. Hearing her "shrill and dreadful scream," he rushes to their bedroom to find "the murderous mark of the fiend's grasp . . . on her neck" (*F*, 164).

In Dickens's redoing, Pip is more vulnerable than the new Mrs. Frankenstein. His roommate, Herbert, is away "on a journey to Marseilles," so Pip is very conscious "of being alone" (*GE*, 310). Alarmed by "a stranger" entering his apartment so late at night, he contemplates ejecting the intruder until Magwitch warns against it. But the returned transport, Mr. Pirrip writes, "grasped" Pip by his hands, not his throat; he wants to reward Pip, not choke him. Ironically, Pip's honeymoon as a London gentleman comes to an end as abruptly as Elizabeth's wedding night on Lake Como.

Stricken with fever in consequence of Elizabeth's violent death, Frankenstein spends "many months" distracted in a "solitary cell." He tells Robert Walton how he awoke to "reason" and "revenge" simultaneously (*F*, 166). These are incompatible, Dickens objected. Embracing both, Frankenstein has learned nothing; his symbolic death and rebirth are wasted. Magwitch's death brings on Pip's nearly fatal illness: "I had a fever . . . I suffered greatly, . . . I often lost my reason," Mr. Pirrip recalls (*GE*, 458). Under Joe's careful nursing, however, Pip gradually recovers and is reconciled to his oldest, truest friend. Frankenstein flees when the monster enters his bedroom; when it enters Elizabeth's, she dies. Whether the monster seizes Pip on the marshes (ch. 1) or tries to clasp him in the latter's apartment (ch. 39), he must stay put each time and cope. Eventually, Pip accepts responsibility for what society has made Magwitch and for what his surrogate father has made him. Magwitch, Orlick, Trabb's boy—Dickens's gallery of monsters for Pip to deal with is Shakespearean in its variations. Darker, deeper, funnier than *Frankenstein,* only *Great Expectations,* Dickens argued, begins to explore Victorian monstrosity in all its tragicomic complexity.

Pip reports "shrinking from Magwitch with the strongest repugnance"; "my blood again ran cold when he again took me by both hands," says Pip (*GE,* 320). Nevertheless, he permits Magwitch to remain overnight. Frankenstein attempts to lock the monster out; Pip locks Magwitch in: "My first care was to close the shutters, . . . and then to close and make fast the doors" (*GE,* 320). Rather than remain in the same room with the monster, Frankenstein escapes to the courtyard, where he spends the night "walking up and down in the greatest agitation" (*F,* 58–59). But Pip must hide Magwitch in his apartment for "about five days" (*GE,* 337) in tacit acknowledgment of their relationship as secret sharers; admitting he is Magwitch's creature while accepting responsibility for the ex-convict, Pip becomes his keeper's keeper.

Frankenstein never confides his "fatal secret" (*F,* 156) to relatives or friends even as their death toll mounts. He would never have had to see "the lifeless form of Henry Clerval stretched before" him (*F,* 149) if he had tipped off his best friend. In Dickens's revision, Pip asks Herbert to assume joint responsibility for Magwitch. Only Pip knows that the ex-convict's money has been paying for Herbert's partnership at Clarriker & Co. Hence the irony in Magwitch's promise that Herbert's loyalty will be rewarded: "[N]ever believe me or mine," Magwitch tells Herbert, "if Pip shan't make a gentleman on you!" (*GE,* 338). Pip's transformation of Herbert from unemployed planner of commercial ventures into successful businessman—"the only good thing I had done," Pip calls it (*GE,* 461)—breaks the pattern of monster-making in *Great Expectations* whereby Compeyson creates Miss Havisham, who creates Estella, just as society spawns Magwitch, who fashions Pip.

In both *Frankenstein* and *Great Expectations,* the monster renders an account of itself that is designed to establish its essential humanity. Frankenstein's monster relates his attempts to befriend the De Laceys ("my beloved cottagers"; *F,* 111); the autodidact also delivers oral book reports on *Plutarch's Lives,* the *Sorrows of Werter,* and especially *Paradise Lost* (*F,* 113). Magwitch tells his life story to Pip and Herbert, who represent polite society. His account of how "a deserting soldier . . . learnt me to read; and a traveling giant . . . learnt me to write" (*GE,* 345) ridicules the unrealistic notion of Frankenstein's monster giving himself a liberal education: "I learned from Werter's imaginations despondency and gloom: but Plutarch taught me high thoughts" (*F,* 112).

Unfortunately, Frankenstein's monster fails to placate his maker: "I compassionated him," Victor says, " . . . but when I looked upon him, when I saw the filthy mass that moved and talked, my heart sickened, and my feelings were altered to those of horror and hatred" (*F*, 126). Similarly, Pip reports of Magwitch that "every hour . . . increased my abhorrence of him" (*GE*, 336). Yet chapter 54 ends with Pip relenting totally. Unlike Shelley's protagonist, he sees the fundamental humanity beneath an unprepossessing appearance.

Pip's reconciliation with Magwitch in chapters 39 through 54 redoes Frankenstein's failure with the monster. Dickens is not brightening Shelley's novel in this regard; on the contrary, he insists upon the harder course, reconciliation over rejection. The bond between Pip and Magwitch is a victory for the latter, whose gratitude toward Pip no longer includes using him to take revenge upon gentlemen. Pip triumphs too in that he accepts an ex-convict's loyalty and love unsnobbishly, never regretting Magwitch's money. "He need never know," Pip resolves, "how his hopes of enriching me had perished" (*GE*, 444).

The biggest benefiter is society. "Please God, I will be as true to you, as you have been to me!" Pip vows to Magwitch after their failed escape attempt. Certain to be tried and found guilty, Magwitch has advised Pip to disown him: "It's best as a gentleman should not be knowed to belong to me now" (*GE*, 444). Unlike Frankenstein, who resists being compassionate, Pip bonds with Magwitch at the worst possible moment; he not only admits to knowing Magwitch but accepts the latter's claim upon him. Dickens recommends a bonding between Haves and Have-Nots in which the former group recognizes the latter's worth; through Pip, the former swears to look after the latter's interests as assiduously as the efforts of hard workers such as Magwitch have furthered its own.

L.J. Swingle has pointed out that Shelley's novel "is a study of the mind in the process of trying to come to terms with the Stranger," the Other or Alien which, in Frankenstein's case, he not only encounters but has created (LJS, 61). For Shelley and Frankenstein, there can be no mutual comprehension between creator and creature. Although we learn how the monster is made, the monster itself, as Stranger or Other, remains an unknown quantity, perhaps an unknowable one, its essential goodness or malignity impossible to determine.[12]

Such a perspective, allegedly tragic, infuriated Dickens, who regards unknowableness of the Other as a failure of imagination. Pip's enlightenment is painful, indeed, disastrous. The minute he realizes who Magwitch is, the minute he fathoms their relationship, his expectations collapse like Misnar's pavilion. Coming to terms with the repulsive outcast is obligatory, however, arguably purgative and therapeutic as well. Society's obtuseness in treating creatures like Magwitch as Aliens must be condemned and corrected. The more one views the unknown as Other, Dickens warns admirers of Shelley's impractical sociology, the more monstrous (that is, unknowable) it becomes. Pip admits Magwitch and allows him to stay because the creature must be accommodated if society is to survive. Shunning Magwitch and his ilk is a fatal mistake, yet *Frankenstein,* Dickens protested, encourages just that.

Shelley, Dickens charged, cannot make peace between master and creature, who harden into implacable enemies; his revision of *Frankenstein* brings them together twice over. Pip and Magwitch cease to be strange to each other thanks to a reversal of roles that Victor never countenances, hence derives little benefit from. Dickens's pair acknowledges each other as both creature and creator; each accepts the other as his creature or responsibility; each is also willing to be dependent on the other. Once Pip alludes to *Frankenstein,* seeing himself in the creature's role and installing the creaturelike ex-convict in the monster-maker's, Dickens disallows Frankenstein's experience of monstrosity as unknowable Otherness.

Actually, Pip achieves a sympathetic understanding of more than one monster. He forgives Miss Havisham in a phrase reminiscent of Frankenstein's: "I stood compassionating her," Pip reports (*GE,* 393) just as Frankenstein says he "compassionated" the monster (*F,* 126) but then changes his mind. In effect, Pip pardons Magwitch a second time by forgiving Miss Havisham. In doing so, he seems to be scolding Frankenstein for callousness. "How could I look upon her without compassion . . . ?" Pip asks.[13]

Frankenstein refuses his creature a mate; Miss Havisham deceives Pip into thinking she is preparing Estella especially for him. Seeking forgiveness for this, Miss Havisham confesses to "monstrous vanities"; she has molded "an impressionable child" into a tool for "vengeance" (*GE,* 396). Yet Pip and Estella eventually reach an understanding, and Miss Havisham, like Magwitch, is reclaimed. Magwitch and Miss Havisham both perish, but not before Dickens reveals their inner drives and the social forces that shaped them. He makes the workings of their minds understandable. Consequently, the four major monsters in *Great Expectations*—Pip, Estella, Magwitch, Miss Havisham—manage to assert a basic humanness.

One finds a profusion of monsters in Dickens's novel, plus the implication that Victorian England's social system is monstrous rather than Cinderella-like. Nevertheless, Dickens's monsters repay psychological examination because their novelist-creator maintains that monstrosity is comprehensible as a socioeconomic disaster; contrary to Shelley, it constituted an unprecedented crisis in social relations, neither a biological dilemma nor an epistemological conundrum.

Victor Frankenstein perishes chasing his creature toward the North Pole; in Dickens's reworking, Magwitch is fatally injured trying to reach the North Atlantic. The difference is that he and Pip attempt to escape together. Technically, Magwitch is arrested for illegally returning to England, but his flight with Pip has the appearance of an unsuccessful elopement; they hasten toward the Continent, where despite the social gap between them, they hope to be allowed to live as father and son.

Frankenstein calls "destruction of the demon" a "task enjoined by heaven" (*F*, 170). Dickens refuses to accept Shelley's protagonist as an avenging angel on a par with Wilkie Collins's Mat Marksman or Walter Hartright. "Revenge kept me alive," Frankenstein tells Walton (*F*, 168); it fuels his pursuit of the monster across barren wastes. Easily misconstrued as a celebration of revenge, such harsh statements are never life-sustaining in Dickens's redoing. He transfers Victor's violent feelings to Magwitch, who experiences them early on in Australia; the thought of someday owning "a brought-up London gentleman," he informs Pip, was the "way I kep myself a going" (*GE*, 319). Having his own creature, not eliminating it, stokes Magwitch's fire.

Not one but two deadly struggles between creator and creature sensationalize the final chapters of *Great Expectations*, putting Shelley's conclusion to shame. Orlick attempts to strangle Pip in chapter 53, and Magwitch drowns Compeyson in the following chapter. Dickens rewrites Shelley by reconciling Pip to Magwitch, then outdoes her by having things both ways: Pip survives a vicious attack by a creature who blames him for all its disappointments, and Magwitch destroys the gentleman-crook responsible for leading him deeper into crime. "Side by side" at their trial, they may easily be seen as master and creature: "[W]hat a gentleman Compeyson looked," Magwitch tells Pip and Herbert, "and what a common sort of wretch I looked" (*GE*, 349).

When Orlick snares Pip in the sluice house, Dickens parodically revises Shelley's child-snatching scene for the third and final time. "Now . . . I've got you!" Orlick swears; it is "as if his mouth watered for me" says Pip (*GE*, 421). One is reminded of little William's fears of being eaten and of Magwitch "licking his lips" at the sight of Pip's plump cheeks (*GE*, 5). Having felled Mrs. Joe and persecuted Biddy, Orlick tries to intervene as violently in Pip's life as the monster does in Frankenstein's. More sensationally than Shelley, Dickens recognizes the monster as his protagonist's dark side, his antisocial self, hence both Pip's creature or creation and his responsibility. While Pip rises in the world, Orlick does his dirty work for him, settling old scores by punishing Mrs. Joe. Later, Orlick robs Pumblechook, Pip's other childhood tormentor.

In the sluice house scene, however, Orlick is not just "a distorted and darkened mirror-image" of Pip, "a monstrous caricature" of the seemingly passive Pip, who is revealed to be "monstrously ambitious" (JuM, 67, 70).[14] Orlick seems to be Magwitch's double as well. Mr. Pirrip presents Orlick as a variation on the theme that snobbery stems from one monstrosity and spawns another; that is, bred from social injustice and inequality, it leads to the desire for revenge. The ex-convict wants to take his place in society through Pip; Orlick simply wants Pip's place. Where Magwitch seeks revenge for not being allowed to become good enough for polite company, Orlick considers himself as good as Pip but unfairly passed over in the latter's favor. His is a snobbery born of acute personal envy:

"You was always in Old Orlick's way since ever you was a child," Orlick grumbles; "You was favoured, and he was bullied and beat" (*GE*, 421, 423).[15]

In a variation on Magwitch's unwelcome return, Orlick lures Pip back out on the marshes, where Magwitch first seized him. In one fell swoop, Orlick attempts to accomplish what Magwitch threatened to do to Pip, what Frankenstein's monster actually does to little William, but what, unaccountably, it never attempts against Victor himself. An aggrieved cinder girl eager to strangle Cinderella, Orlick personifies the violence that Dickens suspects every disgruntled drudge longs to wreak on so-called persons of quality.

Despite Orlick's failure to murder Pip, Dickens eclipses Shelley's child-snatching scene with yet another superior redoing, more suspenseful and more involved psychologically. The monster spells out his anger and frustration, which have been building for years. Pip seems to sense his darker self catching up with him, much as Magwitch's moving into his rooms signified society's sins come home to roost. Unlike both Frankensteins, Victor and little William, Pip is consumed by guilt—"the dread of being misremembered after death" (*GE*, 422). Silently numbering his sins, errors of both omission and commission, Pip makes a full confession, something Shelley never obtains from Frankenstein, the parodic revaluator reminded readers.

Eulogizing Frankenstein's corpse, the monster repents: "Oh, Frankenstein! generous and self-devoted being! what does it avail that I now ask thee to pardon me?" (*F*, 182). Dickens makes the monster's tardy grief seem ridiculous; futile as well as misplaced, it avails nothing. When Pip prays to God for the expired Magwitch, however, two things happen at once: creature intercedes for creator, and respectable society speaks up for the monster it has made. For this double healing to take place, Pip remembers to address his prayer for Magwitch—"O Lord, be merciful to him, a sinner!" (*GE*, 457)—to the creator of them both.[16]

"During these last days," a dying Frankenstein confides in Walton, "I have been occupied in examining my past conduct; nor do I find it blameable" (*F*, 180). This self-exculpation Dickens found laughable. Mr. Pirrip's book-long reexamination of his younger self's delusions and derelictions is unsparing, redolent with guilt, bristling with self-accusation. Pip's self-recrimination becomes clearer and more impressive when seen as a parody of Frankenstein's talent for self-justification.

Frankenstein presents himself as a second Lucifer, the usurping "archangel who aspired to omnipotence" (*F*, 176). "From my infancy," Victor laments, "I was imbued with high hopes and a lofty ambition; but how I am sunk!" Taken in, Walton attempts to elevate Frankenstein's life story into the stuff of tragedy: "What a glorious creature must he have been in the days of his prosperity, when he is thus noble and godlike in ruin! He seems to feel his own worth, and the greatness of his fall" (*F*, 175).

For Frankenstein's posturing and Walton's susceptibility to it, Dickens substitutes the tragicomedy of Pip's Cinderella-like rise; it culminates in a comedown comparable to the collapse of Misnar's pavilion: instead of a fallen angel, we see a failed Cinderella, diminished yet too ridiculous to be tragic. Realistically, Shelley's protagonist cannot be both guiltless and Lucifer-like. In contrast, Pip's life story shifts from *Cinderella* to the Misnar tale because the latter undercuts the former. Lucifer–Frankenstein is implausible, Dickens contended, not so Pip as a cinder girl whose spurious elevation makes him in effect a usurper. *Great Expectations*, not *Frankenstein*, is the cautionary first-person narrative that society should heed as potentially a telling of its own story, Dickens argued. Frankenstein misrepresents his degradation as tragedy: a tumble from high to low. Pip's sudden comedown dismisses Frankenstein's fall and discredits Cinderella's rise, both oversimplifications. Mr. Pirrip's autobiography allegedly constitutes the more pertinent horror story for the 1860s and the more instructive fairy tale.

Preoccupied with her critique of overreaching—Victor Frankenstein as "The Modern Prometheus"—Shelley failed to comprehend the humbler sort of reaching out that, says Dickens, makes the Pip–Magwitch relationship crucial for Victorian society. Each is an overreacher who falls short of his goal yet manages to reach out to the other across gaps of class and generation. *Great Expectations* utilizes the same relationship to punish overreaching and to reward reaching out. Study *Great Expectations*, Dickens exhorted; consign "The Modern Prometheus" to oblivion.

Three times in *Great Expectations* Dickens parodically revalued Shelley's child-snatching scene in which the monster seizes Victor's brother, William: Magwitch upends Pip in the churchyard; he invades Pip's apartments and repeatedly clasps him; Orlick catches Pip "in a strong running noose" at the sluice house (*GE*, 419). With each rewriting, Dickens took a more alarmed look at England's social and moral condition. In the opening chapter, Pip, society's representative, is just a child; he is given time to feed the monster. When Magwitch enters Pip's rooms, the monster's suit is harder to accommodate. At the sluice house, the monster is unpacifiable: in the journeyman's death grip, Pip fears that he and his sort deserve to be choked to death "and despised by unborn generations" (*GE*, 422).

As Orlick fastens Pip to the wall and resolves to destroy every rag and bone of him, the monster becomes a fusion figure, bringing together Frankenstein's creature, *Cinderella,* and the Misnar story. From Magwitch, Orlick takes over the creature's violent role but is also a disgruntled, embittered cinder girl who feels Pip has been favored in his stead. Finally, he reminds one of the giant Kifri, who kills Ahubal, Misnar's brother, after the latter's attempt to usurp the throne costs the enchanters, Ahaback and Desra, their lives. Pip is simultaneously seized by Frankenstein's monster, pummeled by a resentful cinder girl, and menaced by a disgruntled giant. *Great Expectations* parodies *Frankenstein,* subverts *Cinderella,* but maintains a damaging parallel between Pip's rise and the usurpers' attempt to overthrow Misnar.

What, finally, should the modern revaluator say about allusions to *Paradise Lost* in *Great Expectations*? Milton set out to "assert Eternal Providence, / and justify the ways of God to men" (1:25–26). Shelley responded by compelling Victor Frankenstein to feel "what the duties of a creator toward his creatures were" (*F,* 92). Should *Great Expectations* be read as the deciding vote in a debate between Shelley and Milton about accountability—who owes what to whom? To what extent must Dickens uphold Milton in order to rebuke Shelley?

As Dickens's revisionary reading of *Frankenstein,* Iain Crawford argued, *Great Expectations* restores Milton's emphasis on heaven-sent grace; it reaffirms "the operations of divine Providence" (IC, 638). True enough—in novel after novel throughout the 1850s, Dickens relied on providential chastisement, a corrective principle seemingly within the nature of things but whose workings become visible chiefly in retrospect if one shines a "backward light" on events that have led up to the present.[17] Mr. Pirrup's autobiographical bildungsroman does just that. But Dickens was seldom as keen as Wilkie Collins to personify providence by appointing admirable characters its agents.

Jay Stubblefield saw Dickens scolding Shelley for oversimplifying individual responsibility. Her monster defers blame for all his actions to his creator: "On you it rests," the creature berates Frankenstein, "whether I . . . lead a harmless life, or become the scourge of your fellow-creatures" (*F,* 92). No one in *Great Expectations* gets away with such total self-exculpation, although nearly everyone—Pip, Magwitch, Estella, Miss Havisham, even Orlick—tries. Pip may plead that he is the victim of other people's ploys, but Dickens holds him partially responsible for his deeds, Stubblefield maintained. In reply to *Frankenstein, Great Expectations* seconds Milton's "most basic premise": unfavorable conditions never preclude one's ability to make moral and reasonable choices (JS, 235, 239).

Dickens's position on *Frankenstein* vis-à-vis *Paradise Lost* is a subtler, more intricate feat of parodic revaluation than previous commentators perceived. Dickens wants to demolish Shelley in favor of Milton but in ways that promote *Great Expectations* as a better guidebook to human relationships in Victorian England than either *Frankenstein* or *Paradise Lost*.

In this regard, *Great Expectations* has three objectives, the first of which is to reinstate a supervisory agency worthy of the confidence Milton had in providence but without unduly anthropomorphizing it as a paternal or avuncular force. Magwitch and Miss Havisham may be seen as Dickens's parody of providential superintendence as a fairy godparent. The second objective is to distance itself from the preoccupation with creator–creature relationships in both *Frankenstein* and *Paradise Lost*. As a recipe for social ties between individuals or classes, the creator–creature paradigm is wrong per se. It cannot be modified or renegotiated to suit modern times. Although Dickens shares Milton's belief in individual responsibility and deplores Frankenstein's creature's disavowals, the third objective of *Great Expectations* is to propose a new ideal for Victorian society: partnership. That is what the creator–creature relationship between Magwitch and Pip (or Pip and Magwitch) ultimately becomes.

Milton's providence is virtually identical with an all-powerful, all-caring deity whose long-range plans can be explained and defended. As Mary Shelley's supervisory figure, Victor Frankenstein oversteps boundaries, then defaults on his responsibilities. But Dickens emphasizes providence's punitive aspect, personifying it as the sultan "in the Eastern story" that Pip summarizes just before his expectations suddenly collapse (*GE*, 309–10). Misnar's intervention is timed perfectly; as the sultan releases his palace's collapsible ceiling to destroy two would-be usurpers, it symbolizes life's self-corrective capacity, a built-in mechanism that can be activated if things go awry. Unlike Milton's providence, which seeks "to bring forth good" out of evil (1: 161–62), Misnar's pavilion elaborates upon the idea that an "Appointed Time" overtakes not only Krook but "all Lord Chancellors in all Courts . . . where injustice is done" (*BH*, 403).

Contradicting both Milton and Shelley, Dickens asserts that the workings of providence are neither as comprehensible as God's actions in the Old Testament nor as incompetent as Frankenstein's. Nor do agents of providence scramble to do its bidding. In Wilkie Collins's *The Woman in White*, Walter Hartright comes back from the "forests of Central America" to reinstate Laura Fairlie (*WW*, 426); in order to obtain revenge for his sister, Mat Marksman returns to England "after twenty years" of "dodging about the Amazon" (*H&S*, 191). When Magwitch arrives from Australia to further Pip's prospects, however, unrealistic expectations responsible for the latter's Cinderella complex fall apart "in an instant," much like Misnar's pavilion, says Pip (*GE*, 310). Milton's providence is predictable, Shelley's inept, Collins's overly protective—hence all struck Dickens as incredible. Dickens's providence moves in more mysterious ways than Milton's (indeed, the pretense in chapter 38 is that it is oriental, inscrutable.) Although more dependable than Shelley allowed, it is more likely to deputize the ex-convict with a file (ch. 10) or Jaggers (ch. 18) on Magwitch's behalf than to send Pip someone like Hartright or Marksman.

Of the three objectives outlined above, the second seems paramount. Irrevocably wedded to the creator–creature relationship, *Paradise Lost* has nothing pertinent to say about how to improve social conditions in nineteenth-century England, Dickens tells Shelley. Insofar as *Frankenstein* is obsessed with rewriting a seventeenth-century poem, neither, it follows, does she. England's biggest bind, Dickens vociferated, is not theological, biological, or epistemological. It would be misleading for a novelist in 1860 to discuss the disdain of the powerful for the disenfranchised in terms of God's behavior toward Adam. Nor could Dickens accept the gap between Haves and Have-Nots as a scientific experiment gone wrong or an instance of the mind's inability to comprehend Otherness, both of which describe *Frankenstein*.

Exterminating the creator–creature paradigm, removing the most glaring inequalities in the social system—discrepancies between the few who have and the many who lack, for example—should be the social realist's principal concern, not rehashing man's relationship to God as Shelley does in talking back to Milton. Society must cease producing creatures like Magwitch, Dickens contends. Creatures like Pip must recognize their real creator, not providence personified as Cinderella's fairy godparent but exploited souls like Magwitch.

Great Expectations abounds in unsatisfactory creator–creature relationships, all of them more complicated, Dickens believed, than the one in *Frankenstein*. But Dickens ultimately urges readers to stop thinking in such outdated terms altogether. Within Victorian society, that is, on the temporal plane, creator–creature dependency is detrimental to both parties, whether it is one-sided, as Dickens felt happens in *Frankenstein,* or perversely mutual as in *Great Expectations,* where a subclass toils to maintain and enrich the upper class that created it.

Ironic role reversals in the case of Pip and Magwitch make each creator the creature of his creation, each creation the creator of a creature. The Magwitch–Pip connection is thus a parodic worsening of Shelley's reconfiguration of God and Adam as Victor and his monster. Only such a worsening, Dickens demonstrates, can begin to describe the Victorian socioeconomic situation. In effect, a parodic revaluator disqualifies an errant parodic revaluation. Shelley's reconsideration of Milton is alleged to have missed the point. Outdated and irrelevant in 1860, *Frankenstein* begs for reassessment more desperately than its target ever did.

The new paradigm, explains Dickens, should be enlightened partnerships between self-aware, self-reliant individuals. These partnerships must be based on friendship and trust rather than on money, economic necessity, or even love. More than just quarreling with Shelley's revaluation of Milton, Dickens urges readers not to rely upon either *Frankenstein* or *Paradise Lost* to explain civil obligation and social responsibility in nineteenth-century society. They should peruse *Great Expectations* instead. Shelley seemed outmoded to Dickens, hence irrelevant, not just for misconstruing Milton's Old Testament epic but for consulting it in the first place. Dickens sides with Milton against Shelley in support of providence as a reliable director. Nevertheless, he dismisses *Paradise Lost* and *Frankenstein* along with *Cinderella* as inapplicable texts (and contexts) for a realistic discussion of solutions to England's most pressing problems in 1860.

Alluding to *Paradise Lost* throughout *Frankenstein* hardly replaces one creation myth with another, Dickens complained; nor does it bring readers closer to the current state of affairs. Even if Shelley thought she was describing the formation of the proletariat, *Frankenstein* fails to depict the vicious cycle whereby Haves and Have-Nots endlessly create each other: society begets Magwitch, who begets Pip, whose creature and creator is Magwitch. In contrast, substituting the Misnar tale for *Cinderella,* as Dickens does when Pip realizes the former is the better analogue for his career, is a legitimate parodic revaluation; a pertinent fairy tale with a useful admonition replaces a lie.

Paradise Lost opens the monster's eyes to his plight as the botched creation of an irresponsible creator. Reading Milton's poem, the monster tells Victor, "I often referred the several situations, as their similarity struck me, to my own" (*F,* 113). Unfortunately, the monster mistakes poetry for fact, accepting *Paradise Lost* as "true history." For Magwitch to pore over *Paradise Lost* in this way would be a waste of time. The ex-convict's reading skills would be taxed severely. Moreover, were he to emulate Frankenstein's monster and consider himself "Like Adam" (*F,* 113), Magwitch would misread his situation as solipsistically as Pip misjudges his by imagining himself Cinderella.[18]

In short, Magwitch cannot relive *Paradise Lost* any more than Pip can reenact *Cinderella.* Adam's creation story is as ill-fitted to Magwitch's plight as the cinder girl's transformation proves to Pip's. On the other hand, Magwitch is "chrisen'd Abel" (*GE,* 344). Ironically, he becomes in Australia a keeper of flocks, as was his biblical namesake. It is Cain's murder of Abel (not God's creation of Adam) that *Great Expectations* evokes, even though Magwitch does not underline the parallel.[19] When asked Abel's whereabouts, Cain replied with the infamous query, "Am I my brother's keeper?" (Genesis, 4:9).

Magwitch's problems, Dickens insisted, are sociological, fraternal rather than patriarchal; his predicament is society's creation more so than God's. It illustrates a failure of brotherhood, a breakdown of responsibility between man and his fellows, not a rupture of creature from creator. If one must authorize an Old Testament pattern for the contemporary scene, Dickens advised Shelley's admirers, forget Genesis and Shelley's squabbles with Milton over how to retell it; let Cain and Abel—Compeyson and Magwitch—stand for social inequalities and class hatreds that are not only monstrous but actually create monsters. To all appearances, Magwitch is Compeyson's creature whom the gentleman-crook "prays the Judge to be protected from" after their trial (*GE,* 350). But Magwitch was taken on as Compeyson's "man and pardner" (*GE,* 346); that is the relationship Compeyson betrays when his lawyers depict him as Magwitch's tool.

Pip, not Magwitch, alludes to Milton. Twice he compares his situation to

Adam's at the conclusion of *Paradise Lost*. Pip's allusions point to each other as well as to Milton's poem. Arguably, *both* references are ironic. In the first, Mr. Pirrip reveals his younger self's ignorance of the real world and his position in it. In the second, the maturer Pip's reappraisal of the individual's place in nature bears little resemblance to what Shelley's novel says on the subject. Unfortunately, Pip lacks some of the compensations that Milton's Adam and Eve take for granted.

As the "First Stage" ends, Pip has just left Joe and Biddy, an unsatisfactory parting because he regrets his "ingratitude" (*GE*, 158). Once the coach gets under way, however, returning to the forge for a better leave-taking is out of the question. Pip is London-bound. "And the mists had all solemnly risen now, and the world lay spread before me," he observes in the last line of chapter 19.[20] The Miltonic allusion is supplied here in retrospect by Mr. Pirrip since Pip has yet to read *Paradise Lost*. Looking back, the older Pip emphasizes the tragicomedy of a false dawn; that is, a false start. Young Pip thinks the mists are "solemnly rising, as if to show [him] the world" (*GE*, 158). Actually, the former blacksmith's apprentice is a dependent thrice over: Magwitch's puppet, Miss Havisham's dupe, Estella's slave. He leaves behind the grime and heat of a forge not really hellish for a paradise even falser than his overvaluation of Satis House.

Milton ends *Paradise Lost* as follows: "The World was all before them, where to choose / Thir place of rest, and Providence thir guide; / They hand in hand with wand'ring steps and slow, / Through *Eden* took their solitary way" (12:646–49). Adam and Eve have been expelled, sent forth "sorrowing yet in peace," with a "new hope" born from "despair," to quote two earlier passages that help to explain the final lines (11:117, 139). For the naive Pip en route to London, comparison of himself to Adam departing from the garden to enter a brave new world seems grandiose. Unlike Adam and Eve's, Pip's downfall has yet to come.

When Pip and Estella leave the "ruined place" in the novel's final paragraph, Pip repeats the Miltonic allusion from chapter 19: "As the morning mists had risen long ago when I first left the forge, so the evening mists were rising now" (*GE*, 480).[21] One should recognize this exit in the revised ending as Dickens's double revision—not just of Pip's departure from the village years ago, but also of Adam and Eve's from paradise.

Milton's couple take "their solitary way"; no longer alone as in his earlier parting, Pip leaves with Estella. Instead of a false dawn, the "rising" evening mists reveal a "broad expanse of tranquil light" (*GE*, 480), surely a good omen and more symbolic of arrival than departure. This is not really a parting in that Pip foresees no separation from Estella. In short, Dickens reverses Pip's leave-taking from Joe and Biddy and modifies Adam and Eve's from Eden. Satis House and its environs are a "garden of false hopes," it has been argued,[22] from which Pip and Estella are liberated, not exiled.

Pip alludes to *Paradise Lost* chiefly to separate *Great Expectations* from Milton's frame of reference and Shelley's untimely obsession with it. Leaving Satis House behind, Pip and Estella do not enter Milton's divinely regulated arena with its master plan for eventual redemption. Instead, they will immerse themselves in Dickens's tragicomic world of arduous cooperation. Dickens does not deny extraterrestrial oversight of human affairs; indeed, he relies on it for whatever uprightness his universe attains, so "Providence thir guide" still applies. But *Great Expectations* refuses to explicate its future workings on a daily, step-by-step basis. Pip's prophecy of a lifetime with Estella is a plausible prediction by a mature individual. Were there a Miltonic blueprint, however, Pip again would have expectations and the world would have a fairy godparent.

Pip and Estella are both ex-Cinderellas. The future they face will be closer to the cinder girl's than to the life they once anticipated as heir and heiress respectively. Working beneath this self-evident paralleling of Pip and Estella with Adam and Eve, however, is a tacit rejection of the creator–creature relationship still in place at the conclusion of *Paradise Lost*. In *Frankenstein,* creature and creator both perish,[23] hardly an acceptable solution to the human condition, Dickens objected. No fewer than three parodic creators die in this novel—Magwitch, Miss Havisham, and Compeyson, who helped to shape them both. That leaves Pip and Estella, each formerly the creature of a dubious fairy godparent, on their own. Providence has finally brought them together; from now on, the revised ending implies, they must rely chiefly on each other.

Estella beseeches Pip: "[T]ell me we are friends" (*GE,* 480). He replies affirmatively, repeating her exact words as if they are the new formula for ideal personal relationships: "We are friends."[24] Pip and Estella exchange vows of friendship more important than any subsequent nuptials; marry they probably will—indeed, should—but first they move toward the sort of partnership *Great Expectations* celebrates. Variant anticipations of it include Pip and Herbert as roommates and at Clarriker's; Joe and Biddy; the partnership at the forge that Joe reserves for Pip; and above all, Pip and Magwitch, who confound Shelley's creator–creature relationship by becoming mutually supportive, each willingly allied to the other.[25]

"I took her hand in mine, and we went out of the ruined place," Pip relates in the final paragraph's first line (*GE,* 480). It is Dickens's intention that *Great Expectations* and *Paradise Lost* appear to end similarly, whereas his novel differs drastically from *Frankenstein* in this regard. Again, however, Dickens reinstates Milton with a difference; Pip speaks at the very end, where Adam did not, which gives Dickens's protagonist more of a voice in his own fate. The revaluator also redesigns the hand-in-hand motif, pervasive in *Paradise Lost,* for his own purposes. Throughout *Great Expectations,* Dickens insists on shifting from superior clasping subordinate to partner acknowledging partner.

Walking hand in hand frequently carried "overtones of forthcoming sexual activity" for Adam and Eve, John Shawcross has noted (JTS, 193). Pip's action in taking Estella's hand and her acquiescence suggest they will spend the future together. But when Adam takes Eve's hand at their first meeting, it constitutes "a reprise" of God taking Adam's hand at the creation (JTS, 195). The relationship of wife to husband, Milton strongly implies, parallels her husband's to God: Eve is Adam's creature as he is God's.

Pip clasping Estella's hand replaces Magwitch's attempts to grasp Pip's hands—indeed, to take possession of him—on the night of the ex-convict's return. It also replays the trusting gesture when Pip feels Magwitch's "hand tremble as it held mine" after their capture by Custom House agents (*GE*, 444). And it recalls Magwitch's dying act: "With a last faint effort, which would have been powerless but for my yielding to it and assisting it, he raised my hand to his lips" (*GE*, 456).

Paradise Lost tells what happens when Adam forgoes his authority over Eve and, jointly, they seek to overturn God's.[26] Adam should have remained Eve's controller instead of becoming her partner in disobedience, says Milton. But Pip takes Estella's hand in the last paragraph because he offers her a partnership which she does not refuse; Magwitch is not "powerless" at the last, because Pip both yields and assists. Differences between Dickens's pairings and Milton's couple are significant enough to count as revaluations. Pip and Estella begin the world again in a manner closed to Frankenstein's creature and fundamentally different—namely, more pragmatic—from Adam and Eve's fresh start. Applied to social relationships in 1860, the creator–creature paradigm revolted Dickens compared to the new ideal of equality between true partners.

Dickens begins his novel by showing Shelley's admirers what it would really be like to be seized by a monster. He ends by explaining to Miltonists what Pip and Estella's future will be like in a tragicomic universe outside the ruined garden. They must learn to walk the fine line between Miltonic and Smilesian extremes—between the illusion of total dependence on another's benevolent designs and the equally unrealistic determination to rise in the world unassisted; that is, through the use of, or at the expense of, other people.

Breaking down Estella's insistence on continuing as "friends apart" (*GE*, 480), one assumes, will be the next stage in Pip's evolution. Unlike Jane Eyre, whose reversals, invariably fortunate, leave her snobbishly triumphant, Pip has developed from a would-be Cinderella into a dependable colleague. Admittedly, he will be Estella's *second* husband and is merely "*third* in the Firm" at Clarriker's (*GE,* 476; italics added). But Dickens seems satisfied with Pip's moral progress. Formerly another's deluded creature (Magwitch's, Miss Havisham's), he grows into a reliable partner for Herbert and Estella.[27]

Chapter 7
Charlotte Brontë

Of all the allegedly unrealistic novelists whom *Great Expectations* ridicules, none was targeted with more vim than Charlotte Brontë. Dickens's "great revisionary novel,"[1] his most versatile revaluative parody, reserves much of its severest scorn for scenes, ideas, and characters from *Jane Eyre*. Although Dickens detested the Brontës as a duo,[2] he held Charlotte's autobiographical bildungsroman chiefly responsible for establishing the Cinderella complex in Victorian fiction. Jane's story corroborates the cinder girl's rise more reverently than *Oliver Twist* vindicates *The Pilgrim's Progress*.[3] "Both Jane as narrator and *Jane Eyre* as text appear untroubled by [Brontë's] reliance on a version of the Cinderella narrative as the main paradigm for organizing her life story," John O. Jordan has observed (JJ, 30). "Untroubled" is hardly the word. In Dickens's opinion, Brontë embraces the Cinderella paradigm as the ideal analogue for her heroine's stubborn advancement. *Jane Eyre* exhibits none of the saving irony that characterizes Mr. Pirrip's depiction of his younger self.[4]

"In defiance of the accepted canon," Elizabeth Gaskell asserted, Brontë "determined to make her heroine plain, small and unattractive" (*LCB*, 308). But portraying Jane as David against Goliath, or as the perennial Ugly Duckling, cannot weaken the main parallel, Dickens retorted. In his view, Brontë canonized the Cinderella story and the use of Cinderella motifs accelerated thereafter; their recurrence in novel after novel helped both to generate and preserve the era's Cinderella complex—Victorian England's growing misconception of itself as history's fairy godchild.

In *Jane Eyre*, Richard Chase has argued, Brontë created "a culture heroine" (RCh, 111). Actually, she made the cinder girl into one; this redoubtable underdog's ability to maintain her integrity while overcoming all obstacles offered readers a parable for Victorian England's dramatic rise from embattled island at the start of the century to world power less than fifty years later. When

Jane hears Rochester's distant summons and resolves to obey it, she declares: "It was *my* time to assume ascendancy. *My* powers were in play and in force" (*JE*, 474). She hastens to Ferndean not only to succor and marry her prince, but also to fulfill her destiny. One imagines Victorian readers nodding agreement, thinking their country's time for prevalence had come as well.

From novels successful earlier in the century, Dickens singled out *Jane Eyre* for parodic revision because it accomplished what Shelley's *Frankenstein* failed to preclude: the conversion of *Cinderella* from fairy tale to cultural myth. Taking their cues from *Jane Eyre*, novels with Cinderella motifs seemed to promise unstinting upward mobility not just for individuals but for the country as a whole. Until *Great Expectations*, there was little to discourage overly expectant readers from relishing Cinderella-like rises and recoveries in their favorite fictions. These could be read as so many promises (or reassurances) of the reader's growing importance both personally and as a member of a rising nation.

Cinderella is rising, all is well with the world—such is the implicit premise in novels imbued with Cinderella motifs. Unconvinced, Dickens felt obliged to turn Brontë's seminal fairy tale of an orphan who becomes an heiress inside out. *Great Expectations* should be read as a parodic reversal of the cultural paradigm consecrated in *Jane Eyre*: the rise and fall of a real cinder person—a blacksmith's apprentice, also an orphan—whose castles in the air tragicomically collapse.[5]

From its opening scene, *Great Expectations* tries to make *Jane Eyre* appear too good to be true, its storybook world discredited by Dickens's darker reflection of the real one. Thus Jane reads about an imaginary churchyard while Pip is really in one. Snug in the window seat at Gateshead Hall while studying Bewick's "History of British Birds" (*JE*, 20), Jane has drawn the curtain to create a private world. Dickens implies that Brontë's novel is similarly self-contained, a fabrication cut off from actual conditions.

Jane Eyre opens on a "winter afternoon" of "ceaseless rain," but the "quiet solitary churchyard" at "eventide," with its "inscribed headstone" and "broken wall," holds no terrors for the safely ensconced heroine; they comprise an illustration in Jane's book (*JE*, 20–21). Pip shivers outdoors toward evening on a "bleak" December day. Headstones within the churchyard's wall, reprised as actualities, offer the only clues to what his parents "were like" (*GE*, 3–4). Unlike Jane, Pip is attempting to get in touch with the world.

Jane's contemplations are interrupted by John Reed, her late uncle's bullying son, who threatens to drag her from her womblike enclosure. Pip studies the family tombstones until "a fearful man...started up from among the graves" and "seized [him] by the chin" (*GE*, 4). As Magwitch turns Pip upside down, he, not Jane, is torn from the womb of innocent complacency. Although reality intrudes in both instances, only from Dickens's parodic revision does one get a sense of the protagonist's life beginning again in the real world. Pip rightly calls this scene "[m]y first most vivid and broad impression of the identity of things" (*GE*, 3). When John, who is fourteen, strikes Jane, she, only ten, fights back like "a desperate thing" until he "bellowed out loud" for help (*JE*, 24).[6] In sharp contrast, Pip must placate a savage parody of Cinderella's fairy godparent who upends him, calls him "you little devil (*GE*, 4)," and swears, "I'll cut your throat!"

Jane's is a purely domestic crisis, no more serious than sibling rivalry; she emerges with ego intact. Pip comes face to face with a victim of England's unfair socioeconomic system and the discriminatory laws in support of it, a traumatic encounter that reshapes his life. Seized by Bessie and Miss Abbot, Jane is locked in "the red room" lest she assault her "benefactress's son" again (*JE*, 24). Not even recapture and transportation can prevent Magwitch from resuming contact with Pip as the latter's more problematic benefactor. Doubly pivotal, the confrontation on the marshes determines the rest of Pip's life story and the direction of Magwitch's as well. Just as Dickens's real churchyard replaces Brontë's imaginary one, just as Magwitch seizing Pip minimizes Jane's contest with John Reed, Pip's life story upstages Jane's; it allegedly constitutes the truer, sociologically more important autobiography of a would-be Cinderella.

Jane Eyre refuses to be anything but Cinderella and eventually gets her way. On no fewer than three occasions—at Gateshead Hall, Lowood, and Thornfield—she rejects the cinder girl's role; she will not knuckle under to Mrs. Reed, Mr. Brocklehurst, or even Edward Fairfax Rochester. Finally, she is elevated to princesshood as Rochester's second wife. Inasmuch as she acquires the position she feels deserving of all along, Jane seems to regain her rights. Lest Brontë's admirers expect a similarly fortunate, indeed, permanent transcendence of life's difficulties, Mr. Pirrip repeatedly thrusts Pip back into the cinder girl's unenviable position.

"You have no money," John Reed taunts Jane; "you ought to beg, and not to live here with gentlemen's children like us" (*JE*, 23). Jane's snobbery, however, is a match for John's. Unwilling to concede inferiority to anyone at Gateshead Hall, she demands to know, "How is he [John] my master? Am I a servant?" (*JE*, 24) When Pip is invited to "play" at Satis House in Dickens's parodic reformulation, Estella crushes him for the forge-bred boor he is: "[S]he was as scornful of me as if she had been . . . a queen," Pip recalls (*GE*, 58). Assaulted by John Reed, Jane fights back like a man; disconcerted by Estella, Pip cries like a baby. "Why don't you cry?" Estella provokes the departing Pip; "you have been crying till you are half-blind, and you are near crying again now" (*GE*, 66). Estella's otherwise cruel mistreatment of Pip acquires a comic dimension when read as a parodic replay of Jane's improbable thrashing of John.

Dickens considered the Cinderella complex a personal delusion and a cultural mania, yet it gives Jane strength and self-confidence. The armor of her self-esteem is too thick to admit the sufferings of a truly unwanted child. Jane thinks too highly of herself to be downcast, but Dickens substitutes Pip's humiliation at Satis House for Jane's indignation at Gateshead Hall.

In place of Jane trouncing John, Dickens has Pip beat up Herbert. That a country lad from the forge easily outpoints a city boy comes as no surprise, but it undercuts a ten-year-old girl's defeat of a fourteen-year-old bully. On his second visit to Satis House, Pip soundly whips "the pale young gentleman," who, he admits, "did not look very healthy" (*GE,* 91). Although Pip defeating Herbert is more credible than Jane vanquishing John, it remains a ridiculous mismatch. Nor does winning save Pip from the sociopsychological beating Estella continues to administer. Following the fight, she allows the victor a reward, but Pip realizes "that the kiss was given to the coarse common boy as a piece of money might have been, and that it was worth nothing (*GE,* 93).

Instead of Jane's sanctimonious stand at Gateshead Hall, Dickens presents Pip's humiliations at Satis House. For Jane's persistent overvaluation of self, Dickens substitutes Estella's poor opinion of Pip, which the latter is compelled to accept. Servants at Gateshead Hall call Jane "a little toad" (*JE,* 37), but such insults cannot erode her self-confidence. When Estella criticizes Pip's "coarse hands" and "thick boots," he immediately feels "ashamed" (*GE,* 61). Estella brands Pip "a little coarse monster" (*GE,* 82), and he has no recourse but to believe her.[7] The more vulnerable Dickens makes Pip, the more of a fairy tale Jane's invulnerability becomes.

Jane is a simple sort of snob. Dickens's rendition of the Cinderella complex reveals that Pip's confused psychological state has graver consequences. As cinder girl to Estella's Cinderella, Pip feels diminished; he begins to see the world awry, looking down on his truest benefactor: "I wished Joe had been rather more genteely brought up," says Pip, "and then I should have been so too" (*GE,* 63).

Denouncing her oppressors, calling Aunt Reed "deceitful" (*JE,* 47), Jane leaves Gateshead Hall in triumph. Deemed undesirable company for John, Eliza, and Georgiana, Jane shouts that Mrs. Reed's children "are not fit to associate with me" (*JE,* 39).[8] Epiphanically, Jane discovers how exhilarating self-righteousness can be: "[M]y soul began to expand, to exult, with the strangest sense of freedom" (*JE,* 48). Although packed off to Lowood, she declares herself "winner of the field. It was the hardest battle I had fought, and the first victory I had gained" (*JE,* 48).

To remain a potential Cinderella, Dickens objected, Jane must never become a cinder girl in her own eyes. She prevails by retaining control of herself, preserving her sense of self-worth at all costs, standing firm until others weaken. When Dickens rewrites Jane as Pip, fairy tale as tragicomedy, epiphany invariably connotes demotion, the revelation that Pip is less than he had thought. Only in *Cinderella* and novels patterned on it, never in so-called real life, Dickens charged, does the protagonist prove every bit as wonderful as he or she claims. Brontë's efforts to verify Cinderella in 1847 fail spectacularly upon reexamination in 1860.

Each time Jane enters upon a new stage—from Gateshead to Lowood to Thornfield—she moves closer to Cinderella-hood. Transportation for Pip proves more problematic—from forge to Satis House to London to Egypt, a series of ups and downs in place of Jane's steady progress. Jane is sent to Lowood "to be made useful, to be kept humble" (*JE*, 45), a combination, presumably, of cinder girl and Uriah Heep. She stays eight years—six as pupil, two as teacher. Pip serves Joe for four years, at which point he is approximately eighteen, Jane's age upon leaving school. But Pip has truly led a cinder girl's existence. Instead of marrying Pip to Estella, Miss Havisham apprentices him to Joe. With "a black face and hands" when at his "grimiest," Pip experiences a reversion to cinder girl status completely foreign to Jane; it was "as if a thick curtain had fallen on all [life's] interest and romance," Pip moans, "to shut me out from anything save dull endurance any more" (*GE*, 107).

At Lowood, Helen Burns expounds her philosophy of "endurance" (*JE*, 65)—the art of putting up with things. But Jane's philosophy is closer to an eye for an eye: "When we are struck at without a reason," she affirms, "we should strike back again very hard; . . . so hard as to teach the person who struck us never to do it again" (*JE*, 67). Incredibly, says Dickens, *Jane Eyre* posits no situation in which the eponymous heroine cannot "strike back" and win. For Pip, once "the blow was struck" (*GE*, 310), his "stronghold" (hopes, plans, aspirations) falls apart for good.

Brontë's view of personality formation infuriated Dickens. Unlike Helen Burns, who forbears, Jane proposes to harden herself in order to hit back harder than any assailant. She does not mature so much as she continues to toughen, Dickens implied. *Great Expectations* attributes such inflexibility to the youthful Magwitch, a victim of social neglect, who "got the name of being hardened" from prison authorities; "this is a terrible hardened one," officialdom declares (*GE*, 344). According to her own formula, *Great Expectations* retorts, Jane should resemble a transported felon, not Cinderella.

Jane's ultimate deliverance is never in doubt. Before leaving Lowood for Thornfield, she learns that her father's brother, a gentleman well-off, had been at Gateshead looking for her "nearly seven years" earlier (*JE*, 100). Mrs. Reed was "very high with him," so Mr. Eyre left for London and Madeira without making a side trip to Lowood. But once Jane's fairy godfather manifests himself—this happens after a mere ten chapters—her transformation into Jane Eyre, heiress, seems assured.[9]

Dickens lampoons Uncle Eyre's non-arrival twice. Two surrogate fairy godfathers descend on the forge, emissaries as unlike Cinderella's benefactress as is Magwitch, their sender. First the stranger who "stirred his rum-and-water . . . *with a file*" gives Pip two one-pound notes (*GE*, 78); then Jaggers, "the confidential agent of another," tells Pip he is to be "brought up as a gentleman—in a word, as a young fellow of great expectations" (*GE*, 136–37). Which is more credible, Dickens demands, Magwitch endowing Pip from Australia, then coming to visit his beneficiary, or Uncle Eyre, eschewing a fifty-mile detour from Gateshead to Lowood, but sending a sizeable inheritance posthumously all the way from a Portuguese island? Magwitch is a vicious parody of Cinderella's fairy godparent, the point being that such good angels are entirely imaginary, yet he seems real compared to Uncle Eyre. The latter never sees Jane, is never seen by the reader, but news of his generosity arrives just in time to help dissuade Jane from exiling herself as a missionary to India.[10] The archetypal mixed blessing, Pip's Uncle Provis makes nonsense of Brontë's deus ex machina. Within a few months of Magwitch's return, Pip is penniless and en route to Egypt.

The "First Stage" of *Great Expectations* ends with Pip erroneously imagining that a world of opportunity lies before him. As the "Second Stage" approaches completion, Magwitch's reappearance triggers the collapse of Pip's expectations as if they were Misnar's pavilion. Having prevailed at Gateshead and Lowood, Jane's third phase takes place at Thornfield. On her first day as governess she enthuses: "My faculties, roused by the change of scene, the new field offered to hope, seemed all astir. I cannot precisely define what they *expected,* but it was something pleasant; not perhaps that day or that month, but at an indefinite future-period" (*JE*, 105–6; italics added). Collapsing Pip's hopes in the "Second Stage", converting him in the "Third" from gentleman to clerk, Dickens ridicules the facile optimism in Jane's "new field of hope." The fated arrival of catastrophe, described by Pip in the Misnar passage (*GE*, 309–10), overrules Jane's nebulous expectancy.

Jane Eyre, Dickens protests, is unbalanced, all third stage. Hardships at Gateshead and Lowood are overshadowed by eventual successes at Thornfield and Ferndean, which fill the last twenty-seven of Brontë's thirty-eight chapters. In Dickens's revision, after false hopes raised at the end of Pip's "First Stage" come crashing down as the "Second Stage" ends, a "Third Stage" of arduous rehabilitation follows. Tripartite symmetry—stages of nineteen, twenty, and twenty chapters respectively—allow Dickens to define three equally significant phases of the Cinderella complex: misleading rise, precipitate fall, mandatory readjustment, none of which the psychological realist can shorten or prolong.

"Something pleasant . . . at an indefinite future period" (*JE*, 105–6)—it would be difficult to define the Cinderella complex more clearly. Its essence is an open-ended, largely unfounded expectation of good fortune. Nothing so "indefinite" characterizes Pip's disappointment, which arrives on schedule: "All being made ready with much labour, and the hour come" (*GE*, 310), Pip's absurd conception of himself as Cinderella, a parody of Jane's aroused "faculties," abruptly comes to an end when Magwitch returns. Such is the fate of illusion in the real world, Dickens insisted.

⁂

Brontë never alludes to the Misnar story by name. In telling her own story as if it were Cinderella's, however, Jane mistells the Misnar tale. Brontë's improbable novel, Dickens charged, distorts a potential countertext. When *Great Expectations* subverts *Jane Eyre*, the Misnar story replaces *Cinderella* instead of aiding and abetting it.

Jane may be said to take Bertha Mason's place in Rochester's bed, just as the enchanters, having helped Misnar's brother to seize the sultanate, confirm their rise to power by sleeping on the sultan's couch in the royal pavilion. But the roof never caves in upon Jane, Dickens cried in disbelief; the destruction of Thornfield claims Bertha instead. Jane remains a candidate for Cinderella-hood by *not* suffering an untimely collapse.

Throughout *Great Expectations,* Dickens refutes Brontë's celebration of *Cinderella* by setting to rights her mangling of the Misnar tale. Mr. Pirrip depicts his younger self as a would-be usurper because Brontë's heroine steadfastly denies the imputation. Pip's career collapses like Misnar's pavilion because Bertha, not Jane, perishes in Thornfield's collapse. Pip's life story shifts disconcertingly from *Cinderella* to the Misnar tale so that Jane's flattering self-portrait will appear less convincing.

Rochester's mad first wife descends from her attic confinement one night to set fire to the curtains of her husband's bed. Using the contents of Rochester's water basin and her own water jug, Jane extinguishes the blaze. In putting out the fire in her master's bed, Jane ignites one in Rochester himself, who calls her one of the "good genii" (*JE*, 156), which is as close as Brontë comes to acknowledging *The Tales of the Genii*.[11]

As the cinder girl's equivalent, only Jane can save Rochester from being incinerated. Unlike Ahaback and Desra, the two enchanters in *The Tales of the Genii* who have no right to the ousted sultan's couch, Jane preserves Rochester's bed, thus seems to deserve a place in it: she "baptized the couch," Brontë writes, and "succeeded in extinguishing the flames which were devouring it" (*JE*, 153). Salvation for the forty-year-old Rochester lies in being "bewitched" by his daughter's not yet twenty-year-old governess (*JE*, 416). The name "Eyre" connotes both *eery* and *eyrie*: Jane is an uncanny person, not only able to control the elements of fire and water but also strong as a mountain fortress, hence immune to collapse. In parodic contrast, Pip survives fire and water but is badly burned rescuing Miss Havisham and nearly drowns with Magwitch—demythologizations of Brontë's heroine and Cinderella both.[12]

Jane's dousing of the fire that Bertha starts is rife with sexual undertones. Rochester surveys "the bed, all blackened and scorched, the sheets drenched" and he "himself lying in a pool of water" (*JE*, 154). Implications of fiery passions violently subdued, suggestions of superhuman ejaculation—Dickens apparently found these laughable. In Pip's accurate retelling of the Misnar story, the couch's rightful tenant, the sultan, is "aroused in the dead of the night"; a blow from his "sharpened axe" released the deadly ceiling to crush the usurping enchanters in their sleep. An "aroused" ruler's "sharpened axe" turns Jane's water jug into a ridiculous weapon. Jane's heroics to the contrary, Pip compares his loss of prospects to the fate of the enchanters.

As Pip's catastrophe occurs, the parodic revaluator juggles four interconnected texts: *Great Expectations, Jane Eyre, Cinderella,* and the Misnar story. Dickens's novel uses Misnar to demote *Cinderella* and, just as important, to debunk *Jane Eyre*'s misuse of both *Cinderella* and Misnar, namely *Jane Eyre*'s elevation of *Cinderella* and its evasions of Misnar's harsh truths about the precariousness of extravagant hopes. Dickens implies that Brontë's fairy tale novel can only endorse *Cinderella* by presenting a twisted version of Misnar, in which the roof does not cave in on the usurper; instead she is rewarded with an invitation to share the master's bed.

Ironically, Jane describes the destruction of an actual edifice, Thornfield Hall; the caving in of Misnar's pavilion is merely an analogue for the collapse of Pip's unrealistic expectations. Yet these expectations, Dickens contended, actually collapse, whereas Thornfield's fiery end, a false collapse, removes the final barrier between Jane and her prince. The downfall of the sultan's pavilion parodies Thornfield's, exposing Brontë's Gothic climax as a contrived providential retribution that punishes Bertha and Rochester but enables Jane to complete her rise from unwanted stepchild to mistress of Ferndean. Superimpose Pip and Misnar on Jane and Thornfield, Dickens suggests, and Brontë is shown not only to cultivate the fairy tale world of *Cinderella* but also to side with a snob and usurper.

Jane receives an account of the Thornfield disaster from an eyewitness, a "respectable-looking, middle-aged man" (*JE*, 415). He tells how Bertha, having set Thornfield ablaze, leaps from the roof just as the house caves in, blinding and maiming Rochester with its fall (*JE*, 415–17). "Dead as the stones on which her brains and blood were scattered," Bertha has self-destructed, exonerating Rochester from his bigamous attempt to wed the governess and purifying the latter's passion for her employer, heretofore a married man. Magwitch's reappearance, the event Pip considers tantamount to the collapse of Misnar's pavilion, works oppositely. In a heartbeat, Pip's fortune and marital prospects disintegrate; he will never be master of Satis House. Unlike Thornfield, it remains standing after Pip's pavilion-like expectations fall apart but becomes inaccessible forever.

Rochester and Jane find their positions reversed. With one eye knocked out, blinded in the other, one crushed hand amputated, Rochester must forfeit his "state of proud independence" as Jane's would-be "giver and protector" (*JE*, 414). But Estella, heartless as ever, wastes no sympathy on Pip. "Looking at [him] perfectly unmoved" when he informs her that his patron's identity has not been "a fortunate discovery" (*GE*, 360, 357), she becomes more unattainable after Magwitch's return than she seemed before.

Dickens found the first Mrs. Rochester incredible. Said to be "cunning as a witch" (*JE*, 416), Jane's rival recalls the jealous stepmothers of defenseless heroines such as Cinderella and Snow White. In addition, Bertha stalks Jane as desperately as Frankenstein's vengeful creature pursues his creator. Yet she also personifies the younger heroine's insufficiently acknowledged passionate self.

To set fire to Thornfield, Bertha "kindled the bed" in the governess's chamber (JE, 416), as if Rochester's lawful wife, not Jane, were the intruder. To the extent that Bertha is a usurper, Dickens alleged, she remains an outsider, not a credible projection of a monsterlike second self that might compromise Jane as a potential Cinderella.

Every bit as crammed with witches, monsters, and secret sharers as *Jane Eyre*, *Great Expectations* profits from a realistic reorganization of Brontë's material. Bertha's garbled roles are parceled out among Magwitch, Miss Havisham, and Orlick, each of whom causes greater difficulty for Pip's Cinderella complex than Bertha makes for Jane's.

Ten chapters separate Bertha's lawyer's interruption of Jane's wedding (ch. 26) from the eyewitness account Jane receives of Bertha setting fire to Thornfield (ch. 36). Disruption of the marriage ceremony and the destruction of Thornfield are treated as separate events. Actually, lawyerly intervention postpones Jane's rise from cinder girl to Cinderella, whereas the fire facilitates it. Until Thornfield collapses upon Bertha's leap from its rooftop, Cinderella's prince is unavailable; Rochester cannot marry Jane because he is still encumbered with Bertha. Pip's expectations collapse when he realizes he can no longer hope to bond with Estella because he is already permanently bound to Magwitch.

Dickens rewrites Briggs's intervention on Bertha's behalf as Magwitch's unwelcome return on Pip's. Magwitch's manifestation of himself as Pip's secret benefactor, Dickens calculated, would produce a greater shock than Bertha's lawyer's disclosure and be comic too when read as a parodic redoing of Jane's wedding day. The ex-convict's unexpected reappearance, not Bertha's lawyer's, brings down a house; Magwitch's return, the collapse of Pip's expectations, and the caving-in of Misnar's pavilion to which he compares his disappointment, are simultaneous, Dickens noted, not ten chapters apart to disguise their interconnectedness.

In Brontë's fairy tale, not even Briggs's revelation of "an impediment," the "previous marriage" of the story's prince (*JE*, 286), prevents Jane's eventual promotion. Victorian England, Dickens contended, faces a more serious obstacle; like Pip with Magwitch, it has an incriminating prior relationship, one that subjects its conception of itself as a Cinderella among nations to a more severe test than Brontë's for Jane. England cannot be history's bride any more than Pip can be Cinderella, because the prosperity—indeed, the identity—of both Pip and Victorian society is tied to drudges like Magwitch. This tie precludes Pip's marrying Estella or England achieving real greatness because it has all the restraining power of a first marriage.

Great Expectations showed readers a more realistic "impediment" (*JE*, 286) to becoming Cinderella. Injustices done to Magwitch and his kind constitute a genuine hindrance to any conception of oneself or one's country as destiny's bride; Bertha is shown to be a contrived obstruction, a minimal deterrent, no matter how melodramatic Briggs's arrival or her removal upon Thornfield's destruction.

Jane's fairy godfather extricates her from what would have been a bigamous marriage. His quick action preserves her integrity so that she can marry her prince at a later date. When Uncle Eyre receives Jane's letter announcing an imminent union, "Mr. Mason," Bertha's brother, is "staying at Madeira to recruit his health on his way back to Jamaica" (*JE*, 291). Given Uncle Eyre's prior difficulties contacting his niece, Jane's letter reaches him nearly as fortuitously as Mason does Madeira. Learning "the real state of matters" from Mason but too ill to return in person, Jane's uncle dispatches Bertha's brother to Briggs. They reach Thornfield in time to save Jane "from the snare into which [she] had fallen" (*JE*, 291).

Dickens remembered this passage when fashioning Miss Havisham's reply to Pip's accusation that his fairy godmother misled him into expecting marriage to Estella: "You made your own snares. *I* never made them" (*GE*, 358). Magwitch's unexpected arrival in Garden Court (ch. 39) parodies Uncle Eyre's providential prevention of Jane's "false marriage" to Rochester (*JE*, 291); it blocks a marriage that Dickens considered even falser: Pip's Cinderella-like union with a Cinderella-like princess (Estella). Using Magwitch as parodic fairy godparent, Dickens simultaneously subverts *Cinderella*, *Jane Eyre*, and the notion of an avuncular providence. Between them, Magwitch and Miss Havisham, Dickens's twofold parody of Uncle Eyre, sabotage Pip's marital prospects more effectively than Jane's uncle protects hers.

Pip makes the more embarrassing discovery, Dickens argued, just as Magwitch's problematic largesse makes Uncle Eyre's seem too good to be true. Which knowledge is harder to contemplate, *Great Expectations* asks, Jane's that her intended husband already has a wife, or a young snob's that a Victorian gentleman's rank and money seldom come to him untarnished? Who has the more "disgusting secret," to adopt Brontë's words (*JE*, 289), Rochester or Pip? Brontë's parodic revaluator believes that Pip's difficulties are both more realistic than Jane's and of greater consequence for the nation to ponder.

In England, Pip perceives, thousands of unappreciated Have-Nots, such as Magwitch, slave for a handful of Haves like Pip, whose comfortable existence they sustain. *Great Expectations* proscribes this unfair social arrangement for being more reprehensible than bigamy. Allowing unacknowledgeable drudges to sweat lest the privileged individual be denied his comforts is a crazier social situation than being married to a madwoman one must seclude in an attic; it is worse than trying to take a second wife—or so Dickens's parodic response to Brontë asserts.

Upon learning from Rochester the truth of Briggs's disclosure, Jane describes her state of mind in aquatic terms: "[T]he waters came into my soul; I sank in deep mire: I felt no standing; I came into deep waters; the floods overflowed me" (*JE*, 293).[13] Pip states his realization that Magwitch is his fairy godfather in words nearly as watery but not so overwrought: "[D]isappointments, dangers, disgraces, consequences of all kinds, rushed in in such a multitude that I was borne down by them and had to struggle for every breath" (*GE*, 316), like a drowning man.

All night after Magwitch's return, Pip is consumed by guilt for having "deserted" Biddy and Joe in order to live like a gentleman on an ex-convict's money. Calling himself a passenger in a ship "gone to pieces" (*GE*, 320), Pip is beset by what he terms a "sense of my own worthless conduct" (*GE*, 321). Jane too bemoans her "weak ... conduct," her poor judgment in thinking of Rochester as "stainless truth" (*JE*, 292). But her epiphany struck Dickens as less traumatic than Pip's graver yet funnier misjudgment in never imagining a transported felon could be his fairy godparent. *Cinderella* still works as a cultural paradigm if the prince is less than perfect, but not if Dickens disqualifies the fairy godmother, be it Jane's Uncle Eyre or Mat Marksman in Collins's *Hide and Seek*. Pip's misjudgment, moreover, lies not only in thinking too highly of another, as Jane does, but also in overvaluing himself, and in that, says Dickens, Pip mirrors Victorian England's Cinderella complex.

Jane claims she is changed from "ardent expectant woman" to "cold, solitary girl again" (*JE*, 292); that is, from Cinderella back to cinder girl. In Mr. Pirrip's opinion, Pip's reversal is the severer comedown, his life story the only realistic lesson in the dangers and consequences of expectancy. To prove as much, Pip invokes the Misnar story to revise the Biblical analogy Jane uses for her disaster. "My hopes were all dead—struck with a subtle doom, such as, in one night, fell on all the first-born in the land of Egypt," Jane laments (*JE*, 292). Pip's substitutive metaphor, the collapse of Misnar's pavilion for expectations irretrievably lost, is the superior analogue; it, not Exodus, deserves to be called "*the* Eastern story" (*GE*, 309; italics added). Jane's allusion sidesteps the question of personal guilt, Dickens charged. The Egyptian children perished because of Pharaoh's refusal to let Moses and his people go.[14] Similarly, Jane pays for Rochester's duplicity; her Cinderella may be said to be among Egypt's "first-born" (*JE*, 292), indirect victims of another's turpitude. Pip blames himself for deserting Joe in favor of Magwitch. His Cinderella is a social-climbing snob, not unlike Ahaback and Desra, who are pulverized for proclaiming the true sultan's usurping brother. Disappointing nuptials cause Jane to flee Thornfield. Pip's crushed hopes drive him all the way to ten years of bondage in the real Egypt. Jane's "doom" requires "one night"; Pip is demoted from aspiring Cinderella to snobbish usurper—"in an instant" (*GE*, 310).

Bertha Antoinette Mason of Jamaica and Miss Havisham of Satis House are both insane. Both remain hidden away, the latter by choice. Both meet a fiery end. But Brontë gets everything else wrong, Dickens protested. Because "the mysterious lunatic," to use Rochester's phrase (*JE*, 289), is a victim of heredity, her plight lacks extensive social significance. With "idiots and maniacs" in her family "through three generations" (*JE*, 289), how, Dickens asks, can her misfortunes shed light on Victorian England?

In Dickens's parody, Miss Havisham is as monstrous and witchlike as Bertha but clearly a casualty of contemporary society. The wealthy brewer's daughter has been driven mad—swindled out of money and jilted at the altar by the same conniving gentleman (Compeyson) for whose crimes Magwitch takes most of the blame. Rochester is tricked *into* marrying Bertha; Miss Havisham is tricked *out* of marriage and "a pot of money" (*GE*, 346).

Despite Rochester's attempt to rescue her, Bertha dies wild and unrepentant. Having apologized to Pip, Miss Havisham accidentally sets herself aflame: she bursts into "a whirl of fire" (*GE*, 399) that connotes expiation, instant purgatory. Dickens manages to reclaim his madwoman. Yet he strikes down Cinderella motifs in *Jane Eyre* by sending one of Pip's fairy godparents up in flames, then nearly drowns the other.

Pip willingly pardons Miss Havisham. Although the injured party, he seems genuinely embarrassed when his deceitful ex-patron, "kneeling at [his] feet," sheds tears of genuine regret (*GE*, 395).[15] No one in *Jane Eyre* seems capable of such remorse. In particular, Dickens parodies Mrs. Reed's efforts to stave off Jane's grudging absolution. "Love me, then, or hate me, as you will," says Jane, "you have my full and free forgiveness; ask now for God's; and be at peace" (*JE*, 239). Mrs. Reed not only has treated Jane as an unwanted stepchild; she has also tried to keep her from inheriting John Eyre's estate. Still, Dickens interjects, it is unnatural for neither Jane nor Mrs. Reed to back down. Like Cinderella and her wicked stepmother, they inhabit a fairy tale world in which people's fortunes change dramatically, but not people. In contrast, Pip declares to Miss Havisham: "I want forgiveness and direction far too much, to be bitter with you" (*GE*, 395). In place of the cold severity of Jane's forgiveness and Mrs. Reed's imperviousness to it, Dickens insists upon a mutual softening between Pip and Miss Havisham. Pip's scheming fairy godmother becomes a repentant, apologetic one, a parody of *Cinderella* each time.

On the other hand, Pip's rescue of the flaming Miss Havisham has been called an assault. Pip extinguishes her with a vehemence recent critics find akin to "rape."[16] "I threw her down," Mr. Pirrip remembers, and got "the great cloth from the table" over her; "we were on the ground struggling like desperate enemies, and . . . the closer I covered her, the more wildly she shrieked and tried to free herself" (*GE*, 399).

Implications of revengeful rape lessen, however, if one emphasizes Dickens's contempt for Brontë's forgiveness scene between Jane and Mrs. Reed. Cinderella receives a splendid outfit whenever she meets her fairy godmother, but Pip sees Miss Havisham's bridal gown consumed by "a great flaming light" (*GE*, 399). Nevertheless, he behaves throughout like a Christian, whereas Jane acts like a haughty princess. Why would Mr. Pirrip invest with sexual overtones his twenty-three-year-old self's efforts to save a woman more than twice that age? Recounting the calamity more than thirty years after it transpired, does he suddenly realize its true nature, or is he realistically describing how much force was necessary? As Pip grapples with Miss Havisham, he notes "the disturbed beetles and spiders running away over the floor" (*GE*, 399), hardly a rapist's recollection. After Miss Havisham's accident, there is nothing rapacious in Pip's parting kiss reaffirming his forgiveness.

Pip has come to Satis House to obtain nine hundred pounds for Herbert's partnership and to inquire about Estella. "Is she married?" he asks Miss Havisham, whose resounding "Yes" leaves him desolate (*GE*, 396). The combustion of Miss Havisham's bridal gown, a symbol of this superannuated Cinderella's frustrated marital plans, symbolizes Pip's disappointment as well. Its ashy tatters settle on him like remnants of his own false hopes. Smothering the flames soaring around his parodic fairy godmother, Pip extinguishes the vestiges of his Cinderella-like expectations. In the "smoky air," says Pip, "patches of tinder" that "had been [Miss Havisham's] faded bridal dress" were "falling in a black shower around us" (*GE*, 399), making these failed Cinderellas cinder girls again.

Dickens believed Miss Havisham's conflagration would rival—indeed, surpass—Bertha's setting fire to Thornfield. Taken together, Mrs. Reed's death and Bertha's self-destruction assure Jane's rise, removing *two* witches from her path. In Dickens's parody, the combustion of Pip's phony fairy godmother follows closely upon the revelation that a coarse ex-convict is his real patron. Together, these events seal his downfall. He is deprived of the fairy godmother he thought he wanted and acquires an even less suitable replacement: one witch (Mag*witch*) in place of another.

Dickens also accused Brontë of misreading Jane's darker side as an expungeable hidden self. In his opinion, *Jane Eyre* seems to say that unwanted character traits—on the sociopolitical level, undesirables in general—can be externalized and destroyed. Like Bertha, they are foreigners and tend to self-destruct, leaving an uncompromised Cinderella in possession of the field. Orlick menaces Pip more effectively than Bertha resents Jane. A nasty caricature of Pip, Orlick becomes the agent for an even nastier epiphany. The self-knowledge Orlick forces on Pip, the considerable degree of identification with Orlick that Pip is compelled to accept, constitutes the ultimate psychological barrier to his conception of himself as Cinderella. Bertha, Dickens implied, ought to have been an equally earthshaking revelation to Jane.[17]

Cinderella, Dickens realized, cannot have a darker internal self, a hidden antisocial side. She must be one-pointed to the core, free from all internal contradictions, which is how Brontë keeps Jane's personality: a case of undaunted merit awaiting compensation. Realistically, Dickens protested, no individual (or country) can be devoid of inner conflicts or without an underside to his, her, or its makeup.

Orlick does Pip's dirty work in felling Mrs. Joe and robbing Pumblechook. It is as if he acts out Pip's secret fantasies of taking revenge. Bertha, Dickens charged, is simply expendable, the heroine's darker side as scapegoat. Orlick nearly murders Pip. In Dickens's redoing of Brontë, Orlick forces the disillusioned Cinderella to confront his resentful inner self much as Magwitch makes him recognize his parasitism. Thanks to Orlick, Pip is obliged to realize that he harbors within himself a secondary personality not unlike a psychopath.

The night before her wedding, Jane awakens from one bad dream into another: a strange creature enters her bedroom, tries on Jane's bridal veil, then tears it "in two parts," trampling both. This ineffectual bit of sabotage does more than suggest disapproval of Rochester for wanting two wives; it also shows that Jane has two selves, of which Bertha is the less manageable. The intruder's "savage face" reminds Jane of a "Vampire"; "I lost consciousness," she tells Rochester the next morning (*JE*, 281).¹⁸

On "a dark night," the Monday before the Wednesday morning escape attempt with Magwitch, Pip enters the sluice house and is "caught in a strong running noose, thrown over [his] head from behind" (*GE*, 419). In Dickens's improvement upon Bertha's nighttime intrusion, noose replaces bridal veil. Once Orlick seizes his nemesis, Pip must wrestle with his demon. Jane's nightmare occurs in pantomime; Pip's features sound. In place of silent Bertha, Dickens presents a talkative Orlick, eager to air his grievances. There can be no integration of personality without prolonged conversation, Dickens informs Brontë.

Only after Orlick's accusations and much self-recrimination does Pip pass out, dying in effect to his other self rather than having it die for him as Bertha does to simplify matters for Jane. "After a blank," says Pip, "as I recovered consciousness, I knew that I was in the place where I had lost it" (*GE*, 426), the "it" referring not only to "consciousness" but also to his less commendable other self, which he has faced and resisted, expelling his dark side yet setting it free.

When Dickens rewrites the scene in which Bertha invades Jane's bedroom but harms only her wedding finery, Orlick's venom seems to materialize out of Pip himself. The latter remembers "a strong man's breast" being "set against my mouth to deaden my cries"; he feels "a hot breath always close to me" (*GE*, 419), as if the two of them have merged. Having "struggled ineffectually in the dark," Pip reports a losing battle against an alternative version of himself; in other words, unlike Bertha, Orlick is a genuine secret sharer and the doubling of Pip and Orlick is handled with greater psychological dexterity than that of Bertha and Jane.

Bertha's demise, which cancels Jane's second self, is simple subtraction, Dickens opined, not the sort of resonating psychological collision that produces greater self-awareness and moral growth. Dickens accused Brontë of removing a complication not only from Rochester's life but also from his second wife's personality. In contrast, Orlick brings Pip's submerged self to the surface, compelling him to acknowledge complicity in "the attack upon" Mrs. Joe, which Pip supposedly desired even more than Orlick: "[I]t warn't Old Orlick as did it; it was you," the journeyman asserts (*GE*, 423). Pip is forced to see Orlick's Cinderella complex as a grotesquely tragicomic rendition of his own. Incurably envious and spiteful—indeed, a snob—Orlick depicts himself as having been the forge's true cinder girl, with Pip in the stepsister's role: "You was favoured, and he [Orlick] was bullied and beat" (*GE*, 423), Orlick complains.

Jane hears of Bertha's fatal plunge without a pang. "Good God!" she exclaims, yet it is the recounting eyewitness who "shuddered" (*JE*, 417). Jane merely asks for directions to Ferndean, Rochester's new abode, and offers to pay "twice the hire" to be conveyed there "before dark" (*JE*, 418). She could be Cinderella anxious to get to the ball and score her triumph before midnight. Snared by Orlick, Pip says, "I shouted out with all my might" and "struggled with all the force, until then unknown, that was in me" (*GE*, 426). Pip draws upon heretofore unsuspected inner reserves to combat an attempted takeover by his worse self, simultaneously repudiating the latter's Cinderella complex as a grotesquely ludicrous version of his own. Pip cannot cast out the Orlick in himself unless, Jane to the contrary, he first realizes that this alter ego is indeed internal as well as other. Nor can he expel Orlick alone. As rescuers burst in, Pip sees "Orlick emerge from a struggle of men, as if it were tumbling water, clear the table at a leap, and fly out into the night" (*GE*, 426).

Orlick's "leap" is Bertha's redone by a superior psychological realist, Dickens boasted. Bertha jumps to her death out of fire; in Dickens's retelling, Orlick leaps to freedom and seems to "fly" away. His escape is presented as a release for Pip's second self, an expulsion that is also relief and liberation. "Tumbling water" serves as a powerful abluent, more efficacious than the purgation that Bertha's fiery death signifies for Jane. Her second self conveniently commits suicide, whereas Pip is able to cleanse himself of his in an act of acknowledgment, liberation, and expulsion, perhaps in that order. Nevertheless, Pip's story replaces Brontë's oversimplification with a tragicomic universe of dualisms and contradictions in which Pip's rescuers cannot contain Orlick any more than he can kill Pip.

Having regained consciousness, the first thing Pip sees, with much joy, is "the face of Trabb's boy!" (*GE*, 426) Dickens substitutes the visage of this "unlimited miscreant" for the "savage face" to which Jane awakes (*GE*, 245; *JE*, 281). After expelling his darker self, Pip can embrace, and be embraced by, his comic imitator, thereby striking a tragicomic note in coming to terms with two stalkers at once. He is saved from a bad end by his comic double, in whose countenance (as in Orlick's) he must recognize something of himself.[19]

Jane Eyre boasts nothing of similar psychological complexity, Dickens avowed. To triumph as Cinderella, Jane must shed all internal contradiction, all psychological complication. But Pip survives the sluice house because, as in real life, tragic and comic elements alternate within him, neither prevailing definitively over the other even if Trabb's boy, who personifies Pip's sense of his own absurdity, staves off Orlick, the projection of Pip's darker designs. To the extent that Pip's encounter with Orlick and rescue by Trabb's boy cause one to frown with anxiety then smile in relief, they illustrate how tragedy and comedy continuously undercut each other.

In Dickens's parodic reformulation of the Jane–Bertha encounter, Pip has a painful premonition of a future in which only the worst of him survives. Thanks to Orlick, it will appear that Pip "deserted" Herbert and Magwitch even more reprehensibly than he forsook Biddy and Joe. It looks as if only a totally selfish, ungrateful Pip will be, as he puts it, "misremembered" (*GE*, 422).

Putting all thoughts of Bertha's pyromania aside, Jane hastens to Ferndean to become her prince's good "fairy" (*JE*, 427). Pip resolves to "die making some last poor resistance" to Orlick. This decision to hold firm to his better self, without denying its failings, "softened [Pip's] thoughts of all the rest of men," leaving him "melted at heart" (*GE*, 422). Pip achieves a tragicomic perspective: able to oppose yet accept (not excuse) life's inadequacies—including, in his case, an unjust end—he is at peace, ready for life or death, a mature person morally and psychologically.
   Bertha's death allows Jane's personality to solidify. In Dickens's revision, Pip stands fast against his darker self only to melt charitably toward everyone else. His Cinderella complex does not survive the sluice house: softening toward all indicates that he is no longer snob or social climber and may be considered cured.

Pip's realistic failings, not just the dramatic failure of his ill-fated hopes, expose Jane's false modesty. Sporting her "usual Quaker trim" (*JE*, 135), Jane looks unimpressive next to Blanche Ingram, "clad in white" like a bride-to-be. But appearances do not concern Jane, confident of greater inner worth. Rochester's "intended" lacks a single "opinion of her own"; Miss Ingram, Jane decides, "was too inferior to excite" jealousy (*JE*, 188). A parody of such hypocritical reticence, Pip is consumed with envy of Bentley Drummle, whom he considers "sulky," "sluggish," "awkward," "idle," and "a blockhead"—"half a dozen heads thicker than most gentlemen" (*GE*, 202). Which is more believable, Dickens asks, Jane's feigned indifference to Blanche, or Pip's outspoken contempt for Drummle?
   The more Jane protests, the more Dickens ridicules her coy reluctance to become her story's princess. Thus he refuses to credit Jane's disdain for the jewels and dresses her future husband desires to shower upon her. Jane tells readers how she resisted Rochester's "efforts to masque [his] plebeian bride in the attributes of a peeress" (*JE*, 278). When his fairy godparent's agent suggests a new wardrobe, Pip immediately buys one.
   On Saturday night, Jaggers recommends "new clothes" for the trip to London; Pip goes "down town on Monday" to order them (*GE*, 139, 143). The eagerness with which Mr. Trabb serves Pip gives the latter his "first decided experience of the stupendous power of money" (*GE*, 150). In a comic reversal of gender stereotypes, a male Cinderella hastens to acquire the finery that a female Cinderella declines. Not just here but throughout, *Great Expectations* alleges, Jane makes herself much too good to be true. Pip's snobberies grow increasingly amusing as they expose Jane's attempts to deceive the reader and herself.
   "He has left you all his property, and . . . you are now rich," says St. John

Rivers when he informs Jane of Uncle Eyre's legacy. "I! rich?" Jane asks. "Yes, you, rich—quite an heiress," Rivers assures her (*JE*, 373). Jaggers's rigmarole— "What I have to do as the confidential agent of another, I do"; "I am the bearer of an offer . . ."; "Bear in mind then, that Brag is a good dog, but Holdfast is a better"; "And the communication I have got to make is that he has great expectations" (*GE*, 136–37)—parodies the monosyllabic exchange between Rivers and Jane. On crucial questions of growth and development, Dickens's prolixity implies, *Jane Eyre* invariably oversimplifies.

Dickens rewrites Rivers's good news as Jaggers's problematic announcement. Dismissing *Jane Eyre* and *Cinderella* simultaneously, he redefines Jane's experience of being "lifted in a moment from indigence to wealth" (*JE*, 373). "Silence succeeded" Rivers's bulletin, Jane writes, for "one does not jump, and spring, and shout hurrah! at hearing one has got a fortune"; instead, she moralizes, one "begins to consider responsibilities, and to ponder business; on a base of steady satisfaction rise certain grave cares—and we contain ourselves, and brood over our bliss with a solemn brow" (*JE*, 373–74). Not so Pip. His more animated response makes Jane sound like Pecksniff.

On hearing Jagger's announcement, Pip reports, "Joe and I gasped" (*GE*, 137). Then Pip proceeds to do all the things Jane proscribes. "My dream was out; my wild fancy was surpassed by sober reality," he exults. "My heart was beating so fast, and there was such a singing in my ears, that I could scarcely stammer" (*GE*, 137). Pip's reaction—rapid heartbeat, dizziness, broken speech— pours scorn on Jane's. Her sedate brooding, her all-too-businesslike satisfaction, appears absurd, too good to be true, as is her inheritance itself, Dickens alleges, and the very notion of a fairy godfather, even if Uncle Eyre really is her uncle whereas Magwitch is not Pip's.

Great Expectations is more reliable than *Jane Eyre* because it treats Pip less flatteringly than Brontë represents Jane. The young snob is horrified to learn that his money originates from an ex-convict who earned it in Australia, but Jane's "solemn" acceptance of John Eyre's bequest is no less reprehensible. According to Beth Newman, Jane must know that her money was earned from sugar produced by slave labor (*JE*, 12). Making Pip appear snobbish makes Jane seem hypocritical; her deceptive self-restraint, Dickens inveighed, imparts false gravity to the novel's fairy tale resolution.

Not surprisingly, *Great Expectations* and *Jane Eyre* come to different conclusions. Dickens's second ending can be read as a parodic subversion of Brontë's finale. Thus, Jane's self-congratulatory announcement, "Reader, I married him" (*JE*, 437), yields to Pip's less definite forecast: from Estella, he says, "I saw no shadow of another parting" (*GE*, 480).

Jane calls Rochester "a lamp quenched," one "whose gold-ringed eyes cruelty has extinguished" (*JE* 496, 487). Rochester's orbs see nothing, nor can Jane see anything in them. "What I had never seen before," Pip declares, "was the saddened, softened light of the once proud eyes" (*GE*, 478). He records a deepening in Estella, a mellower outlook reflecting his own. Yet Pip refuses to predict the "perfect accord" that Jane attributes to herself and Rochester.

Through Pip's self-imposed shortsightedness, Dickens scoffs at Rochester's miraculous recovery. Within two years, without medical supervision, he progresses from "a sightless block," for whom all is "haze" and "cloud," to a man whose happy future with Jane, always "the apple of his eye," can be easily foreseen (*JE*, 424, 439). Which is the sounder prognosis, Dickens asks, that of a novelist who brings Rochester out of the shadows to "recovered" sight (*JE*, 440), or Mr. Pirrip's cautious confession of what he cannot see (namely, "no shadow of another parting"; *GE*, 480)? If the latter, clarity and truthfulness belong to *Great Expectations* and Dickens can say he is the more insightful novelist.

As Jane's tale "draws to its close," she has "been married ten years" (*JE*, 439), roughly the time Dickens keeps Pip in Egypt before reconciling him with Estella. Dickens's pair needs a decade even to contemplate the bliss Jane and Rochester have enjoyed. Unlike Brontë's couple, who have at least a "first-born" (*JE*, 440), Pip and Estella seem fated to remain childless; little Pip is the son of Biddy and Joe.

Although Jane enjoys waiting on Rochester, Brontë underlines her graduation to Cinderella. "Let me leave you an instant," Jane tells Rochester, "to make a better fire, and have the hearth swept up" (*JE*, 425). But Jane issues these commands instead of executing them herself. Reunited with Rochester at Ferndean, she repeatedly tries to "comb out" the "shaggy black mane" of her "sightless Samson" (*JE*, 427, 420). Just as *Frankenstein* needlessly invokes *Paradise Lost*, *Jane Eyre*, Dickens fumed, misuses *Samson Agonistes*. Rochester not only survives Thornfield's collapse ("there was a great crash—all fell"); Samson to the contrary, he also regains his eyesight after marrying the "fairy-born" Jane (*JE*, 418, 427). Again Brontë fails to take an "Eastern story" (*GE*, 309) correctly into account. For Rochester (Samson's experience with Delilah notwithstanding) as for Jane, collapse is not the all-changing calamity Pip suffers.

Jane's allusion to Milton insulates her Cinderella complex from collapse. Samson revenged himself and recovered his former glory by pulling down the Temple of Dagon on the Philistines. But Thornfield claims Bertha, not Jane, and Rochester's role in the proceedings is Samson-like without proving fatal. Pip's palace, Dickens replies, falls solely and ignominiously upon him, just as Misnar's pavilion destroyed the usurpers.

Reinjured in the struggle with Orlick, Pip's "throbbing" left arm, already burned "to the elbow" rescuing Miss Havisham, is violently swollen and inflamed" (*GE*, 427). The "crash" of Thornfield costs Rochester "one hand so crushed that ... the surgeon had to amputate it directly" (*JE*, 418). Pip's injuries are less severe than Rochester's; nevertheless, the abundance of hand imagery in Dickens's novel owes something to the latter's missing extremity.

As chapter 37 ends, Rochester "stretched out his hand to be led." Jane relates that she "took that dear hand" and they "entered the wood, and wended homeward" (*JE*, 437). In Dickens's parodic rendition, not only must Pip confiscate Estella's hand, but their destination seems less certain. "I took her hand in mine," Pip says, "and we went out of the ruined place" (*GE*, 480). Dickens rewrites Jane's sense of homecoming at Ferndean as Adam and Eve exiting paradise. He laughs at Brontë's ending by darkening it considerably.

Rochester calls himself a "ruin" (*JE*, 433), but neither he nor "the blackened ruin" of Thornfield, says Dickens, can rival Pip's destroyed hopes, which resemble Misnar's collapsed pavilion. "The old lightning-struck chestnut-tree in Thornfield's orchard" supplies Rochester with a symbol for his altered state (*JE*, 433).[20] In declaring herself "bent and broken" (*GE*, 480), however, Estella surpasses Rochester with a description of the internal injuries she and Pip have sustained, damages to heart and soul beyond Rochester's ken. As a "ruined place" (*GE*, 480), Satis House connotes psychologically painful disappointments, lost illusions and, in consequence, a soberer, tragicomic worldview that mocks Brontë's fairy tale ending.

Dickens's final picture of Pip and Estella, two victims of the Cinderella complex walking hand-in-hand toward an uncertain future, replays Brontë's sylvan scene in which Cinderella motifs still work. Before kneeling to Jane in supplication and devotion, Rochester confesses to wearing beneath his cravat her "little pearl necklace" (*JE*, 435), Brontë's facsimile for a glass slipper.

Dickens's hand imagery carries the day. From a "softened" Estella, Pip receives "the friendly touch of the once insensible hand." He is reminded "of the pressure" with which Magwitch acknowledged "the last words he had heard on earth," news that his daughter is still alive (*GE*, 478, 456). In clasping Estella's hand, Pip feels Magwitch's grip again as well. This exceeds anything Jane can accomplish with Rochester: "I arrested his wandering hand, and pressed it in both mine" (*JE*, 422). Jane presses one hand within two, but Pip's hand receives a double pressure, one from a hand formerly "insensible" and another from beyond the grave.

Great Expectations also parodies the "mysterious summons" that recalls Jane to Thornfield (*JE*, 436). Totally forlorn because, as he says, "I could nowhere find you," Rochester exclaims "Jane! Jane! Jane!" Miles away at Moor House, she not only hears his voice but telepathically transmits her reassuring reply, "I am coming: wait for me" (*JE*, 436).[21] Staggered by Magwitch's more difficult return from Australia, Pip starts to believe he saw it coming: "I began either to imagine or recall that I had had mysterious warnings of this man's approach . . . for weeks gone by" (*GE*, 321). Pip's "mysterious warnings" prior to Magwitch's late-night return replace Jane's "mysterious summons at midnight." Only after a severe shock does Pip's mind begin to work as irrationally as Jane's. Magwitch's reappearance causes Pip to lose proud-eyed Estella as surely as the crash of Thornfield costs Rochester his eyes.[22] Pip's exclamation of loss and disappointment, "O Estella, Estella!" (*GE*, 318), never escapes his lips. Not surprisingly, she neither hears nor comes. Nevertheless, Pip's inward cry seems designed to stifle Rochester's implausible appeal, "Jane! Jane! Jane!"

Pip's extraordinary reencounter with Estella is no less far-fetched than Jane's reunion with Rochester, but Dickens ridicules the latter to enhance the former's credibility. Pip has been gone "eleven years"; Jane less than one. Her journey to Thornfield requires no more than three or four days. Yet Pip, presumably returning all the way from Egypt, enters "the old garden" the very evening on which Estella comes to "take leave of it" for the last time (*GE*, 479). Pip's fortuitous reconciliation with Estella is made to appear providential compared with Jane's supercharged rush toward Rochester. Fate schools Pip and Estella separately for a decade before they meet again. How can either of Brontë's characters have improved greatly during their few months apart? Dickens asks.

When Jane appears in Rochester's room instead of the customary servant, he grasps her fingers; then, Jane continues, "[M]y arm was seized, my shoulder—neck—waist—I was entwined" (*JE*, 422). Pip, it has been noted, not only retains Estella's hand but also connects its touch with the sympathy he felt from Magwitch's as the latter lay dying. From the "touch" of the newly returned ex-convict, however, Pip initially "recoiled . . . as if he had been a snake (*GE*, 317). When Orlick seizes Pip, "my arms," says the latter, were "pulled close to my sides . . . while I was fastened tight to the wall" (*GE*, 419), the ultimate negative reworking of Jane's serendipitous entwinement.

As Elizabeth Gaskell noted, Charlotte Brontë expressed "strong . . . admiration" for Thackeray (*LCB*, 320), whom she hailed in her preface to the second edition of *Jane Eyre* as "the first social regenerator of the day" (*JE*, 19). To this coveted accolade, Dickens felt more entitled. As long as Brontë was read with respect, however, her tribute to Thackeray would nominate Dickens's rival as the era's premier social critic. Dickens had a long-standing grievance to settle with Brontë that her reliance on *Cinderella* doubtless exacerbated.

Brontë ranked Thackeray as the period's most powerful moral force—not just a denouncer of society's ills but a "prophet-like" writer as "dauntless and daring" as any who came "before the throned Kings of Judah and Israel." Having praised "the Greek fire of [Thackeray's] sarcasm," Brontë prayed that society might "take his warnings in time" (*JE*, 18). As the 1850s ended, Dickens saw himself, not Thackeray, as the Victorian equivalent of Micaiah, who warned Israel of defeat when others promised victory. Substituting the Misnar tale for *Cinderella*, collapse in place of going from rags to riches, *Great Expectations* issued Dickens's sternest warning to date: England's continued ascendancy among nations was no more assured than Pip's patent of gentility.

Inasmuch as Brontë corroborated *Cinderella* throughout *Jane Eyre* and Thackeray deployed Cinderella motifs in *Pendennis*, neither could supply the admonishing voice the 1860s required, Dickens insisted. The more unreliable *Great Expectations* made *Jane Eyre* appear—that is, the more deftly it reduced the latter to fairy tale—the less trustworthy Thackeray, whom it endorses, became as well.

That *Jane Eyre* tried to outdo *Oliver Twist* and, along with *Pendennis*, was often identified as a source for *David Copperfield*, aggravated Dickens's hostility toward Charlotte's best-known novel.[23] The "orphan's myth" as created by Dickens in *Oliver Twist*, is not unlike *Cinderella*; positing the protagonist's temporal situation as a hardship, both works advise perseverance until deliverance arrives.[24] The cinder girl, however, gets soiled before her fairy godmother providentially appears; little Oliver remains unstained in word or deed.

On the path to salvation, everyone is an orphan sooner or later—solely responsible for oneself. The orphan may meet thieves and prostitutes, as Oliver does, or religious hypocrites and a would-be seducer in Jane's case, but soul and personality remain inseparable—indeed, identical; keeping the former unsullied is equivalent to developing the latter. Like Bunyan's Pilgrim, Oliver and Jane are simply passing through; progress consists in doing so unscathed.

Neither Jane nor Oliver is an evolving child; each comes into money by preserving unchanged an essential God-given integrity. The difference is that Charlotte Brontë conceived of Jane as a ball of fire aggressively defending her uprightness against all comers. A shuttlecock between Fagin's world and Mr. Brownlow's, the passive Oliver is less deserving than Charlotte's feisty alter ego, or so *Jane Eyre* implies. The world is an unfriendly place in both *Oliver Twist* and *Jane Eyre*, but the meek, Brontë informs Dickens, never inherit it. Dickens's critique of temporal reality may be disregarded because he has no idea how his younger characters are to survive in it.[25]

Dickens supposedly learned from Jane how to create his first realistic child. F.R. Leavis noted uncanny resemblances between *Jane Eyre* and *David Copperfield*: for Mrs. Reed, Miss Murdstone; for Mr. Brocklehurst's boarding school, Mr. Creakle's; for Helen Burns, Traddles; for Jane's wanderings until taken in by relatives and renamed Jane Elliott,[26] David's difficult journey to Aunt Betsey's, where he becomes Trotwood Copperfield. Leavis concluded "that David Copperfield inherits from Jane Eyre in these respects" (QDL, 109). By

1860, however, it seemed less imperative to separate David from Jane than to demonstrate that the creation of Pip marked an advance on both. Even if Copperfield were another Jane or was patterned on the hero of Thackeray's *Pendennis,* he is definitely not Pip's prototype, Dickens maintained; instead, Pip furnishes a corrective for all three (Copperfield, Pen, Jane).

F.R. Leavis mistook Jane's vigorous acts of self-preservation for personality development. She "develops," he argued, "by the laws of her own being and in accordance with the pressures brought to bear on her" (QDL, 109). *Great Expectations* attempts to expose Jane's life story as a prolonged act of self-justification in which she pits her unrelenting sense of self-worth—indeed, her inherent superiority—against all external pressures that might lessen it.[27] Mr. Pirrip composes the first post-Darwin bildungsroman, the first story of a young person's growth and development since *The Origin of Species* (1859) was published. Pip develops not by the laws of his own being but in accord with Darwin's. Whereas Jane struggles to keep from changing or being changed, Pip, unlike his "five little brothers" who died in infancy, continually adjusts; he never gives up "that universal struggle" (*GE,* 3) for existence which the *Origin* designates nature's first principle.[28]

Natural selection, wrote Darwin, "can produce no great or sudden modifications; it can act only by short and slow steps" (*OS,* 117). The theory of evolution, *Great Expectations* contends, rules out Cinderella-like ascent once and for all. Natural selection precludes a three-day transfiguration from servant girl to princess. Consequently, it renders unbelievable—that is, unscientific—novels patterned on such transfigurations. Pip sees earthly existence from a perspective as providential and evolutionary as it is tragicomic; every life, he says, is a "long chain of iron or gold, of thorns or flowers" that is formed daily "link" by link (*GE,* 73). Through Pip, Mr. Pirrip speaks not just of the sort of chain that Joe might forge but of a chain reaction in which events, always both a result and a cause, produce pleasure ("gold," "flowers") and pain ("iron," "thorns"), occasions for laughter and tears.

Great Expectations anticipates what modern Darwinians call "punctuated evolution": a series of starts and stops wherein wholesale extinctions and recoveries interrupt periods of slow development. Hence Jaggers's announcement changes Pip's lifestyle in chapter 18 and Magwitch's return does so again in chapter 39. Evolution, it appears, sanctions neither *gradualism* nor *catastrophism;* instead, it applies each to the other in constantly varying proportions that render unidirectional movements such as Cinderella's miraculous rise scientifically simpleminded. For survival through adaptation, Dickens repeatedly suggests, being "softened" (*GE,* 314) is a better metaphor than hardening. Yet Pip evolves in a world prone to moments of traumatic epiphany and providential comeuppance.[29]

To be "naturally selected," in Darwin's view, a creature must be able to "vary however slightly in any manner profitable to itself" (*OS*, 37). This is something that Jane cannot—indeed, will not—do. Success for her means being resistant to variation. *Jane Eyre*, Dickens remonstrates, denies the very idea of what Darwin terms "profitable deviations" (*OS*, 109). Whether refusing to become Rochester's mistress or St. John Rivers's missionary companion, Jane obeys her cardinal rule: "care for myself," to use her phrase (*JE*, 312), a respect for a finished product to which others must defer.[30] "To have yielded" to Rivers's entreaties, Jane congratulates herself, "would have been an error of principle" (*JE*, 397, 408). Not surprisingly, as one commentator has noted, Rochester is "moulded ideally to suit Jane's needs" (KB, 130).

Having recalled his "Havisham days," the time spent with Miss Havisham and Estella, Pip asks, "How could my character fail to be influenced by them?" (*GE*, 96) Jane, Dickens emphasizes, never acknowledges such impress. From confrontations with John Reed, his mother, Mr. Brocklehurst, Rochester, and St. John Rivers, she emerges unchanged. Thanks to her "independent maturity" (SG, 484), she springs to life fully grown and resists all setbacks, including any sense of identification with Bertha, which would give her personality a dark complication. Jane Eyre personifies the concept Darwin most vehemently denied—namely, that "each species has been independently created" (*OS*, 38)—for she is one of a kind.

"Though rank and wealth sever us widely," Jane remarks of herself and Rochester, "I have something in my brain and heart, in my blood and nerves, that assimilates me mentally to him" (*JE*, 178). To Dickens's amazement, Rochester agrees. The morning after Jane accepts his marriage proposal to go from "plain, Quakerish governess" to "Jane Rochester," he praises her for having "mutinied against fate and claimed your rank as my equal" (*JE*, 257, 261).[31] He lauds her Cinderella complex. Pip never ceases to recognize in others attributes superior to his own: Joe's unselfishness, for example, or Biddy's love, even Magwitch's greater, if twisted, capacity for loyalty. *Great Expectations* opines that Jane mutinies against modern science, not "against fate." On the one hand, her personality never changes; on the other hand, her circumstances change dramatically and she is transformed in one jump from orphan governess to wife and heiress.

Almost always, Pip comes off second best. He thrashes Herbert yet winds up "third in the firm," second to Herbert, who is Clarriker's partner. Pip runs second to Drummle with Estella and second again to Joe for Biddy. "I often wondered how I conceived that old idea of his inaptitude," Pip confesses regarding Herbert, "until I was one day enlightened by the reflection, that perhaps the inaptitude had never been in him at all, but had been in me" (*GE*, 476). The more chastened Pip becomes, the more humble his revised self-estimate, the bigger snob Jane appears. The more frequently he settles for second place, the more convincingly Dickens mocks Jane's triumphs. Pip's autobiography defeats hers by denying its hero her string of victories. In short, Jane rises but never develops; Pip falls yet evolves. The falling and evolving countermand both *Jane Eyre* and *Cinderella*.[32]

No gap exists between Jane as child and her older self as adult narrator; they see eye to eye, Dickens noted. Mr. Pirrip gradually closes the gap between his naive younger self and the mature autobiographer. Pip develops from the target of his older self's unsparing irony into the tragicomedian who writes *Great Expectations*. *Jane Eyre* has been called "the struggle of an individual consciousness toward self-fulfillment" (DL, 114). *Great Expectations* replaces it with Pip's struggle, which is more complicated, often humiliating—indeed, the autobiography of a failure judged by materialist standards—but morally and scientifically, says Dickens, more realistic than *Jane Eyre*, hence fitter to be read and reread.

After reading Darwin, Goldie Morgentaler has argued, Dickens jettisoned heredity as a "determining factor in the formation of the self"; in *Great Expectations*, he is no longer "a heredity determinist" (GM, 708).[33] Throughout his thirteenth novel, Dickens emphasizes like never before the "formative effects of environment"; "adoption, adaptation," and life's "vagaries" shape Pip (GM, 712), whereas Jane is as predestined for princesshood as is Bertha for madness.

Realism, heredity, and inheritance become interrelated issues. Jane's identity is her real inheritance; she triumphs by holding onto her good opinion of herself until, like Cinderella's, her real worth is proclaimed. Although Jane inherits a fortune while Pip does not, Dickens tries to disinherit her through him. He wants Brontë excluded from the list of Victorian realists because her idea of personality formation was antiquated after 1859. Despite looking backward, boasts Dickens, his novel accommodates new ideas about the individual's growth and development, ideas to which hopelessly irrelevant Cinderella stories such as Brontë's can never adapt.

Two additional Darwinian dictates apply: 1) "if any one species does not become modified and improved in a corresponding degree with its competitors, it will be exterminated"; 2) "the more diversified in habits and structures" a species, "the more places [it] will be enabled to occupy," that is, its ability "to encroach on places occupied by others" will know no bounds (OS, 72, 74). For "any one species" in the first decree, read novels with Cinderella motifs; in the second, consider *Great Expectations* the epitome of the diversified encroacher.

Darwin's theory of evolution allowed Dickens to put the "realism wars" of the 1850s (HR, 2–3) into scientific perspective; reviewed in light of natural selection, they became a struggle for existence that only the fittest, a novelist such as himself, deserved to survive. Novels confirming *Cinderella* did not mea-sure up once Darwin had spoken. In contrast, *Great Expectations* was extremely versatile, adaptability itself: melodramatic—indeed, sensational—politically poignant, a searing critique of the Victorian socioeconomic system, a tragicomic fictional autobiography of a reformed snob, a grotesque monster story, a tale of revenge that fosters reconciliation. Thanks to Darwin, works from earlier in the century—*Frankenstein* and *Jane Eyre* in particular—could be considered usurpers. Outdated sociologically, biologically, psychologically and yet the instigator of a harmful popular trend—namely, the use of Cinderella motifs—Brontë's novel invited extermination through revaluation for occupying its niche undeservedly.

Chapter 8
Emily Brontë

Dickens shared the distaste some of Emily Brontë's contemporaries expressed for her fascination with devilish behavior, which supposedly leaves a "moral taint" on *Wuthering Heights*.[1] "Appropos of Miss Hogarth saying that [*Jane Eyre*] was an unhealthy book," Dickens declared that he "had not read" Emily's novel either because "he disapproved of the whole school."[2] Practitioners of the Gothic mode were ineffective socially—in Dickens's opinion, incapable of bringing about desirable change. Although Dickens's novel is as sensational as Emily's and Charlotte's, both of which he doubtless read, he considered Magwitch and Miss Havisham, not to mention Orlick, more urgent manifestations of antisocial energy than Heathcliff. Schemes concocted by Dickens's diabolical characters point to, or are products of, glaring social deficiencies. Consequently, Dickens's probings into deviant behavior—Magwitch's perverse plan to refine Pip, Orlick's devilish attempt to murder him—are healthful; that is, imbued with a psychological realist's curiosity and driven by a reformer's zeal.

Jane Eyre and *Wuthering Heights* were not the sort of novels Dickens felt Victorian readers needed. That both had been written during one of "the most harrowing and dangerous [decades] of the entire century" (RA, 89) yet lacked a crusading social conscience rendered them hopelessly obsolete by 1860. Each Brontë depends on a different facet of the century's favorite fairy tale. Jane rises like Cinderella, according to one Brontë; the other shows Hindley and then Heathcliff reducing a rival to cinder girl status. *Jane Eyre* encouraged readers to fantasize about duplicating Cinderella's ascent; *Wuthering Heights* invited them to watch a former cinder person get even by reducing his enemies or their progeny to that unhappy state. Although Emily's book beat *Jane Eyre* into print, Dickens damned this revenge tragedy as an unwholesome corollary to Charlotte's improbable Cinderella story.

Emily helped Charlotte to suffuse the nineteenth-century British novel with

Cinderella motifs. In Charlotte's fairy tale world, the heroine rises by standing firm, resisting detractors; Heathcliff, a vengeful cinder person, dreams of raising himself in order to lord it over his persecutors and their descendants. Emily's revenge fantasy, Dickens fumed, exposes the nastiness concealed in Jane's Cinderella-like autobiography about demanding one's desserts.

To ridicule Hindley's crude designs on Heathcliff and the latter's retaliation against Hareton, Dickens substituted the vengeful child-rearing schemes that Magwitch and Miss Havisham devise for Pip and Estella, ill-fated projects that he insisted are subtler psychologically and more pertinent sociologically. Unable to rise personally, Magwitch makes use of a deputy, as does Miss Havisham, but not in the clumsy way Hindley abuses Heathcliff in order to punish old Earnshaw or Heathcliff mistreats Hareton to get even with Hindley. On the contrary, Pip is to have every refinement that Magwitch's money can buy; with no heart for men to break, an invincible Estella can never be fooled the way Compeyson jilted Miss Havisham.

One Brontë, Dickens alleged, oversimplifies the process of getting ahead; the other appears unduly intrigued by the equally perilous process of getting even. Admittedly, parodic revaluation can be defined as self-promotion (Jane's specialty) through a rival's demotion (Heathcliff's forte). Nevertheless, Dickens rejects Jane's wonderful capacity for rising and Heathcliff's terrible resolve to reduce his opponents as twin manifestations of snobbery.

Having contrived a fairy tale about revenge, Emily resorts to unmotivated forgiveness, a futile expedient that Dickens considered her most grievous departure from narrative realism. Heathcliff simply abandons his debasement of Hareton. In Dickens's reworking of Emily's material, a disgruntled Magwitch assails the upper class from start to finish; he enriches Pip, thus creating an artificial gentleman, and drowns Compeyson, thereby destroying a pernicious one. Pip's ongoing negotiations with Estella replace the facile alliance that springs up between Hareton and Cathy. In Dickens's opinion, Mr. Pirrip has written his century's premier revenge tragicomedy; *Great Expectations* not only deplores Emily's obsession with retaliation, but also denigrates her mishandling of the reconciliation process.

Characters, locale, theme—Dickens reworked aspects of all three, outclassing Emily's blusterings with a corrosive sensational realism. He took exception to Brontë's exotic setting and the overdrawn characters the Yorkshire moors seem to spawn. *Great Expectations* "is [Dickens's] *Wuthering Heights*," Frederick Page maintained; "the moors are . . . part-author of the one book, and the Kentish marshes . . . of the other" (FP, ix). Actually, Dickens replaces Brontë's wind-blown landscape with the sobering "marsh country," a "dark flat wilderness" of dikes, ditches, and mud (*GE*, 3).

In Brontë's high-strung universe, "atmospheric tumult" from Yorkshire's "stormy weather" (*WH*, 25) supplies an operatic background for the Heathcliff–Catherine relationship in which hypertensive passions suggest "the clash of cosmic forces."[3] On the marshes in Dickens's darker world, socially verifiable terrors lurk, grimmer realities than Emily's Gothic novel imagines: starving escaped convicts such as Magwitch, for instance, or Orlick, a jealous psychopath.

Psychology in *Wuthering Heights*, the much vaunted collision between cold and hot temperaments, was elementary, Dickens maintained, not elemental. In contrast, Pip's Cinderella complex epitomizes a national failing. Heathcliff's parentage remains forever obscure and *Wuthering Heights* is provincial throughout, but all England has a hand in making Pip. Engendered in the marsh country with help from Australia, his Cinderella complex burgeons in London. Its collapse drives him all the way to Egypt.

A social critic bent on becoming a more convincing psychological realist, Dickens rejected the idea of characters driven by "psychological forces" in lieu of social ones.[4] He believed that the social shaped the psychological. Such is surely the case with the Cinderella complex; in this disturbed mental state, one does not look for victims to degrade, Dickens scolded. Instead, Pip longs to relive *Cinderella*—and Magwitch helps him—not because being a Cinderella is as feasible as Charlotte considers it, but because society's Haves and Have-Nots both wrongly imagine that being loved and experiencing happiness are consequences of material success. By 1860, Dickens realized, rising in the world had become the ultimate revenge.

"It was one of their chief amusements to run away to the moors," Nelly Dean tells Lockwood of Heathcliff and Catherine Earnshaw as children (*WH*, 59). When they venture too near Thrushcross Grange, however, they are captured by the Lintons. Their bulldog, Skulker, "his huge, purple tongue hanging half a foot out of his mouth," seizes Catherine by "her ankle"; a servant calls Heathcliff "an out-and outer," a "foul-mouthed thief" who will "go to the gallows" for disturbing the household (*WH*, 61).

In *Great Expectations*, Dickens rewrote Brontë's opening, darkening it effectively. Pip is "seized" not by the ankle but "by the chin"; his captor is not Skulker but Magwitch, a real down-and-outer seemingly destined for the "gibbet," which Pip sees him "limping" toward at chapter's end (*GE*, 4, 7). The escaped prisoner dubs Pip a "little devil" and a "young dog" (*GE*, 4, 5), epithets more vicious than the insults hurled at Heathcliff.

In *Wuthering Heights*, it is difficult to decide who is more frightened, Heathcliff and Catherine or the Lintons. Perched on a flowerpot outside their window, the youngsters make "frightful noises" to terrify them (*WH*, 61).[5] Pip, Dickens stipulates, is traumatized for life, thanks to a pivotal incident that

Dickens considered the superior blend of comedy with gravity. Catherine's "five weeks" of convalescence at Thrushcross Grange (*WH,* 63) divide her from Heathcliff the way Pip's visits to Satis House alienate him from the forge; they precipitate the mismatches that cause prolonged misery to Edgar and Isabella, not just to herself and Heathcliff. But Dickens expects readers to find Pip's few seconds in Magwitch's grasp a life-changing experience more momentous than Catherine's. Pip and Magwitch, Dickens tells Brontë, are the Victorian novel's tragicomic mismatch, its bona fide odd couple, not Catherine Earnshaw and Edgar Linton (or Heathcliff and Isabella).

After Skulker catches Catherine, the Lintons and Earnshaws stare at each other like creatures of two different species; residents of Thrushcross Grange and visitors from Wuthering Heights might as well be inhabitants of different planets. Dickens rejects such artificial differentiation, branding it both sociologically counterproductive and psychologically suspect. The tremendous gap that yawns between Pip and the convict, Dickens contends, is greater than that separating Catherine from Edgar and more imperative for the social critic to investigate. When village lad meets escapee from the hulks, Dickens shows Brontë a genuine collision of two different worlds.

Dickens abhors the psychological oversimplifications he found in Brontë's dichotomous world. He demonstrates what an odd pairing really is. Pip and Magwitch not only represent opposing classes but exude socioeconomic significance. *Wuthering Heights,* Dickens jeered, thinks that tragedy happens when unlikes wed. To discredit such self-defeating nonsense, two characters in *Great Expectations,* more dissimilar than Catherine and Edgar, manage to bond. Which juxtapositioning is more thought-provoking, its components harder to reconcile, the parodic revaluator asks—Wuthering Heights and Thrushcross Grange, which are next door to each other, or an orphan from a Kentish village and a coarse, violence-prone criminal doing fourteen years at hard labor?

Dickens's odd couple revaluates odd couplings in *Wuthering Heights.* Brontë is accused of fabricating phony divisions and ignoring more complicated real ones. Instead of exploring the gap between Haves and Have-Nots, the more exigent opposition, Emily manufactured incompatibilities between imaginary psychological types. According to Catherine Earnshaw, she and Edgar Linton are as unlike each other as "lightning" and "moonbeam" (*WH,* 86). To render such classifications ludicrous, Dickens finds nothing contrary to nature in the mutual regard that develops between a terrified boy, now a London gentleman, and a hardened criminal, now an illegally returned transport. The Pip–Magwitch relationship, stranger and more self-contradictory than pairings in Brontë, is not only certified as plausible but seems essential for society's survival.

Thanks to Pip and Magwitch, Dickens boasted, *Great Expectations* breaks down real-life barriers separating social classes instead of grossly inflating fanciful oppositions between fiery temperaments and cooler ones. In *Wuthering Heights*, Dickens implied, encounters between opposites, no matter how melodramatic, are of no consequence economically, politically, or sociologically. Dickens derided star-crossed unions between Brontë's trumped-up dissimilars—so-called "children of the storm" (Catherine, Heathcliff) and "children of calm" (Edgar, Isabella),[6] pseudopsychological distinctions more suited to fairy lore than to realistic fiction. Victorians were advised to examine closely the links that Pip and Magwitch forge, and ignore the alliances on which Brontë squanders her talents;[7] namely, Catherine Earnshaw's unsalutary union with Edgar Linton in marriage and Heathcliff's morbid reunion with Catherine through death.

Edgar Linton and Catherine Earnshaw are "as different as . . . frost from fire," Catherine proclaims to Nelly Dean (*WH*, 86). Dickens protested Brontë's use of fire and water imagery to reinforce her novel's spurious oppositions. For Emily, Dickens laughed, there are fire people and water people and never the twain shall meet. Were she realistic, novelists like himself, critical of divisions within society and pushing for a stronger sense of partnership and community, would be well advised to give up.

Pip struggles to master both of Emily's antagonistic elements, putting out fire and melting ice. In chapter 49, for example, he tackles Miss Havisham, who comes "running at [him], shrieking, with a whirl of fire blazing all about her" (*GE*, 399). He also reverses the evil she has done Estella: "I stole her heart away and put ice in its place," Miss Havisham confesses (*GE*, 397). In the revised ending, Estella tells Pip, "I have given it [that is, his love] a place in my heart" (*GE*, 479). Whether extinguishing his fairy godmother, defrosting a Cinderella's frozen heart, or floundering in the Thames with his other fairy godparent, Pip realistically braves the elements Brontë treats grandiosely as psychological principles.

Her supercharged hero and heroine yearn to shuffle off this mortal coil in hopes of spending eternity together. Such escapist behavior was not only morbid in Dickens's estimation, the cultivation of a death wish, but a dead end for society. Upon leaving "the ruined place," which is "to be built on . . . at last" (*GE*, 479–80), Pip and Estella must also be constructive, immersing themselves in the everyday in order to rebuild their lives, allegedly the harder course.

Brontë's novel ends with a glimpse of its major characters' tombstones. *Great Expectations* corrects this unhealthy situation despite beginning and ending in graveyard-like surroundings: the marsh churchyard at the start, the "old garden" belonging to Satis House for the final scene (*GE*, 478). On both occasions, Pip is obliged to go forth, first on a mission of mercy for Magwitch, the second time hand-in-hand with the ex-convict's daughter, now in his care. Putting Little Nell and Paul Dombey behind him, Dickens twice rebuts the impression throughout *Wuthering Heights* that life's goal is an early grave. Brontë, he insinuates, was wrong to bury Heathcliff and Catherine and even more unrealistic, it will be shown, to create in Hareton and Cathy a fresh start, a prelapsarian pair, as if *Wuthering Heights,* instead of continuing, could begin over again like a fairy tale, with another Heathcliff and Catherine.

"Nelly, I *am* Heathcliff," Catherine cries early in the story (*WH,* 87). In *Great Expectations,* such outbursts are given to Pip, who diagnoses his mental state more convincingly. After a visit to Satis House to see his former playmate, now "an elegant lady," Pip admits that "it was impossible for me to separate [Estella], in the past or in the present, from the innermost life of my life" (*GE,* 236).[8] Which is the more levelheaded statement, Dickens asks, Catherine's fervid declaration of biological interchangeability for herself and Heathcliff, or Pip's realization that Estella has been a permanent but external influence, helping to shape his inmost self?

Neither act of identification, Catherine's or Pip's, brings unmitigated delight. "He's always, always in my mind," Catherine adds, "not as a pleasure, . . . but, as my own being" (*WH,* 87). Yet Pip's is the more poignant discomfort, Dickens argued, in that it resonates sociologically, clarifying the Cinderella complex. "Truly," says Pip, "it was impossible to dissociate [Estella's] presence from all those wretched hankerings after money and gentility that had disturbed my boyhood" (*GE,* 236).

Pip's need for Estella and for "money and gentility" are intertwined in his Cinderella complex to the point where rampant materialism acquires a sexual aspect, while sexual attraction is tainted by insatiable materialistic desires. Such interchanges go beyond anything Emily could prefigure with Catherine and Heathcliff. The all-consuming need they profess for each other, Dickens marveled, appears to be neither sexual nor materialistic; it is morally ambiguous, too unrealistic to be judged right or wrong, yet definitely irrelevant socially.

"You are part of my existence, part of myself . . . you cannot choose but remain part of my character, part of the little good in me, part of the evil," Pip harangues Estella upon learning her decision to accept Drummle (*GE,* 362–63). Although Estella forms "part" of Pip's "character," Heathcliff supposedly permeates Catherine's very "being." Only Pip's situation, Dickens claims, is plausible. The impression Estella has made on Pip has a profound bearing upon the protagonist's moral health and society's. How Pip handles his "wretched hankerings" (*GE,* 236) is more important than Catherine's sense of physical identification with Heathcliff because Pip's condition encapsulates the general dementia, his era's Cinderella complex; Catherine's psychological predicament, which Brontë thinks is biological, begins and ends with her, Dickens implies.

The solution to Catherine's problem and his own, Heathcliff decides, is to be buried beside her. He arranges for one side of each coffin to be "struck . . . loose" so that their dust will eventually combine. Heathcliff foresees himself "dissolving with her" (*WH*, 246), finally becoming one with Catherine. Revolted, Dickens accuses Emily of once again looking for a morbid solution. He has clearly forgotten, perhaps outgrown, his youthful desire "to be buried in that same grave" with Mary Hogarth, his wife's younger sister, who died suddenly in 1837, when she was seventeen and he twenty-five (J, 1:197).

By novel's end, Estella is asked to become part of Pip as his partner for life, Dickens chides Brontë, not to decompose with him in the grave. Thanks to Emily's unacceptable novel, *Great Expectations* is greatly concerned with partners and partings; that is, with becoming part of someone as opposed to living apart. Pip refuses to predict "another parting" from Estella, objects to their continuing "friends apart," and seems intent on becoming her marriage partner (*GE*, 479–80). This, says Dickens, is a more sensible paradigm for human behavior than Heathcliff's or Catherine's egotistical eagerness to dissolve into another who is supposedly really oneself.

The difference is between the responsible rededication of tragicomedy and a Romantic morbidity that Dickens found sickly. It offended the reform-minded novelist as much as Emily's fascination with devilish scheming did. Pip and Estella are not encouraged to dissolve and commingle; instead, they soften toward each other, each becoming increasingly receptive. The "softened light" in Estella's "once proud eyes" (*GE*, 478) gives Pip his signal to resume courtship. The parodic revaluator's alternative to dissolution, softening is socially commendable, a return to life; it renders Heathcliff's idea of commingling absurd as well as depressing.

As partners who will not part in this world, Pip and Estella will become part of each other, an extended parody of the Heathcliff–Catherine postmortem fusion, which is made to seem impractical, unhealthy—indeed, ghoulish. The more firmly Pip refuses to relinquish Estella's hand as they proceed out of the cemetery-like garden, the more life-affirmingly tragicomic *Great Expectations* becomes, despite Pip's crushed expectations and a "bent and broken" Estella (*GE*, 480). The more determinedly Dickens sent his couple back into this world as if they were Adam and Eve after the Fall, the more escapist, the more inapplicable to the Victorian scene, indeed, the more morally tainted he made Heathcliff's anxiety to get inside Catherine's coffin. Bathed in "tranquil light" (*GE*, 400), the revised ending eschews Emily's atmospheric tumults while enlivening her funerary conclusion.

Despite the allegedly cosmic reverberations of the Heathcliff–Catherine relationship, *Wuthering Heights* ends indoors with the former confined in his room to await the latter's spirit. *Great Expectations* concludes outside, in "the old garden" at Satis House (*GE*, 478). Heathcliff can find no one to stay with him except Catherine's ghost, "an unearthly vision" that has been stalking him (*WH*, 280). "There is *one* who won't shrink from my company!" he exclaims (*WH*, 282). In Dickens's reformulation, Pip is startled to spy "a solitary figure" in "the desolate garden-walk" (*GE*, 478). Instead of a spectral Catherine calling through Heathcliff's window, Pip encounters a flesh-and-blood Estella who utters his name and responds to her own.

Coming up to her, Pip feels "the friendly touch of the once insensible hand." Estella is not only living but more alive than before (*GE*, 478). When Nelly enters Heathcliff's chamber, she notes that "one hand . . . rested on the sill; . . . and when I put my fingers to it, I could doubt no more: he was dead and stark!" (*WH*, 283) Dickens substitutes Pip's reunion with Estella for Heathcliff's rejoining Catherine. The "softened light" in Estella's eyes, with Pip "bending" protectively over her, replaces the "frightful . . . gaze of exultation" Nelly finds on the face of Heathcliff's corpse, whose eyes, she adds, "would not shut" (*GE*, 478, 480; *WH*, 283). Dickens's ending flirts with the supernatural—is Pip seeing a ghost?—only to parody Emily's far-fetched conclusion, which is made to seem morbid, unearthly, totally without reference to problems of the real world.

When Pip describes how he and Estella "went out of the ruined place," its "low quiet mounds" suggest a burial spot (*GE*, 480). But two former Cinderellas, electing to remain with each other above ground, turn their backs on the graveyard of the past, to which Dickens consigns *Wuthering Heights*'s creepy kirkyard conclusion. Having discovered "three head-stones on the slope next the moor," Lockwood wishes Edgar, Catherine, and Heathcliff a peaceful rest. He doubts that "any one could ever imagine unquiet slumbers for the sleepers in that quiet earth" (*WH*, 285). Why romanticize slumber as life's goal and reward? *Great Expectations* asks. Had Dickens stuck with an earlier version of Pip's final line— "I saw the shadow of no parting from [Estella] but one" (*GE*, 480, n. 2)[9] — stress on arduous but curative continuance until death would be stronger. Postponing his demise indefinitely in order to remain active alongside Estella, Mr. Pirrip would have jibed even more derisively at Brontë's socially ineffective, death-oriented fairy tale.

As things stand, *Great Expectations* and *Wuthering Heights* both end with a narrator's prophecy. That Lockwood's is probably wrong and Pip's correct is supposed to influence one's overall response to their respective stories. Most readers expect the ghosts of Heathcliff and Catherine to walk the moors.[10] Dickens invites one to contrast what Lockwood cannot imagine with what Pip says he cannot foresee. Only the first is a failure to envision. Dickens also appoints himself the superior miracle worker. Whereas Brontë reunites two children of the storm, *Great Expectations* reunites a village blacksmith's apprentice, briefly a London-educated gentleman but now working in Egypt, with a financially strapped widow, daughter of a murderess and a convicted felon, who was raised to be an heiress.

In any successful but unfair social system, such as England's in the 1800s, one is either victim or criminal, sometimes both (Magwitch) or each in turn, as is Miss Havisham. Pip discovers that he has been gull and extortionist: the dupe of Magwitch's designs and the pampered beneficiary of the laboring classes, whom Magwitch represents. Given such conditions, Dickens continues, revenge and forgiveness become all-important concerns. How to get even? That is the question snobs ask themselves. How is one to get over having been slighted, how to stifle the resentment from feeling unjustly deprived? Solving such conundrums seemed as crucial as deciding whether to expand the suffrage or determining how to reform the penal code, but only wrong answers can be found in *Wuthering Heights,* Dickens criticized.

Throughout Brontë's novel, characters take revenge by "proxy" (*WH,* 137). Heathcliff marries Isabella to punish her brother, Edgar, for marrying Catherine. In no time, he turns the refined Isabella into a "little slattern" (*WH,* 138), a cinder girl. Revenge by proxy, characters in *Wuthering Heights* realize, works even better if the instrument used is a child; a vengeful upbringing punishes not just the instrument one employs but also the target for whom it stands. Hindley gets even with his father by demoting Heathcliff in the Earnshaw household from family favorite to farmhand; eventually, Heathcliff does likewise to Hareton, thereby punishing his former persecutor by coarsening his son.

"I have a fancy to try my hand at raising a young one," Heathcliff declares, eyeing Hareton with malice aforethought (*WH,* 226). Magwitch and Miss Havisham could make similar statements regarding Pip and Estella. Exacting revenge through another's upbringing, all four adults just mentioned conduct villainous experiments in child raising. But Dickens's pair constitutes a parodic revaluing of Emily's, which is deemed amateurish both psychologically and sociologically.

Arguably, the title of Dickens's thirteenth novel refers to the high hopes that Magwitch and Miss Havisham entertain of settling old scores, not just to Pip's craving for new horizons. *Great Expectations* scrutinizes no fewer than *three* sets of inordinate expectations. All three programs—Pip's, Magwitch's, Miss Havisham's—subvert *Cinderella.* Victorian England's notion that fate is working overtime to promote and protect a former stepchild among nations is increasingly difficult to credit when one watches Miss Havisham mislead Pip and warp Estella while Magwitch devises a benefaction that confuses gratitude and vengeance.

Emily's concept of revenge comes under heavy fire. Which is the psychologically more insidious way of getting even with society, Dickens asked, to *degrade* one's victims as Hindley and Heathcliff do, or to *upgrade* them, if only temporarily, as a false benefit to them and as an affront or affliction to others? Is it more diabolical to demote or promote, to create artificial Cinderellas or unhappy cinder girls? Which process, Dickens demands, resembles the way fate has treated so-called great civilizations?

Old Earnshaw, Hindley's father, brings home a cinder person, "a dirty, ragged, black-haired child" he claims to have discovered "starving, and houseless" in Liverpool's streets (*WH*, 51). From this charitable deed, the first of the novel's experiments in upbringing, all complications spring. Unfortunately, Earnshaw's motives remain unclear, his godfatherly interest in Heathcliff, unlike Magwitch's in Pip, an unsolved mystery.

No well-made tale, Dickens objected, should have for one of its pivotal events an inexplicable encounter that takes place offstage. The famous opening of *Great Expectations* remedies this deficiency. Brontë's omission may even account for the boasting in Dickens's disclosure to Forster: "I have got in the pivot on which the story will turn" (*PL*, 9:325). Dickens turns Emily's causal event upside down: unlike the benevolent Earnshaw, Magwitch seizes Pip, yet the latter succors the former, contrary to Emily's fairy tale in which, faithful to *Cinderella*, a fairy godfather rescues a child. Ironically, Pip's eventual benefactor is in worse condition than Heathcliff when Earnshaw found him. By water, mud, stones, and thorns, the escaped convict has been "soaked ... smothered ... lamed ... cut ... stung ... and torn" (*GE*, 4).

Hindley regards Heathcliff "as a *usurper* of his parent's affection and his privileges" (*WH*, 53; italics added). In Dickens's retelling, Pip recognizes himself as the usurper. Upon Magwitch's return, the London gentleman is forced to identify with Misnar's enemies in "the Eastern story" (*GE*, 309), the pretenders to the sultan's throne. Dickens suggests that the would-be Cinderella, be she Pip or Victorian England, always sports a usurper's presumption, an unproducible patent or mandate.

Catherine's diary records Heathcliff's expulsion from the family circle after Earnshaw's death: Hindley "won't let him sit with us, nor eat with us any more; and, he says, he and I must not *play* together ... and swears he will reduce him to his rightful place" (*WH*, 40; italics added). In *Great Expectations*, Pip is selected to be Estella's playmate. Mrs. Joe obeys Miss Havisham's request: "She wants this boy to go and *play* there" (*GE*, 52; italics added). Pip's invitations to Satis House—where he is made to feel common, is "beggared" at cards, and has his heart broken (*GE*, 62)—accomplish a more diabolic reduction than

Hindley's banishment of Heathcliff or Heathcliff's subsequent beggaring of Hareton.

Reduced from family favorite to field laborer, Heathcliff bears "his degradation pretty well at first" (*WH*, 58). Soon, however, his Cinderella-hood evaporates, leaving a cinder person in its stead; Heathcliff's "childhood's sense of superiority, instilled into him by the favours of old Mr. Earnshaw, was faded away," Nelly Dean reports (*WH*, 76). When Pip is apprenticed to Joe and the sessions at Satis House cease, Pip cannot forget them. "In a moment some confounding remembrance of the Havisham days would fall upon me, like a destructive missile," says Pip, who describes in detail the scattering of his wits (*GE*, 131). The phrase "fall upon me" is a premonition of greater misfortune. When Magwitch reappears, Pip repeats it: "[M]y stronghold dropped upon me" (*GE*, 310), edificial collapse in place of mere fadings away.

Miss Havisham's designs on Pip and Estella make the Lintons' transformation of Catherine from tomboy to Cinderella appear as motiveless as old Earnshaw's rescue of Heathcliff. Once Hindley has "brought Heathcliff so low," Catherine determines that "it would degrade [her] to marry [him], now"; marrying Edgar, she stands to become "rich, and . . . the greatest woman in the neighbourhood" (*WH*, 84, 86). Dickens imparts to Pip both Heathcliff's feeling of debasement and Catherine's eagerness to rise through marriage. Heathcliff's growing sense of inferiority and Catherine's increasing appetite for refinement are concentrated in Pip and scrutinized more intensively, making him the compleat snob. Pip leaves Joe and Biddy behind more reprehensibly than Catherine forsakes Heathcliff.

To make Catherine's resolve to wed Edgar seem facile, Dickens delves into Pip's deep-seated awareness that he is crazy to prefer Estella to Biddy: it "was clear that Biddy was immeasurable better than Estella" (*GE*, 131). Despite behaving irrationally, Pip inhabits a world wherein moral measurements are possible. Catherine's choice, *Great Expectations* suggests, eludes moral judgment. One can only say that she goes contrary to her nature, fidelity to one's nature being the only law *Wuthering Heights* acknowledges. Dickens reworks the Catherine–Heathcliff–Edgar triangle as Pip–Estella–Biddy. Watching a stormy personality deciding between its like or an alien calm struck Dickens as meteorology, not inner weather. Pip's heartfelt admiration for Biddy loses out to cravings that Victorian readers were supposed to recognize as their own.

"If I marry [Edgar] Linton," Catherine rationalizes, "I can aid Heathcliff to rise" (*WH*, 87). Dickens transfers Catherine's good intentions to Pip, whose efforts to raise Joe meet with the latter's stubborn resistance. Brontë believes Catherine, but Mr. Pirrip exposes the hypocrisy in his younger self's Cinderella complex, the pretense that one rises unselfishly as the means to "emancipation" (a word Pip uses; *GE*, 145) for others.

Upon Catherine's return from Thrushcross Grange, Heathcliff is awed by her "grand dress" and speaks enviously of Edgar Linton: "I wish I had light hair and a fair skin, and was dressed, and behaved as well, and had a chance of being as rich as he will be!" Heathcliff exclaims (*WH*, 67). Dickens rejects this outcry as garden-variety jealousy. Pip's determination "to be a gentleman on [Estella's] account" (*GE*, 128) conflates Heathcliff's awe of Catherine and dislike of Edgar into a psychologically complex mixture of lust and aspiration. A risen Pip will settle accounts with Estella. Ironically, Pip's nemesis proves to be not someone as effete as Edgar Linton, but the boorish Bentley Drummle, who is more of a Frankenstein's monster than Heathcliff.[11]

After Catherine marries Edgar, Heathcliff returns from a three-year absence, having somehow acquired money and polish. He had been able "to raise his mind from the savage ignorance into which it was sunk" (*WH*, 94). Heathcliff "would certainly have struck a stranger as a born and bred gentleman," says Nelly (*WH*, 138). Dickens redoes this improbable self-transformation as Pip's Cinderella-like rise, which does not last. In addition, readers are made privy to Pip's internal state before, during, and after his rising. Brontë, Dickens points out, never investigates Heathcliff with the degree of interiority Mr. Pirrip supplies for Pip.

Heathcliff's mysterious self-overhaul is so incredible, Dickens insinuates, that Brontë could only incorporate it provided the changes, especially those inside Heathcliff's skull, are never described in much detail and happen somewhere unspecified. Dickens found Lockwood's speculations a ridiculous smokescreen: "Did [Heathcliff] finish his education on the Continent, . . . get a sizer's place at college . . . escape to America . . . or make a fortune . . . on the English highways?" (*WH*, 94) This list of improbabilities cannot persuade readers that Brontë has a realistic answer, Dickens charged. When Nelly admits she "didn't know how [Heathcliff] gained his money," one savors the parody of her ignorance in Magwitch's admission to having been "sheep-farmer, stock-breeder, other trades besides, away in the New World" (*GE*, 315).

Heathcliff is a cinder person, capable of self-help, whose offstage rise makes him more than a match for his enemies. Through Pip's life story, Dickens debunks this revenge fantasy. Thanks to Emily and Charlotte, connections were established as early as 1847 between rising, self-help, and *Cinderella,* not to mention snobbery and revenge. In all of these interrelated subjects, Dickens alleged, the sisters, amateur psychologists at best, took an unsound interest.

In Dickens's estimation, Brontë's underdeveloped social conscience could only imagine socially irrelevant acts of vengeance that damn the targeted individual directly or by proxy while leaving systems intact. Demotion, in other words, destroys the immediate enemy, whereas vengeful or parodic promotion can threaten social structure. When Magwitch elevates Pip from unlettered blacksmith's apprentice to London gentleman, or Miss Havisham raises a convict's daughter to be a regal heiress, they shake society to its foundations, overturning its assumptions about worth. Transforming two Have-Nots into problematic Haves, a pair of revenge-seeking fairy godparents subverts the Victorian ethos, imperiling society's veneration for rank, money, and the rewards that privilege supposedly commands—a comfortable London existence, for example, or the love of a beautiful woman.

"I'm trying to settle how I shall pay Hindley back," swears Heathcliff; "I don't care how long I wait, if only I can do it, at last" (*WH*, 70). Dickens shifts Heathcliff's perseverance to Magwitch, a more unsettling portrait of the disgruntled drudge; he gets even with society, striking back not just for himself but for an entire class.[12] Upgrading Pip to gentleman status, Magwitch rises vicariously; he revenges himself upon gentlemen in general, not just Compeyson in particular. The ex-convict's success, albeit shortlived, reduces Heathcliff's degrading of Hareton to a personal vendetta of meager social consequence.

Emily's pattern of revenge, Dickens objects, is repetitive, not just prosaic. Heathcliff reduces Hareton much as Hindley degraded Heathcliff. When Magwitch promotes Pip, he secures for the former blacksmith's apprentice advantages that Compeyson and his kind refuse to bestow on persons like Magwitch. For such cunning, unprecedented revenge, once is enough. Because an ex-convict infiltrates the upper ranks vicariously—that is, by proxy—the socioeconomic system stands revealed as a hoax, an unnatural order masquerading as the nature of things.

Unlike Heathcliff's reuse against Hareton of Hindley's plots against him, Miss Havisham's child-raising scheme does not merely duplicate Magwitch's. She appears to do with Magwitch's daughter exactly what the ex-convict does with Pip—use a child to settle a grievance. By proxy is precisely how Miss Havisham seeks to break men's hearts, thereby loosening the stranglehold she believes males have on her sex. But when Estella's fairy godmother has her heart broken again, a woman does it. Miss Havisham's debacle with her adopted daughter, who cannot love her, is a variant on both Magwitch's bonding with Pip and her original misfortune.

In sum, revenge plots in *Great Expectations*, intricate in themselves, become more psychologically complex when read as parodic reconsiderations of retaliation schemes in *Wuthering Heights*. Pip and Estella are upgraded more disastrously than Heathcliff and Hareton are degraded. Together, Pip's fairy godparents ruin him financially and shatter his heart. In place of Emily's dichotomies—stormy Earnshaws versus languid Lintons—Dickens installs characters with serious internal conflicts. Magwitch reveals his by devising a tangled revenge scheme that simultaneously repays Pip for a kindness and society for its neglect. Although Miss Havisham sets out to shield Estella, she turns her into a weapon against men that ultimately harms Miss Havisham herself. Life is more of a tragicomedy than a revenge tragedy, Dickens insisted. *Great Expectations* depicts a darker world than Emily's but is full of unforgettable psychological portraits and recognizable socioeconomic problems.

Magwitch dies believing Pip will thrive on the fortune of an illegally returned transport. Either a gypsy brat or the bastard of a sailor and a prostitute,[13] Heathcliff learns to manipulate inheritance law with lawyerly expertise. Which is more realistic, Dickens asked, Magwitch's ignorance and loss, which keep him the victim of social injustice, or Heathcliff's knowledge and gain, without which revenge in *Wuthering Heights* would be impossible?

Unwisely, Edgar Linton's father secured his estate to his own daughter, Isabella, ahead of his son's daughter, Cathy (the second Catherine). Thus Heathcliff's child by Isabella inherits Thrushcross Grange instead of Edgar's child by Catherine. Amazingly, Heathcliff has figured all this out and uses the situation to his advantage. Having made Hindley his creditor, Heathcliff not only gains control of Wuthering Heights but reduces Hareton, the legitimate heir, to "little else than a beggar," as Mr. Kenneth informs Nelly (*WH*, 168). Linton, Heathcliff's sickly, unwanted child by Isabella, obligingly dies after naming his father heir to Thrushcross Grange.

In short order, Heathcliff dispossesses Edgar Linton's daughter, Cathy, and impoverishes Hareton, Hindley's son. "The guest was now master of Wuthering Heights," Nelly announces; Hareton, by rights "the first gentleman in the neighbourhood, was reduced to a state of complete dependence on his father's inveterate enemy; and lives in his own house as a servant" (*WH*, 169). Unless Cathy marries Linton, Heathcliff threatens, she will be "a young chit [who] has no expectations" (*WH*, 190). When she does marry Heathcliff's son by Isabella, Heathcliff seems to be punishing her mother for marrying Edgar.

Pip not only must forfeit Magwitch's fortune but also misses out on Satis House; Miss Havisham never intends to marry him to Estella. He is promoted, upgraded initially, as Miss Havisham's fairy godchild and Estella's intended, whereas Heathcliff and Hareton are "reduced" (*WH*, 169); through Magwitch, Pip is given "great expectations" (*GE*, 137), unlike Cathy who has none. Yet contrary to Cinderella, Pip winds up en route to Egypt without mate or money.

"Now, my bonny lad, you are *mine*!" gloats Heathcliff. "And we'll see if one tree won't grow as crooked as another, with the same wind to twist it!" (*WH*, 169) Heathcliff plans to punish Hareton exactly the way Hareton's father debased Heathcliff. He "appeared to have bent his malevolence on making

[Hareton] a brute; he was never taught to read or write; never rebuked for any bad habit which did not annoy his keeper" (*WH*, 176). Magwitch's program for Pip parodically reverses not just Hindley's for Heathcliff but Heathcliff's for Hareton. It also reverses society's neglect of Magwitch. Mr. Pocket tutors Pip in subjects (and manners) required for matriculation at Oxford and Cambridge. Heathcliff deforms Hareton from heir to bumpkin. Magwitch has "lived rough, that [Pip] should live smooth"; toiling by proxy for Pip, he elevates the latter to "a brought-up London gentleman" (*GE,* 317, 319).

"I want the triumph of seeing *my* descendant fairly lord of their estates; my child hiring their children, to till their fathers' lands for wages," declares a vengeful Heathcliff (*WH,* 185). Brontë draws on *Cinderella* for Heathcliff's inspiration to reduce his enemies' children to cinder girls. Dickens dismissed this as the crudest form of tragedy, in which those on top are abruptly knocked to the bottom. Heathcliff's "revenge" upon the "representatives" (that is, children) of his foes (*WH,* 273) is unimaginative, purely personal: his child in place of Edgar's daughter and Hindley's son.

Instead of displacing society's Haves, Magwitch determines to deceive them into accepting Pip as one of their own. This is tragicomic revenge, wickedly funny as well as serious and subversive. The snobbish ex-convict tells Pip how "that there hunted dunghill dog wot you kep life in, got his head so high that he could make a gentleman" (*GE,* 317). Rather than downgrade his oppressors, Magwitch gives himself the pleasure of hobnobbing with them vicariously. His diabolical program reduces Heathcliff's to child's play, Dickens boasted. Perverse and ill-fated though they may be, Magwitch's machinations betray a reformer's intent: the ex-convict demonstrates that only superficial differences—Pip's unearned advantages rather than innate merit—separate the social outcast from the wealthiest socialite. Finally, Magwitch exhibits a zest for his task that outshines Heathcliff's sullen—indeed, morbid—masochism.

"I've a pleasure in him!" Heathcliff says of Hareton. "He has satisfied my expectations" (*WH,* 193). (Dickens's title indicates that he registered Brontë's second use of this key word within a dozen pages.) "If [Hareton] were a born fool," Heathcliff continues, "I should not enjoy it half so much—But he's no fool; and I can sympathize with all his feelings, having felt them myself—I know what he suffers now, for instance, exactly—it is merely a beginning of what he shall suffer, though. And he'll never be able to emerge from his bathos of coarseness and ignorance. I've got him faster than his scoundrel of a father secured me, and lower" (*WH,* 193).

Dickens objected to the implausible psychology behind Heathcliff's use of such expressions as "pleasure" and "enjoy." Why, he asks, would a former cinder girl such as Heathcliff want to reexperience "coarseness and ignorance" all over again vicariously? Heathcliff brags of knowing "exactly" what Hareton suffers (*WH*, 193), a dubious gratification. Magwitch's satisfaction in raising Pip may be perverse, but it makes nonsense of the intense joy Heathcliff claims to derive from reliving his own torments by proxy through Hareton's. Magwitch typifies the outcast unable "to emerge from . . . coarseness and ignorance (*WH*, 193)," says Dickens, yet he tries to do so through Pip.

Hareton does not just suffer in Heathcliff's place, Dickens marveled; the latter elects to suffer all over again through the former. More credibly, Magwitch tries to leave his drudgelike past life behind in Australia. He salivates at the prospect of enjoying, through Pip, high society and a glamorous marriage. One can hear tragicomic exuberance in Magwitch's voice when he finds Pip in "lodgings . . . fit for a lord!" or when he promises his protegé the company of "bright eyes . . . if money can buy 'em" (*GE*, 317, 318). The more boisterously Magwitch behaves, the more masochist than sadist Heathcliff becomes as he savors a lugubrious revenge. As a commentary on Heathcliff's glum musings regarding Hareton, Magwitch's glee seems almost healthy.

"I've got him faster than his . . . father secured me, and lower," Heathcliff exults (*WH*, 193). He has kept Hareton illiterate. Magwitch takes pride in asking Pip "to read to him," something in a "Foreign language" even though the ex-convict will not understand a word. The latter scene, Dickens contends, is much funnier yet infinitely sadder. Heathcliff is dismissed as a brooding egotist reopening his old wounds. Through Pip, Magwitch acquires the gift of tongues. With a "fiendish laugh" at having turned "gold" into "paving-stones" (*WH*, 193), Heathcliff relishes Hareton's dispossession. Magwitch looks about him in Pip's apartments with a proprietary air "as if he had some part in the things he admired" (*GE*, 312). Which is the socially more disturbing alchemy, Dickens asks, Heathcliff reducing gold to stone, or Magwitch turning a blacksmith's apprentice into a London gentleman?

It is characteristic of revenge schemes to have a fatal flaw, Dickens explains to Brontë; that is why his are tragicomic. Magwitch's plan to be Pip's fairy godparent backfires, unlike Heathcliff's scheme to be Hareton's evil supervisor, which simply runs out of gas. The ex-convict never savors high society through Pip because the latter demurs; Pip realizes that he cannot maintain an exalted position with a returned transport for his sponsor. Haves, Dickens implied, could not in conscience continue to live off Have-Nots if they faced the truth of their economic position.

Psychologically more complex than Heathcliff's and of greater social importance, Magwitch's revenge scheme is tragicomically self-defeating. Once he succeeds in making Pip a gentleman, the latter must repudiate the favor either because as a gentleman, he is too snobbish to accept an ex-convict's money

(Pip's immediate response), or because the manner in which Haves live off Have-Nots is morally repugnant, a perversion of partnership. This is Pip's eventual perspective as he and Magwitch become more like father and son.

Magwitch cannot repay Pip and infiltrate society's upper levels unless Pip continues to masquerade as Cinderella and ignores the increasingly insistent parallels between his life story and the tale of Misnar's pavilion. But the shock occasioned by Magwitch's reappearance knocks Pip from one fairy tale into another. That the failure of Magwitch's designs is an inevitable consequence of their success solicits from the reader a bitter smile.

Contemplating Heathcliff, Nelly is "amazed at the blackness of a spirit that could brood on and covet revenge for years" (*WH*, 196). In Dickens's estimation, Magwitch and Miss Havisham, especially the former, deserve this doubtful distinction. Moreover, Heathcliff inexplicably gives up. "Now would be the precise time to revenge myself on their representatives," Heathcliff acknowledges, referring to Hareton and Cathy. He has the children of his old tormentors at his mercy. But "I have lost the faculty of enjoying their destruction," he adds (*WH*, 273). Brontë, Dickens stated, uses a feeble sort of forgiveness—forgiveness by default—to end a socially irrelevant novel with unrealistic expediency.

Revenge is not a "faculty," Dickens tells Emily, not an intellectual or emotional capacity that must be used regularly lest it atrophy. It is a self-defeating tragicomic phenomenon—a form of aberrant behavior caused by unbearable social conditions. Eradicate social injustices, Dickens argues, and there will be less need for desperados like Magwitch to meditate revenge. Fewer social inequalities will mean healthier states of mind.

Dickens's resolution of Magwitch's quest for revenge is psychologically more complicated than Heathcliff's decision to quit. The returned transport is remorseless yet "softened" (*GE*, 444); that is, he both persists and relents. From the mixture of kindness toward Pip and hatred for society in Magwitch's plan for getting even, the former finally predominates, but not until Magwitch has settled with Compeyson, drowning him with his own hands. In the Custom House galley, their escape attempt having failed, Pip swears: "Please God, I will be as true to you, as you have been to me!" (*GE*, 444). This declaration of love and loyalty binds London gentleman and social outcast with the force of a marriage vow. It overshadows any conceivable union between frost and fire, moonbeams and lightning, in *Wuthering Heights*. No union in Brontë, Dickens maintains, can surpass this one.

Having informed Pip of Estella's marriage, Miss Havisham apologizes for breaking his heart; that is, for having harmed him the way Compeyson did her. "Until I saw in you a looking-glass that showed me what I once felt myself, I did not know what I had done," she explains (*GE*, 396). Dickens rewrites Heathcliff's delight in the subjugation of Hareton as Miss Havisham's regret for hurting

Pip—for ruining his hopes vicariously through Estella. Miss Havisham's remorse exposes the psychological absurdity of Heathcliff's professions of continuous joy in vicarious suffering.

Wuthering Heights to the contrary, *Great Expectations* refuses to allow a character who sees his or her own pain reproduced in another to take unmitigated pleasure in the sight, even if he or she is the inflicter. In Dickens's profounder psychological study, Miss Havisham, observing herself in brokenhearted Pip as in "a looking-glass," is immediately overcome with regret (*GE*, 396), not suffused with delight as is Heathcliff studying Hareton in the exact plight that formerly was Heathcliff's.

Pip's "repugnance" to Magwitch "all melted away," he beholds in a "hunted wounded shackled creature" a "much better man," he confesses, "than I had been to Joe" (*GE*, 443). In the ex-convict's loyalty, Pip perceives, as in a mirror, what should have been his conduct toward Joe. Breaking Pip's heart has gradually worked a cure for Estella's heartlessness. In the final sentence of the original ending, she assures Pip that "suffering... had given her a heart to understand what [his] heart used to be" (*GE*, 482).[14]

According to Dickens, the psychological realist worth his salt knows that putting oneself in another's place leads to compassionate understanding. Emily's novel did not seem unwholesome to Dickens just because of its fascination with Heathcliff's cruelties. Even worse is his determination to savor his miseries over again through another's suffering. Heathcliff relives his own pain by inflicting its equivalent on his victims to the point where he appears to be experiencing them again literally. Unlike *Wuthering Heights*, *Great Expectations* is a healthy book because it employs proxies in the rehabilitation process. Pip's unrequited love for Estella cures Miss Havisham of her snobbish desire to ruin men. Magwitch's unswerving loyalty to Pip convinces the latter that his neglect of Joe and Biddy has been reprehensible.

Dickens condemned *Jane Eyre* and *Wuthering Heights* for being psychologically primitive and politically conservative, just like *Cinderella*. The fairy tale's heroine goes from servant to princess without bringing extremes closer together, without worrying about the persistence of sharp social divisions. Whether glorifying Jane's promotion or watching Heathcliff savor Hareton's demotion, the Brontës never think to foster greater understanding between Haves and Have-Nots.

Wuthering Heights, Dickens's parodic revisions suggest, is hardly "a masterwork of 'realistic' fiction" as Hillis Miller called it,[15] but a Gothic revenge tragedy that simply extinguishes itself. Forgiveness at the end of Emily's novel seems as preposterous as the introduction of Heathcliff into the family circle at the start. Thomas Vargish's enthusiasm to the contrary, Dickens would never have called Heathcliff's abandonment of revenge Emily's "crowning achievement" (V, 15).[16]

Heathcliff accuses Catherine of "Having levelled [his] palace" by marrying Edgar (*WH*, 111).[17] In contrast, Mr. Pirrip rewrites this levelling as the traumatic collapse of his younger self's marital and economic expectations; they cave in upon Pip as fatally as Misnar's pavilion fell upon the sultan's enemies in "the Eastern story" Pip summarizes (*GE*, 309–10). Dickens's determination to reshape Emily's outdated material into a timely admonishment is nowhere clearer than in the redesigning of Heathcliff's "palace" as Misnar's pavilion. The latter reduces the former to an insignificant edifice. Reassigned to Pip, Heathcliff's marital disappointments have far-reaching sociological consequences.

Heathcliff's "palace" is "levelled" while he watches from outside, Dickens mocked. "The roof of [Pip's] stronghold" collapses "upon" him (*GE*, 310), a trap his exorbitant expectations (and society's encouragement of them) have laid. In Brontë's unlikely story, Heathcliff's disappointments *precede* his transformation into a gentleman, in effect propelling him upward. In Dickens's corrective retelling, disappointment puts a sudden end to Pip's rise, demolishing his misconception of himself as someone special.

Pip's would-be fairy godparent collapses his protegé's "stronghold." Magwitch's return, ostensibly a well-intentioned visit from a father to his "dear boy" (*GE*, 315), has a devastating impact on Pip's fortunes. From Dickens's perspective, only Have-Nots, not girlfriends, can destroy the privileges and prospects of the Haves, whose Cinderella-like existence their drudgeries support. The collapse of Pip's expectations, on a par with that of a sultan's pavilion, reduces Catherine's intentional leveling of Heathcliff's "palace" to a minor disaster.

Mr. Pirrip is careful to distinguish the intentional breaking of Pip's heart (Estella's doing) from the unpremeditated collapsing of his "stronghold" (*GE*, 310), which is Magwitch's fault. Pip's lengthy synopsis of the Misnar tale separates his discovery that Estella intends to marry Drummle (ch. 38) from his epiphanic realization that a social outcast is his patron (ch. 39). The synopsis of the Misnar tale in the final paragraph of chapter 38 serves as a dividing line between the two but applies to the latter.

In chapter 38, Pip's courtship of Estella begins to break down at Satis House and finally does so during an Assembly Ball at Richmond. Immediately, Pip turns to a graver misfortune: "And now that I have given the one chapter to the theme that so filled my heart," he writes of Estella, "I pass on, unhindered, to the event that had impended over me longer yet" (*GE*, 309). "Unhindered" means that Dickens, unlike Brontë, can move beyond his characters' emotional entanglements to deal with more important social issues. Pip's heart may be "filled" with pain, but not to the exclusion of distressing revelations about Victorian England's social and economic life, which are absent from Brontë.

The "event," as Pip calls it, refers not only to his sudden awareness of dependence upon an uncouth ex-convict, but also to the uncovering of embarrassing absurdities in England's socioeconomic system. Snobs such as young Pip, it turns out, are profoundly indebted to the very underclass of exploited individuals upon whom they look down. This discovery of interconnectivity, Dickens insisted, is more disturbing than Catherine's realization of elemental oneness with Heathcliff. Choosing Edgar Linton over Heathcliff, it follows, can never be as serious a denial of reality, or as potentially fatal a gesture, as the reluctance of England's Haves, personified here by Pip, to embrace undesirables such as Magwitch.

The epiphany that Magwitch's return triggers, says Pip, "had begun to be prepared for" when Estella's "baby intelligence was receiving its first distortions from Miss Havisham's wasting hands" (*GE*, 309). From one point of view, Dickens keeps Pip's misfortunes as suitor separate from his disappointments in gentility. From another perspective, however, he links them as the results of comparable "distortions." Pip both separates and subtly connects his traumatic letdown and Estella's unnatural upbringing. Being Estella's unwanted suitor and having Magwitch as an unwanted fairy godfather are both consequences of Pip's desire to rise like a Cinderella, which has distorted his personality as grievously as Miss Havisham misshaped Estella's.

As a palace leveler, Dickens proclaimed, *Wuthering Heights* could not compete with *Great Expectations*. He rewrote the leveling of Heathcliff's "palace" much as he redid Emily's revenge plots: to brand *Wuthering Heights* an obsolete novel, sociologically useless for 1860 and psychologically incredible.

By 3 August 1861, when the last installment appeared, Dickens was confident that *Great Expectations* had developed into full-fledged tragicomedy. Having been humbled severely *after* their risings, Pip and Estella are no longer Cinderella material; nevertheless, like Adam and Eve, they appear resolved to make the most of their remaining opportunities.

Although it takes three generations—from old Earnshaw's through Heathcliff's to Hareton's—*Wuthering Heights*, Dickens grumbled, still substantiates *Cinderella*. Hareton's recovery will complete the rise that old Earnshaw tried to give Heathcliff but that Hindley rescinded and that Heathcliff at first denies to Hindley's son. Hareton and Cathy, an Earnshaw and a Linton, will again own Wuthering Heights and Thrushcross Grange. The atmospheric tumultuousness on the Yorkshire moors having spent itself, nothing much will have changed. Initially, Hareton's attempts to spell and figure, his "endeavor to raise himself," excite Cathy's scorn (*WH*, 257). Soon, however, she asks to be his teacher and they become "sworn allies," their "radiant countenances bent over the page" (*WH*, 267).[18]

Cathy makes the overture. "I must show [Hareton] someway that I like him, that I want to be friends," she tells Nelly (*WH*, 267). When Hareton accepts her offer to tutor him, she attaches a proviso: "And you'll be my friend?" Not surprisingly, Nelly confesses to Lockwood that "the crown of all my wishes will be the union of those two" (*WH*, 268).

Agreeing with Nelly, several modern commentators have designated the Cathy–Hareton educational experiment the novel's finest moment, a "correction" process to reverse the earlier downgradings suffered by Heathcliff and Hareton (WG, 371). For U.C. Knoepflmacher, Brontë's couple provides a "Victorian" solution to a novel whose first half is "Romantic" (*L&D,* 104–5). Cathy's tutorials have even been celebrated as Emily's revision of "the Miltonic myth of the fall" (G&G, 295). This time, Eve does Adam a favor by feeding him from the Tree of Knowledge.

Great Expectations, Dickens insisted, is the apogee for tragicomic reversals, not *Wuthering Heights*, which it doggedly corrects. Pip has traveled from Joe's forge to Satis House, London, and Egypt; now he reverses the trajectory, returning from Egypt to reconcile with Estella in the ruined garden not far from the forge. In revising Pip's fleeting reunion with Estella in the first ending, Dickens gave his novel a more congruent conclusion; the second ending is both more Victorian than the first and yet protomodern; unlike the final parting in Piccadilly that Dickens originally described, it rounds off the story, which paradoxically remains open-ended. One is left with both a stronger sense of resolution and the expectation of more to come. Just as important for Dickens, the revision discredits Emily's supposedly Victorian ending to a Gothic novel as more of the same—pure fairy lore.

When Dickens rewrites the reconciliation of Hareton and Cathy as Pip's reunion with Estella, he cancels the former's radiance. His Adam and Eve are older, not to mention sadder and wiser. Estella's is a more problematic overture than Cathy's; although she asks for Pip's friendship ("tell me we are friends"), she expects to "continue friends apart" (*GE,* 480). Pip's actions appear to revise this prospectus. But instead of Nelly's crowning wish, Mr. Pirrip leaves readers with his younger self's tentative prognostication: "I saw no shadow of another parting from her" (*GE,* 480). The final form of the novel's last line, positive though it undoubtedly is, relies on an emphatic negative ("*no* shadow"; italics added). The effect is to curtail the statement's optimism and check Nelly Dean's euphoria.

On one hand, Emily seems to say, storm and calm, fire and frost, never mix. Life is a tragedy of polarized opposites. On the other hand, this one more Victorian, the reconciliation of Hareton and Cathy (the Earnshaw–Heathcliff faction with the Linton group) implies that each new generation affords another chance for uniting the wildness of the natural element and the cultural refinements of civilization. Dickens rejected both propositions.

Haves and Have-Nots, *Great Expectations* argues, constitute the most serious division plaguing society in 1860. Dickens presents it tragicomically in that his polar opposites turn out to be mutually dependent. The gap separating them must be bridged, Dickens insisted, but it would be ridiculous to believe in fresh opportunities for doing so generation after generation, as if little Pip, son of Joe and Biddy, were to meet another convict out on the marshes.

Through Hareton and Cathy, Emily may be said to give youth back to Heathcliff and Catherine so that they can start over. Only in a fairy tale could this happen, Dickens retorted. Through Pip and Estella, who resolve to soldier on, Dickens ridiculed Brontë's resolution for abandoning social and psychological realism in favor of fairy lore: a new Adam and Eve in Hareton and Cathy, another possibility in Hareton's case for a Cinderella story of rise and recovery. In short, Dickens charged that *Wuthering Heights* revises the Miltonic myth by turning Adam and Eve into Cinderella. An old-fashioned, self-absorbed Gothic melodrama, *Wuthering Heights* gave no impetus to social reform; although more preoccupied with revenge than with rising, its unwholesome story line endorsed *Cinderella* after all.

Synopsis A
Summary of the Tale of Misnar's Pavilion

The table of contents for Sir Charles Morell's *The Tales of the Genii: or, The Delightful Lessons of Horam the Son of Asmar* (London: Henry G. Bohn, 1861) gives the title of the sixth tale as "The Enchanters; or, Misnar the Sultan of the East" (136–225). It is subdivided into three sections: "The History of Mahoud," "Continuation of the Tale of the Enchanters," and "The History of the Princess of Cashmere." Within, tale VI bears a slightly different subtitle, "The Sultan Misnar of India," which also serves as the running title atop right-hand pages. In addition, subtitles for the first two sections of VI seem to have been transposed.

Misnar's investiture fills the first four pages (136–39). Subtitled "The Continuation of the Tale of the Enchanters; or, Misnar the Sultan of the East," the next fourteen pages chronicle Misnar's struggles against rebellious enchanters and end with the sultan's enchantment (140–53). At this point, Mahoud, who has also been transformed into a reptile, tells Misnar his life story. But "The History of Mahoud" (154) is introduced as tale VII when Morell is still writing VI.[1] "The Continuation of the Tale of the Enchanters," provided as a subtitle on page 140, better describes events *after* Mahoud completes his narrative. Otherwise, Morell's account of the construction of Misnar's pavilion, including the deaths of the usurpers Ahaback and Desra, occur within Mahoud's tale and not as the climactic continuation of Misnar's (204–16). To add to the confusion, "The History of the Princess of Cashmere," the third part of the sixth tale according to the table of contents, becomes tale VIII in the text.

Morell wrote the Misnar story to recommend prudence, which is the virtue both the youthful sultan and his vizier must acquire or perish. In Henry Fielding's genre-shaping novel *Tom Jones,* which Dickens admired, the eponymous hero also learns to behave prudently. Conceivably, Dickens meant to devalue Victorian expectancy by contrasting Pip's aspirations with eighteenth-century prudence.

Given that life is tragicomic, Dickens asked, which is more advisable, circumspection, or expectation? Only after Pip's prospects collapse does he learn from "the Eastern story" to build a realistic "stronghold" (*GE,* 309–10). Having secured Herbert's partnership in Clarriker and Co., he obtains a berth for himself as clerk to this firm's "Eastern branch" (*GE,* 476); for eleven years in this less spectacular Eastern story, he toils in Egypt before returning to propose to Estella.

Comparing the Misnar story with Cruikshank's retelling of fairy tales in the *Fairy Library,* Dickens decided that 1) fairy tales convey their message best in the course of a good story; 2) lessons in improving one's general attitude (that is, how to take a more prudent approach to life) are worth more than narrower, more specific injunctions; 3) inventing fairy tales is superior to redoing existing material, unless revision is purgative—parodic revaluation of *Cinderella* in "Frauds on the Fairies" to embarrass Cruikshank, or reworking Cinderella's rise as the collapse of Misnar's pavilion to question the nineteenth-century's Cinderella complex.

As "The Enchanters" begins, Misnar, youthful and unbearded, ascends India's throne upon the death of "mighty Dabulcombar" (*TG,* 136). At a tribunal of the wisest men in the kingdom, the prophet Zeuramaund predicts that "dark clouds of evil" are gathering. Misnar is advised to "cut off" (138) his younger brother, Ahubal, but finds fratricide repugnant. One of several hostile enchanters attending the tribunal threatens that "the powers of enchantment shall prevail" against Misnar (139). Evil agents at the tribunal include Ahaback, Ulin, and Kifri, who resolve to torment him.

The new sultan sends Ahubal to a remote castle under house arrest. En route, Misnar's younger brother is rescued by five thousand rebel horsemen; Misnar's attempt to be prudent fails (142). When one of the southern kingdoms revolts in support of Ahubal, Misnar dispatches Horam to quell the disturbance while he proceeds to Mecca to consult Mahomet's seal (144).

Distracted by mysterious foresters, Misnar unwisely keeps an assignation with Noradin, ostensibly a beautiful virgin in their troupe but actually the enchantress Ulin in disguise. Ulin transforms Misnar into a toad (152). A similar fate has befallen Horam, the Princess of Cashmere, and Mahoud. The last mentioned tells his fellow toads how he squandered his inheritance, then imprudently became Bennaskar's lieutenant in the latter's attempt to ravish Hemjunah, the beautiful Princess of Cashmere. Each of the toads realizes it has been guilty of "imprudence" (171): the princess in listening to Bennaskar, Mahoud in assisting him, Misnar in yielding to Noradin's blandishments, and Horam in operating on his own as a secret agent instead of remaining, as instructed, at the head of the sultan's army.[2]

Having released Misnar from "toadhood," Shemshelnar, a holy man, counsels the young sultan to be more "prudent and vigilant" (173). Shortly thereafter, not fooled by Ulin's disguise as a lady in distress, Misnar smites her with his sword, thereby dispelling Horam's enchantment. By the time Misnar reaches his army's encampment, Horam is again in command of the loyalists against Ahubal's rebel forces. Happuck, Ulin's brother, fails to assassinate Misnar, but another enchanter on Ahubal's side, Ollomand, conjures new wealth and weaponry for further uprisings (191).

"Prudent Tasnar" foils an attempt on Ahubal's life made by one of Horam's female slaves. But Tasnar foolishly returns to Misnar disguised as the murderous slave and is slain by Horam when he tries to assassinate the sultan (201). News arrives that two powerful enchanters, Ahaback and Desra, have banded together against Misnar. They encourage Ahubal's troops to "erect a sumptuous pavilion" for their prince as proof of his superiority (204).

Lest this palace attract followers to Ahubal's standard, Horam deploys some of Misnar's troops to build "such a pavilion as shall far outshine in splendour every glory upon earth" (205); it will be "the most magnificent spectacle that art could achieve" (206). While the soldiers are preoccupied with this architectural counterstroke, the armies of Ahubal unite with those of Ahaback and Desra, an unfavorable development for which Misnar blames Horam.

Misnar's pavilion is made of crimson velvet, into which was worked in gold the deaths of enemy enchanters (Ulin, Happuck, Tasnar, etc.). Other features include gold carpeting, four massive gold pillars, and a ceiling studded with jewels and diamonds beneath which Horam positions two sofas "of the richest workmanship" (206). When Ahubal receives word that Misnar's "glorious pavilion" exceeds his, Ahaback and Desra promise to "dispossess" Misnar of this superior palace.

In the ensuing battle, the rebel armies gain the upper hand, compelling Misnar to retreat to the mountains where Horam's divisions, instead of joining the fray, have set up defensive positions. Misnar's lavish pavilion falls into rebel hands. Ahubal rewards Ahaback and Desra by allowing them to sleep in it.

Horam wakens Misnar in "the dead of night" and takes the sultan into "a spacious cavern" in the mountains (210). He gives Misnar an axe to sever a rope from a ring of iron. When cut, the rope flies "with great swiftness" through a hole in the rock (211); otherwise, nothing seems to have happened. The next morning, a disgruntled Misnar is preparing to have Horam hanged when news comes that Ahaback and Desra are dead, having been crushed on the sofas by the collapse of Misnar's pavilion. With Ahubal's forces "in the utmost consternation," Misnar's troops fall upon them, routing the insurgents once and for all.

Reinstated, Misnar's vizier asserts that "prudence and not force" has defeated the powers of enchantment. He tells the sultan how and why he built such an alluring trap, the key device being "a concealed ... massy stone ... sawn out of the solid rock" and "hung upon four pillars of gold" so that it "covered the whole pavilion" (213). Equally important, the rope that "upheld this massy stone," Horam explains, "passed through one of the gold pillars into the earth beneath, and by a secret channel cut in the rock was carried onward through the side of the mountain, and was fastened to a ring of iron in a cave hollowed out of the rock" (213).

All of this ingenious but backbreaking construction was completed on a tight schedule during a lull in the fight against Ahubal. Not only is Misnar's collapsible pavilion a clever ploy; it was built precisely to specifications and finished within the allotted time. Horam expected that Ahaback and Desra, "puffed up with their success," would be imprudent enough to fall into the vizier's carefully prepared trap.

Enraged at the deaths of the two enchanters, the giant Kifri dashes Ahubal against the rocks and tosses his body down the mountainside. When Kifri commits suicide, the last vestige of opposition to Misnar's rule appears to have disappeared. Horam and Misnar rescue the Princess of Cashmere, who becomes sultana of India.

Synopsis B

Chapter-by-Chapter Summary of *A Day's Ride*[1]

1. After an undistinguished first year, Potts resolves to spend the long vacation from Trinity College, Dublin, traveling about Ireland on horseback, thanks to a legacy of one hundred pounds from an uncle.

2. He concludes the first day's ride at the "Lamb" in Ashford, where he joins a group composed of Lord Keldrum, Father Dyke, Oxley, and Hammond, all of whom easily see through his pretensions to be a person "of some note" (*ADR*, 17).

3. Inebriated and boastful, Potts loses Blondel, his rental horse, to Father Dyke at backgammon.

4. The next morning, hung over, Potts sets out on foot after Father Dyke.

5. Potts is befriended by Edward Crofton and his sister, Mary, at their cottage, "the Rosary."

6. Their cousin, Rose, overhears Potts eulogizing himself.

7. Potts intercepts Dyke's letter about winning a horse that he has sold to its former owner for a hefty sum. Dyke calls Potts a fool.

8. Potts flees to Wales by boat. Its garrulous captain gives him a letter of introduction to Bob Rogers, his brother, a skipper based at Malta.

9. In a farewell note to Crofton, Potts invents "great expectations" (*ADR*, 86) from an uncle who is allegedly dying. At the train station in Milford, he assists Kate Herbert. She is journeying to London, then to Brussels to become companion to a widow. They travel to London in different carriages. Potts overhears the story of Sir Samuel Whalley's disappearance; Kate, he realizes, is the disgraced industrialist's younger daughter.

10. Having been misdirected, Potts follows a lady in mourning by mistake for Kate; he goes to Dover by train and across to Ostend.

11. The captain of the channel packet rescues Potts from the lady in mourning's irate husband, "the most jealous man in Europe" (*ADR*, 124).

12. Potts reaches Hesse-Kalbbratonstadt in northern Germany; he bears Grey Buller's despatches, which got mixed in with his luggage on the Dover train.

13. Calling at the British legation, Potts meets Miss Herbert again, who remembers him from Milford. Mistaken for a diplomatic courier, Potts is invited to dine by Sir Shalley Doubleton.

14. Potts dines with the ambassador.

15. Sir Shalley instructs Potts to escort Mrs. Keats and Kate to Lake Como.

16. Dressed as a courier, Potts undertakes his mission. Kate deflates his literary ambitions.

17. Potts takes a dislike to Mrs. Keats.

18. Potts tells Kate that he is an important messenger eagerly expected at Constantinople.

19. Mrs. Keats suspects that Potts may be of consequence.

20. Potts describes his method of building "castles in Spain" (*ADR*, 194). Mrs. Keats mistakes him for a nobleman in disguise.

21. Kate does not share Mrs. Keats's delusions.

22. The journey continues.

23. At a German inn, Potts behaves absurdly when a real nobleman compliments Kate.

24. The journey proceeds.

25. Potts meets Vaterchen, a German clown, and young Tintefleck, a pretty Moorish circus rider, both vagabonds.

26. Potts converses with his new friends.

27. Mrs. Keats, a snob, is insulted when Potts presents them.

28. She leaves Potts behind. He sends half the money he has left back to Dublin to pay for Blondel.

29. Potts joins Vaterchen and Tintefleck on their rambles.

30. Vaterchen tells his life story.

31. Potts continues with Vaterchen and Tintefleck.

32. Potts flirts with Tintefleck, now called Catinka.

33. Mistaken for gypsies, Potts and his friends cause a disturbance in the hotel at Constance, a lake between Germany, Austria, and Switzerland. Potts meets Harpar, the Englishman, at the police station. He takes Potts and his friends to breakfast, then attempts to borrow ten pounds from Potts, who declines. Potts follows Harpar to Lindau, Austria.

34. Having outpaced Vaterchen and Catinka, Potts nevertheless fails to overtake Harpar. At Lindau, an unidentified guest pays for his dinner.

35. The guest, Crofton, and his sister are searching for Whalley, whom their late uncle repented of ruining financially. Sir Elkanah names Whalley's alleged widow his legatee. Potts reveals that he knows Kate Whalley's story and has

been her fellow traveler. He is to search for Whalley in Savoy and Upper Italy then rejoin the Croftons in Rome. Surmising Potts's feelings for Kate, Mary hopes that he will persuade her to accept Sir Elkanah's reparations. Miss Crofton brings Potts one hundred pounds from his father, who has remarried.

36. Still at Lindau, Potts reencounters Harpar conducting an experiment lakeside with two model ships, causing each to sink to the bottom. Potts invites Harpar to dine and loans him ten pounds.

37. Potts overhears the count from chapter 23 telling of additional conversations with Miss Herbert; his story includes disparaging references to Potts, who challenges him.

38. Vaterchen and Catinka intervene to save Potts from Prince Max of Swabia. Potts snubs Catinka and they separate; she has been given a brooch, presumably by Prince Max.

39. Potts travels the Upper Rhine valley as it descends to the German plains.

40. Potts is arrested by two horsemen.

41. Potts is imprisoned at Feldkirch by mistake for Harpar, who has been outlawed for assaulting Rigges, his former associate and traveling companion.

42. From his cell at Innsbruck, Austria, Potts sees a circus performing in the center of town; a "pretty Moorish girl" rides Blondel (*ADR*, 396).

43. Potts is jailed in the Ambras Schloss until he can be identified by Rigges, who never appears.

44. Potts is interrogated by a young Englishman who secures his release, Rigges having dropped charges. Potts confesses that he is neither Harpar nor "Pottinger," the name he assumed in chapter 9, but simply Potts. The English official is Grey Buller, whose despatches Potts carried off.

45. Having located Kate with Mrs. Keats on Malta, Potts admits to being a druggist's son and professes his love. Daughter of a self-made man, Kate is receptive. He delivers a note from Miss Crofton. Kate has already heard from Whalley; she reports several possible sightings of him. Potts promises to find her father.

46. Potts overhears George Buller, Kate's cousin, reading her a letter from Grey, his brother, who describes Potts as a "sublime snob" (*ADR*, 430); Kate defends him. Bob Rogers, who is to transport Potts to Russia, challenges George on Potts's behalf.

47. Rogers informs Potts of his appointment to duel with Buller. Potts escapes to Constantinople by ship.

48. At Odessa, Potts hears of a circus girl who eloped with the prince who paid thirty thousand piastres to buy her a horse (Blondel). Potts finds Harpar at Sebastopol; posing as an American contractor, he has been badly injured yet cannot communicate with Russian doctors. Passing for a surgeon, Potts tends Harpar with directions from a German-speaking Russian physician. Harpar

survives, but Potts is stricken with seven weeks of fever. When Harpar and Potts finally compare notes, the latter tells of being imprisoned as the former. Harpar reveals that Rigges has died. Potts outlines his efforts to find Whalley. Harpar identifies himself as Whalley. By raising sunken liners, he has regained wealth and reputation. Whalley departs for home, leaving Potts unrewarded and in tears. Potts wanders Europe on a legacy from his late father. In Paris he is snubbed in excellent French by a stuck-up Catinka. She refuses to recall their former association but has provided Blondel a splendid retirement. Potts receives Kate's letter of invitation; he leaves to join her permanently in Wales, his starting point in chapter 7. He has parlayed a day's ride into a life's romance.[2]

Notes

Preface

1. Robert B. Partlow distinguished Mr. Pirrip, the narrator "as I am now," from Pip, the narrator "as I was"; the former relates to the latter as a "close" to a "distant view" (RP, 124–25). According to Sylvia Manning, one needs the older narrator to deal with "the confusion and misunderstanding of the younger Pip. The distance between the two [narrators] diminishes with the progress of the book" (SM, 192).

2. Pip's "greatest achievement," Bert G. Hornback maintained, is "the way he organizes his life into meaning, not just for himself but as a moral lesson for us" (BH, 129).

1. Misnar versus Cinderella

1. "How we must read *Great Expectations*"—Q.D. Leavis's title for chapter 6 of *Dickens the Novelist*—fares better in the interrogative. Change the imperative to "should," transpose it and "we," add a question mark, and one has the query that *Dickens's* Great Expectations attempts to answer. *Great Expectations,* Leavis asseverated, "is the Dickens novel the mature and exigent are now likely to re-read most often and to find more and more in each time, perhaps because it seems to have more relevance outside its own age than any other of Dickens's creative work" (QDL, 289). Twelve pages earlier, however, Leavis's opening statement sounded equally adamant to the contrary: "It must have been very much easier to read *Great Expectations* adequately—that is, with a sympathetic and intelligent comprehension of the spirit in which it was written and of what it was actually about—in Dickens's own day, or in any time up to the present, than it evidently is now." Can a novel distinguished for continuing significance be increasingly difficult to comprehend? Does one perceive additional relevance in *Great Expectations* each time one rereads it if it has become steadily harder to understand "the spirit" governing its composition? Should the Dickens novel with the most to say to posterity tax the reader's sympathy and intelligence more severely today than at any time since 1861? *Dickens's* Great Expectations was begun in response to Leavis and out of admiration for

Great Expectations. The challenge was not to resolve an apparent contradiction but to grapple with conflicting statements, verifying one in the course of remedying the other. *Dickens's* Great Expectations reaffirms the perennial importance of *Great Expectations* by rendering this masterpiece richer and "easier" for the next age to appreciate. Leavis rightly insists that Dickens meant to depict "the growth of a moral sensibility" (QDL, 299); yet she reduces to a single theme the many socioeconomic as well as autobiographical factors that influenced this multipurpose novel. Pip may be "the Everyman of the Victorian middle class" and "the end of the road that began with Robinson Crusoe," as Sylvia Manning has argued; the goal of *Great Expectations,* however, is not merely "the exposure of a whole class" (SM, 197), but also of the kinds of fiction that soothed it, Cinderella stories especially. Dickens critiqued inordinate expectancy to rend "the fabric of values and attitudes necessarily erected by a complex commercial and industrial society" (RD, 128). One should add that he also sought to discredit novels he felt were upholding those attitudes and values.

2. According to Michael C. Kotzin, "Pip begins by being Cinderella . . . then imagines himself playing a different role"—Prince Charming to Estella's Sleeping Beauty (MK, 57). Had Pip connected Jaggers's announcement (ch. 18) with the money he received earlier from the stranger who stirs his drink with a file (ch. 10), it has been argued, disillusionment might have come sooner: "a wrenching reimagining of himself" (LF, 165). On the other hand, Pip's traumatic self-realization at age twenty-three in chapters 38 and 39 seems appropriate; not until he believes himself to be Cinderella can he rethink his situation in terms of the Misnar story.

3. Technically, *Cinderella* is a story of riches recovered: the daughter of a wealthy man is rescued from enslavement at the hands of his second wife (AD, 296). Like most subsequent readers, Walt Disney included, Dickens considered the cinder girl's seemingly meteoric rise from servant to princess the gist of the story.

4. Substitution of the Misnar story for *Cinderella* lays to rest objections to Pip as an unreclaimed self-deceiver who has "not only deceived himself in the past," but "continues to do so even as he tells the story of his previous self-deceptions" (JJ, 29). Pip, one feels, "is hard on himself to exactly the right (the convincing) degree" (DT, viii). His life story does not suggest "the impossibility of ever distinguishing completely between truth and falsehood" (JJ, 29); Mr. Pirrip's decision to undercut *Cinderella* with the Misnar story is one such distinction for himself and society. Peter Brooks's well-known essay to the contrary, Dickens's most expertly plotted novel is not "an abandonment of the attempt to read plot"; Pip has not "outlived plot, renounced plot, been cured of it." Granted, he has "misread the plot of his life," but Mr. Pirrip has not. In the last paragraph of chapter 38, he brings Pip's misreading to an abrupt halt; see PB, 113–42.

5. This may be the most under-annotated passage in *Great Expectations*. Customarily, it receives a note of two or three lines. See, for examples, Carlisle (JC, 291); Louis Crompton, ed., *Great Expectations* (New York: Bobbs-Merrill, 1964), 338; and R.D. McMaster, ed., *Great Expectations* (New York: Odyssey Press, 1965), 307. Charlotte Mitchell's note in the Penguin Classics edition (DT, 501) is a welcome exception, although it too ignores the allusion's centrality. Edgar Rosenberg gave the Misnar tale a concise summary (N*GE*, 235); David Paroissien devoted half a page to it (C*GE*, 301–2).

6. *Cinderella* is one of only twenty-five tales by the Brothers Grimm in which children are abused (JZ, 120). Their number is much higher in Dickens.

7. For a summary of "The Enchanters; or, Misnar the Sultan of the East," see Synopsis A. Stanley Friedman found Pip's "brief account" of the Misnar story inconsistent. Pip supposedly "identifies with *both* Misnar and the latter's foes"; Dickens abused his source "to fuse the role of the sultan and his enemies" so that Pip can be blameworthy like the latter and a hero like the former (SF, 216–18). According to Peter Merchant, Dickens discovered the "main elements" for chapter 38's last paragraph in George Eliot's *Silas Marner*. See "From Eliot to Dickens: The Descent of the Stone Slab in *Great Expectations*," *The Dickensian*, 95 (summer 1999), 132, 136–37. Eppie's arrival at Silas's cottage allegedly inspired Magwitch's appearance in Pip's apartments. The golden-curled child is "a message" of hope and concern from the "Power presiding over [Silas's] life" (*SM*, 115); for Pip, however, Magwitch's return is a major disaster. Eliot's novel was published on 2 April 1861. Chapter 38 came out on 11 May, probably too soon to be a reaction. In writing *Great Expectations,* Dickens generally "managed to keep . . . six weeks ahead of publication" (N*GE*, 397).

8. In "Before the Curtain," a prefatory note, Thackeray ruled out tragicomedy as a legitimate response to contemporary life; not even a "reflective" person, he predicts, will be "oppressed" by hilarity as he (or she) traverses *Vanity Fair*. "An episode of humour or kindness" may amuse occasionally, "but the general impression," he insists, is bound to be "more melancholy than mirthful" (*VF*, xxix).

9. In chapter 7, before Pip has been apprenticed, he reports his fanciful impression that his earnings as "odd-boy about the forge" were to be "contributed eventually towards the liquidation of the National Debt" (*GE*, 44). It had risen alarmingly during the Napoleonic Wars (1805–1815).

10. Janice Carlisle recognized that "Victorian Britain offers a success story on a national scale" (JC, 6), but never mentioned *Cinderella;* instead, she paralleled Pip's success story with "the foundling legend. According to this ancient plot, a child of royal birth is mistakenly or purposely set in circumstances below his or her station. In similar fashion, Pip, a boy raised by simple village folk and intended for life as a blacksmith, tells the story of discovering that he has finer prospects" (JC, 4–5). William F. Axton has argued that Pip's story is based on the rise and fall of George Barnwell, the eighteen-year-old protagonist in George Lillo's bourgeois tragedy, *The London Merchant; or The History of George Barnwell* (1731) (A, 117). At first diligent and loyal, Barnwell embezzles from his employer to please Milwood, a whore. She persuades him to kill his rich uncle but turns him in after the crime to save herself. In chapter 15, Mr. Wopsle reads "the affecting tragedy of George Barnwell" to Pip in its entirety. During the evening-long recital in "the Pumblechookian parlour," Wopsle and Mr. Pumblechook regard Pip's "unoffending self" as a potential Barnwell (*GE*, 116–17). *Cinderella* and the foundling legend have much in common, but Pip has not been "set" below his rightful station by parties unknown. The Pip–Barnwell parallel is important not as something that Pip suddenly perceives but as part of the persecution he suffers throughout childhood. Closer to the mark, Humphry House insisted that Dickens disappoints Pip's expectations as "an expression of disgust at the groundless optimism and 'progressive' hope of mid-Victorian society" (HH, 64).

11. Carlyle's utopia in Book II of *Past and Present* is the twelfth-century Benedictine Abbey of Bury St. Edmunds, an orderly, efficient contrast to an allegedly misgoverned England in 1842. As *A Child's History of England* (1851–1853) makes clear, Dickens did not romanticize his nation's past.

12. Hilary Shor has called Estella's life a rewriting of the story of the fairy princess with emphasis on "its darker side" (VD, 541). Margaret Flanders Darby argued that the heroine's development—her understanding of herself, Pip, and Miss Havisham—exceeds Pip's. See MFD, 215, 217.

13. To underscore Estella's financial comedown, Dickens added greed to the list of Drummle's deficiencies: "pride, brutality, and meanness" in the original ending (*GE*, 481) was changed to "pride, *avarice*, brutality, and meanness" in the revision (*GE*, 477; italics added).

14. Charles Perrault's version of *Cinderella* introduced a glass slipper (JZ, 142). When Cinderella rushes off for the third time in the Brothers Grimm, she leaves behind a slipper of "pure gold" (*BG*, 90). Glass seems preferable as a symbol of virginity (AD, 111). With one shoe on and one off, Miss Havisham is forever poised to try on a glass slipper. For Perrault, see note 41 below.

15. Cinderella is a cinder wench because "in the evening, when she was exhausted from working," her stepmother "took away her bed, and she had to lie next to the hearth in the ashes. This is why she always looked so dusty and dirty and why they all called her Cinderella" (*BG*, 87).

16. Include Orlick and Trabb's boy among the parodies of Cinderella. Orlick tracks Pip's upward progress as if it should have been his, as if Orlick were the cinder girl and Pip his stepsister. Trabb's boy is the apprentice who never aspired to go to London and become a gentleman.

17. An 1820 edition of the *Tales,* possibly the one that Dickens read as a boy, has "translated from the Persian by Sir Charles Morell" on its title page. But a six-page introduction, the "Memoirs" of the Reverend James Ridley, begins: "It is, perhaps, quite unnecessary to inform our readers that *Sir Charles Morell* . . . was an assumed name"; the real author feared "the composition of Tales would be thought inconsistent with the clerical character."

18. Harry Stone catalogued Dickens's use of Cinderella motifs (HS, 60, 94, 169, 256). Huang Mei included Dickens on a list of male writers whose heroines are the Cinderella type; Esther Summerson, Lizzie Hexam, and Jenny Wren are her examples (HM, 27), two of which postdate *Great Expectations.*

19. In the Brothers Grimm story, both stepsisters mutilate themselves in order to squeeze a foot into Cinderella's slipper; on Cinderella's wedding day, birds pluck out the sisters' eyes. Perrault's kindlier cinder girl forgives her stepsisters and marries them to great lords at court (AD, 21).

20. J. Hillis Miller pointed out several reworkings of *Oliver Twist* in *Great Expectations* (*OT,* xxiv). Pip too asks for more. But Oliver is undernourished; Pip expects Miss Havisham's money, Estella in marriage, and rank as a gentleman. Fagin and Monks try to sully Oliver; Mrs. Joe and Pumblechook instill Pip's Cinderella complex, insinuating that his "fortune may be made by his going to Miss Havisham's" (*GE,* 53).

21. "If you were to be very persevering and were to work hard, you might some day come to live in it," Dickens reports his father saying as they walked past Gad's Hill (*UT,* 62).

22. Most of this litany of disappointments was composed by Morris Golden (MG, 54, 56, 167).

23. Probably Charles Perrault's.

24. Dickens's parody was doubly biting because Cruikshank was a reformed alcoholic—not just a traducer of fairy tales, but also a self-righteous moralizer. "Once a hilarious climber of lampposts and wallower in gutters," Cruikshank had become "a fanatical teetotaler" (J, 2:619). In Cruikshank's *Cinderella,* the heroine takes the pledge to abstain from alcohol at age four (HS, 13).

25. See "The World is Too Much With Us; Late and Soon." The sonneteer regrets that in "Getting and Spending, we lay waste our powers." His wish to behold "Proteus rising from the sea" or to "hear old Triton blow his wreathed horn" anticipates Dickens's desire to awaken the Fancy with fairy tales.

26. In *David Copperfield* and "Frauds on the Fairies," Dickens sounds like Bruno Bettelheim. Throughout *The Uses of Enchantment: The Meaning and Importance of Fairy Tales,* a title Dickens might have liked, Bettelheim argued that tales convey the "advantages of moral behavior . . . by implication"—without being overtly didactic, they enrich the inner lives of children, helping them to cope with their problems through a process of ruminating and fantasizing. They make "positive psychological contributions to the child's inner growth" (BB, 5–12). However, Bettelheim's thesis that *Cinderella* gives children relief from sibling rivalry (BB, 239) would not have impressed Dickens.

27. Copperfield must learn to make wiser emotional choices (see Gwendolyn B. Needham, "The Undisciplined Heart of David Copperfield," reprinted in *DC,* 794–805). Having lauded Smollett, Fielding, Goldsmith, Cervantes, Le Sage, and Defoe, Copperfield adds "the Arabian nights and the Tales of the Genii" as stories that did him "no harm" (*DC,* 54).

28. Dickens never abandoned fairy lore. Cynthia DeMarcus has explored his reliance on *Little Red Riding Hood* for "the fairy-tale structure of *Our Mutual Friend*" (DeM, 17). Also, see Charles Forsyte, "*Drood* and the Bean-stalk," *The Dickensian,* 80 (1984), 74–88.

29. Hailing *Great Expectations* as a work that "restores Mr. Dickens and his readers to the old level," *The Saturday Review* praised the forty-nine-year-old novelist for having the "courage and resolution it demands to note the comic in life and manners amid the tragedy and farce of declining years" (*SR,* 69). K.J. Fielding noted: "Dickens produced his greatest work only to have it hailed by the critics as a welcome return to the old manner" despite "all that was new in the novel" (KJF, 220–21).

30. Martin Amis singularized tragicomedy as "a genre which literature finds hard to do and rarely attempts" (*I,* 199). But Richard J. Dunn has awarded *Our Mutual Friend* high marks for "tragi-comic fusion" (RJD, 155); Dickens's last completed novel blends "terror and comedy in grotesque tragicomedy" that captures mid-century England's "absurdity" (RJD, 147).

31. Cf. Horace Walpole's famous epigram (1776): "This world is a comedy to those that think, a tragedy to those that feel."

32. Contending that modernists such as Joyce, Synge, O'Casey, and Beckett consti-

tute a "tradition ... whose mode is tragicomic," Kathleen Ferris describes their "humor" as "dark, bitter, and satiric" (KF, 11).

33. Cf. John Cunningham's observation that "Dickens's comedy implies the operation of a theistic providence that can use pain to effect joy" (JCu, 43).

34. Randall Craig's definition of a tragicomic outlook corroborates Garis: "a trenchant perception of human limitation and suffering, combined with an empathic and amused acceptance of them" (RC, 13). Elsewhere, discussing tragicomedy in Arnold Bennett's *The Old Wives' Tale,* I argue that Bennett redeems the life process, which steadily renews itself, but not individual existence, which always ends in defeat (that is, death). On one hand, life is always subtraction; on another, broader plane, the process triumphs despite—indeed, because of—individual failures. Less approving, Dickens thought it more realistic to entertain mixed feelings about both the lot of individuals and the nature of life in general rather than to assign tragedy to the one, comedy to the other. See Jerome Meckier, "Distortion Versus Revaluation: Three Twentieth-Century Responses to Victorian Fiction," *Victorian Newsletter,* No. 73, (spring 1988), 3–8.

35. According to Craig, tragicomedy presupposes "the fundamental theatricality of existence" (RC, 34); in short, the world is a stage whereon tragedy and comedy are always playing simultaneously. For J. Hillis Miller, *Great Expectations* is "the most unified and concentrated expression of Dickens's abiding sense of the world" (JHM, 247).

36. A.E. Dyson insisted "there are few scenes in literature more ineffaceable than the picture of Pip working in his high chamber on this dire night, and his first intimation of a visitor on the stair" (AED, 234).

37. Pip alludes to *Paradise Lost,* 12:646–47. In the manuscript, the Miltonic echo is even clearer: "And the mists had all solemnly risen now, and the world was before me."

38. When Pip extinguishes Miss Havisham's burning bridal dress, Robert M. Polhemus refers to "Oedipus and Jocastâ" (RMP, 157). Bettelheim detected Oedipal conflicts in *Cinderella,* citing the girl's disappointment with her father and with her mother too for turning into a wicked stepmother. Anny Sadrin discussed Pip's Oedipal guilt in the penultimate chapter of *Parentage and Inheritance in the Novels of Charles Dickens* (Cambridge: Cambridge Univ. Press, 1994). Earlier, she called *Great Expectations* "an oedipal novel with Telemachus in the leading role" (AS, 122). Harry Stone traced "the interrelated networks of cannibalistic motifs" in Dickens's novel, calling offenses such as Pip's "the sin of feasting on others"; see *The Night Side of Dickens: Cannibalism, Passion, Necessity* (Columbus: Ohio State Univ. Press, 1994), 15, 136.

39. Ross Dabney found moral corruption spreading in two ways in *Great Expectations:* "by overt act ... and by seepage from a generally corrupt society. The direct line of infection runs from Compeyson, through Miss Havisham and Magwitch, through Estella, to Pip, who is rotted by his expectations" (RD, 128).

40. See "Cinderella" in Jack Zipes's translation of the Brothers Grimm (*BG,* 86–92). The first volume of *Kinder- und Hausmärchen* (*Children's and Household Tales*) was published in 1812, the year of Dickens's birth; the tales began appearing in English translations in 1823, when Dickens was eleven.

41. There is no fairy godmother in *Aschenputtel—Cinderella* as written down by the Brothers Grimm. In Cinderella's riches-to-rags-to-riches story, her well-to-do fa-

ther is apparently powerless to prevent his new wife and her two daughters from degrading Cinderella to servant status. Presumably, the two white pigeons that splendidly and miraculously clothe Cinderella each day of the Prince's three-day festival are emissaries from her late mother. The archetype for Magwitch appears in Charles Perrault's version of the fairy story, *Cendrillon—Cinderella, or the Little Glass Slipper* (AD, 14–21). Perrault's collection of eight fairy tales was translated into English by Robert Samber in 1729. He used Perrault's alternate title, *Mother Goose Tales* (*Contes de Ma Mère l'Oye*), instead of the less appealing *Histoires ou Contes du Temps Passé*. Perrault's tales were widely disseminated throughout the British Isles in a variety of formats, so Dickens undoubtedly knew the fairy godmother version of *Cinderella* from childhood. Harry Stone places Magwitch in the "godfatherly tradition"; Dickens meant to associate the ex-convict with the godmother figure in Perrault's story (HS, 24–25).

42. In 1859, the Royal College of Surgeons began issuing "certificates of fitness" to practicing dentists, raising their standing socially and professionally. The comparison of Magwitch to a dentist is Mr. Pirrip's idea; it could not have occurred to Pip.

43. Dickens tampered with the law to aggravate this tragic possibility. Between 1827 and 1830, eight returned transports were convicted, but none was executed; see Edward Gibbon Wakefield, *Facts Relating to the Punishment of Death in the Metropolis* (1831). Edgar Rosenberg noted that Magwitch's offense had "ceased to be *de facto* capital by the time the action of the novel takes place" (*NGE,* 243, n. 7). The death penalty for returning illegally was abolished in 1834. Although transportation to South Wales ended in 1840, the last hulk was not broken up until Dickens's birthday in 1859 (MEd, 27).

44. Eliot's warlike intentions can be discerned from "The Natural History of German Life," published in the *Westminster Review,* 66 (July 1856), 51–79. Dickens, she declared, lacks tragicomic perspective; the "psychological character" of his creations suffers because "he scarcely ever passes from the humorous and external to the emotional and tragic" without substituting "unreality" for "artistic truthfulness."

45. In *The Communist Manifesto,* Karl Marx maintained that history boils down to the class struggle between Haves and Have-Nots. The Pip–Magwitch relationship shows Dickens not to be a Marxist when it comes to solutions. Marx believed in a society solely of Haves: some have more than others, but all make decent livelihoods. This would suit Dickens, but he never advocates the abolition of private property or an end to the class system by force. Marx thought both steps inevitable. In Marxist terminology, Dickens remains a bourgeois socialist—a reformer who desires to make the advantages of the status quo available to all, hence a bourgeoisie increasingly without a proletariat instead of Marx's ideal: a new state with a proletariat but no bourgeoisie. In the Marxist utopia, all ties are strictly economic. See Vladimir Pozner's introduction to Karl Marx and Frederich Engels, *The Communist Manifesto* (New York: Bantam, 1992), xii-xiv.

46. When Beaty referred to the "parodic destruction of preceding novelistic worlds," he was not alluding to intense hand-to-hand competitions between Victorian novelists, each insisting his or her world best reflects the real one; instead, he echoed the Russian Formalist Mikhail Bakhtin: Charlotte Brontë, Thackeray, and others supposedly demolished "precedent novel conventions" mainly by coining new kinds of plots, inventing new ways to tell stories (JB, 220).

2. Lever

1. *All the Year Round* was not invariably "a writing workshop" in which, according to Sutherland, Dickens collaborated with fellow novelists in a friendly manner (JAS, 177–78).

2. Ada Nisbet observed that "discussions of Dickens' relationships with other contemporary novelists such as *Charles Lever,* Elizabeth Gaskell, George Eliot, Poe, Thackeray, and Trollope have in general been of more biographical than critical interest" (italics added; AN, 111). In George Ford's update, *Victorian Fiction: A Second Guide to Research,* only Ruth apRoberts mentions "the early Lever" as an analogue for Trollope's Irish novels (GF, 159).

3. Lever was sufficiently famous to be one of only five writers burlesqued in William Makepeace Thackeray's *Mr. Punch's Prize Novelists* (1847). According to legend, Thackeray intended to include Dickens but got cold feet. Lever retaliated by caricaturing Thackeray as Elias Howle in *Roland Cashel* (1850).

4. For most of his fictions, beginning with *Dombey and Son* (1846–1848), Dickens outlined each installment; he also jotted down things to be done in future chapters. *Harry Lorrequer* established the pattern for Lever's novels: throughout most of the story, this officer on leave simply roams about Ireland. Lever tried to improvise a more coherent plot in *The O'Donoghue* (1845) and actually planned *The Knight of Gwynne* (1846–1847) in advance. Critics consider novels such as *Sir Joseph Carew* (1855) and *The Fortunes of Glencore* (1857) better constructed than Lever's earlier serials, but improvements seem negligible.

5. A chapter-by-chapter synopsis of *A Day's Ride* can be found in Synopsis B.

6. Contributing an increasingly Thackerayan novel to Dickens's journal was an affront of sorts in that Dickens and Thackeray were rival editors in 1860, the former conducting *All the Year Round* while the latter presided over the *Cornhill Magazine.*

7. In choosing a name, Lever may have been thinking of Pott, cantankerous editor of the *Eatanswill Gazette* in *Pickwick Papers.* There is also Wilkie Collins's parodic autobiography of a pretentious painter: "A Passage in the Life of Mr. Peruguino Potts" in *Bentley's Miscellany* (February 1852), but Collins's source could be the same as Lever's.

8. Edgar Rosenberg found Potts too gullible for a picaro; Lever's rambling plot and "sloppy construction" are "secondary characteristics" of picaresque (NGE, 415). Still, Potts's misadventures seem to fall within the confines of what Edgar Johnson, discussing *Pickwick Papers,* called "picaresque realism" (J, 1:174). Rosenberg is of two minds about *A Day's Ride;* having damned it for "a slapdash novel" without coherence or sense of direction, he deems it "worth salvaging in volume form" (NGE, 412, 417).

9. When Dickens edited *Bentley's Miscellany* in the late 1830s, he required new serials to follow those that were nearing completion. *Oliver Twist* had to wait to move into the lead-off spot. In a monthly magazine, however, positioning may not have been as vital to a new serial's success. The final four installments of *Oliver Twist* surrendered pride of place to William Harrison Ainsworth's *Jack Sheppard* (1839); by then, Ainsworth had assumed the editorship.

10. Johnson stated that "the protraction of Lever's story . . . reduced Dickens's readers . . . to desperation" (J, 2:966).

11. "Of all first chapters," Swinburne rightly asked, "is there any comparable for impression and for fusion of humour and terror and pity and fancy and truth to that which confronts the child with the convict on the marshes in the twilight?" (S, 31).

12. Robert Garis emphasized a "melancholy, mildly humorous acceptance of the world's insufficiency" as the tragicomic core of *Great Expectations* (RG, 212), but not Thackeray's melancholia, said Dickens, nor Lever's humor.

13. That an uncritical Lever took "unalloyed delight" in this sort of misunderstanding was Lionel Stevenson's verdict in *The English Novel: A Panorama* (LS, 252).

14. This was Thackeray's epithet for Victorian England (BS, 45).

15. Joe behaves almost as badly when he accompanies Pip to Miss Havisham's (ch. 13).

16. Michael Cotsell hails Pip as "one of the great achievements of Western literature" (MC, 7). For William F. Axton, Pip is the "textbook case," a snob both "insecure and pretentious"; see WFA, 280, 281.

17. Not surprisingly, Edgar Rosenberg's survey of the Dickens–Lever interchange ("Lever's Long Day's Journey Into Night"; NGE, 410–22) does not discuss the editor-novelist's parodic revisions of his inept contributor.

18. In Philip Marcus's opinion, Pip's reaction was not supposed to be shared by readers of *All the Year Round,* to whom Dickens had given "anticipatory clues" (PM, 65–67). Surely Dickens had things both ways: surprise for readers who did not expect Magwitch, confirmation of their worst fears for those who did.

19. Edward Said's reading of the Pip–Magwitch association as a parable in which England's wealth is owed to slavery and exploitation in other countries is far-fetched (ES, 13–14). It seems more prudent to second Humphry House on "Pip's parasitism": like his allowance from Magwitch, the Victorian age's wealth and progress are revealed to be "parasitic on the drudgery of an exploited working-class, a hideous underworld of labour" (HH, 64). Grahame Smith traces "the sources of wealth that created the luxurious ease of much of the Victorian world" to "the degrading labour of men, women and children" in coal mines, the steel industry, and factories in general. In *Great Expectations,* "wealth is rooted in criminal exploitation" (GS, 176–77). Magwitch relates to Pip and polite society much as the Morlocks relate to the Eloi in H.G. Wells's *The Time Machine.* Returning from down under (Australia), Magwitch foreshadows the Morlocks emerging from their subterranean tunnels to cannibalize the Eloi. Writing about coal miners in northern England, George Orwell contended that "all of us *really* owe the comparative decency of our lives to poor drudges underground" (WP, 42). According to Stephen Ingle, Orwell believed that "it is on the backs of those who inhabit this [underground] world that the rest of us are able to live our lives of comparative coziness"; the relationship is "parasitic," not "symbiotic" (SI, 47).

20. See Synopsis A for a summary of "The Enchanters; or, Misnar the Sultan of India" in *The Tales of the Genii: or, the Delightful Lessons of Horam, the Son of Asmar* (1764). Ironically, Wemmick, whose Walworth self feels snobbish contempt for urbanites, is a successful castle builder; his "little wooden cottage," with its top "cut out and painted like a battery mounted with guns" (GE, 206), offers a positive variation on Pip's pavilion-like expectations and Potts's castles in Spain. Wemmick is a more practical builder than Potts: "I am my own engineer, and my own carpenter, and my own plumber,"

he says (*GE,* 107). But he takes the precaution of collapsing his castle daily lest it interfere with his duties: "[W]hen we got to his place of business," Pip marvels, "he looked as unconscious of his Walworth property as if the Castle and the drawbridge and the arbour and the lake and the fountains . . . had all been blown into space together" (*GE,* 209).

21. Cf. Harry Stone's remarks apropos of *David Copperfield* (HS, 197).

22. This paragraph and those surrounding it are taken almost verbatim from my essay "Dickens, *Great Expectations,* and the Dartmouth College Notes," *Papers on Language and Literature,* 28 (spring 1992), 120–21, 131.

23. This paragraph and several after it come with minor alterations from my essay "Charles Dickens's *Great Expectations:* A Defense of the Second Ending," *Studies in the Novel,* 25 (spring 1993), 47–49; for the argument that Bulwer was not the instigator for a revised ending, see pp. 39–42.

24. Not only has Robert L. Patten discussed the circulation of *All the Year Round* (RLP, 292); his chart showing Dickens's earnings from the journal appears on p. 464.

25. In fall 1868, Dickens began a tour of readings from his own works for Chappell's: one hundred performances for eight thousand pounds.

26. MS in the Free Library of Philadelphia.

27. Seven hundred fifty pounds is precisely the amount Dickens subsequently gave for *The Moonstone;* either he grossly overpaid Lever, or Collins's novel was a bargain.

28. Ironically, *Hard Cash* proved too sensational. Reade graphically depicted abuses in the Victorian asylum; the public's unwillingness to spend time and money on lunacy reform revealed a materialistic outlook potentially fatal to society, Reade alleged. Shocked and displeased by Reade's stark realism and harsh critique, readers stopped buying *All the Year Round,* lowering circulation by three thousand copies weekly. Nevertheless, the "loss of sales represented only three per cent" (AG, 146). This drop cannot be compared with the ongoing slide that Lever caused. Outraging readers, one may argue, was preferable to boring them and more in keeping with the mission of Dickens's journal. Reade never became a full-fledged rival of Dickens and Collins; nevertheless, *Hard Cash* deserves to be read as a revaluation of Collins's use of the asylum in *The Woman in White.*

29. These condolences sound heartfelt, but in Dickens's "pleasure in his power over the problem of serialization," Grahame Smith detected an "ill-concealed delight at the failure of others to master it, even when this involved the fortunes of his own publication" (GS, 37).

30. On the other hand, Dickens persuaded his publishers, Chapman and Hall, to issue hardcover editions of both *A Day's Ride* and Lever's next novel, *The Barringtons,* which was dedicated to Dickens. According to Stevenson, Lever made the dedication because he had heard "rumours" that he was "jealous" of Dickens and thought it politic to defuse them (*CL,* 249).

31. Dickens's handling of *A Day's Ride* has been compared to his dealing with Elizabeth Gaskell's *North and South* in *Household Words* six years earlier. Lever was dealt with more leniently, J. Don Vann has argued, because he tolerated editorial interference (*VPR,* 69–70). Actually, Dickens complained privately about both but remained complimentary whenever he wrote either in an editorial capacity. After *A Day's Ride,* Lever continued to publish articles in *All the Year Round,* but these were paid for upon accep-

tance, not commissioned (J, 2:966). Unable to strike back in fiction, Lever kept Dickens under surveillance in letters to John Blackwood. He branded *Our Mutual Friend* "disagreeable reading," its characters "more or less repugnant" (7 March 1865; ED, 2:91). He envied the "hatfulls of money" Dickens made in America (January 1868; ED, 2:210). On 15 April 1870, he asked if Blackwood had read *Drood* (ED, 2:277). Lever's letter, dated 9 July 1870, contained a spiteful eulogy: Dickens "was a man of genius and a loyal, warm-hearted, good fellow; but he was not Shakespeare" (ED, 2:284–85).

3. Thackeray

1. On the other hand, an entry for "June 11th" in Nathaniel Hawthorne's notebook during his visit to England (1855) sums up Dickens's imperiled position, which even a transatlantic visitor, who never met Dickens, could sense: "Dickens is evidently not liked nor thought well of by his literary brethren—at least, the most eminent of them, whose reputation might interfere with his." Thackeray, Hawthorne added, "is much more to their taste" (*EN*, 118). Throughout his early fiction, Thackeray "parodied and transformed elements from Dickens' novels" (MCr, 232); in the *Yellowplush Correspondence* (1838), he rewrote *Pickwick Papers*, whereas *Catherine* (1839–1840) parodies Newgate novels such as *Oliver Twist*, itself a commentary on this sub-genre. Dickens "did not really care much for the writings of Thackeray," Edgar Johnson has remarked, yet "he always spoke well of them" (J, 2:1132). As did most Victorian realists, Dickens expressed unfavorable opinions through revaluative parody, literary criticism in the form of an allegedly more truthful counterstroke. Thus one questions K.J. Fielding's observation that "Dickens was extraordinarily silent about his major rival novelists"; he never said "anything of the slightest interest" about Thackeray ("CA," 80). Similarly, criticisms of Dickens are scattered throughout a handful of Thackeray's letters and appear in several reviews of Newgate novels for *Fraser's Magazine*, but Thackeray "was usually careful in his public comments to speak favorably of Dickens's works" (CM, 21). George Worth marveled "at the silence [regarding *Great Expectations*], at least in their published letters, of novelists like Eliot and Thackeray" (W, xiii). Actually, *Denis Duval* (1864) reconsiders the subject of great expectations (*AW*, 411). In Thackeray's last novel, unfinished at his death, the hero's mother resolves "to make him a gentleman" (*DD*, 392) and succeeds; it is smugglers' money that gives her son a start. Duval, a retired naval officer, tells his story in old age. He credits Agnes, his prize in life, for helping him to rise. Not only does Duval's wife have Copperfield's second wife's first name, but like Biddy at the forge, she grows up in the Duval household. Her mother, Madame de Saverne, is referred to as "the lady in white" (*DD*, 312). Thackeray describes her as a continental Miss Havisham, "in a white wrapper, her hair flowing down her back," and wearing one white shoe (*DD*, 325). In *Hidden Rivalries in Victorian Fiction: Dickens, Realism, and Revaluation*, Thackeray is not dismissed as a rival for Dickens (see pp. 243–48); instead, the argument is that the vision and practice of other Victorian novelists, principally George Eliot, remain more antithetical to Dickens's. Eliot's competitions with Dickens constitute the more profound rivalry; nevertheless, 1) Thackeray was "the first substantial rival of [Dickens's] career" (ML, 77); 2) most Victorians, readers and critics alike, considered Dickens and Thackeray arch-rivals; 3)

Thackeray certainly did so. In a letter to his mother after the success of *Vanity Fair*, he positioned himself "at the top of the tree . . . and having a great fight up there with Dickens" (*LPP*, 2:233).

2. Reprinted in 1848 as *The Book of Snobs*, Thackeray's fifty-two installments ran anonymously in *Punch* (1846–1847) as *The Snobs of England*. *The History of Pendennis*, twenty-four monthly parts in twenty-three monthly installments, appeared between November 1848 and December 1850 (JDV, 137). *David Copperfield*, twenty monthly numbers in nineteen installments, started six months after *Pendennis* (May 1849) but finished one month sooner, in November 1850 (JDV, 68), due to a three-month hiatus caused by Thackeray's serious illness at the end of 1849.

3. Humphry House called snobbery "that delicate, insinuating, pervasive class-consciousness which achieved in England a subtle variegation and force to which other countries . . . have scarcely aspired" (HH, 64). Altick found Victorian novelists at mid-century "especially concerned with the anxieties, envy, insecurity, *snobbery*" stemming from ambiguities of rank and wealth in a time of social flux (RA, 17; italics added). But not everyone agrees with House's characterization of Pip's moral evolution as "a snob's progress" (HH, 64). A.E. Dyson and Patricia R. Sweeney swell the chorus denying that snobbery is a Dickensian concern. The former opts for guilt as the subject of Dickens's moral exemplum (AED, 233); the latter seconds Sylvère Monod's objection that Dickens seldom used "snob," a slur Thackeray is credited with virtually inventing (PRS, 55). See Monod's retrospective, "*Great Expectations* a Hundred Years After," *The Dickensian*, 66 (1960), 133–40. In Sutherland's opinion, the idea of snobbery "was in the air in the late 1830s and early 1840s, and Thackeray distilled it" (*BS*, 236).

4. In Micael M. Clarke's estimation, *Barry Lyndon* marks the culmination of Thackeray's early parodies, yet "many people thought Thackeray meant Barry to be likeable" (C, 40). Potts's fabrications imitate Lyndon's.

5. Thackeray's famous remark that if his books "are true," Dickens's "must be false" originally appeared as a quote in *Lippincott's Magazine* during Thackeray's second American reading tour. For Thackeray's statement in full, see WCP, 22. Modern critics subtly endorse Thackeray's view. Speaking of Warrington's wife in *The Virginians*, Jack P. Rawlins observed that in Thackeray, "the good-hearted female does not turn into . . . Cinderella," as she presumably would in a Dickens narrative (JPR, 232). Judith Fisher claims Thackeray offers the more modern idea of moral action in which characters operate as cultural conditions indicate (JF, 112), as if Pip and Magwitch were not products of society. John Reed opined that Thackeray is the more believable administrator of justice; in Dickens, providence metes out punishments rarely as rehabilitative as Thackeray's (JR, 257). As if in response to Thackeray, Ruskin asserted that "the things [Dickens] tells us are always true." In the *Cornhill Magazine*, a journal being edited by Thackeray, Ruskin, writing of *Hard Times* in August 1860, insisted on Dickens's unsurpassed veracity: he "is never mistaken"; he has been "entirely right in his main drift and purpose in every book he has written," especially on "social questions." Dickens's "view," Ruskin concluded, "was finally the right one, grossly and sharply told." Grahame Smith has reprinted the relevant passage from Ruskin's essay in the Everyman edition of *Hard Times* (London: Dent, 1994), 327.

6. Similarly, Thackeray's sketch for the covers of the monthly numbers of *Vanity

Fair depicted the author as "A Fool Addressing Other Fools." Thackeray's talent for self-parody, especially when formulating upper-class attitudes toward art, displeased Dickens, who felt that sufficient revaluation could be expected from one's rivals. Dickens took seriously the artist's obligation to improve the world. Mark Cronin has suggested that the dilettante, Henry Gowan, in *Little Dorrit* is a parodic rendition of Thackeray's genteel idler, Clive Newcome. See "Henry Gowan, William Makepeace Thackeray, and 'The Dignity of Literature' Controversy," *Dickens Quarterly*, 16 (January 1999), 105, 108.

7. "In the mid-nineteenth century," P.D. Edwards has argued, "a 'snob' was generally a person of low rank putting on upper-class airs, not (as in modern usage) an upper-class person looking down on his or her social inferiors." See n. 30 (p. 461) to Elizabeth Braddon's *Aurora Floyd* (New York: Oxford Univ. Press, 1996). Dickens and Thackeray agree that snobbery is both subservience to superiors and haughtiness to inferiors, often by the same person.

8. Jerome H. Buckley compared the interplay between Mr. Pirrip and his younger self to "a dramatic monologue" (JHB, 53), thus underscoring Dickens's willingness to probe psychologically.

9. Dickens's portrait of a young snob, not Lever's or Thackeray's, has left its imprint on subsequent bildungsromans. *Stephen Hero*, the original title for *Portrait of the Artist as a Young Man*, links Joyce's novel to both *David Copperfield* and *Vanity Fair*: the latter "A Novel Without a Hero," whereas David wonders if he can present himself as one. But Joyce wrote with *Great Expectations* primarily in mind. After Stephen emerges from the confessional (ch. 3), Joyce echoes Dickens's Miltonic allusion at the end of the First Stage; "and life lay all before him" (*PA*, 145) recalls Pip's "and the world lay spread before me" (*GE*, 158). Dedalus is contemplating a hearty communion breakfast of pudding, eggs, and sausages, so Joyce may be laughing at Milton and Dickens both. In *Tono-Bungay*, H.G. Wells pays tribute to *Great Expectations* throughout his account of George Ponderevo's disappointments. George's fight with Archie over Beatrice (Wells's Estella) is modeled on Pip's combat with the "pale young gentleman" (*GE*, 91); Uncle Teddy's magazine, "The Sacred Grove" (*TB*, 211), borrows its title from "a club called the Finches of the Grove" (*GE*, 272), to which Pip and Herbert belong. Neither Wells nor Joyce, however, surpassed the tragicomic double perspective that Dickens obtains by allowing Mr. Pirrip both to dramatize and comment upon his younger self's behavior. In Joyce, Stephen's experiences, such as his martyrdom at the hands of Father Dolan in chapter 1, seldom seem as momentous in retrospect; the mature novelist undercuts his young protagonist's traumatic moments. The grown-up Pip gives his mistakes and misjudgments, albeit the stuff of comedy, their due weight.

10. In Doris Alexander's opinion, Dickens disliked Thackeray's literary parodies in *Punch* because they "do no honor to literature or literary men" (DA, 2). In the early parodist, Micael M. Clarke found the makings of Thackeray the realist (C, 67–68).

11. M.R. Ridley's introduction to the Everyman edition of *Pendennis* sounded the same warning: Thackeray adopts a "temperately cynical air," stripping disguises from shams but "with a tolerance"; "now condemning, now excusing," Thackeray "had too warm a heart to be a true cynic" (*Pen*, viii–ix). For Gordon N. Ray's critique of the Snob Papers, see *UA*, 348–83.

12. Juliet McMaster reads Thackeray's parody of Lever's *Charles O'Malley*, in *Punch*, as a form of "flattery"; she pointed out that Thackeray used an episode from Lever's novel as a model for the duel scene in *Barry Lyndon* and alluded to *O'Malley* again in the Waterloo chapter of *Vanity Fair* (McM, 310, 328, 331).

13. For more on Thackeray's objections to Jerrold and his radical satirical brethren, see CM, 30–31.

14. "There are many disagreeable things in society," Thackeray pontificated, "which you are bound to take down and to do so with a smiling face" (*Pen*, 1:10). Dickens considered this attempt at stoicism shameful, if not akin to resignation.

15. This phrase appeared in Thackeray's letter of "6? May 1851" thanking David Masson for his review of *Pendennis* and *David Copperfield* in *The North British Review* (May 1851; 57–89). Thackeray states of Dickens's novels: "I don't think he represents Nature duly" (*LPP*, 2:772).

16. Perhaps Dickens found a hint for Magwitch's Australian occupation in Warrington's uncle, who took "a sheep-farm" in New South Wales and "made a fortune" (*Pen*, 1:290). Miss Havisham's father was a wealthy brewer; Pip notices "a large brewery," no longer operational, "at the side" of Satis House (*GE*, 64–65). Foker's *pater* makes a fortune with "Foker's Entire"; his son and heir acquires the sobriquet "young lord of the vats" (*Pen*, 1:163). Captain Strong shares his surname with Dr. Strong, whose academy Copperfield attends. Blanche Amory's real name is Betsy, as is David's aunt's; Miss Costigan's first name, Emily, duplicates that of David's childhood playmate. When Foker's romance with Miss Amory falls through, he hastens "to the Pyramids" for solace (*Pen*, 2:390); Pip goes to Egypt after losing Estella and Biddy. Lever may have taken a hint from Miss Costigan, who discloses the real name of a fellow thespian: Potts (*Pen*, 1:52). Like Pen, Potts is the son of an apothecary. One of the "old bucks" at Bays's Club is Mr. Blondel (*Pen*, 1:369), the name given to Potts's horse.

17. Thackeray draws the parallel between Pen and "the artful Lovelace" (*Pen*, 2:96).

18. It is difficult to explain Major Pendennis's sudden avowal of firsthand knowledge of Australia; he insists that he saw Altamont "in Sydney a convict" long after the latter's "reported death in the bush" (*Pen*, 2:263).

19. Altamont is frequently referred to as "the gentleman in the black wig" (*Pen*, 1:267, for example). This disguise fools no one: "His copious black hair was evidently surreptitious," Thackeray observes (*Pen*, 1:389).

20. The book Mrs. Pocket treasures is *Debrett's Peerage* by John Field Debrett; first published in 1784, in Dickens's day it was still the essential guide to the British nobility. Mrs. Pocket is yet another travesty of Cinderella. Her husband values her as a "treasure for a prince" (*GE*, 188).

21. The manuscript reads "there were no better words that I could say beside his bed through my rush of tears." On second thought, Dickens deleted Pip's tears, but they indicate sincerity on Pip's part, not snobbery.

22. Edgar Harden referred to this story several times in the index to his *Annotations for the Selected Works of William Makepeace Thackeray* (New York: Garland, 1990), 2:621. Oddly, he does not discuss Pen's allusion in his comments on chapter 72 of *Pendennis* (1:650). In the illustrated capital for chapter 52 of *Vanity Fair*, one actually

sees Alnaschar kicking over the tray of glass. Thackeray also mentions the incident in chapter 3 of that novel. The illustration features a tray, not a "basket"; in *Pendennis*, the contents are "porcelain," not glass. The would-be glass merchant has no name in the Norton edition of *The Arabian Nights*, but Thackeray's translation gave him one. Perhaps Thackeray used an English translation of Antoine Galland's early eighteenth-century French version.

23. Sutherland conceded that a shadowy editor censors Pen's "confessions" so that much of his "inner life stays forever inner" (*TW*, 55).

24. "In *Pendennis*," wrote R.D. McMaster, "though not in the first person . . . Thackeray's delight is in depicting the violent convictions and infatuations of adolescence and shading them with the mellow wisdom of the Old Fogy" (RMcM, xxii).

4. David Copperfield

1. Ellen Moers inverted the parodic revaluation process, mistaking *Pendennis* for an "influence" on *Great Expectations:* "Dickens and Thackeray come more closely together in these two books than in any others . . . the similarities between Pip and Pen are remarkable" (EM, 245).

2. Pen represents the youthful Thackeray, frivolous and undecided about a vocation, whereas Warrington stands for the worldly-wise Thackeray trapped in a sad marriage to Isabella Shaw. Only by dividing himself into Pen and Warrington could Thackeray insure the latter's integrity and allow the former to get the girl in the end (CHM, 252–53).

3. Pen comes to London at twenty-three (*Pen*, 1:274), Pip's age when Magwitch returns and Potts's when he sets out on his ride.

4. Computations regarding Copperfield's age come from Gwendolyn B. Needham; see GBN, 796.

5. Ella Kusnetz has argued for "the writing of *Great Expectations*" as "the last stage of [Pip's] self-reclamation" (EK, 154).

6. In Shaw's opinion, Carlyle "roused" Dickens from his bourgeois optimism ("P," xxi). But Dickens lost his lightheartedness throughout the 1840s, beginning traumatically with his disillusionment in America.

7. Elsewhere, Shaw contended that "*David Copperfield*, once Dickens's pet book, was wiped out by *Great Expectations*" ("GBS," 118). For E. Pearlman, *David Copperfield* "has been inverted" in *Great Expectations*, which "stood . . . *David Copperfield* on its head" (EP, 191). In his afterward to the Signet edition (1963), Angus Wilson called *Great Expectations* a social and personal "recantation" of *David Copperfield*'s "prematurely mellow, over-cozy, self-satisfied note" (AW, 524).

8. The embarrassing convict, Pip's "second father" (*GE*, 317), returns from the continent to which Dickens conveniently shipped Mr. Micawber, a caricature of his own impedimental parent. For the opening scene of *Great Expectations*, Dickens may have drawn on the episode wherein the pawnbroker "rushed out of a den behind [his shop], and seized [David] by the hair," exclaiming "Oh, my lungs and liver . . . Oh, goroo, goroo!" (*DC*, 161)

9. When the blacking warehouse "was removed" to Chandos Street, young Dickens, working near a window "for the light's sake," tied up the pots of blacking so briskly that passers-by stopped to watch: "I saw my father coming in at the door one day when we were very busy," Dickens recalls in the Autobiographical Fragment, "and I wondered how he could bear it" (F, 1:37). When at last John Dickens rescued his son from servitude, "it may have had," Dickens speculated, "some backward reference . . . to my employment at the window" (F, 1:38).

10. Arguably, Pip has a third unsatisfactory fairy godparent in Pumblechook, who misrepresents himself as "the founder of [Pip's] fortunes" (*GE*, 231).

11. Because *David Copperfield* was such a trendsetter, Buckley ranked it higher than *Pendennis*, but not ahead of *Great Expectations*, whose "narrower focus" permits Dickens to achieve "a much fuller characterization of the narrator" (JHB, 43).

12. This paragraph conflates Buckley's "broad outline" (JHB, 17) with his equally helpful "standard formula for the bildungsroman" (*DC*, xi).

13. Cf. Dickens's long-lasting resentment toward his parents, especially his mother, for consigning him to Warren's and for wanting him to continue even after John Dickens "quarrelled" with the proprietor: "I never afterwards forgot, I never shall forget, I never can forget . . ." (F, 1:38).

14. When Wemmick asks Pip not to describe for Jaggers his marriage to Miss Skiffins, he explains that Jaggers "might think my brain was softening" (*GE*, 451). Earlier, however, Jaggers and Wemmick catch each other softening toward Pip, whose passion for Estella touches them both. They exchange "odd looks" (*GE*, 443), suspecting each other's business self to be "the most cunning imposter in all London." Having "melted" momentarily, they quickly recover; each regrets "having shown himself in a weak and unprofessional light to the other" (*GE*, 446).

15. Initially, Dickens was of two minds concerning self-help, an idea that Smiles's best-seller glorified but did not invent. In George Ford's opinion, Dickens divides characters in *Bleak House* into those capable of self-help and the truly helpless, such as Jo, whom private charities and state agencies must support (RR, 93–94). Disapproval falls heaviest on Richard Carstone and Harold Skimpole for failing to utilize their capabilities. Ford considered Copperfield a paragon of self-help, a prototype of Smilesian perseverance who is constantly energized (RR, 95). According to Robin Gilmour, the later Dickens's disillusionment with most things Victorian came to include Smiles. Self-help was "one of the mainstream Victorian notions" to which Dickens was initially indebted (B-C, 71); *David Copperfield* celebrated "the self-help values of hard work, earnestness, and perseverance," but *Great Expectations* is Dickens's "most profound commentary on Victorian civilization and its values," hence a major rethinking of self-help (B-C, 84, 94). Janice Carlisle reminded readers that Dickens's father began life as the son of servants. John Dickens not only rose to be a clerk in London's Navy Pay Office, he also married the daughter of an important official there. His career seems to prove that inequalities of status could be overcome if one possessed a strong character and made a great effort (JC, 7). Nevertheless, one doubts that Charles Dickens viewed his debt-ridden, improvident, sponging father from a Smilesian perspective.

16. Smiles alludes to the Greek biographer, Plutarch (A.D. c.50–c.125), who wrote

Parallel Lives, a series of anecdotes comparing famous Greeks and Romans, in order to isolate the moral qualities of great persons.

17. In J. Hillis Miller's view, this is "the truth which lies at the very center of *Great Expectations:* all the claims made by wealth, social rank, and culture to endow the individual with true selfhood are absolutely false" (JHM, 271).

18. In the preface to the 1869 Charles Dickens Edition, he referred to *David Copperfield* as his "favourite child." "Of all my books," he stated, "I like this the best" (*DC,* 766). However, such attachment did not preclude revaluation.

19. In Trollope's *The Three Clerks* (1858), the disreputable Undy Scott, having been discredited, hurries off "to Hamburg perhaps, or to Ems" after "collecting what little he might" from wife and family (*TC,* 535). Pip goes all the way to Egypt.

20. Smiles idolized railroad engineers, citing the construction of England's railroads as the greatest example he knew of material progress. His *Life of George Stephenson, Railway Engineer* (1858) went through five editions the first year. Smiles worked for the railroad line on which the Staplehurst accident occurred in June 1865. Ellen Ternan filed a damage claim for injury to her dress, giving her mother and Dickens as witnesses; until then, according to Smiles, no one at the railway office knew that Dickens was on the train. Smiles denies the accident contributed to Dickens's death five years later: "He died most probably from too much work, too much reading of his works, and too much unrest" (*SS,* 245).

21. Although Kenneth Fielden agreed that Smiles "reduced" the triumphs of great men "to a few moral qualities" that anyone can emulate, he defended *Self-Help* against charges of materialism and success worship; see "Samuel Smiles and Self-Help," *Victorian Studies,* 12 (December 1968), 155–76.

22. Asa Briggs listed energy, cheerfulness, prudence, and industry as Smiles's four qualities for a good character (AB, 25).

23. Charles Darwin's *The Origin of Species* and *Self-Help* both appeared in 1859, hence their topical conflation in Mr. Pirrip's mind in 1860, a double allusion his younger self could not have made.

24. Not until chapter 13, after a dozen chapters of success stories, did Smiles belatedly salute gentleness and self-respect in "Character—The True Gentleman."

25. The expression "great expectations" appears early in *Self-Help,* one of several places Dickens could have encountered it in 1859 or 1860 (*SH,* 5).

26. Christopher Clausen connected self-help with the snobbery involved in aping one's betters; Smiles's anecdotes and biographical sketches of well-known people who had risen from humble origins were intended to prove that one "could not merely imitate gentlemen or ladies but actually belong to their number, provided one worked diligently to acquire middle-class values and habits." See "How to Join the Middle Classes: With the help of Dr. Smiles and Mrs. Beeton," *The American Scholar* (summer 1993), 405, 408.

27. Dickens disbelieved Smiles whenever the latter denigrated the craze to become genteel, recommending, instead, acceptance of one's lot: "There is a dreadful ambition abroad for being genteel"; "we have not the courage to go patiently onward in the condition in life in which it has pleased God to call us" (*SH,* 290–91).

28. Magwitch is based partly on success stories of real-life convicts who thrived down under; Dickens could claim to be writing their composite biography. For example, Samuel Terry (1776–1838), an illiterate Manchester laborer transported for theft, grew so wealthy as pub keeper and moneylender that he was nicknamed "the Rothschild of Botany Bay" (RH, 334–35). No successful convict returned from Australia to settle old scores, however. In *David Copperfield*, the Micawbers, Mr. Peggoty, Em'ly, Martha, and Mrs. Gummidge not only flourish in Port Middlebay (Melbourne) but remain there.

29. Not even Magwitch is entirely self-made. From his first "hiring-out," he tells Pip, "I got money left me by my master (which died, and had been the same as me)" (*GE*, 318). Pip is thus the recipient of funds from *two* ex-convicts, Magwitch and his master, while Herbert unwittingly collects from both of Pip's fairy godparents, Magwitch and Miss Havisham. Dickens not only invents a pair of unforgettable grotesques to caricature the fairy godparent; he also employs Magwitch's master's gift to Magwitch and Miss Havisham's money for Herbert to ridicule self-help as an equally implausible phenomenon.

5. Collins

1. Were the evidence Rance provides more persuasive, Dickens would still have ample motive to downgrade *Self-Help;* namely, to outdo Collins's subversion of Smiles.

2. *Hide and Seek* takes place mostly in 1851, but the seduction, abandonment, and death of Mary Grice, Madonna's mother, occurred between April 1827 and March 1828; that is, roughly about the time of Magwitch's unexpected return to England. When Mat first sees Madonna, she is "twenty-three" (*H&S*, 289), the same age as Pip and Estella in the "Third Stage" of *Great Expectations*.

3. Catherine Peters pointed out that "part of [*Hide and Seek*] was written on an extended visit to Dickens and his family in Boulogne during the summer of 1853" (*H&S*, xi). Collins, she added later, spent "a third of 1853 in close companionship with Dickens" (CP, 129). But *Hide and Seek* was not serialized in *Household Words* as has been claimed (NGE, 393).

4. "So close" in some particulars are descriptions of the circuses in *Hide and Seek* and *Hard Times* that Catherine Peters hypothesized a real-life model in common: Dickens and Collins "were remembering the same circus act, perhaps one they had seen together" (*H&S*, xiv).

5. Bounderby's alleged sufferings exceed Magwitch's, which they also resemble. Compare Bounderby's fabrications (*HT*, 18) with the ex-convict's account of his childhood and early youth (ch. 42). Bounderby calls his young self a "vagabond" whom "everybody . . . knocked . . . about and starved"; similarly, Magwitch, the perennial vagrant, was "took up, took up, took up." Bounderby "learnt his letters from the outsides of shops" and told time "from studying the steeple clock of St. Giles's Church, London, under the direction of a drunken cripple, who was a convicted thief, and an incorrigible vagrant." Magwitch credits "a deserting soldier . . . hid up to the chin under a lot of taturs" with having "learnt [him] to read" and "a traveling Giant" with teaching him to write. Bounderby remembers himself as "one of the most miserable wretches ever seen";

Magwitch recalls "a ragged little creetur as much to be pitied as ever I see." Bounderby's resumé—"Vagabond, errand-boy, vagabond, labourer, porter"—reads like Magwitch's: "Tramping, begging, thieving, working" (*GE*, 344–45).

6. Madonna shines like Cinderella, but her mother bore a cinder girl's indignities. At the rector's, Madonna is "dressed in a white frock, with a little silk mantilla over it" (*H&S*, 74), all traces of the circus performer eliminated. But Mrs. Peckover, a benign, capable Mrs. Gamp, describes meeting Mary Grice when Madonna was still her babe in arms: Mary's "gown was very dusty, and one of her boots was burst, and her hair was draggled all over her face . . . but we saw somehow that she was a lady" (*H&S*, 80).

7. The debate pits *No Name* against *Bleak House*. Magdalen Vanstone (*NN*) may be read as a parodic replacement of Esther Summerson (*BH*). Both illegitimate women qualify as victims of society whose plights resemble Cinderella's, but Collins replaces what he considered Dickens's conventional rendition with a cinder girl whose struggles to regain respectability make her a complex instance of self-help; that is, a borderline villainess. The passive Esther is allegedly too modest and self-sacrificing to be named for the Jewish Queen of the King of Persia who saved her people from annihilation; in contrast, a rehabilitated fallen woman provides Collins's Cinderella with a psychologically more complicated biblical antecedent. Magdalen's audacity on her own behalf repeatedly mocks Esther's meekness. Nevertheless, Collins has Captain Kirk rescue Magdalen much as Woodcourt is Esther's salvation.

8. In her biography of Collins, Catherine Peters asserted that he took Forgues's advice and "never again wrote so Dickensian a novel as *Hide and Seek*" (CP, 158); in fact, his attempts to surpass and supplant Dickens had only begun. Also see Emile Forgues, "William Wilkie Collins," *Revue des Deux Mondes,* 12 (Oct.–Dec. 1855).

9. One of Zack's failures to adopt "commercial pursuits" involves three weeks of clerking in "a Tea Broker's office" in London (*H&S*, 45). In the manuscript of *Great Expectations,* Herbert plans to trade with China mainly for tea.

10. Bounderby gets excited only from the neck up; Dickens notes Bounderby's "great puffed head and forehead, swelled veins in his temples, and such a strained skin to his face that it seemed to hold his eyes open, and lift his eyebrows up" (*HT,* 17).

11. See *HR*, 49–92, wherein Gaskell's industrial novel, *North and South,* is construed as a parodic revaluation of *Hard Times,* which it followed in *Household Words*.

12. "My scalp's on the top of a high pole in some Indian village, anywhere you like about the Amazon country," Mat tells Zack (*H&S*, 187). Collins apparently thought that the Amazon tribes shared Cooper's Indians' penchant for scalping.

13. Much of the fault in *Hide and Seek* lies with Joanna Grice, Mary's aunt and the novel's equivalent of a wicked stepmother. She intercepted Carr's letters, without which Mary believed she had been deserted by her lover. Dickens reused "Arthur" for Miss Havisham's half brother's first name (*GE*, 351). Arthur Havisham helps Compeyson to obtain money from Miss Havisham before he cruelly disappoints her expectations of marriage.

14. Dickens makes a rare slip here; in the next chapter, Magwitch's "door opened," says Pip, "and he came out" for breakfast (*GE*, 328). This is impossible unless Pip has unlocked it.

15. Before switching to a "black velvet skull-cap," Mat wore "an old yellow handkercher" to shield his scalped head (*H&S*, 188). Mat is described as "having objections to a wig" (*H&S*, 182), but "disguising wigs" are key items in Magwitch's scheme for remaining unrecognized in London (*GE*, 331).

16. Mat's "gruff chuckles, . . . the nearest approach he was capable of making towards a civilized laugh" (*H&S*, 290), are redone as the catch of gratitude in Magwitch's throat when he accepts food and a file from Pip: "Something clicked in his throat . . . And he smeared his ragged rough sleeve over his eyes" (*GE*, 19).

17. Beggar my Neighbour is a juvenile game for two players. Each holds half the deck face down. Players take turns turning up cards, placing them in the common pile until either one draws an ace or a face card. Then the other must pay a quota to the pile: four cards for an ace, three for a king, two for a queen, one for a jack. If these quota cards are tens or below, the player of the high cards puts the common pile under his or her own, and turning up resumes. If an ace or face card appears in the quota, the player formerly with high card must give a quota. Excitement mounts when high cards follow each other until the last captures all, the winner taking possession of the entire pack.

18. Collins exposes Thorpe much as Dickens explodes Bounderby: just as the self-made manufacturer has a self-sacrificing mother, the castigator of illegitimacy fathered an illegitimate child. Thorpe fell out with Blythe because he assumed Madonna was the painter's illegitimate daughter (*H&S*, 415).

19. In a letter dated 23 June 1861 from Gad's Hill, Dickens informed Collins that he had yielded to Bulwer's anxieties and altered "the extreme end" of *Great Expectations*, "after Biddy and Joe are done with . . . You shall see the change when we meet," Dickens promised (*PL*, 9:428).

20. One can point to other examples of Dickens appearing to respond to Collins by speaking first. Students in Blythe's drawing academy are required to sketch "the Dying Gladiator," a statue from 150 B.C. (*H&S*, 145). Dickens alludes to it when Mr. Pocket drops upon a sofa "in the attitude of the Dying Gladiator" (*GE*, 196). But the allusion is not in response to Collins, who introduced this sculpture for the 1861 edition, perhaps in acknowledgment of Dickens's many reworkings of material from *Hide and Seek*.

21. After 1861, Miss Havisham offered an unintentional yet striking contrast to the popular image of Queen Victoria, forever in black to mourn Prince Albert.

22. Forster subsequently became a Lunacy Commissioner; Collins dedicated *Armadale* (1864–1866) to him.

23. Variations on the theme of wrongful confinement pinpoint Mary Elizabeth Braddon's *Lady Audley's Secret* (1862) and Charles Reade's *Hard Cash*, which appeared in *All the Year Round* (1863), as reconsiderations of *The Woman in White*. In the final chapter of *Love's Madness: Medicine, the Novel, and Female Insanity, 1800–1865* (Oxford: Oxford Univ. Press, 1996), Helen Small argued that both *Great Expectations* and *The Woman in White* capitalized on "lunacy panics" of the 1850s, the fear of individuals being committed through faulty diagnoses.

24. Collins used several Cinderella motifs in *The Woman in White:* 1) a persecuted heroine, 2) receives help, as if by magic, 3) from a princely rescuer, 4) who finds proof of her noble identity, 5) and marries her; see BFL, 119.

25. In choosing the transported felon to represent society's reluctance to accept responsibility, Dickens was working on borrowed time. The most severe penalty under the law next to execution, transportation would be abolished in 1867 (PC, 7).

26. Miss Havisham, Estella, and Pip are also irreverent variants of Sleeping Beauty. Miss Havisham will never awaken from her self-imposed comalike state. Pip confuses Estella's heartlessness with a dozing heart: "When should I awaken the heart within her, that was mute and sleeping now?" he wonders (*GE*, 244). Ironically, Pip's moral conscience naps from the time he begins moving up in the world until Magwitch returns to prompt a moral awakening of the sort Dickens prescribes for society at large. But the anti-Cinderella parody is stronger and more pervasive.

27. For Collins's attacks on propriety, see *HR*, chapter 4, which is based on my earlier essay "Wilkie Collins's *The Woman in White*: Providence against the Evils of Propriety," *Journal of British Studies*, 22 (fall 1982), 104–26.

28. The other unforgettable dramatic scene was Carlyle's account of the women's march to Versailles in *The French Revolution*. Catherine Peters has suggested "the sudden appearance of Magwitch to Pip at the beginning of *Great Expectations*" as "a third" (CP, 208).

29. Dickens also replays Walter's midnight encounter with Anne as Arthur Havisham's hallucinatory dread of his sister, to whom he helped Compeyson do "a bad thing" (*GE*, 347). "Late at night" in his room, Arthur imagines that he sees Miss Havisham advancing toward him "all in white," with "a shroud hanging over her arm," which she intends to put on him.

30. Dickens's opening scene also attempts to eclipse Collins's piece de resistance to end the Second Epoch when Walter, returned from eighteen months or more in Central America, discovers Laura looking at him over her own tombstone (*WW*, 431). An escaped convict, Dickens countered, was more likely to be lurking in a deserted cemetery than a disenfranchised heiress.

31. When Mr. Wopsle's great-aunt dies, Biddy leaves the aunt's "miserable little shop" and "hopeless circumstances" for a better life at the forge. "What a drudge she had been until" then, Pip reflects (*GE*, 125).

32. Sophia Andres believes that Walter, shocked by his initial encounter with Anne, begins to undergo a Jungian process of individuation; see "Pre-Raphaelite Paintings and Jungian Images in Wilkie Collins's *The Woman in White*," *Victorian Newsletter*, No. 88 (fall 1995), 28–36.

33. Sir Percival's incineration makes him a despicable martyr to the proprieties. It is also Collins's attempt to eclipse Krook's spontaneous combustion (*Bleak House*). When Miss Havisham sets herself on fire (ch. 49), Dickens has the final word on self-combustion.

34. Anne's fatal resemblance to Laura in both looks and dress—they are "twin-sisters . . . the living reflection of one another" (*WW*, 120)—inspires Fosco's plan for "the complete transformation of two separate identities" (*WW*, 620). Like Cinderella, Laura may be said to have two stepsisters. Technically, she and Anne are half sisters; they have the same father, although neither Philip Fairlie nor his wife, who befriends Anne, knows she is his child by Mrs. Catherick. Mr. Fairlie was also Marian Halcombe's mother's second husband. So Laura and Marian are actually stepsisters, not blood-related as are Laura and Anne, yet Marian calls Laura her half sister (*WW*, 60).

35. On one hand, being overdressed, as Joe seems to be when he accompanies Pip to Satis House (ch. 13) or visits him in London (ch. 27), is evidence that clothes cannot change a cinder person into Cinderella; on the other hand, in a society obsessed with externals, a good set of clothes can distinguish an allegedly genteel person from the rogue he actually is. When Compeyson and Magwitch are both in the dock, the former's "black clothes and his white pocket-handkercher," recalls Magwitch, made everyone conscious of "what a common sort of wretch I looked" (*GE*, 349).

36. Unlike Anne Catherick, Pip cannot keep his new clothes clean; having toured Newgate with Wemmick, Pip finds (or imagines) "prison dust" "soiling" his clothes. "I shook it out of my dress," he states, but feels "contaminated" (*GE*, 263).

37. "There are strong hints," Catherine Peters pointed out, "that Sir Percival, like Ruskin, leaves his bride as virginal as he found her" (*CP*, 221); Pip will have to undo the physical and psychological damage done to Estella by Drummle, "who . . . used her with great cruelty" (*GE*, 477).

38. When Magwitch's return destroys Pip's hopes of marrying Estella, his nautical despair parodies Walter's happiness: "I began fully to know how wrecked I was, and how the ship in which I had sailed was gone to pieces" (*GE*, 320).

39. According to Stanley Friedman, Pip's discovery of Estella's parentage reawakens his expectations and confirms his belief in providence, thus facilitating reunion in the revised ending. But Pip's exclamation to Herbert—"the man we have in hiding down the river is Estella's father" (*GE*, 405)—startles the exclaimer as much as the discovery that Magwitch is his patron; reunion with Estella is over a decade away. See "Estella's Parentage and Pip's Persistence: The Outcome of *Great Expectations*," *Studies in the Novel*, 19 (winter 1987), 410–21.

6. Mary Shelley

1. According to W. Laurence Gadd, Dickens put the "stone lozenges" (tombstones) from St. James at Cooling into the churchyard of St. Mary the Virgin, his parish church at Gad's Hill (*LG*, 21, 23; *GE*, 3).

2. Curt Hartog referred to Estella as Miss Havisham's "Frankenstein monster" (*CH*, 249).

3. Chris Baldick has called *Great Expectations* a "Frankensteinian exercise" in which Dickens can be seen "pondering the full modern significance of monstrosity" mainly "as a presence beneath our skins" (*CB*, 117, 120).

4. "I had made the monster," Pip says of his servant, "and had clothed him . . . I had to find him a little to do and a great deal to eat; and with both of those horrible requirements he haunted my existence" (*GE*, 218).

5. George Levine believes that Pip identifies with Victor but not with the monster; in his repulsion of the creature, Pip "is emulating Victor Frankenstein's 'horror' and lack of fellow-feeling" ("AH," 22). Chris Baldick observed that Pip "loses his allusive bearings and is unable to consign Magwitch to the realm of monstrosity when he knows that he belongs there himself" (*CB*, 119–20).

6. This is the passage frequently cited to characterize Mary Shelley as a radical reformer, a proto-Marxist. *Frankenstein* is set in the second decade of the nineteenth

century, the argument goes, in order "to identify Frankenstein's monster with the emerging proletariat" (WM, 303). A product of the new industrial order, this work force appeared monstrous to observers in Shelley's day; an unnatural creation, it had no collective identity or genealogy and belonged to no known species (WM, 310).

7. One hesitates to call Shelley's novel a bildungsroman. Yet after only four letters from Robert Walton to Mrs. Saville, his sister, *Frankenstein* becomes Victor's life story as told "in his own words" to Walton (F, 37).

8. Forster's review of *Great Expectations* may have been written by Henry Morley; see the *Examiner*, 20 (July 1861), 452–53.

9. Johanna M. Smith has called Frankenstein's monster a rebel against "a privileged class parasitic on the laboring class" (F, 16). In an "ironic reversal," William Montag has argued, parasites and laborers succumb to a "new kind of servitude" to science and technology (WM, 306).

10. As William F. Axton put it, the gentlemen class "has created a system of criminal justice calculated to heap with blame and punishment those creatures of its own making" (WFA, 287).

11. Johanna M. Smith dubbed Frankenstein's monster's potential mate a "monsterette" (F, 15). Equally egregious is her argument that "society produces monsters not so much by systematic oppression as by inept parenting" (F, 4). Victor Frankenstein she later calls " a Bad Parent" (F, 280).

12. L.J. Swingle placed *Frankenstein* and its monster "in the literary context of the Romantic period"; citing examples from Keats, Byron, Shelley and others, he argued that "the fundamental question posed by the Stranger concerns the human mind's ability to know things . . . the problem of knowledge"; see LJS, 56–60.

13. Confident of his superiority to Shelley, Dickens equates comprehension with compassion, treating the subject tragicomically—seriously in one episode, less so in the next. In chapter 54, Magwitch reacts to Pip's vow of fidelity with "that old sound in his throat—softened now, like all the rest of him" (GE, 444). When Pip takes leave of Wemmick after the latter's marriage in chapter 55, he is implored not to mention the festivities to Jaggers lest he "think my brain was softening," says Wemmick (GE, 451). Comprehension, compassion, softening—these are not unrealistic goals, Dickens persisted, even if Wemmick's is presented ironically as a shameful lapse.

14. Besides offering the best-known explanation of Orlick—he is Pip's "double, *alter ego,* or shadow"—Julian Moynahan defined "the great expectation fantasy": the dream of huge, easy success that haunted imaginations in the increasingly commercial and industrial nineteenth century; in short, the Cinderella complex (JuM, 67, 69). One's "final judgment" on Victor Frankenstein, Mary Lowe-Evans has recommended, should be that "an essentially good man . . . has been led astray by ambition" (L-E, 228). In Dickens's opinion, Pip is the more pertinent portrait of such a person.

15. For a history and description of Dickens's model for the sluice house, see LG, 25–38; the sluice house is clearly the most desolate of the dark, spooky settings with which Dickens replaces Shelley's sunlit child-snatching scene. On the other hand, John Clubbe has noted the prevalence of foul weather in *Frankenstein;* for the argument that "the coldest summer ever recorded in Europe" is "the single most determining influ-

ence upon" the creation of Shelley's novel, see "The Tempest-toss'd Summer of 1816: Mary Shelley's *Frankenstein*," *Byron Journal,* 19 (1991), 27, 31, 34.

16. Pip quotes Luke 18:13; see chapter 3, endnote 21 above.

17. For the melodramatic realist, all art is an imitation of the ways of providence; I have argued previously that "His artistry, although vastly humbler than Milton's, nevertheless illuminates God's ways and stands as their explanatory justification." Dickens told Collins that their "business" is "to show by a backward light what everything has been working to." See *HR,* 97, 93.

18. According to Bernard Duyfhuizen, Milton's text "plays an important role in educating the creature to the point where he can question Victor Frankenstein in much the same fashion that Adam queries God" (BD, 478). Thus for her epigraph, Shelley quotes *Paradise Lost,* 10: 743–45: "Did I request thee, Maker, from my clay / To mould me man?" Adam demands. "Did I solicit thee / From darkness to promote me?"

19. Is Magwitch a Bible reader? Pip's "terrible patron" possesses "a greasy little clasped black Testament" but Pip says he "never knew him to put it to any other use" than "to swear people on" (*GE,* 332). Neither Magwitch nor Pip remarks on the ex-convict's unusual first name, which Dickens had trouble with; the manuscript reveals him exploring several alternatives, "George" and "Willum" among them, before deciding on "Abel." Edgar Rosenberg considered Dickens's difficulty in picking Magwitch's first name proof of its unimportance to both author and character: "Much—too much, I think—has been made of Magwitch's Christian name" (N*GE,* 462). Yet why discard two prior choices in favor of a name fraught with biblical significance and pointing to a shepherd's life? Could Dickens simply have ignored what Rosenberg dismisses as Magwitch's "pastoral pursuits down under" (N*GE,* 463)? "I was a hired-out shepherd in a solitary hut," says Magwitch, "not seeing no faces but faces of sheep" (*GE,* 317). "Abel" also suggests "able," which Magwitch is for himself in Australia, but only parodically as Pip's enabler. For the importance of "the Cain–Abel" story to Dickens, see Wendy Jacobson, "The Genesis of the Last Novel: *The Mystery of Edwin Drood," Dickens Studies Annual,* 25 (New York: AMS, 1996), 197–210.

20. After the De Laceys depart and the creature burns their cottage, he quotes *Paradise Lost*: "And now, with the world before me," asks the monster, "whither should I bend my steps?" (*F,* 120) But the monster's recollection lacks the irony that Mr. Pirrip imparts to Pip's similar quotation in chapter 19. Dickens rewrites not only Shelley's scene but her use of Milton in it as well.

21. The two allusions reveal the unique relationship between Mr. Pirrip and his younger self. Only the older, nominal author of *Great Expectations* could insert the Miltonic reference that ends chapter 19. The educated Pip who speaks as the novel concludes is qualified to quote *Paradise Lost.* But in chapter 59, Pip builds on an earlier allusion he could not have known about in the ruined garden, because Mr. Pirrip had yet to commence his autobiography, much less chapter 19. Strictly speaking, no mists rise in the final lines of Milton's epic. Dickens may have been thinking of the cherubim who descend by "Gliding meteorous, as Ev'ning Mist" glides "o'er the marsh"(12:628–30).

22. J. Hillis Miller described Pip and Estella "accepting their exile from the garden of false hopes" (JHM, 278).

23. Technically, only Frankenstein is dead, but the creature, having declared he will die "soon," disappears into the "darkness and distance" (*F*, 185).

24. When Biddy asks Pip if he has "quite forgotten" Estella, she inquires "as an old, old friend" (*GE*, 477).

25. Anticipations do not include Wemmick and Jaggers, but Wemmick and the Aged seem worthy of inclusion, the former taking pains to assign his ancient father a partner's responsibilities, no matter how trivial.

26. Curiously, young Pip suffers from Adam's complaint, not uxoriousness exactly but domination by women; he is subjected to the tyrannical Mrs. Joe, the deceiving Miss Havisham, and a queenly Estella.

27. Once Estella and Pip learn "how to be friends," Bert G. Hornback has argued, *Great Expectations* can end (BH, 121). *Great Expectations* not only considers friendship superior to love and thus a prerequisite for the latter, but partnership is the ideal form friendship can take.

7. Charlotte Brontë

1. This is James Kincaid's appellation in "Pip and Jane and Recovered Memories," *Dickens Studies Annual*, 25 (New York: AMS, 1996), 213. Jane's autobiography is discussed as a "recovered memory plot," whereas Pip's is "a Freudian repression plot" (212–13).

2. On an undated piece of Gad's Hill stationery, Dickens is reported speaking as follows: he "had not read Jane Eyre and said he never would as he disapproved of the whole school. [This apropos of Miss Hogarth saying that it was an unhealthy book] He had not read Wuthering Heights. . . ." See Jerome Meckier, "Some Household Words: Two New Accounts of Dickens's Conversation," *The Dickensian*, 71 (January 1975), 5–20.

3. Cinderella's plight as an unwanted stepchild and Jane's situation as a dependent at Gateshead Hall are practically identical. Jane's uncle (her mother's brother) has died, leaving her at the mercy of a surrogate mother, an aunt who is not her blood relative. Every inch the wicked stepmother, Mrs. Reed reneges on the promise she made her dying husband to "rear and maintain [Jane] as one of their own children" (*JE*, 28). These include Eliza and Georgiana, perfect equivalents for Cinderella's stepsisters. Exploring "the Cinderella pattern" in *Jane Eyre*, Robert Keefe noted "how closely the plot approximates pure wish fulfillment on the author's part"; "the novel can be seen as a sort of literary courtroom in which Brontë defends her heroine against an accusing world and proves her innocent" (RK, 112, 124).

4. Dickens's retelling of *Cinderella* prefigures Joyce's mythical method. Pip both is and is not Cinderella, just as Leopold Bloom's adventures parallel Ulysses's but are always much smaller. Joyce uses parallels with Ulysses to elevate and deflate Bloom simultaneously; when Dickens rewrites *Cinderella* in terms of the Misnar story, Pip's resemblance to the usurpers in the latter tale increasingly interferes with parallels between his rise and Cinderella's. Arguably, Brontë anticipates the mythical method by paralleling Jane Eyre and Cinderella, whereas Dickens complicates matters by using competing analogues.

5. From Brontë's day to this, novelists remain preoccupied with *Jane Eyre*. Dinah

Craik's *Olive: A Young Girl's Triumph Over Prejudice* (1850) has been termed a "reworking" of *Jane Eyre*, both its "companion and countertext," according to Cora Kaplan (*O*, x). Olive is ultimately as much a Cinderella as Jane, only more convincing and deserving in Craik's opinion. Craik's "The Half-Caste: An Old Governess's Tale" features two Cinderellas. Jane Eyre reappears as Cassia Pryor, short, meek, yet resourceful. Zillah Le Poer, an heiress half-English, half-Indian, is a triumphant version of Bertha Mason; "my poor Cinderella," as Cassia calls her, Zillah marries Mr. Sutherland, whom Cassia also loves (*O*, 341). *Wide Sargasso Sea* (1966) tells the first Mrs. Rochester's story, the events leading up to *Jane Eyre*. Jean Rhys's "pre-quel" augments *Jane Eyre* with an account of Bertha's girlhood and marriage. Also see Janice Rossen, "On Not Being Jane Eyre: The Romantic Heroine in Barbara Pym's Novels," *Independent Women* (New York: Harvester, 1988), 137–56.

6. Calling Jane "a sullen Cinderella, an angry Ugly Duckling," Sandra M. Gilbert glossed "Eyre" as "ire" (SG, 478).

7. Both *Jane Eyre* and *Great Expectations* allude to *Frankenstein* through the monster imagery they share. Frequently called "fiend" and "monster," Jane rejects all such derogation: "[A]m I a monster?" she demands of Mrs. Fairfax, who doubts Rochester's affection for her (*JE*, 263). "I have no particular reason to suspect myself of having been a monstrosity," says Pip, echoing Jane (*GE*, 67). He confesses shortly afterward to one exception: "Towards Joe, and Joe only, I considered myself a young monster" (*GE*, 70).

8. Not surprisingly, all three Reed children end unhappily. Financially ruined, John commits suicide. Eliza marries a wealthy old man for his money; Georgiana converts to Roman Catholicism and takes the veil—a fate Jane considers worse than death.

9. Perhaps so little can be made of Pip's name because so much is implicit in Jane's: air, ire, heir, for examples. "Eyre" is almost palindromic, but "Pip" is truly so—the same whether read backwards or forwards. Pip's name is just Pip, "nothing longer or more explicit" (*GE*, 3), hence its bearer is immune to transfiguration.

10. Many of Jane's travails seem unnecessary. John Eyre writes Mrs. Reed to declare Jane his heir, but her evil stepmother suppresses the letter for three years (*JE*, 238). Jaggers conceals the identity of Pip's benefactor for roughly twice as long, but the suspense is genuine and the lengthier suppression useful to complete Pip's gentrification. Jane's inheritance, twenty thousand pounds, is nearly as grand as Bertha's dowry (thirty thousand pounds). On the other hand, Rivers informs Jane that she has inherited "twenty thousand pounds" yet she tells Rochester her uncle left her "five thousand pounds" (*JE*, 374, 423). Perhaps she has divided it with her three Rivers cousins.

11. *Jane Eyre* evinces no shortage of fairy tale allusions. When Jane and Mrs. Fairfax wander down a long passage on the third floor, where Bertha is confined, the former hears a "mirthless," "preternatural" laugh; she imagines herself in "a corridor in some Bluebeard's castle" (*JE*, 114). "When you came on me in Hay Lane last night," says Rochester of his first encounter with Jane, "I thought unaccountably of fairy tales" (*JE*, 128). Arguably, *Jane Eyre* is a miraculous blending of Sleeping Beauty (her "soul sleeps," says Rochester; *JE*, 147) and Cinderella to correspond with her employer's ultimately benign conflation of Bluebeard and Prince Charming.

12. Essays on Brontë's symbolic use of the elements are legion. For a similar con-

cern in *Great Expectations*, see Paulette Michel-Michot, "The Fire Motif in *Great Expectations*," *Ariel*, 8 (1977), 46–69, and William H. New, "The Four Elements in *Great Expectations*," *Dickens Studies*, 3 (October 1967), 111–21. In *Great Expectations*, fire imagery seems uppermost. Joe's forge depends on fire; Magwitch remembers being abandoned by someone who "took the fire with him" (*GE*, 344); Pip feels compelled to confess his lies about seeing a "black velvet coach" at Satis House "[b]efore the fire goes out" (*GE*, 68, 70); "Burn me if I know! declares Orlick (*GE*, 234); at the Blue Boar, "neither of us," says Pip of himself and Drummle, "could relinquish the fire" (*GE*, 355). "Fittingly," however, "the climax of the novel," Jerome Hamilton Buckley has argued, "comes with the death struggle on the dark river; as the convict Magwitch is lifted prostrate from the Thames, Pip, himself drenched, his pride drowned, 'melts' with a deep compassion. . . . the watery 'baptism' is clearly related to the events of a moving narrative; yet not a little of the emotional effect may spring from free association with the established images of spiritual renewal"; see *The Victorian Temper* (New York: Vintage, 1964), 100–101. For Dickens, Robert G. Garnett suggests, the ideal is to be neither cold (water, ice) nor passionate (fire), but each as required; see "The Good and the Unruly in *Great Expectations*—and Estella," *Dickens Quarterly*, 16 (March 1999), 24–41.

13. Jane alludes to Bunyan. See *The Pilgrim's Progress* (New York: Washington Square Press, 1961), 151.

14. See Exodus, chapters 11–12.

15. Miss Havisham's "kneeling" regretfully to Pip replays his kneeling in homage before his "fairy godmother" on his last visit to Satis House before going to London (*GE*, 156).

16. According to Curt Hartog, "Pip's rescue" of Miss Havisham "dramatizes a rich nexus of psychological intentions, the core being a symbolic revenge—rape—aimed at violating and degrading Woman in order to free the self from fixation" (CH, 259–60); Pip attempts to get even with all the women who have mistreated him—not just Miss Havisham, but also Mrs. Joe and Estella.

17. Bertha has been called "Jane's truest and darkest double: the angry aspect of the orphan child, the ferocious secret self Jane has been trying to repress ever since her days at Gateshead" (SG, 492). For an overview of Bertha, see Laurence Lerner, "Bertha and the Critics: The Character of Bertha Mason in *Jane Eyre*," *Nineteenth-Century Literature*, 44 (1989), 273–300.

18. The "tradition of the double," Martin Trapp has argued, includes "nocturnal appearances" and a tendency for "self-destruction" (MT, 40). Dickens reused Jane's first glimpse of a vampirish Bertha for Pip's first meeting with Miss Havisham in the latter's darkened room. Both scenes feature dressing tables, candles, bridal outfits, and a marriage gone awry. "Ghastly" appears in both places (*JE*, 281; *GE*, 58–59). Miss Havisham's "dark eyes" make Pip want to cry out even more than Bertha's "red eyes" terrify Jane.

19. According to Helen von Schmidt, "the figure who most conspicuously mocked [Pip's] romantic conception of himself is also—and perhaps by virtue of that role—his rescuer" (HvS, 89).

20. The chestnut tree may derive from *Frankenstein*, in which Victor, fifteen, sees

lightning strike: "On a sudden I beheld a stream of fire issue from an old and beautiful oak ... and so soon as the dazzling light vanished, the oak had disappeared, and nothing remained but a blasted stump" (*F*, 45).

21. Brontë claimed that Jane's hearing Rochester from miles away was "a true thing; it really happened" (*LCB*, 401); when winds wailed around the parsonage, Charlotte supposedly heard the voices of her dead sisters' souls. See, also, Ruth Bernard Yeazell, "More True than Real: Jane Eyre's Mysterious Summons," *Nineteenth-Century Fiction*, 29 (1974), 693–717.

22. In the version of *Cinderella* recorded by the Brothers Grimm, both stepsisters have their eyes "pecked out" on Cinderella's wedding day (*BG*, 92), her rise capped by their blinding. Rochester has "one eye ... knocked out" and loses sight in the other (*JE*, 418); atoning for all Jane's oppressors, he suffers the stepsisters' fate.

23. That *Jane Eyre* and *David Copperfield* still run together in the critical imagination seems clear from Clara L. Peterson, "*Jane Eyre* and *David Copperfield*: Nature and Providence" in *The Determined Reader: Gender and Culture in the Novel from Napoleon to Victoria* (New Brunswick, N.J.: Rutgers Univ. Press, 1986), 82–131.

24. F.R. Leavis coined the term "orphan's myth" in a note on "*Oliver Twist, Jane Eyre* and *David Copperfield*," Appendix B in *Dickens the Novelist* (QDL, 108). "Whatever ... Dickens ... may or may not have said ... about Currer Bell's first novel, which rivalled *Vanity Fair* in the reception it received from both reviewers and reading-public," Leavis added, "he, like everyone else in the literary world, must have read it with the kind of respect we know was accorded it by novelists as different as George Eliot, Thackeray and Lockhart." Leavis's remarks—he is right to surmise that Dickens must have known *Jane Eyre*—fail to take into account the nineteenth-century novelist's competitive nature.

25. For additional evidence, Brontë could have pointed to Oliver's friend Dick, Smike in *Nicholas Nickleby*, Little Nell in *The Old Curiosity Shop*, and Paul Dombey in *Dombey and Son*.

26. Arlene Young, however, preferred to compare Jane's wanderings after fleeing from Mr. Rochester with those of Frankenstein's monster upon rejection by its creator; for example, the monster observes the De Laceys through a small aperture just as Jane, outside Moor House, watched the Rivers family inside (AY, 327, 333).

27. Karen Chase has pointed out that Brontë "explores personality by allowing the individual to expand," whereas Dickens "shows no interest in having his characters assimilate new traits." He supposedly "prefers to contract the expressive range of his characters" (KC, 135). Actually, Jane swells until her concerns become ubiquitous. Chase dubs Jane's maturation "a process of incorporation by which the central character consumes the work and takes on its every feature. Jane is everywhere" (KC, 135). Brontë's heroine is "a boundless whole" chiefly in that her self continually "widens its extension." Such self-aggrandizement, Dickens counters, does not constitute greater self-understanding or increased psychological depth. He presents Pip's "self as a rigorously bounded part which achieves significance only by entering a pattern of relations" (KC, 135). But the "pattern" complicates the personality it restricts, affording greater interi-

ority instead of added breadth. It is not expansion versus contraction but specious growth as opposed to genuine internal development. Jane gets bigger, whereas Pip, his illusions crushed, gets deeper, Dickens believed, not just smaller. Parodic revaluation is a "process of incorporation" (to use Chase's words) in which *Great Expectations* "consumes" *Jane Eyre;* it "takes on" this rival's features in order to reshape them into something more credible.

28. Charles Darwin titled chapter 3 of *The Origin of Species* "Struggle for Existence," using the phrase throughout the chapter interchangeably with "the struggle for life" (*OS,* 48–49).

29. In *The Descent of Man,* which Dickens did not live long enough to read, Darwin advocated softening when he wrote: "The moral nature of man has reached its present standard, partly through the advancement of his reasoning powers . . . but especially from his sympathies having been rendered more tender and widely diffused through the effects of habit, example, instruction, and reflection." See the excerpt from *The Descent of Man* in Appleman's edition of *The Origin of Species* (*OS,* 201). For a discussion of gradualism and catastrophism in Victorian fiction, especially as a point of contention between George Eliot and Dickens, see *HR,* 249 ff.

30. Calling personality development the subject of "an on-going debate" between Dickens and Brontë, Helen von Schmidt found in *Great Expectations* and *Jane Eyre* "two almost wholly opposite models of the self and its relation to the world" (HvS, 84): identity formed through relations with others versus identity one is born with and must protect.

31. G. Armour Craig has argued that "in every relationship Jane rises from inferiority to superiority" (GC, 476). Jane Eyre and Mr. Rochester "begin their relationship as master and servant," Sandra M. Gilbert has written, but "prince and Cinderella" are soon "democratically equal" (SG, 485, 487). Although Jane calls marriage to Rochester "a fairy-tale—a daydream" come true, Anny Sadrin considers *Jane Eyre* "Brontë's 'modern' version of *Pamela*"; see "The Trappings of Romance in *Jane Eyre* and *Great Expectations,*" *Dickens Quarterly,* 14 (June 1997), 69–91.

32. Frederick Karl questioned whether *Jane Eyre* can be called a bildungsroman because its heroine is "inflexibly right from the beginning." He regretted Brontë's "failure to allow change"; Jane grows "only chronologically, not emotionally or mentally" (FK, 98). Yet Michael S. Kearns quotes G.H. Lewes's admiration for Brontë as a psychological novelist, particularly the "deep significant reality" of *Jane Eyre.* See "Revealing Surfaces, Predictable Depths: Mind as Entity in Brontë and Dickens" in *Metaphors of Mind in Fiction and Psychology* (Lexington: Univ. Press of Kentucky, 1987), 140–41.

33. Morgentaler correctly billed *Great Expectations* as "a reassessment of *Oliver Twist*" (GM, 713), but it revaluates *Jane Eyre* and *David Copperfield* just as vehemently. Disappointingly, George Levine, in his chapter on "Dickens and Darwin," mentioned *Great Expectations* only once; see *Darwin and the Novelists* (Cambridge: Harvard Univ. Press, 1988), 147. A few months after *The Origin of Species* appeared, Levine noted, *All the Year Round* gave it "a remarkably fair-minded review" (p. 129). For a less Darwinian reading of Dickens's conception of the life process, see *HR,* 254–56.

8. Emily Brontë

1. A "moral taint" is a quote from an unsigned review in the *Literary World* (*WH*, 291). Similar reservations appear in contemporary reviews reprinted in Miriam Allott, ed., *The Brontës: The Critical Heritage* (London: Routledge, 1974).

2. Georgina's aversion seems to be based on personal experience; see endnote 2 in chapter 7 above.

3. *Wuthering Heights* is never about good and evil, wrote Linda H. Peterson; instead, it recounts "the clash of cosmic forces transcending human morality" (*WH*, 11).

4. Just three years before Dickens commenced *Great Expectations*, Peter Bayne's essay on *Wuthering Heights* stressed the "psychological forces" behind Heathcliff's actions; see *EBC*, 401.

5. The captured Heathcliff is greatly impressed by the Lintons' drawing room. He describes "crimson-covered chairs and tables, and a pure white ceiling bordered by gold, a shower of glass-drops hanging in silver chains from the centre, and shimmering with little soft tapers" (*WH*, 60). Dickens redid the unlettered boy's precocity for interior design as the "lies" Pip tells Pumblechook and Mrs. Joe about his first visit to Satis House; among its many splendors are a "black velvet coach" kept inside to rival the Lintons' indoor waterfall (that is, chandelier) and "cake and wine on gold plates" (*GE*, 68).

6. In David Cecil's classic explication, *Wuthering Heights* pits "children of the storm" against "children of calm," its primary concern being the "destruction" and "re-establishment" of each sphere's harmony. Cecil called it "the culminating achievement of a whole civilization" (DC, 153, 182). Nearly every subsequent analysis of Emily's dichotomies is a variation on Cecil; for example, the substitution of nature and culture for storm and calm and the dubious argument, attributed to Emily, that society's movement from the natural to the cultural "must be won anew, or simply repeated from generation to generation" (WG, 373–74).

7. When arguing against Mrs. Gaskell's *North and South* six years earlier in *Hard Times*, Dickens repudiated in advance her suggestion that labor and management relate to each other by imitating domestic paradigms: brother to brother, husband and wife (*HR*, 51–53). In making Magwitch and Pip, Have-Nots and Haves, like father and son, Dickens was not reversing himself—he found Mrs. Gaskell's models much too optimistic; now he charges that Brontë's pairings belong to her own fairy tale world.

8. Q.D. Leavis connected Pip's protestation, "You are part of my existence, part of myself" (*GE*, 362) with Catherine's cry, "I *am* Heathcliff" (*WH*, 87). Leavis praised "Dickens's intelligent reuse of a passage that had lodged in his memory" (QDL, 302), in effect a parodic reconsideration.

9. Dickens wrote "no parting from her but one" in manuscript and proof.

10. The last line of Brontë's novel should be explicated as the final indication of Lockwood's naivete. For a fuller discussion, see Peter D. Grudin, "*Wuthering Heights*: The Question of Unquiet Slumbers," *Studies in the Novel*, 6 (winter 1974), 389–407.

11. Although good-looking, Heathcliff is often likened to a "Monster"; his "sharp cannibal teeth" make him a carnivorous predecessor to Magwitch. See *WH*, 157, 161.

12. Arnold Kettle contended that Brontë enlists sympathy for Heathcliff as the representative of the working classes (AK, 144); even if this were plausible, Magwitch makes a better standard-bearer. Kettle's blue-collar Heathcliff is part of his attempt to bolster the relevance of *Wuthering Heights* as an early Victorian text: a novel "about England in 1847" (AK, 130). For proof that nineteenth-century cinder persons toiled in droves to make life easier for their betters, see Adrian Bristow, *George Smith: The Children's Friend* (Chester: Imogen Press, 1999). It chronicles Smith's efforts on behalf of laboring children in the newly industrialized era, especially so-called brickyard children who worked ten hours a day from age ten or younger in the Midlands brickyards. Some carried as much as sixteen tons of clay a day. Haves depended upon Have-Nots for the construction of their very homes.

13. Given conditions in Liverpool at the time of old Earnshaw's visit, Peterson suggested these origins for Heathcliff (*WH*, 12).

14. In the revised ending, Estella says that "suffering . . . has taught me to understand what your heart used to be" (*GE*, 480). This is not quite as powerful as her statement in the original version.

15. As a realistic "masterwork," J. Hillis Miller has argued, *Wuthering Heights* gives "to an unusual degree" the unique "pleasure of realistic fiction," namely the "illusion that one is entering into a real world by way of the words on the page"; see "*Wuthering Heights:* Repetition and the 'Uncanny'" in Peterson's edition (*WH*, 371).

16. Thomas Vargish applauded the new "depth" and increased "aesthetic value" Emily Brontë gives to the concept of revenge. Heathcliff, he argued, is a great teacher; he seeks to educate his enemies "to conditions which he recreates from his own experience of degradation and loss." By "reproducing" in Hareton the "degradation" suffered from Hindley, Heathcliff supposedly delivers a "parodic comment" on Hindley's perverse behavior; similarly, Heathcliff marries Cathy to his invalid son, Linton, to parody the "grotesque mismatch of Catherine with Edgar" (V, 7, 13, 14).

17. "Having levelled my palace," Heathcliff's full accusation reads, "don't erect a hovel and complacently admire your own charity in giving me that for a home" (*WH*, 111). The "hovel" in question is the future domicile of Heathcliff and Isabella. Mr. Pirrip's choice of an oriental analogue for Pip's career may have been influenced by Nelly's attempt to console the recently demoted Heathcliff: "You're fit for a prince in disguise," Nelly tells the frowning farmer. "Who knows, but your father was Emperor of China, and your mother an Indian princess, each of them able to buy up, with one week's income, Wuthering Heights and Thrushcross Grange together?" (*WH*, 67)

18. Instead of Cathy's tutoring, another facile expedient in Dickens's opinion, consider Biddy's less successful efforts to instruct Pip (ch. 10) and the latter's total failure with Joe (ch. 7). Only when Biddy teaches Joe to read, a feat not shown, does capable instruction reach deserving pupil.

Synopsis A

1. According to the table of contents, VII should be "Sadak and Kalasrade"; within the text it is IX, although there are only supposed to be eight tales.

2. Behaving imprudently, losing one's circumspection, Morell implies, is tantamount to falling under a spell or being enchanted.

Synopsis B

1. I follow the one-volume Roberts Brothers edition (1898) instead of the two-volume Chapman and Hall edition (1863) in which, as with their *Great Expectations*, chapter numbering begins over again in the second volume. Chapters 1 through 23 in volume 1 of *A Day's Ride* are followed by chapters 1 through 25 in volume 2.

2. Serial divisions for *A Day's Ride,* including overlap with Great Expectations: 18 August: 1–2; 25: 3–4; 1 September: 5; 8: 6; 15: 7; 22: 8; 29: 9; 6 October: 10; 13: 11; 20: 12; 27: 13–14; 3 November: 15; 10: 16–17; 17: 18–19; 24: 20–21; 1 December: 22–23 (*GE*, 1–2); 8: 24–25 (3–4); 15: 26–27 (5); 22: 28–29 (6–7); 29: 30–31 (8); 5 January: 32 (9–10); 12: 33 (11); 19: 34 (12–13); 26: 35 (14–15); 2 February: 36 (16–17); 9: 37 (18); 16: 38–39 (19); 23: 40–41 (20–21); 2 March: 42–43 (22); 9: 44 (23–24); 16: 45–46 (25–26); 23: 47–48 (27–28).

Index

Ainsworth, William Harrison, 243n 9
Alexander, Doris, 248n 10
Allcott, Miriam, 265n 1
All the Year Round, 41–42, 44–47, 68, 71–75, 243n 1, 244–46nn 18, 24, 28, 31, 255n 23, 264n 33
alter ego, 195–96
Altick, Richard D., 247n 3
Amis, Martin, 240n 30
Andres, Sophia, 256n 32
Antic Hay (A. Huxley), 25
apRoberts, Ruth, 243n 2
Arabian Nights, The, 95, 249–50n 22
architectural symbols: revaluation of Spanish castles (*A Day's Ride*), 64–65, 68. *See also* Misnar's pavilion
Arkwright, Richard, Sir, 111
Armadale (Collins), 255n 22
Astrophel and Stella (Sidney), 68
asylums, Victorian, 142–44, 147, 149, 153, 245n 28, 255n 23
Avery, Gillian, 10, 11
Axton, William F., 238n 10, 244n 16, 258n 10

Bakhtin, Mikhail, 242n 46
Baldick, Chris, 257nn 3, 5
Barringtons, The (Lever), 245n 30
Barry Lyndon (Thackeray), 44, 76–77, 247n 4, 249n 12
Baynes, Peter, 265n 4
Beadnell, Maria, 15
Beaty, Jerome, 39, 242n 46
Beggar-my-Neighbour, 134, 255n 17
Bennett, Arnold, 241n 34
Bentley, Richard, 42
Bentley's Miscellany, 42, 243nn 7, 9
Bettelheim, Bruno, 15, 240n 26, 241n 38
Bible references, 175–76, 191, 259n 19
bildungsromans, 48, 97–108, 122, 248n 9, 251n 12, 258n 7, 264n 32
Blacking Warehouse. *See* Warren's Blacking Warehouse
Blackwood, John, 245–46n 31
Blackwood's Magazine, 20, 240n 29
Blain, Virginia, 128
Bleak House (Dickens), 9, 251n 15; as social realism, 10, 11, 20, 45
Bluebeard, 261n 11
Book of Snobs, The (Thackeray), 67–68, 76–83, 247n 2
Bradbury and Evans, publishers, 37, 42
Braddon, Mary Elizabeth, 248n 7, 255n 23
Briggs, Asa, 252n 22
Bristow, Adrian, 266n 12
Brontë, Charlotte, 180–205
Brontë, Emily, 206–27

Brontës: The Critical Heritage, The (Allcott), 265n 1
Brooks, Peter, 237n 4
Browne, Hablot K., 37
Brownlow-Fagin polarity (*Oliver Twist*): Magwitch vs., 22
Buckley, Jerome H., 104, 248–51nn 7, 11, 12, 261–62n 12
Bulwer-Lytton, Edward, 70–71, 74, 245n 23
burlesque, literary, 82

Cardwell, Margaret, 100–101
Carlisle, Janice, 238n 10, 251n 15
Carlyle, Thomas, 10–11, 77, 239n 11, 250n 6, 256n 28
Carnegie, Dale, 110
catastrophism, 202, 264n 29
Catherine (Thackeray), 246–47n 1
Cecil, David, 265n 6
Chapman and Hall, publishers, 245n 30
Charles O'Malley (Lever), 42, 249n 12
Chase, Karen, 263–64n 27
Chase, Richard, 180
Chesterton, G.K., 56, 76, 80
child-rearing schemes, 207, 214–15, 218
Children's and Household Tales (Zipes), 241n 40
Child's History of England, A (Dickens), 239n 11
child-snatching scenes, 155–56, 158, 162, 164, 165, 170
"Christabel" (Coleridge), 33
Christmas Carol, A (Dickens), 19
Christmas dinners, 22–23, 51
churchyards, 155, 181–82, 210–11, 213
Cinderella, 3, 237–42nn 3, 4, 6, 14, 15, 19, 38, 40, 41; as bildungsroman, 104–5; parodic revaluation of, 2–3, 16–20, 109, 239–40nn 16, 23, 24, 26
Cinderella complex, 2, 12–13, 28–32, 239n 20; C. Brontë's complicity in, 180, 183, 185; Collins's complicity in, 124–26; personified by Pip, 99–100, 102–4, 208, 211, 251n 10; Thackeray's complicity in, 83–86; Victorian England and, 18–20, 118–19, 124, 130, 139–43, 156, 256n 26
Cinderella motifs, 6, 8, 9–12, 29–32, 237nn 2, 4, 239n 14; in *David Copperfield* revaluation, 14, 20, 77, 86, 98–100, 109, 240n 26; in Dickens's life and work, 14–20, 239n 18; in *Frankenstein* revaluation, 158–60, 162; in *Hide and Seek* revaluation, 127–29, 130, 254n 6; in *Jane Eyre* revaluation, 2, 156, 180–90, 192–201, 204–5, 260–64nn 3–6, 11, 22, 31; in *Pendennis* revaluation, 85, 86–91; in Victorian novels, 2, 5, 8–12, 129–30, 156–57, 238n 10; in *The Woman in White* revaluation, 138–54, 255n 24; in *Wuthering Heights* revaluation, 206–7, 211, 214, 219, 227
circus life: in Dickens and Collins, 125–27, 253n 4
Clarissa (Richardson), 87, 249n 17
Clarke, Micael M., 247n 4, 248n 10
Clausen, Christopher, 252n 26
clothes philosophy, 29–31, 148–53, 158, 196, 257nn 35, 36
Clubbe, John, 258–59n 15
Coleridge, Samuel Taylor, 33
Collins, Wilkie, 75, 123–54, 243n 7, 245nn 27–28, 253–56nn 3, 4, 8, 18–20, 24, 27, 30
Communist Manifesto, The (Marx and Engels), 242n 45
Cornhill Magazine, 243n 6, 247n 5
Cotsell, Michael, 244n 16
Craig, G. Armour, 264n 31
Craig, Randall, 241nn 34–35
Craik, Dinah, 260–61n 5
Crawford, Iain, 173–79
creator-creature relationship, 156, 160–65, 170, 173–75, 258n 10
Cronin, Mark, 97, 247–48n 6
Cruikshank, George, 16–19, 229, 240n 24
Cunningham, John, 241n 33

Dabney, Ross, 241n 39
Darby, Margaret Flanders, 239n 12

Darwin, Charles, 112, 202–6, 252n 23, 264nn 28, 29, 33
daughter figures: Lear-Cordelia relationship, 11–12
David Copperfield (Dickens), 97–108, 247–49nn 2, 9, 15, 250–52nn 4, 7, 8, 11, 15, 18; *Cinderella* motifs in, 2, 14, 20, 77, 86, 98–100, 109, 240n 26; fairy tales in, 13–14, 240nn 26–27; *Jane Eyre* and, 201
Day's Ride: A Life's Romance, A (Lever), 1, 2, 41–75, 244n 17, 267nn 1–2; publication of, 245–46nn 30–31; snobbery in, 67–68, 76–78, 244nn 14, 16
Debrett's Peerage, 93, 249n 20
DeMarcus, Cynthia, 240n 28
Denis Duval (Thackeray), 246–47n 1
dentists, 31, 242n 42
Descent of Man, The (Darwin), 264n 29
Dickens, Charles: as editor, 41–42, 71–75, 243nn 6, 9, 245–46nn 24, 29–31; on fairy tales, 240nn 26, 28; literary reputation of, 36–40; Shaw on, 100–101, 250n 6; as social critic, 10–11, 45, 120, 208, 242n 45, 247–48n 6
Dickens, Henry, Sir, 143
Dickens, John, 15, 240n 21, 251nn 9, 13, 15
Dickens the Novelist (Q.D. Leavis), 236–37n 1
Dombey and Son (Dickens), 43, 56, 243n 4, 263n 25; *Cinderella* motifs in, 14; as social realism, 11
Douhault, Mme. de, 142
"*Drood* and the Bean-stalk" (Forsyte), 240n 28
Dublin Literary Gazette, The, 42
Dublin University Magazine, 42, 44–45
Dunciad, The (Pope), 82
Dunn, Richard J., 240n 30
Duyfhuizen, Bernard, 259n 18
Dyson, A.E., 241n 36, 247n 3

Edwards, P.D., 248n 7
elements, 190, 191–93, 208, 210, 226, 261–62n 12
Eliot, George, 33–34, 43, 242n 44, 246–47n 1

"Enchanters; or, Misnar the Sultan of the East, The." *See* Misnar's pavilion
Engel, Monroe, 104
England, Victorian. *See* Victorian England
English Novel: A Panorama, The (Stevenson), 244n 13
Estella (*Great Expectations*). *See* Pip-Estella relationship

failure, 104, 105, 108, 109, 121–22
Fairy Library (Cruikshank), 16, 229, 240n 24
fairy tales: in Dickens's life and work, 13–20. *See also Cinderella*; Misnar's pavilion
Fancy, 16–19, 127, 240n 25
farce, tragic. *See* tragic farce
Ferris, Kathleen, 240–41n 32
Fielden, Kenneth, 252n 21
Fielding, Henry, 228
Fielding, K.J., 240n 29, 246–47n 1
fire imagery, 191–93, 210, 261–62n 12
Fisher, Judith, 247n 5
Fitzpatrick, W.J., 42, 44
Flaubert, Gustave, 25–26
Ford, George, 243n 2, 251n 15
forgiveness, 106–7, 114, 136–37
Forster, John, 21, 36, 48, 71–72, 75, 100, 215; on *Frankenstein* revaluation, 163, 258n 8; views on psychiatric theory, 141–42, 255n 22
Forsyte, Charles, 240n 28
Fortunes of Glencore, The (Lever), 243n 4
foundling legend, 238n 10
Frankenstein (M. Shelley), 1, 155–79, 181, 257–60nn 1–6, 9, 11, 12, 14, 15, 18, 20, 23, 261–63nn 7, 20, 26
Fraser's Magazine, 246–47n 1
"Frauds on the Fairies" (Dickens), 16, 229, 240n 26
The French Revolution (Carlyle), 256n 28
Friedman, Stanley, 238n 7, 257n 39
friendship, 104, 106–7, 114

Gadd, W. Laurence, 257n 1
Gad's Hill Place, Rochester, 15, 37, 122, 240n 21

Galland, Antoine, 249–50n 22
Garis, Robert, 7, 24, 241n 34, 244n 12
Garnett, Robert G., 261–62n 12
Gaskell, Elizabeth, 43, 129, 180, 200, 245–46n 31, 254n 11, 265n 7
gentility, 92–95, 113, 147–48, 156, 157, 258n 10; Smiles on, 252nn 24, 27
George Smith: The Children's Friend (Bristow), 266n 12
Gilbert, Sandra M., 261n 6, 264n 31
Gilmour, Robin, 118, 251n 15
Golden, Morris, 240n 22
Gothic novels, 206, 208, 223
gradualism, 202, 264n 29
Grudin, Peter D., 265n 10

"Half-Caste: An Old Governess's Tale, The" (Craik), 260–61n 5
Hamlet (Shakespeare), 26, 32, 101
hand imagery, 199, 213
Hard Cash (Reade), 75, 245n 28, 255n 23
Harden, Edgar, 249–50n 22
Hard Times (Dickens), 125, 247n 5, 254n 11, 265n 7; as social realism, 10, 11, 18, 20, 45
Harrison, Frederic, 69
Harry Lorrequer (Lever), 42, 243n 4
Hartog, Curt, 257n 2, 262n 16
Haves and Have-Nots, 1, 28, 35, 242n 45; in *Cinderella* revaluation, 119; in *A Day's Ride* revaluation, 63; in *Frankenstein* revaluation, 157, 159–60, 163–64, 168; in *Jane Eyre* revaluation, 190; in *Pendennis* revaluation, 85; in *Self-Help* revaluation, 121; in Thackeray revaluation, 80; in *The Woman in White* revaluation, 147–48; in *Wuthering Heights* revaluation, 209, 218, 220–21, 224–25, 227, 265–66nn 7, 12
Hawthorne, Nathaniel, 246–47n 1
Hidden Rivalries in Victorian Fiction: Dickens, Realism, and Revaluation (Meckier), 246–47n 1
Hide and Seek (Collins), 125–38, 253–54nn 2–4, 8, 13
History of England (Macaulay), 10

History of Pendennis, The (Thackeray). See *Pendennis*
Hogarth, Catherine, 15, 37
Hogarth, Georgina, 129
Hogarth, Mary, 15
Hop-o'-my-Thumb (Cruikshank), 16, 18
Hornback, Bert G., 65, 107, 236n 2, 260n 27
Houghton, Walter, 69–70, 165
House, Humphry, 238n 10, 244n 19, 247n 3
Household Words, 16–17, 37, 42, 43, 44, 45, 245–46n 31, 253n 3, 254n 11
How to Win Friends and Influence People (Carnegie), 110
Huang Mei, 239n 18
Huxley, Aldous, 25

individual responsibility, 173–74
Ingle, Stephen, 244n 19
insanity, 139–48, 191
institutionalization, wrongful, 142–43, 147, 149, 153, 245n 28, 255n 23
ironic comedy. See tragicomedy
Isherwood, Christopher, 67

Jack Sheppard (Ainsworth), 243n 9
Jackson, T.A., 35
Jane Eyre (C. Brontë), 1, 180–205, 260–64nn 1–13, 17, 18, 21–27, 30–33
Jerrold, Douglas, 81, 82–83, 249n 13
Joe (*Great Expectations*). See Pip-Joe relationship
Johnson, Edgar, 41, 243nn 8, 10, 246–47n 1
Jordan, John O., 180
Jorrocks's Jaunts and Jollities (Surtees), 44
Joyce, James, 248n 9

Kaplan, Cora, 260–61n 5
Kaplan, Fred, 75, 101
Karl, Frederick, 264n 32
Kearns, Michael S., 264n 32
Kettle, Arnold, 266n 12
Kincaid, James, 260n 1
Kinder-und Hausmärchen (Zipes), 241n 40
King Lear (Shakespeare), 11–12

"King of the Golden River, The" (Ruskin), 19
Kingsley, Charles, 68
Knight of Gwynne, The (Lever), 243n 4
Knoepflmacher, U.C., 226
Kotzin, Michael C., 237n 2
Kusnetz, Ella, 250n 5

Lady Audley's Secret (Braddon), 255n 23
Langbaum, Robert, 23–25
Leavis, F.R., 201–2, 263n 24
Leavis, Q.D., 236–37n 1, 265n 8
Lerner, Laurence, 262n 17
Lever, Charles, 41–75, 243nn 2–4, 7, 8, 10, 244nn 12–13, 245–46nn 27, 28, 30, 31
Levine, George, 157, 257n 5, 264n 33
Lewes, G.H., 264n 32
Life and Labour (Smiles), 118
Life of George Stephenson, Railway Engineer (Smiles), 252n 20
Lippincott's Magazine, 247n 5
Literary World, 265n 1
Little Dorrit (Dickens), 247–48n 6; as social realism, 10, 20, 45
Little Red Riding Hood, 240n 28
Lodge, David, 33
London Merchant; or The History of George Barnwell, The (Lillo), 238n 10
Lovelace (*Clarissa*), 87, 249n 17
Love's Madness: Medicine, the Novel, and Female Insanity, 1800–1865 (Small), 255n 23
Lowe-Evans, Mary, 258n 14
Lunacy Commission, 142, 255n 22
Lund, Michael, 97
lying: Pip vs. Potts, 48–49

Macaulay, Thomas Babington, 10–12
MacKay, Carol Hanberry, 97
Madame Bovary (Flaubert), 25–26
madness, 139–48, 191
Madonna (*Hide and Seek*), 126–29, 254n 6
Magwitch, Abel (*Great Expectations*): compared to Bounderby (*Hard Times*), 253–54n 5; compared to Brownlow-Fagin (*Oliver Twist*), 22; compared to Frankenstein's monster, 163–65; first name of, 176, 259n 19. *See also* Pip-Magwitch relationship
Manning, Sylvia, 236–37n 1
Marcus, Philip, 244n 18
Martin Chuzzlewit (Dickens), 14, 56, 68
Marx, Karl, 100, 114, 242n 45
Marxist literature, 257–58n 6
Masson, David, 249n 15
McGowan, John P., 106
McMaster, Juliet, 249n 12
McMaster, R.D., 250n 24
mental patients, 139–43, 147, 149
Merchant, Peter, 238n 7
Michel-Michot, Paulette, 261–62n 12
Miller, J. Hillis, 223, 239n 20, 241n 35, 252n 17, 259n 22, 266n 15
Milton, John, 28, 173–79, 198, 259nn 17, 18
Misnar, the Sultan of India (Dickens), 13–14
Misnar's pavilion, tale of, 2–9, 39, 228–31, 238n 7, 267nn 1–2; in *Cinderella* revaluation, 18–20, 237n 4; in *David Copperfield* revaluation, 121; in *A Day's Ride* revaluation, 64–65, 68, 244–45n 20; in *Frankenstein* revaluation, 156–57, 159–60, 168, 172–73, 174; in *Great Expectations*, 127; in *Jane Eyre* revaluation, 185, 186–89, 191, 198, 201; in *Pendennis* revaluation, 95; in *The Woman in White* revaluation, 148; in *Wuthering Heights* revaluation, 224
Mitchell, Charlotte, 237n 5
Modern Painters (Ruskin), 33
Moers, Ellen, 250n 1
Monod, Sylvère, 247n 3
monstrosity, 155–65, 169–73, 257–58nn 2–6, 9, 11, 12, 261n 7, 265n 11
Montag, William, 258n 9
Moonstone, The (Collins), 245n 27
Morell, Charles, Sir, 14, 228, 239n 17, 267n 2

Morgentaler, Goldie, 204, 264n 33
Morley, Henry, 258n 8
Mother Goose Tales (Perrault), 241–42n 41
Moynahan, Julian, 258n 14
Mr. Punch's Prize Novelists (Thackeray), 243n 3
Mystery of Edwin Drood, The (Dickens), 240n 28

narcissism, 161
"Natural History of German Life, The" (Eliot), 242n 44
natural selection, 112, 202–6
Needham, Gwendolyn B., 250n 4
New, William H., 261–62n 12
Newman, Beth, 197
Nicholas Nickleby (Dickens), 14, 263n 25
Nisbet, Ada, 243n 2
No Name (Collins), 75
North and South (Gaskell), 129, 245–46n 31, 254n 11, 265n 7
North British Review, The, 249n 15
Novels by Eminent Hands (Thackeray), 82

O'Donoghue, The (Lever), 243n 4
Oedipus Rex (Sophocles), 28–29, 32, 241n 38
Old Curiosity Shop, The (Dickens), 11, 14, 263n 25
Old Wives' Tale, The (Bennett), 241n 34
Olive: A Young Girl's Triumph Over Prejudice (Craik), 260–61n 5
Oliver Twist (Dickens), 201, 243n 9, 264n 33; *Cinderella* motifs in, 14–15, 18, 20; parodic revaluation of, 239n 20, 246–47n 1; tragicomic elements in, 21–22, 23
Origin of Species, The (Darwin), 202–6, 252n 23, 264nn 28, 29, 33
orphan's myth, 201, 263n 24
Orwell, George, 244n 19
Our Mutual Friend (Dickens), 240nn 28, 30

Page, Frederick, 207
Pamela (Richardson), 82

Paradise Lost (Milton), 28, 173–79, 212, 226, 241n 37, 259nn 20, 21
Parallel Lives (Plutarch), 121–22, 251–52n 16
parodic revaluation, 1, 6–7, 38–40, 128, 242n 46; of *Cinderella*, 2–3, 16–20, 102, 109, 124–25, 138–54, 229, 239–40nn 16, 23, 24, 26; of *David Copperfield*, 97–122, 250nn 7–8; of *A Day's Ride*, 41–75, 244n 17; Dickens-Collins rivalry, 124–29, 135–36, 254–56nn 7–9, 18–20, 30, 33; of *Frankenstein*, 155–79, 257–60nn 1–6, 9, 11, 12, 14, 15, 18, 20, 23; of *Hide and Seek*, 125–38, 253–54nn 2–4, 8, 13; of *Pendennis*, 56, 68, 83–96, 97–99, 122, 250n 1; of *The Woman in White*, 138–54, 255–56nn 23, 24, 29, 30, 32–34; of *Wuthering Heights*, 206–27, 265nn 5, 7, 8, 11, 17, 18
Paroissien, David, 237n 5
Partlow, Robert B., 236n 1
partnerships, 174–75, 212
"Passage in the Life of Mr. Perugino Potts, A" (Collins), 243n 7
Past and Present (Carlyle), 239n 11
Patten, Robert L., 73–74, 245n 24
Peale, Norman Vincent, 110
Pearlman, E., 250n 7
Peerage, British, 93, 249n 20
Pendennis (Thackeray), 2, 76–77, 201, 202, 248–50nn 11, 14–24; parodic revaluation of, 56, 68, 83–96, 97–99, 122, 249n 20, 250nn 1–3
perfectibilitarianism, 69
Perrault, Charles, 239nn 14, 19, 240n 22, 241–42n 41
perseverance, 108, 109, 111, 112, 123
Peters, Catherine, 128, 129, 253–57nn 3, 4, 8, 28, 37
Peterson, Clara L., 263n 23
Peterson, Linda H., 265–66nn 3, 13
picaresque realism, 48, 243n 8
Pickwick Papers (Dickens), 37, 243nn 7–8; parodic revaluation of, 246–47n 1
Pilgrim's Progress, The (Bunyan), 180, 201, 262n 13

Pip-Biddy relationship, 52, 102, 144–46, 216, 256n 31, 260n 24
Pip-Estella relationship: in *David Copperfield* revaluation, 106–8, 114, 119; in *A Day's Ride* revaluation, 70; in *Jane Eyre* revaluation, 182–83, 200; in Thackeray revaluation, 78–79; in *The Woman in White* revaluation, 146–47, 153–54, 257nn 38, 39; in *Wuthering Heights* revaluation, 211–13, 216–17, 224, 266n 14
Pip (*Great Expectations*), 238n 9, 250n 5; as Cinderella figure, 13, 32, 150–53; as parody of self-help, 112–14; as snob, 79–81; as tragicomic figure, 26
Pip-Joe relationship, 21; contrasted with Pip-Magwitch relationship, 48; monstrosity of, 261n 7; in *Pendennis* revaluation, 92–93; in *Self-Help* revaluation, 114–16; as study of snobbery, 49–50, 53, 244n 15
Pip-Magwitch relationship, 22–23, 107, 244nn 18–19; in *Cinderella* revaluation, 6, 29–32; contrasted with Pip-Joe relationship, 48; in *A Day's Ride* revaluation, 57–58, 62–65; in *Frankenstein* revaluation, 155–73, 177–79, 257–59nn 5, 13, 19; in *Hide and Seek* revaluation, 133–37, 254–55nn 14–16; *Oedipus Rex* relationships compared to, 27–29, 32; in *Pendennis* revaluation, 83–86, 88–92, 94–95, 249n 21; in *Self-Help* revaluation, 117–19, 253nn 28–29; as study of snobbery, 34–36, 54, 79–80; in *The Woman in White* revaluation, 256n 28; in *Wuthering Heights* revaluation, 207, 208–9, 214, 215, 219–25, 265n 7
Pip-Orlick relationship: in *Jane Eyre* revaluation, 195–96
Pirrip, Mr. (*Great Expectations*), 3, 14, 24–25, 80–81, 173, 259n 21; on bildungsromans, 105–6, 112, 122, 252n 23; in *Pendennis* revaluation, 80–81, 96, 248nn 8–9
pivotal structure, literary, 91–92, 144, 182, 208, 215

Plutarch, 109, 121–22, 251–52n 16
Poe, Edgar Allan, 42
Polhemus, Robert M., 241n 38
Portrait of the Artist as a Young Man (Joyce), 248n 9
Power of Positive Thinking, The (Peale), 110
Prince Charming, 261n 11
providence, 173–74, 259n 17
psychological novels, 264n 32, 265n 4
psychological social criticism, 141–48, 206, 208, 223
Punch, 78, 81, 247–49nn 2, 10, 12
Punch's Prize Novelists (Thackeray), 82
punctuated evolution, 202

railroad engineers, 252n 20
Rance, Nick, 253n 1
Rawlins, Jack P., 247n 5
Ray, Gordon N., 82, 248n 11
Reade, Charles, 75, 245n 28, 255n 23
realism, 33, 36, 123–24, 156–57, 204, 207–8, 223
Reed, John, 247n 5
Reform Bill of 1832, 120
"Remonstrance with Dickens," 20
revaluative parodies. *See* parodic revaluation
revenge: in *Frankenstein* revaluation, 156, 157–58; in *Wuthering Heights* revaluation, 206–8, 214–15, 217–23
Rhys, Jean, 260–61n 5
Ridley, James, 14, 239n 17
Ridley, M.R., 248n 11
"Rime of the Ancient Mariner, The" (Coleridge), 33
Roland Cashel (Lever), 243n 3
Romantic literature, 258n 12
Rose, Phyllis, 37
Rose and the Ring, The (Thackeray), 19
Rosenberg, Edgar, 56, 71, 237n 5, 242n 43, 243n 8, 244n 17, 259n 19
Rossen, Janice, 260–61n 5
Royal College of Surgeons, 242n 42
Ruskin, John, 19, 33, 247n 5

"Sad Fortunes of the Rev. Amos Barton, The" (Eliot), 33–34

Sadrin, Anny, 73, 241n 38, 264n 31
Said, Edward, 244n 19
Samber, Robert, 241–42n 41
Samson Agonistes (Milton), 198
satire, Dickensian. *See* tragicomedy
Saturday Review, The, 100, 240n 29
scalping, 129, 254–55nn 12, 15
Scenes of Clerical Life (Eliot), 33
Self-Help (Smiles), 108–9, 110–12, 120–22, 123, 251–52nn 15, 21, 23, 25, 253n 1; parodic revaluation of, 109–10, 112–20, 125
serialized fiction: in *All The Year Round*, 41–51, 71–75, 243nn 1, 10, 245–46nn 27–31; in *Bentley's Miscellany*, 243n 9; Dickens and Thackeray, 76–77, 91–92, 243n 6, 247n 2; in *Household Words*, 253n 3, 254n 11
Shakespeare, William. *See Hamlet; King Lear; Tempest, The*
Shamela (Fielding), 82
Shaw, George Bernard, 55, 70–71, 100–101, 250nn 6–7
Shaw, Isabella, 250n 2
Shéhérazade, 95, 249–50n 22
Shelley, Mary, 155–79, 181, 257–58n 6
shipwreck, 153, 257n 38
Shor, Hilary, 239n 12
Sidney, Philip, Sir, 68
Silas Marner (Eliot), 238n 7
Sir Joseph Carew (Lever), 243n 4
Sleeping Beauty, 256n 26, 261n 11
Small, Helen, 255n 23
Smiles, Samuel, 108–22, 251–52nn 15–16, 20–22, 24–27
Smith, George, 266n 12
Smith, Grahame, 244n 19, 245n 29, 247n 5
Smith, Johanna M., 258n 9, 11
snobbery, 1, 34–36, 157–58; in *A Day's Ride* revaluation, 49–50, 51–56; in *Frankenstein* revaluation, 163; in *Hide and Seek*, 133–34; self-help and, 252n 26; in Thackeray revaluation, 67–68, 76–83, 92–96, 244nn 14, 16, 247–48nn 2, 3, 7, 9, 11
Snobs of England, By One of Themselves,
The (Thackeray), 76, 78, 81, 247n 2. *See also Book of Snobs, The*
social classes, 209–10, 265–66nn 7, 12
social criticism: in Dickens's novels, 16–20, 45, 242n 45; of Victorian England, 2, 5, 9–11, 35–36, 141–48, 244n 19
softening influences: in *Great Expectations*, 106–7, 137, 251n 14; in *Hide and Seek*, 127, 136–37; in *Jane Eyre* revaluation, 192, 196, 199, 202; in *Wuthering Heights* revaluation, 212, 213
Sophocles. *See Oedipus Rex*
Spanish castles (*A Day's Ride*), 64–65, 68
Spencer, Alexander, 42, 43
Staplehurst railroad accident, 252n 20
Stephenson, George, 108, 252n 20
Stevenson, Lionel, 41, 244n 13, 245n 30
Stone, Harry, 2, 101, 104, 239n 18, 241–42nn 38, 41, 245n 21
Stone, Marcus, 37
St. Patrick's Eve (Lever), 42
Strange Story, A (Bulwer-Lytton), 74, 75
Stubblefield, Jay, 173
success, 109, 111, 112–13
Surtees, Robert Smith, 44
Sutherland, J.A., 41, 76, 81–82, 92, 243n 1, 247n 3, 250n 23
Sweeney, Patricia R., 247n 3
Swinburne, Algernon, 244n 11
Swingle, L.J., 168, 258n 12

Tale of Two Cities, A (Dickens): serialization of, 45–47; as social realism, 10
Tales of the Genii, The, 2, 4, 13–15, 65, 121, 186, 228, 239n 17, 244–45n 20. *See also* Misnar's pavilion
Tales of the Trains (Lever), 43
Tavistock House, 37
temperance tracts, 16, 240n 24
Tempest, The (Shakespeare), 23–25
Ternan, Ellen, 100, 122, 252n 20
Terry, Samuel, 253n 28
Thackeray, William Makepeace, 19, 76–96, 242n 46, 246–50nn 1–24; C. Brontë's views on, 200–201; on snobbery, 67–68, 244n 14; tragicomedy and, 8–9, 238n 8, 244n 12

Three Clerks, The (Trollope), 252n 19
Time Machine, The (Wells), 244n 19
Tom Burke of "Ours" (Lever), 42
Tom Jones (Fielding), 228
Tono-Bungay (Wells), 248n 9
tragic farce, 2, 25–34
tragic irony. *See* tragicomedy
tragicomedy, 2, 20–34, 240–41nn 30–35; Dickens vs. Thackeray, 8–9; Eliot on, 242n 44; Isherwood on, 67; Thackeray on, 238n 8
transportation (punishment), 31, 88–89, 142, 242n 43, 256n 25
Trapp, Martin, 262n 18
Trollope, Anthony, 252n 19

Utilitarian philosophy, 16–17, 114

Vanity Fair (Thackeray), 9, 68, 247–50nn 6, 9, 12, 22, 263n 24
Vann, J. Don, 245–46n 31
Vargish, Thomas, 266n 16
verisimilitude, 23
Victoria, Queen, 255n 21
Victorian England: Cinderella complex and, 18–20, 118–19, 129, 180–81, 189, 201, 214–15; madness in, 139–48, 255n 23; snobbery in, 79–81, 85, 244n 14, 247n 3; social criticism of, 2, 5, 9–11, 35–36, 238n 10, 244n 19, 251n 15; socioeconomic system, 159–61, 163–65, 173–75, 182, 205, 209, 257–58nn 6, 9
Victorian Fiction: A Second Guide to Research (Ford), 243n 2
Victorian novels, 36–40, 243n 2; Cinderella motifs in, 2, 5, 8–12, 129–30, 156–57, 238n 10; Darwin and, 264n 29; parodic revaluation in, 82, 128, 246–47n 1; snobbery in, 56, 247n 3; as social realism, 123–24
von Schmidt, Helen, 262n 19, 264n 30

Wakefield, Edward Gibbon, 242n 43
Walpole, Horace, 240n 31
Warren's Blacking Warehouse, 15, 103, 122, 251nn 9, 13
water imagery, 190, 210, 261–62n 12
Wedgwood, Josiah, 111
Wells, H.G., 244n 19, 248n 9
Wemmick (*Great Expectations*), 244–45n 20
Wide Sargasso Sea (Rhys), 260–61n 5
Wills, W.H., 16, 17
Wilson, Angus, 106, 250n 7
Woman in White, The (Collins), 2, 138–54, 245n 28, 255–56nn 23, 24, 29, 30, 32–34; serialization of, 43, 45–46, 74
Wordsworth, William, 17, 240n 25
working classes, 209–10, 265–66nn 7, 12
"World is Too Much With Us; Late and Soon, The" (Wordsworth), 17–18, 240n 25
Worth, George, 246–47n 1
Wuthering Heights (E. Brontë), 2, 206–27, 265–66nn 1–8, 10–13, 15–18

Yeast (Kingsley), 68
Yeazell, Ruth Bernard, 263n 21
Yellowplush Correspondence (Thackeray), 246–47n 1

Zipes, Jack, 19, 241n 40